DAVID A. LYNN
GCA Technology Division

AIR POLLUTION — THREAT AND RESPONSE

Addison-Wesley Publishing Company

Reading, Massachusetts • Menlo Park, California
London • Amsterdam • Don Mills, Ontario • Sydney

ISBN 0-201-04355-6
BCDEFGHIJK-MA-7987

PREFACE

This book is a relatively nontechnical introduction to the field of air pollution and its control. It treats the subject in greater detail and thoroughness than is usually possible when air pollution is considered as only one aspect of our entire environmental problem, but with much less detail than some texts give to the more classic engineering aspects of the topic. It is intended to provide enough material for a one-semester or two-quarter course dealing with air pollution alone, but it has been designed so that it can also be useful as a resource in more general courses.

As with any text, these goals reflect my prejudices concerning the important needs for educated women and men in my field. The choice to include, and in fact emphasize, the nonengineering aspects of the topic reflects my feeling that the air pollution problem can no longer be viewed as primarily an engineering problem, or even primarily a technical problem, but must be seen as a social problem. This feeling has dictated not only a broad coverage, but also a somewhat uneven coverage perhaps, with traditional engineering topics being slighted in favor of the biological, legal, and especially the political aspects of the problem. The more traditional material is, of course, the more readily available, both in technical texts and in the reservoir of experienced teachers in the field, so that I have spent more effort in filling the gaps in other areas.

The decision to deal with air pollution alone in a relatively isolated setting requires some defense, I feel, given the general recognition of the need for a broad, generalist viewpoint in dealing with complex problems, and my firm agreement with that philosophy. The question is one of breadth versus depth, a classic argument to which I have nothing new to contribute. A broad, general understanding of public issues must be part of the education of most of our citizens if progress and orderly change are to be part of our civilization. Environmental concerns are a prominent current example, and there is a growing number of formal courses, anthologies, and other texts available to meet these needs. There is also a need, however, for a somewhat greater depth on the part of a somewhat more select group of people. These include individuals employed in environmental fields, perhaps only peripherally, and especially those citizens who wish not only to support the adoption of sound environmental solutions, but also to understand and perhaps to participate in the formulation of those solutions. There is a variety of public interest groups and other public participation mechanisms that are increasingly available to such persons, as well as the classic letter-writing and informed voting, but the problems are often technical, and effective participation often requires more than a generalist's overview. I have long felt there was a gap in the center of the breadth-versus-depth continuum, and it is my hope that this book will contribute to filling it.

Turning to more tangible considerations, it has been my intent to make this book a flexible tool rather than a rigid guide. The material has been organized into 13 chapters roughly arranged into five groups. The five groups, and to a large extent the individual chapters also, are intended to be interchangeable or skippable as individual tastes and needs warrant. The first three chapters, dealing with history, overview, definitions, and meteorology, are introductory in nature. Chapters 4 and 5 consider the effects of pollution, both the fairly well-known effects and the merely suspected ones. Chapters 6 and 7 consider the measurement of pollution levels and the study of the resulting information. These areas are particularly attractive for class research projects and so have been considered in somewhat more detail than is necessary for a simple understanding of air pollution. General information on typically measured levels of air pollution has been included in Chapter 3, so that the two chapters on measurement might be the first candidate for omission if shortening is required. Chapters 8 and 9 deal with the two major categories of pollution sources and the technical aspects of the various measures used in their control. Chapters 10–13 focus on the legal and social mechanisms available for ensuring that the technical control measures are in fact used.

At the end of each chapter are a set of exercises and a brief discussion of suggested further reading. References in square brackets refer to the bibliography at the back of the book. The exercises, though numbered sequentially, are of several different types. The "Review Questions" are factual questions about the material presented in the chapter; they are intended as a way of reviewing students' grasp of the factual information as such. The coverage is intended to be extensive rather than highly selective, and one who can answer the bulk of these questions has a quite good knowledge of the facts. The correct response can usually be found in the text.

In contrast, the "Thought Questions" involve bringing to bear knowledge from another field, another chapter, or general everyday knowledge and hence are less readily verified. The purpose of these questions is to help establish bridges with various other ideas and fields of knowledge and with one's everyday life, and to keep us reminded that nothing is very well isolated nowadays. These questions are generally factual, but because of the variety of other subject areas concerned, there is no reason why all of these questions should be easy for everyone, though hopefully many will be.

The "Discussion Questions" are designed to extend our thinking to the implications of the facts we have learned and to challenge our imaginations in situations that haven't occurred yet. They are usually questions to which there is no right or wrong answer, as they often involve moral judgments or each individual's personal viewpoint. Nor do they usually admit of a brief answer, as most of them involve numerous undefined side issues or alternatives. The hoped-for benefits to be derived from thinking or writing about these questions are the refinement of our viewpoints on controversial issues and a sharpened awareness of the complexities of those issues. If discussion can be arranged as adversary debates, this would be useful, I feel.

In most chapters, there are also some "Problems." These are distinguished by being quantitative, by requiring calculations of some sort. They tend to be as varied as the questions, though far fewer, ranging from simple illustrations of quantitative points to others requiring quantitative knowledge from other areas.

The "Project Suggestions" are miscellaneous ideas for individual or group projects that would likely take more than a few hours to pursue. They are also a quite varied group, depending on the chapter, and often depending on the geographical location of the reader. To an extent, many of them are suitable for "term paper"-type projects, some of which can be planned or coordinated together through the term.

The body of knowledge that is called "air pollution" has been developed over many years by many people, both scientists and ordinary citizens. The structures and perspectives that I have used in relating this knowledge have been developed over a number of years through contact and discussion with many individuals. From among these, I should like to express particular debts due to Dr. B. J. Steigerwald, who first attracted me to the air pollution field, and to Raymond Smith, whose opinions over the years had a significant effect on my views.

For their helpful comments during the preparation of the manuscript, I would like to thank Professors Sigmund P. Harris of Los Angeles Pierce College, P. Aarne Vesilind of Duke University, Steven M. Slater of the University of New Hampshire, and especially Samuel J. Williamson of New York University. My deepest appreciation, however, must go to my wife, Carol, who in a very real sense made the entire effort possible, not only by typing and retyping, but also by tolerating the many other difficult burdens imposed by such a project.

Waltham, Massachusetts   D. A. L.
November 1975

CONTENTS

1

The Air Pollution Problem

Introduction   2

Historical Perspective   3

The Present   9

Exercises   15

Further Reading   15

2

Air Pollution Meteorology

The Atmosphere   18

Horizontal Motions and Circulations   21

Vertical Temperature Inversions   29

Air Pollution Climatology   36

Exercises   37

Further Reading   38

3

The Pollutants—Their Properties and Prevalence

Particulate Matter and Sulfur Oxides   42

Carbon Monoxide   52

The Photochemical Pollutants   55

Other Pollutants   70

Relative Significance of the Pollutants   74

Exercises   76

Further Reading   79

4

Effects on Human Health

Health Effects and Health-Effects Research   82

The Human Respiratory System   86

Health Effects of Particulate Matter and SO$_2$ 95

Health Effects of Carbon Monoxide   100

Health Effects of the Photochemical Pollutants   104

Health Effects of Other Pollutants   107

Is Air Pollution Really As Bad As They Say?   115

Exercises   118

Further Reading   121

5

Ecologic and Economic Effects

Effects on the Physical Environment   124

Effects on Other Living Things   136

Economic Effects   142

Exercises   148

Further Reading   149

6

Measuring Air Pollution

Introduction   152

Measuring Particulate Pollution in the Ambient Air   155

Measuring Gases in the Ambient Air   159

Automatic Sampler-Analyzers   165

Measuring Pollutants at Their Source   173

Exercises   174

Further Reading   176

7

Monitoring Networks and Data Analysis

Monitoring Networks   178

Data Processing   179

Data Analysis   189

Exercises   194

Further Reading   196

8

Pollution from Stationary Sources

Basic Approaches to Emission Control   198

Fuel Combustion   207

Solid-Waste Disposal   224

Industrial Process Sources   227

Summary   233

Exercises   233

Further Reading   235

9

Pollution from Mobile Sources

Vehicular Emissions   238

Controlling Conventional IC Engines   246

Alternatives to the Conventional IC Engine   254

Other Alternatives   258

Exercises   261

Further Reading   263

10

The Legal Basis for Air Pollution Control

Traditional Common-Law Remedies   266

Governmental Control Programs   272

Citizen Suits: The Changing Law   279

Exercises   285

Further Reading   286

11

Governmental Air Pollution Control Programs

Introduction   290

Air Pollution Control Functions   291

Federal Air Pollution Functions   299
A Systematic National Program   307
Summary   317
Exercises   318
Further Reading   321

12

Control Strategy: Economics and Public Policy

Introduction   324
How Much Control Do We Need?   325
Which Sources? The Implementation Plan   328
How Fast Should We Do It?   333
Who Pays for the Control, and How?   335
How Do We Organize to Do It?   337
Exercises   341

13

Epilogue: Why?   343

Bibliography   349

Glossary   365

Index   369

1
THE
AIR POLLUTION
PROBLEM

Carnegie Library of Pittsburgh

INTRODUCTION

The atmosphere that surrounds the planet Earth is one of the factors that makes our planet hospitable toward life. The average human makes use of about 30 pounds of air each day, using it to oxidize food for energy and warmth. This life-sustaining atmosphere is a mixture of gases that is held around the surface of the earth by the gravitational attraction of the planet's mass. Because it surrounds us so intimately, we've used it without thought to burn not only the food in our bodies, but also the coal in our furnaces and the gasoline in our cars. And almost equally without thought, we've used it to carry away our wastes—not only the carbon dioxide we exhale, but also the wastes from the furnaces and the cars and from our thousand other activities. The atmosphere is, however, limited; although it seems essentially infinite from our individual human perspective, only a relatively thin layer a few miles thick is accessible to us for our use in sustaining life and diluting wastes.

It's our purpose in this book to consider the relationship between these two uses—how we use our air for dumping wastes and how that might interfere with our use of it for sustaining life, in the broadest sense. It will be our purpose in the first three chapters to get an introductory view of the air pollution problem, how the air itself is involved, and what the pollution actually is. We'll begin shortly by looking backward briefly, to get some historical facts and perhaps some perspective. First, however, a thought on the scale of that perspective. Implicit in the very concept of air pollution is the assumption that there is something basically "right" or "good" about some certain composition of the atmospheric mixture. Within the scale of human life on the earth, the atmosphere's composition (Table 1–1) has been stable and has in fact been "good" in the sense that it was suited to us. It is important to remember, however, that in an evolutionary context this has not always been the case. The first living organisms formed

TABLE 1–1
Composition of dry air

Gases	Percent of volume
Nitrogen	78.03
Oxygen	20.99
Argon	0.94
Carbon dioxide	0.03
Balance*	0.01
	100.00

* Includes hydrogen, helium, neon, krypton, xenon, and the various pollutants.

or created millions of years ago would find our air hopelessly polluted with lethal oxygen, and we would have not cared for theirs. Life and the atmosphere have clearly evolved side by side on our planet, and may continue to do so, though this is little consolation in our present troubles.

HISTORICAL PERSPECTIVE

There are references in classical and earlier records to the ill effects of "noxious airs" from one source or another, and these are frequently noted to suggest that the problem of air pollution is an old one. I think we do ourselves a disservice, however, by citing these ancient references. It serves only to imply that pollution is an inevitable concomitant of any civilization, no matter how unlike our own, and so makes our task seem much more difficult than it really is. Actually, however, there is no evidence before the twelfth century that suggests anything at all like the pollution problem as we think of it today. Most of the references are to accidental or catastrophic incidents, rather than to any ongoing community problem.

The Industrial Revolution

The history of air pollution as we know it today begins with the Industrial Revolution, or more accurately, with the entire broad spectrum of economic and social change that began slowly in the eleventh century, produced the steam engine and factories by 1800, and is really still with us today. Many things changed: the knights and barons of manorial splendor gave way to the merchants and traders of the booming cities; the rigid church orthodoxy gave way to the shopkeeper artisan, then the factory worker; but most important from our viewpoint, the use of wood as the primary fuel of civilization gave way to the increasing use of coal.

The use of coal and the many other social and economic aspects of the early industrialization are complexly interwoven; the growth of industrialization spurred coal production, while the availability of coal speeded the growth of industrialization. The overall effect, however, was an increasing burning of coal and a growing concern with the smoke and sulfurous odors that resulted. Through the entire time, there were periodic attempts at banning, taxing, or regulating its use. In 1661 John Evelyn, one of the prominent scientists of the day, wrote an excellent essay deploring the problem in London at the time, and by 1820 there were regulations controlling the nature of burning in industrial furnaces. But all in all, there was really little that could be done to significantly alleviate the problems, short of turning back the process of industrialization, and that no one was willing to do, if it was even suggested.

The Twentieth Century

In the United States, the late 1800s had brought the first smoke-control laws, beginning with Chicago in 1881. By 1912 such laws had been passed by most of the largest American cities. But the dramatic focus of events, which then later becomes the thread of history, continued to be in Britain. There, high pollutant levels and the damp climate, with the resultant frequent, severe fogs, made the problem most acute. Sometime before World War I, an anonymous citizen of London coined the word "smog" for the mixture of smoke and fog he was breathing, and the speed with which the word became popular no doubt reflected the severity of the problem in the public mind.

By and large, the United States and the rest of Europe saw the smog problem in England (when they saw it at all) largely as a uniquely British phenomenon. After all, London's fogs were well known, and a little smoke would of course make it worse, but it didn't do all that much harm, and besides, it couldn't happen anywhere else. But then it did—in Belgium in the winter of 1930, in the deep, narrow, highly industrialized valley of the Meuse River. Beginning on Monday, December 1, a period of five days of abnormally high pollution killed 63 people and made several hundred others ill with acute pulmonary attacks. In what has since become a familiar pattern, this five-day period was characterized by a tremendous accumulation of smoke and other pollutants, which seemed never to disperse at all in the muggy, breezeless air. By the third day, many people were ill and dying; most of the deaths were among the elderly or those with preexisting lung or heart trouble. Cattle, birds, and even rats were killed.

The causes of such occurrences have since become so well known (and so often repeated) that such an incident has come to be called a "classic episode." At the time, however, the causes weren't understood; many and various explanations were offered, most of which seemed designed to exonerate the industrial establishments in the valley. Sulfur dioxide was blamed by some, but more recent knowledge has shown that impossibly high levels of SO_2 would be needed to cause that much damage alone. In retrospect, a more likely answer involves hydrofluoric acid with the SO_2, although the precise truth can never be known or proved.

Lacking a good explanation, people could do little but wait and see what happened next. But what happened next was not to answer any questions. The Great Depression settled over the economic life of the world, industrial activity ground to a lower level if not to a halt, and those who thought about the Meuse Valley in the early 1930s no doubt were readily convinced that it was a totally unique occurrence.

The next brief glimpse into the history of air pollution control occurs in the United States, in St. Louis. American cities, especially those on the great inland waterways, tend to develop heavy industrial economies fueled almost exclusively by coal. As the depression limped to a close in the late 1930s, St. Louis (along with Pittsburgh and many other cities) found itself increasingly burdened with the unpleasant effects of massive coal-burning. The most striking effect to the public then, and surely the most to us today, was the reduction in sunlight caused by black smoke in the air. In the winter, when residential use of coal furnaces was added to industrial use of coal, it was not at all unusual to find that street lights and automobile headlights were needed at noon. By the late 1930s community demands for an end to the darkness at noon caused the passage of a law regulating the quality of fuel permitted to be used. After 1940, when the law became effective (with strict enforcement), the situation was greatly improved, and citizens reaped not only the psychological gain of being able to see across the street, but also the economic benefit of reduced electric bills, less dry cleaning of clothes, and so on.

This early victory in St. Louis, however, was not to be immediately repeated in other cities; the attention of the United States was drawn to Europe, Pearl Harbor, and World War II. The war, which of course had a major impact on almost every aspect of life, had its implications for air pollution, too. Not only was concern over pollution understandably buried under other worries, but the massive war mobilization brought the country out of the depression and started a technological boom which is with us yet. Every existing productive resource was turned to high gear and poured into the war effort. New industries were born overnight; the Japanese cut off supplies of rubber from southeast Asia, and the need for a synthetic substitute built "Rubbertown" on the outskirts of Louisville, Kentucky. The atomic age was born in secret, and electric power plants began fueling the uranium-processing industry. In a hundred ways, the war extended our capacity to pollute the environment, but no one noticed; understandably, the eyes of the country were on the war, and little publicity on the productivity of our industrial machine would be forthcoming at such a time, anyway.

As a result, when the war ended in 1945, the American public was surprised to find a sizeable problem in an area of life that most of them hadn't thought of for a while. In Pittsburgh, "The Smoky City" for half a century, public protest and civic concern brought a successful smoke-control program similar to that enacted in St. Louis earlier. Other cities, large and small, began to take notice of their problem, which was almost always the same: dirty, black smoke, sulfurous odors and irritation from the burning of soft coal, and various other visible or smelly effluents from various sources.

At the same time, on the West Coast, a new problem was rearing its head, although at the time it wasn't recognized as new. The sprawling urban area in the Los Angeles Basin of southern California had had its share, and more, of the wartime boom; during the war, Angelenos had increasingly found their mountain view hidden behind a grey haze which made their eyes water and smart and frequently mottled and wilted flowers and crops. In 1945, with the war out of the way, public demand for something to be done about the "smog" soon resulted in legislation creating the Los Angeles County Air Pollution Control District. In 1947 regulations were passed to control the emission of smoke and SO_2, the primary suspects in the smogs of London, the Meuse Valley, and St. Louis.

Then, as if to confirm the urgency felt in Los Angeles, Pittsburgh, and elsewhere, the first obvious killer smog in the United States struck in October 1948. The dubious honor went to Donora, Pennsylvania, a small industrial town of 12,000 in the valley of the Monongehela River about 30 miles south of Pittsburgh. From October 27–31 pollutants from the town's homes, a zinc smelter, a steel mill, and a sulfuric acid plant accumulated in the windless valley. Within two days 40% of the people were sick, and by the third day, 20 had died.

In many ways the "Donora episode" marked the beginning of the modern air pollution control cause in the United States. It told the public and the authorities that the deaths in the Meuse Valley were not a unique occurrence and that a city didn't need to be big and foggy like London to have killing smogs. The Donora incident also drew the federal government into the air pollution field. The Public Health Service, the chief medical agency of the federal government, made a retrospective medical study of the populace of Donora, and from this ultimately developed the present program of the Environmental Protection Agency (EPA).

In the meantime, however, the major confrontation was shifting to Los Angeles. In direct contrast to the experience of St. Louis and Pittsburgh, control of smoke and SO_2 in Los Angeles had not diminished the symptoms, and it was beginning to be apparent that Los Angeles "smog" was different from that experienced elsewhere. The use of coal in southern California had never been extensive, as in the East near the coal fields; hence, the control of coal-produced pollution was not major and was readily completed. When that little control failed to do anything, the authorities next attacked SO_2 pollution from the combustion of oil, which *was* the major fuel used in the area. In fact, Los Angeles is one of the largest petroleum processing and consumption centers in the nation, and control of pollution from the refineries, etc., was no simple task. It was undertaken, however, and pursued successfully. But controlling this SO_2 also made little headway in reducing the symptoms.

At about this time, Professor A. J. Haagen-Smit of California Institute of Technology demonstrated in the laboratory that the effects seen in the Los Angeles atmosphere could be reproduced by shining ultraviolet light on a mixture of chemicals totally different from SO_2. The chemicals thus demonstrated to be the culprits were oxides of nitrogen and various hydrocarbons, which are emitted from several types of sources that burn organic material. The Los Angeles community once again knuckled down, as it were; hydrocarbon pollution from the petroleum refineries was reduced, and the private backyard burning of household garbage and trash was banned.

But even these measures failed to curtail the eye-watering and mountain-obscuring. The scientific and pollution control authorities increasingly came to recognize that the source of the problem was much closer to home than they had realized. The process of elimination brought the realization that ordinary, everyday automobiles were the principal problem. Automobile exhaust includes, among other things, both of the ingredients of the "smog"—oxides of nitrogen and hydrocarbons. The sprawling Los Angeles area, however, is probably more dependent on motor vehicles than is any other city, and to prohibit autos would grind the city to a halt. Thus, a way had to be found to eliminate or reduce the exhaust pollution without eliminating the cars. This brings us conceptually to the present, as far as Los Angeles pollution is concerned. Since the 1950s, effort has been expended toward the control of the pollution from the automobile, but to date the final solution is not in.

The rising role of automobile pollution has had an effect on the vocabulary of air pollution. The massive publicity given the Los Angeles problem, and the initial confusion, caused the word "smog," coined in England for the "smoke-fog" pollution, to become associated in this country with the photochemically caused pollution of the Los Angeles Basin, which involves neither smoke nor fog. To minimize any confusion, the word is now generally used only with a modifier; the phrase "London smog" means the smoke-SO_2-fog miasma that affects primarily coal-burning areas, and the phrase "Los Angeles smog" or "photochemical smog" means the "newer" variety caused by auto exhaust. The word "smog" alone is still used frequently as a slang term for air pollution in general.

Returning now to our chronological narrative as the second half of the century opens, there is one more distinct event that has come to be a part of the history of air pollution. In 1952, almost as though it meant to defend its name against the usurper from California, the London smog struck again. During and after four days of "pea-soup fog" in December, there were 4000 excess deaths; as before, they were mostly among the ill and the elderly. By now, modern science was a little better prepared—measurements of the pollution were made (SO_2 reached 1.3 ppm), sophisticated actuarial techniques produced the death statistics, and weather observations were being routinely gathered. This information helped greatly in defining the typical "air pollution episode." It didn't, of course, help those killed by the smog. Nonetheless, the 1952 London episode, the most catastrophic yet, had the one good effect of paving the way for the Clean Air Act, England's major air pollution control legislation.

The 1950s saw in the United States the establishment of a formal federal air pollution program and a gradual increase in the number of state and local control efforts. The early sixties saw the first partial control of emissions from autos in California and in December 1962, the first worldwide-scale episode. This episode was really a sequence of nearly simultaneous occurrences of severe air pollution in the eastern United States, Western Europe, and Japan; to the delight of the news media, the stagnation hit Washington, D.C., just prior to a major National Conference on Air Pollution and thereby helped the passage of a major law the following year. The latter half of the sixties saw a greatly increased effort by control authorities, supported by a major federal financing effort, stringent new legislation, and a greatly increased level of public interest and support.

With the public awareness that both flowed from and helped produce the student activism of the late 1960s and early 1970s came a new perspective, one that placed air pollution in a broader environmental context, interwoven with problems of water pollution, solid-waste disposal, noise and radiation hazards, and concern with the overall quality of life. This perspective was reflected in the consolidation of environmental programs in the federal Environmental Protection Agency (EPA) and similar state organizations. Although the more technical problems of the various environmental areas may still need to be solved separately, the broader environmental perspective can't help but clarify and move us closer to solving the fundamental economic and social problems that are the root of our difficulties.

No sooner had this new perspective begun to settle in for the long haul, however, than the context within which we must make our environmental decisions was broadened again. The "energy crisis" has called into question some of the initial environmental decisions recently made; air pollution, in particular, is closely related to our production and use of energy, both in the use of fuels for heat and electric power and in the use of gasoline for motor transport. The shortage of oil forced those electric power plants that could to change over to burning coal, and antipollution restrictions on home heating oils had to be relaxed. In the other direction, the gasoline shortage has had commuters more and more embracing car-pooling, mass transit, and smaller cars—pollution-reducing measures that had often been heartily rejected less than a year earlier. The energy crisis has been eagerly seized upon by pollution control opponents of varied stripe, and there is no more clear concensus on the questions they raise than there is on the cause of the oil shortage itself. The conflict has surely served, however, to emphasize that environmental questions, like those about energy use, reach to the very core of our daily lives. But this is all much too recent to fit under "history"; details will come in other chapters, and perspective will have to come at some point in the future.

These new perspectives we've just mentioned relate to the place of air pollution within broader areas of concern; the air pollution control field itself, our more narrow concern here, is somewhat less fluid. At some ill-defined time in the sixties, once the two types of smog had been recognized and were being dealt with realistically, there was a certain jelling in the field that produced a structure still largely unchanged in basic concepts, though changing continually in detail and emphasis.

THE PRESENT

As we consider this structure, certainly the most logical place to begin is with a definition of our topic. Air pollution is usually defined as the presence in the outdoor atmosphere of a substance or substances, put there directly or indirectly by an act of man, in such an amount as to be detrimental to his health, safety, or welfare, or as to interfere with the full use and enjoyment of his property. Such a definition sounds rather legalistic, but each phrase contributes its own specific point and warrants elaboration.

"...in the outdoor atmosphere..." In practice, only the outdoor ambient atmosphere is considered in the term air pollution; two indoor atmospheres, the workplace atmosphere and the domestic or home atmosphere, are considered separately. The first of these is treated in a field called occupational health or industrial hygiene. The second, the domestic atmosphere, is generally not treated in any systematic way by any group at the present, largely because there has seemed to be relatively little need. Some work on pollutants in domestic atmospheres has been done by air pollution people, and it is possible that our definition will someday be expanded.

"...by an act of man..." Man is not the only agent able to put substances into the atmosphere; there are many natural processes that do so, such as pollination, volcanoes, dust storms, and forest fires, which, for purposes of definition, are excluded here. There are also a few pollutants, sometimes called "secondary," that are not put into the air by man, but are formed naturally in the air from the "primary" pollutants that *are* put into the air by man. The principal example is the photochemical smog of Los Angeles, formed in the air from substances emitted from automobiles. These secondary pollutants *are* included in the definition. The crux of the distinction between these two groups is whether they are controllable. Substances put into the air by man are presumably controllable by man and hence any secondary pollutants are controllable. Since our purpose is to control pollution, it seems pointless to begin by defining into our subject natural events that are not controllable. This is not a hard and fast defini-

tion, nor universally accepted; some would include all events and then relegate the uncontrollables to a subset called "natural air pollution." Actually, if one pursues the details far enough, there emerges a fuzziness in the concept of controllable also. The duststorms in the "dust bowls" of the Southwest were caused by man's disregard of nature; some forest fires are natural and some are caused by man.

"...in such amounts..." Traditionally, a foreign substance in the air has been called "pollution" if it causes any type of harm and "contamination" if it is either intrinsically harmless or present in such small amounts as to be effectively harmless. This traditional "amounts to interfere" clause is thus something of a hedge in the sense that it defines pollution in terms of a possibly ill-definable effect. As we become increasingly aware of the very, very delicate balance of life on our planet, it is being realized that we might be more prudent to adopt a "fail-safe" philosophy, which regards any atmospheric contamination as guilty unless proved harmless, or more realistically, to question the entire concept of whether there should really be any distinction between "pollution" and "contamination," between harmful and not. As a passing footnote, it seems likely to me that the word "pollution" has come into such common use that the general public would probably, at first hearing, feel that the less-common "contamination" is worse than "pollution."

"...a substance or substances..." Another aspect of the definition is raised by the use of the word "substances," which implies tangible chemical entities and excludes other offensive things that might come through the air to assault us, such as excessive noise or perhaps television commercials. The former is a legitimate subject in the area of environmental health; the latter is, at least so far, not in this province, although its mention does remind us that the air is full of intangible as well as tangible substances.

Another significant aspect of the phrase "substance or substances" is its lack of modifiers. Ten years ago, this would have been phrased "foreign substances" or "substances not normally present." However, more recently we have come to recognize that too much of a very natural atmospheric constituent, put there by an act of man, may be detrimental also and hence should be included in our definition. The principal example of this presently is the increase in the atmospheric carbon dioxide content, caused by our massive consumption of fossil fuels.

The Pollutants

Strictly speaking, one might expect the word "pollutant" to mean a specific chemical substance, which it does, but it's also used in a slightly broader sense to include groups and classes of chemicals, as we'll see shortly. Of the many substances and groups of substances that are pollutants of concern to one degree or another, six are presently considered major, in the sense that they have been known longest and studied most, and they are the ones toward which the most control effort is being directed. This distinction has been formalized by the federal government; under the terms of the Clean Air Act, the Environmental Protection Agency (EPA) has legally established National Ambient Air Quality Standards for these six pollutants, standards that reflect the concentration levels of the pollutants that are believed to be safe. The first two of the six, particulate matter and sulfur oxides, are involved in the London smog. The other four have come into prominence via their association with the automobile—carbon monoxide because of its known toxicity; hydrocarbons, nitrogen oxides, and oxidants because of their involvement in Los Angeles or photochemical smog.

Particulate matter. This pollutant wins the privilege of being first by virtue of being the most obvious pollutant; it is what most people think of when they hear the phrase "air pollution," because it is responsible for the most conspicuous aspects of pollution—the visible plume from a smokestack, the gray haze obscuring a distant view, and the dust and dirt on windowsills or in eyes. The word "particulate" itself derives from "particle" and is used to include all solid or liquid substances in the air. There is a tremendous variety of such material in the air, primarily solid rather than liquid. It comes from a wide variety of sources, in all sizes, shapes, colors, textures, and chemical compositions, and can remain suspended in the air for periods ranging from a few seconds to a few years.

Particulate matter is usually divided into two categories—"suspended particulates" and "dustfall," or "settleable dust." The first includes the smaller particles, which remain suspended in the air for a significant length of time; the second, the larger particles that settle out on the ground relatively quickly. The distinction between the two categories is obviously blurry, but is useful in practice.

Sulfur oxides. This pollutant, written as SO_x in chemical shorthand, is a combination of two gases—sulfur dioxide (SO_2) and sulfur trioxide (SO_3) —and particulate sulfates (SO_4). Most of this pollutant is emitted to the atmosphere as sulfur dioxide, but it is chemically converted to SO_3 and sulfates in the air, thus making it difficult to make a clear-cut distinction in talking about the various forms. Along with particulate matter in the form of smoke, sulfur oxides have been implicated in the smogs of London, the Meuse Valley, Donora, etc.

Carbon monoxide. CO is a gas produced primarily by the combustion of gasoline in internal-combustion engines. In the frequent cases of accidental death or suicide by running an auto in a closed garage, CO is the specific cause of the suffocation. It does this by interfering with the blood's ability to carry oxygen from the lungs to the brain and the rest of the body.

Nitrogen oxides. This pollutant is a pair of closely related chemical compounds, nitric oxide (NO) and nitrogen dioxide (NO_2), both gases. Oxides of nitrogen are a by-product of the combustion of any fuel, the heat of the combustion causing the chemical combination of nitrogen and oxygen, both natural constituents of the air. Oxides of nitrogen are of concern primarily because they are ingredients in the production of photochemical smog.

Hydrocarbons. The other ingredient of photochemical smog, hydrocarbons, is less well defined than are the other pollutants. The hydrocarbons are a huge class of chemical compounds lumped together because of the complicated nature of measuring them separately. Not all of the compounds in the group are actually involved in the smog, and some have other effects besides smog. Because of these complications, the grouping of these compounds into one "pollutant" is less desirable than is true for the other groupings (we'll return to this point in greater detail in Chapter 3).

Photochemical oxidants. The last of the six "major" pollutants, photochemical oxidants constitute the only pollutant which is not directly emitted to the air by human activities; rather, these oxidants are chemically formed in the air. An oxidant is any chemical capable of causing a certain type of chemical reaction (oxidation) to take place; as such, the very definition of the pollutant depends on the chemical means employed to measure it. The reason for concern with oxidants is that several of the substances known or believed to cause the ill effects of photochemical smog are oxidants, and hence they are included in a measurement of the oxidizing potential of the air. The two most common of these oxidants are ozone (O_3) and peroxyacetyl nitrate (PAN for slang). As with hydrocarbons, it would be better to measure the various compounds separately, and this is increasingly becoming the case.

The Effects of Air Pollution

Having defined pollution in terms of its deleterious effects, we should now consider briefly the types of effects that are known to be possible. There are effects on all forms of life, including humans, and various effects on nonliving materials. These effects range from very immediate—obvious when they occur—to very slow, insidious effects that are apparent only after years or perhaps can only be inferred from indirect evidence. Sometimes, the effects are synergistic in nature, with simultaneous exposure to more than one pollutant causing combined effects greater than the total of the effects caused separately.

   The effects usually considered most important are those that involve human health. They are generally one of two types—either a nonspecific irritation of the respiratory tract or systemic poisoning by a specific biologically active compound. The extreme example of the former is the death and illness during a London-type smog episode; of the latter, carbon monoxide suffocation. The more subtle, long-term effects on human health are at present not so well defined and are recognized from either laboratory studies with animals or statistical studies of large groups of people. There are also effects on humans other than health damage; the most apparent are the psychological degradation caused by living in an unpleasant environment and the possibility of long-range damage to our ecology.

Economic costs are the other principal type of effect traditionally considered. There are many effects of pollution that are principally economic, such as the accelerated deterioration of materials or the damage to commercial farm crops. There are also the economic aspects of biological effects, such as the lost work time and the economic costs of sickness and medical care.

In the last decade or two, wholly different groups of effects, those on our physical environment and on other living species, have been increasingly discovered, and these are now beginning to receive more serious attention. Many segments of society now recognize that human life should be viewed in the context of the entire *biosphere*, the entire life-supporting portion of our planet, including the lower atmosphere, the water, and that upper portion of the solid crust that is involved with biological processes. Although adopting this viewpoint is more urgent with respect to other environmental concerns, such as the effects of pesticides on wildlife, it is also meaningful for our purposes.

Sources of Air Pollutants

By our definition, pollution can result only from human action. Although almost every conceivable human activity seems able to produce pollution of some sort, the primary sources of air pollution emissions are the combustion of fuels and the various manufacturing processes, each of which includes a wide range of activities. We burn fuels of various types for almost every activity we carry on: gasoline for transport; coal, oil, and gas for heating our buildings, generating electricity, providing heat for cooking, and so on. The use of gasoline produces some particulates, much of the hydrocarbons and nitrogen oxides, and hence much of the photochemical smog, and almost all the carbon monoxide. Coal and oil combustion produces most of the sulfur oxides and particulates. Natural gas is the "cleanest" fuel; gas combustion does produce a fair amount of nitrogen oxides, but not as much as the use of gasoline in autos.

The industrial-processes category is the smaller of the two, producing only half as much particulate matter as fuel combustion, one fourth the

SO_x, and smaller portions of the other pollutants. On the other hand, the nature of pollutant emissions from process sources is less consistent than that from fuel combustion, is harder to deal with, and includes the greater share of the less-than-major pollutants.

It is true, however, that the image of the factory as the vast majority of the pollution is not completely accurate. The pollution caused by individuals and their activities is at least as significant as the process losses and industry's share of the pollution from fuel combustion, although of course the individual doesn't have much opportunity to do anything about it. Actually, trying to put the blame on one or another segment of our society is a relatively futile enterprise; the most accurate generalization is merely to say that our materialistic standard of living, created by our industrial economy, is the villain, and the most appropriate action is to set out doing something about it.

What we generally want to do about the pollutant sources is to "control" them, that is, to reduce or eliminate their emissions. This is done either by changing the source in some way, e.g., by using a different fuel, or by removing some of the pollution from the effluent before it is released to the air.

The Scope of Our Topic

Our definition of air pollution has just led us directly to three of the major areas of technical interest in the field: (1) the identification and measurement of the pollutants themselves; (2) the study of the effects they cause on our health and otherwise, and (3) the identification and control of the sources emitting the pollutants. There is another major technical area, meteorology, that arises implicitly. The motions and other properties of the atmosphere determine the concentration of pollution in the air and hence what effects will arise from specific emissions of pollutants from their sources. This is an important role—Los Angeles' severe pollution problem, for example, is caused in large measure by adverse meteorological factors — and consequently, air pollution meteorology is an area of major interest.

Beyond these technical areas of interest, however, there are other areas that are important to the control of air pollution. These are the legal and administrative procedures adopted by society to control air pollution. Just as the technical aspects of air pollution pose very interesting scientific and engineering problems and questions, so too do the nontechnical aspects raise serious and challenging problems of public policy and social administration. These latter aspects of the pollution problem, considered in later chapters, are in my view an important, integral part of the overall topic on which we're about to embark.

EXERCISES

Review Questions

1. What point in time is described as the beginning of our air pollution problem?
2. When were smoke-control laws first introduced in this country? When did St. Louis and Pittsburgh conduct their famous clean-up campaigns?
3. Name and distinguish between the two types of "smog."
4. Briefly describe a classic episode. When and where was the first one in the United States?
5. List several elements of the definition of air pollution used here.
6. List the six major pollutants discussed. Which are involved in each of the two smog types?
7. What broad types of pollutant effects were noted?

Thought Question

8. Why is the carbon dioxide we exhale not considered pollution? What happens to it?

Discussion Questions

9. It is sometimes suggested that air pollution should be defined very generally, e.g., "the presence of something in the air that shouldn't be there." List some arguments for and against making this change, and then make your own choice on the issue.
10. Do you consider more important the study of the effects of air pollution or the study of means of controlling pollution sources? Why? From what viewpoint did you make your decision? What viewpoint might give a different view?

Project Suggestion

11. If you have access to a library's file of back newspapers from one of the appropriate cities, look up the stories concerning the smog episodes or the smoke-control programs.

FURTHER READING

Most of the books listed in the "General" section of the Bibliography have something to contribute to an overall understanding of the general environmental movement, the increased public awareness, that we've referred to. Commoner's *The Closing Circle* [4] is probably the best by a single author; *No Deposit — No Return* [10] the best multiauthor sampler. Wise's *Killer Smog* [22] is a fascinating narrative of the 1952 London smog; unfortunately, no comprehensive history of pollution, as history, has been written yet. Virginia Brodine [2] treats a 1969 episode in depth in narrative style; [75] treats the major 1962 episode, and [80] another in 1966, both in a somewhat more technical vein. The 1661 essay by John Evelyn is entitled "Fumifugium: or the Inconvenience of Aer and Smoake of London Dissapated, together with Some Remedies Humbly Proposed." Humble or otherwise, Evelyn's proposed remedies were not stupid, but they were not followed either. His essay has been published and republished in various places over the centuries; try the nearest large research library.

2

AIR POLLUTION METEOROLOGY

Columbus Ohio Dispatch, Courtesy EPA

This second introductory chapter deals with the air and how its nature and behavior affect the pollution we put into it (and breathe out of it). There are two reasons for devoting a chapter to meteorology so early in the text. First, of course, is the need for various bits of meteorological knowledge throughout the rest of the discussion; since the air is the medium we are polluting, some basic background will underlie many of the subsequent topics, and it is much easier to pursue all the meteorological topics together, in one logical whole. Beyond this, however, meteorology is an area we meet regularly in our everyday lives, and it may be a little more comfortable to begin with something familiar.

THE ATMOSPHERE

The atmosphere that surrounds the earth performs two basic types of functions for us. It shields and protects us from some of the harmful things coming to our planet from outside, and it functions as a medium of storage and distribution for many substances that are part of the vital processes of the earth. The first of these roles is of only indirect concern in air pollution, being largely a function of the upper atmosphere rather than that lower portion with which we are normally concerned. These functions of the upper atmosphere are nonetheless crucial, involving shielding the surface of the earth (and us) from meteors and some of the harmful types of radiation, primarily ultraviolet and cosmic rays.

The second type of atmospheric function, the storage and distribution of various substances, applies to many of the components of life in the biosphere. The atmosphere stores and distributes water vapor and heat energy to moderate our climate. It stores and distributes oxygen and CO_2; in fact, if we view the atmosphere a little differently from the way we usually do, its "function" of providing us with oxygen to breathe is really just a relatively small part of the larger oxygen-CO_2 distribution cycle that involves all forms of life. The atmosphere, of course, also stores and distributes the various contaminants that we put into it, and it is this function that is of primary interest in air pollution. The behavior of the atmosphere is the one factor that by itself completely determines whether our pollution will hang around to haunt us or will blow away (to bother someone else).

Physical Nature of the Atmosphere

In Chapter 1 we noted briefly that the atmosphere is a mixture of gases held to the planet by gravitational attraction, and we tabulated its composition in Table 1–1. The total mass of the atmosphere amounts to 5.7×10^{15} (5,700,000,000,000,000) tons of air. Though this is a tremendous number, as are all global numbers, the atmosphere is nonetheless a relatively thin shell around the earth. Not only is it spread over 198 million square miles of earth surface, but also the vast majority of the atmosphere is compressed into a thin layer near the bottom. Thus, the pressure, density, and mass of the atmosphere decrease strikingly as one rises above the surface. Figure 2–1 illustrates the vertical variation of the temperature in the atmosphere and how it is divided into layers by fairly abrupt temperature changes; only the lowest level, the troposphere, is routinely involved in our weather and hence in air pollution.

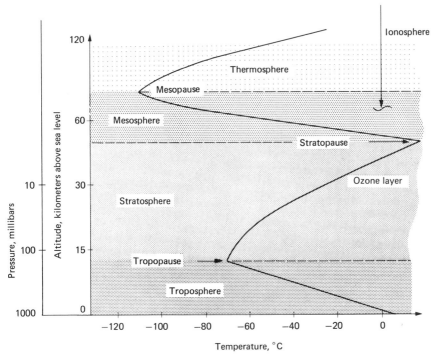

Fig. 2–1. The vertical structure of the atmosphere. The several layers of the atmosphere, determined primarily by the phenomena that occur there, are separated from one another by changes in the slope of the graph of temperature vs. altitude. In the lowest level, the troposphere, the temperature decreases with increasing altitude until at the tropopause (10–12 km), the temperature is −70°C. The next layer, the stratosphere, is characterized by increasing temperature, since near the top of the layer is a region where the ultraviolet solar radiation is absorbed by ozone. This makes the stratopause a warm area of the atmosphere and also provides an effective shield, keeping the harmful ultraviolet radiation from the ground. (J. Spar, *Earth, Sea, and Air*, 2d ed., Reading, Mass.: Addison-Wesley, 1965, p. 98.)

Radiation and Heat Balance

The earth receives radiant energy from the sun, uses it in various ways, and then radiates it back out into space. The nature of the radiation, and the difference between the incoming and outgoing radiation, is involved with air pollution in three ways. First, the imbalance in the distribution of the incoming and outgoing energy provides the driving force behind the motions of the atmosphere, which control the dispersion of substances in the air. Second, the way in which the solar radiation is absorbed by the earth is involved in understanding the vertical variation in the temperature of the atmosphere. Third, as we will see in Chapter 5, the possibility exists that our pollution may even alter the radiation balance.

The imbalance in the distribution of incoming and outgoing radiation is the result of the geometry of a sphere. The incoming energy is a unit cross-section of the sun's rays, about two calories* per square centimeter per minute, and is distributed over a larger area near the poles than near the equator, as seen in Fig. 2–2(a). Thus, at the higher latitudes the amount of solar radiation received per unit surface area is less than at the equator, with the effect proportional to the cosine of the latitude. In contrast, the outgoing radiation is distributed much more uniformly with latitude, as shown in Fig. 2–2(b). In order for these two situations to exist simultaneously, there must be a major transfer of heat energy from the equatorial regions toward the poles; one of the ways this is accomplished is through the motion of the atmosphere. As it eddies and whirls about, the air carries excess heat north and south away from the equator; in this sense, we say that the imbalance of radiation is the driving force behind all atmospheric motions.

The immediate fate of the solar energy arriving at the earth is also of interest. The surface of the earth, with its covering atmosphere and clouds, presents a very mixed reception to the incoming sunlight. Some of the solar energy is absorbed by the air, some by the clouds, and some by the earth, and some is reflected back out into space. Figure 2–3(a) indicates how the incoming radiation is distributed, on the average, between absorption by the ground (47%) and the atmosphere (19%) and reflection back into space (34%). The most significant point concerning air pollution is that the majority of the radiation that is absorbed is absorbed by the ground, the earth, rather than by the atmosphere. This means that the air itself is generally warmed from the bottom, where it touches the warmer earth, rather than by the sun; in turn, this means that during daylight hours the air nearest the ground is usually the warmest, a point we shall see to be significant. Figure 2–3(b) presents a similar breakdown of the radiation leaving the earth. Here, we note that the radiation leaving the ground goes first primarily to the atmosphere, then back out to space, rather than being radiated directly out into space. We will return to this point in Chapter 5.

---

* These are calories with a lower-case "c," the physicists' unit for measuring energy; the dietary Calories, with a capital "C," are 1000 times larger.

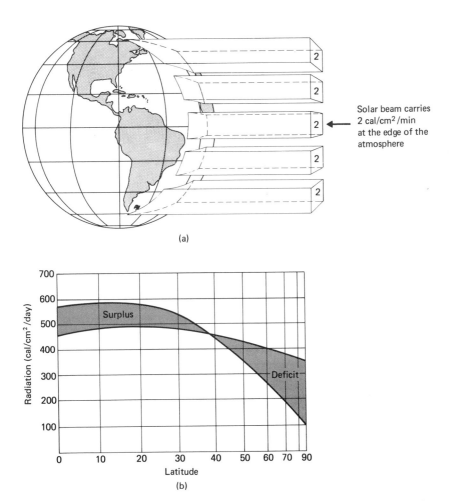

Fig. 2–2. Global temperature imbalances caused by uneven distribution of incoming solar radiation: (a) distribution of incoming radiation varies with latitude (J. A. Day and G. L. Sternes, *Climate and Weather*, Reading, Mass.: Addison-Wesley, 1970, p. 144); (b) distribution of outgoing energy, much more even, results in excess energy at the equator, a force that drives the winds toward the poles. (A. Miller and J. C. Thompson, *Elements of Meteorology*, Columbus, Ohio: Charles E. Merrill, 1970. p. 83. Reprinted by permission.)

HORIZONTAL MOTIONS AND CIRCULATIONS

For most of us, the horizontal motion of the air, which we sense as wind, is the most familiar aspect of the air, and it is also of primary significance in air pollution. The speed of the wind determines how much the pollution is diluted and blown away, while the direction of the wind determines in

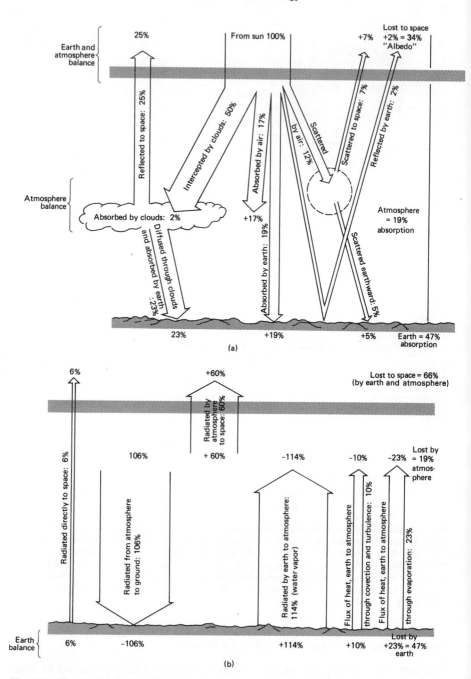

Fig. 2–3. The heat balance of the earth: (a) distribution of incoming radiation—34%, the "albedo," is reflected, and 66% is absorbed, more by the earth than by the air; (b) distribution of outgoing radiation—reradiation, in a different form, of the 66% originally absorbed. (A. Miller and J. C. Thompson, *Elements of Meteorology*, Columbus, Ohio: Charles E. Merrill, 1970, pp. 74–75. Reprinted by permission.)

which direction this dilution and spreading takes place. The latter of these effects is obvious, but sometimes the first requires a little thought. If a pollution source is emitting at a certain rate, that is, emitting a certain amount of pollution per unit time, that much pollution will be distributed into however much air comes by in that same unit time. This determines the concentration of the pollutant, the amount of pollutant in a certain amount of air. Thus, when the wind speed doubles, say, the amount of air coming past the pollution source doubles, and the resulting concentration will be only half what it had been. In this sense, the amount of wind is a primary determinant of the concentration of pollution in the air down-wind of a pollution source.

The driving forces behind all the motions in the air are temperature imbalances, large or small, which cause differences in pressure, since warm air is lighter than cooler air. The atmosphere responds, by moving, to the forces caused by these pressure differences; in moving, the air then brings into play other forces that further modify its motion. The dynamics and interactions of these various forces are quite interesting, but for brevity are omitted here; of primary interest in our consideration of air pollution are the resulting motions themselves.

The motion of the air at any point is the composite result of many motions of different sizes, ranging from global circulations over half a con-

TABLE 2–1
Scales of motion in the atmosphere

Name	Typical horizontal dimensions	Description
Planetary	1000–10,000 km	Primary global circulation patterns; caused by global-scale temperature imbalances, they are nearly permanent.
Synoptic	100–1000 km	Traveling cyclones and anticyclones in the middle latitudes; also caused by global temperature imbalances, they last for several days or sometimes weeks.
Mesoscale	1–100 km	Small convective cells driven by local temperature imbalances, such as the land-sea breeze, mountain-valley breezes, and thunderstorms; generally last at most several hours.
Microscale	1 cm–1 km	Small turbulent eddies; caused by surface roughness— buildings, trees, and smaller effects; each eddy lasting a few minutes at most, these are major factors in the mixing of pollutants.
Molecular	10^{-6} cm	Sound waves and natural molecular motions in a gas.

tinent to dust devils over half a driveway and even smaller. For convenience in discussing such a wide range of motions, meteorologists have arbitrarily classified them into groups by size or scale, as listed in Table 2–1.

Planetary Circulations

The largest motions are the planetary circulations, the overall average movements of the air over global-scale distances. They are the primary carriers of heat energy from the equator toward the poles and in fact are produced as a direct result of the temperature imbalance between the equator and the poles. This is most easily seen by visualizing these circulations on a stationary, nonrotating earth; they would then appear as vertically circulating air masses, or thermal cells, as shown in Fig. 2–4(a). Such a model of atmospheric circulation was proposed as early as the eighteenth century by the Englishman Sir George Hadley; consequently, the thermal convection cells are called Hadley cells. The earth's rotations, however, break these cells up into three smaller circulations, as shown in Fig. 2–4(b), the middle one being rather weak. The temperature differences between the oceans and the continents further break up the center cell into two, large, semipermanent, circulating high-pressure systems, one centered in the North Atlantic and the other over the North Pacific, as

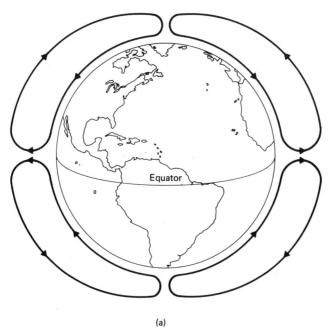

(a)

Fig. 2–4. Global air circulations: (a) on a nonrotating earth, a giant convection cell of air at the equator, warmed by maximum solar radiation, would rise and move northward, to be replaced by cooler air coming south at the surface (S. Williamson, *Fundamentals of Air Pollution,* Reading, Mass.: Addison, Wesley, 1973, p. 123); (b) the earth's rotation creates three smaller convection cells at various latitudes (J. Spar, *Earth, Air, and Sea,* 2d ed., Reading, Mass.: Addison-Wesley, 1965, p. 109).

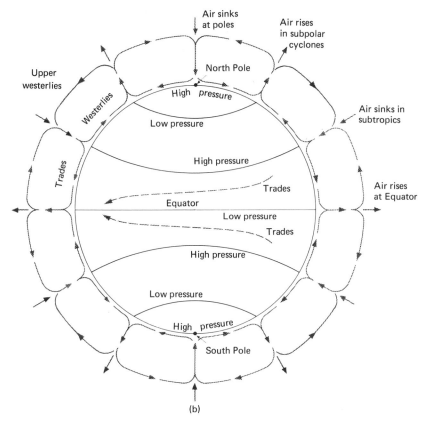

Fig. 2–4 (cont.)

shown in Fig. 2–5. There are no well-defined global circulations over the continental areas, just the turbulent flow of traveling weather systems.

The planetary circulations are of major importance in defining the type of human life on various parts of the earth. In particular, the two oceanic circulations largely determine the climate of the areas on their periphery. Winds blow clockwise around such high-pressure areas in the Northern Hemisphere; this means that the land on the eastern edge of such a system gets cool, dry air from the north. This wind pattern contributes to the glorious coastal climates of California and Spain, but it also causes the interior deserts of North Africa and the southwestern United States. In contrast, the western edges of the high-pressure systems bring moist, tropical air from the south, causing the hot, humid climates in Southeast Asia and the Gulf coast of the United States.

These two semipermanent air masses, huge as they are, also have their effects, sometimes very local ones, on air pollution. As the North Pacific high travels slightly southward in the fall and winter, it brings to the

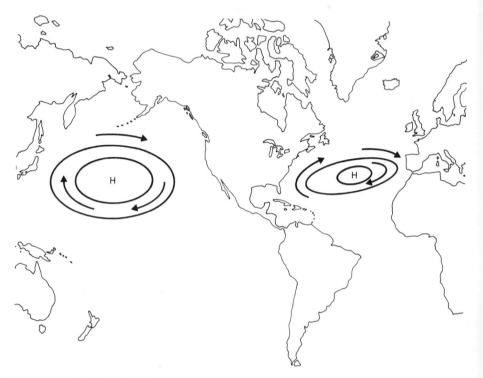

Fig. 2–5. The two global high-pressure systems.

Los Angeles Basin the peculiarly adverse meteorology that helps make its smog problem; similarly the Atlantic, or Bermuda, high has an effect on atmospheric stagnations in the East, as we'll see later.

Synoptic Motions

Somewhat smaller than the global circulations are synoptic motions, which consist mainly of rotational motions ranging in size from 100 to 1000 km. These synoptic motions are the traveling weather systems, described on the television weather shows, that come from the northwest, move eastward across the continent, then swing north again; as each such weather system passes by, it determines the weather in a given spot for two or three days. Over the midlatitude continental areas, such as those in the United States, these systems replace the global circulations in carrying heat north from the equator. In this sense, synoptic motions can be viewed as turbulence in the otherwise relatively smooth global circulation pattern.

Though it is somewhat oversimplified to do so, these traveling air masses are often distinguished as either high- or low-pressure systems, or just "highs" and "lows." More technically, a low-pressure system is known as a cyclone (hurricanes, etc., are extreme cyclones), whereas a high-pressure system is called an anticyclone. The patterns of air flow in such systems are consistent and result from the interactions of several different forces. Without going into great detail, we can characterize low-pressure cyclones in the Northern Hemisphere as counterclockwise rotations, with the air flowing generally inward toward the center and then upward. This rising tends to cause precipitation, and traveling low-pressure systems are frequently stormy (remember a sailor's interpretation of a falling barometer). In contrast, the high-pressure anticyclones rotate clockwise, and the air tends to diverge, or spiral outward, toward the lower pressure. This means that at the center of the system, the air must be replaced by air coming down (subsiding) from higher altitudes. In general, high-pressure systems are associated with fair, pleasant weather.

But, of course, these systems also have their significance in air pollution. One of the factors in Los Angeles' meteorology is that these moving systems don't come; conversely, the high winds such systems bring down across the Great Plains save the midsection of the country (including Chicago, the "Windy city") from having far worse pollution problems than it does. In the East, when a traveling high-pressure system bumps into the Bermuda high, we have a stagnation, a period of adverse meteorology (adverse with respect to air pollution, that is).

Mesoscale Motions

The next smaller motions, the mesoscale, are approximately the size of our urban areas. Since friction with the ground is a factor in these smaller movements, an area's topography begins to have some effect, but the mesoscale motions are nonetheless driven primarily by temperature imbalances. Included in this group of motions, along with thunderstorms, which we shall need to ignore, are two localized phenomena—the land-sea breeze and the mountain-valley wind, both of which have significant impact on local air pollution. These phenomena are shown in Fig. 2–6.

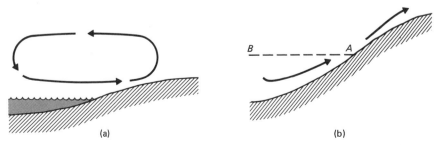

Fig. 2–6. (a) Land-sea breeze; (b) mountain-valley wind.

Coastal areas often develop circulations that are driven by the temperature differences between the land and the ocean, as shown in Fig. 2–6(a). In the morning, the sun warms the land much more rapidly than it does the water; the warmer air over the land tends to rise and is replaced by cooler air from over the ocean (a sea breeze). As the sun goes down, the land cools faster than the ocean does; sometimes, though not too frequently, the warmer air over the ocean tends to rise and is replaced by cooler air over the land (a land breeze). The sea breeze has an impact on air pollution in two ways. First, it can play a major role in carrying pollution generated near downtown water areas to inland areas. Second, if an evening land breeze has carried the pollution out to sea, a morning sea breeze can bring the pollution back to the land.

Mountain-valley winds are quite similar to sea breezes. However, the temperature differences that drive the mountain-valley winds are caused by differences in heights. Figure 2–6(b) shows that since point A is closer to the surface, the air there is warmer than at point B. The warmer air at A rises, creating a morning breeze up the side of the valley; the reverse can occur in the evening. Since pollution sources are often located on valley floors, this pattern of circulation is likely to move pollutants about in unexpected ways.

Microscale and Molecular Motions

The two smallest scales of motion should be mentioned for the sake of completeness, although their effects on air pollution are much simpler. The microscale motions include the dust devil and similar small-scale turbulence; although they have a very important role in mixing and dispersing the pollution as it is emitted from the sources, there are so many of them, in relatively random occurrence, that they can be discussed only as part of larger mixing phenomenon. The smallest motions, those of individual molecules in the air, have no significance in air pollution.

Before we leave the subject of horizontal air motions, we should digress briefly. Friction with the earth's surface is one of the several forces that act on moving air; in the case of the mesoscale and smaller motions, friction has a significant effect in slowing down the wind. This raises an important question. If friction with the earth's surface slows the wind down, why doesn't the wind just keep slowing and finally stop? Under normal conditions, the surface wind is kept moving, despite friction, by mixing with faster-moving air from above. When there is a significant reduction in the amount of vertical mixing, the winds at the surface become disconnected from the upper winds, and they do in fact slow down and essentially stop. This is one of several factors that constitute the typical meteorological conditions associated with classic smog episodes.

VERTICAL TEMPERATURE INVERSIONS

Vertical air movements are completely different from the horizontal movements of winds. Vertical distances are much smaller than horizontal distances, and vertical motions are dominated by completely different forces. The vertical pressure difference caused by gravity is far greater than any of the horizontal pressure gradients caused by temperature differences. However, since gravity is essentially constant, it is still the temperature imbalances that cause the air to move; the resulting motion, however, is quite different from the horizontal wind.

Compared with horizontal winds, vertical motions are less rapid, more random, and are sustained over much shorter periods of time. However, this vertical motion is a crucial aspect of the atmosphere's ability to mix and dilute pollutants. In effect, vertical motions determine how much of the atmosphere's depth will be available to disperse our pollution, and since this *mixing depth* ranges more widely than does the speed of the wind, it is often the most important factor in determining the air's capacity to disperse pollution. Therefore, we will look fairly carefully at the factors, primarily the temperature gradient, governing vertical motion in the air.

Temperature Gradient

The vertical temperature gradient, often called the lapse rate, is the rate at which the temperature changes with increasing height. Figure 2–1 showed that the air generally gets progressively cooler as the altitude increases, at least for the first few miles. This is a result of the basic laws of physics relating the pressure, volume, and temperature of gases, as well as of the fact that the air is heated from the bottom up. The reversal of this trend at the tropopause is caused by a totally different phenomenon, the absorption of radiation by ozone. Before sounding balloons reached that height to make actual measurements (around 1900), it was assumed that the atmospheric temperature just got colder and colder on out into space.

The quantitative rate at which the temperature decreases with height, that is, the slope of a graph of temperature vs. height, determines whether the pollution we emit at ground level will be mixed through a mixing depth of perhaps 5000 feet to produce relatively low concentrations, or whether it will be confined to a relatively thin layer, say, only a few hundred feet deep, producing much higher concentrations. If the temperature decreases more than 1°C with each 100 meters additional height (5.4°F per 1000 feet), the air will mix and stir about violently, dispersing pollutants fairly evenly through a large volume of air. On the other hand, if the rate of temperature decrease is less than 1°C per 100 meters, or if the temperature actually increases with height, the air will tend to remain the way it is, mixing will be inhibited, and pollutant concentrations will be higher. This one specific rate of vertical temperature decrease, the 1°C per 100

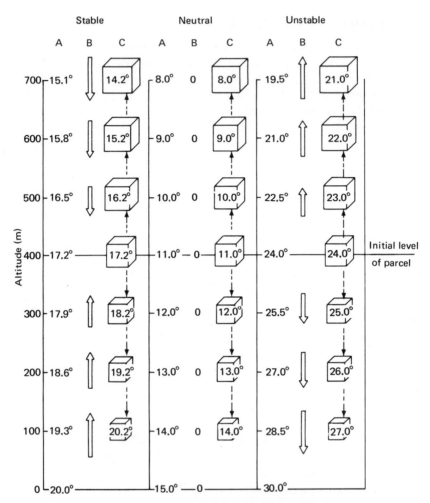

Fig. 2–7. The adiabatic lapse rate. This rate is the amount of temperature change that takes place in a parcel of air as it is moved vertically, and the motion of the parcel is determined by the relation between its own temperature and that of the surrounding air. Thus the left-hand column shows that the temperature decreases as the air parcel rises, at a rate greater than that of the surrounding air; therefore, the parcel is cooler and heavier than its surroundings and tends to sink back, as indicated by the arrows. (A. Miller and J. C. Thompson, *Elements of Meteorology*, Columbus, Ohio: Charles E. Merrill, 1970, p. 113. Reprinted by permission.)

meters, is known as the adiabatic lapse rate.* The reasons for its special significance, though interesting, are not crucial to our air pollution discussion; an intuitive explanation is presented in Fig. 2–7.

---

* Actually, this is the *dry* adiabatic lapse rate; if the air is very humid, saturated with moisture, a slightly different figure is appropriate.

The significance of the vertical temperature profile to air pollution is shown in Fig. 2–8, which illustrates several different profiles and their effect on a single pollution source. The slope of line A (adiabatic) is 1°C per 100 meters; at this adiabatic rate, the atmosphere is neutral with respect to mixing. Line B is superadiabatic, representing a temperature decrease more rapid than adiabatic. If the atmosphere had a temperature gradient like B, it would mix about violently of its own accord—the warmer, lower air rising, and the cooler, upper air coming down. Actually, the atmosphere never gets a B-type slope very much different from A, because as soon as it begins to shift that way, the resulting mixing rearranges the air in such a way as to reestablish a profile close to adiabatic. The slope of line C is less than that of line A and thus represents a decrease in temperature less than adiabatic; in this case, the air would not mix by itself and would be unlikely to mix very much, even if the mixing were started by an outside influence. The fourth profile in Fig. 2–8, line D, slopes the opposite way, indicating that the air temperature actually goes *up* with increasing height. This condition is known as an inversion—the warm air is above the cool air, and the slope of the graph is in the opposite direction from its normal position. In this inversion condition, any mixing

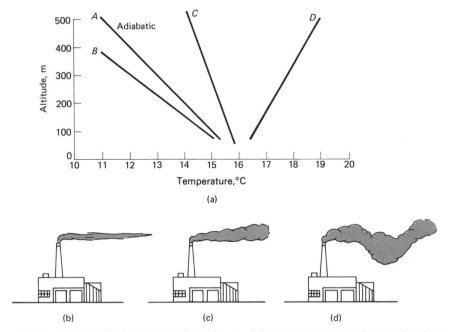

Fig. 2–8. Relationship between various slopes of the temperature gradient and various rates of atmospheric mixing and pollutant dispersal: (a) various temperature-gradient profiles; (b) stable, stratified plume produced by the most adverse gradient, an inversion (line D); (c) plume produced by gradient by adiabatic rate (line A); (d) violently mixed plume produced by a superadiabatic gradient.

in the air, even that caused by outside factors such as turbulence, is actively suppressed; therefore, the air remains very still, and the pollution remains at the height at which it was emitted.

Because inversion conditions were involved in the killer smogs mentioned in Chapter 1 and are partially the cause of Los Angeles' special problem, they have become fairly well known in the popular literature. Indeed, the word "inversion" is somewhat overused and overemphasized. With a bit of thought, one can realize that the line in Fig. 2–8 can be rotated to many various positions to the right of *A* and that any of these will represent some degree of inhibition of the vertical mixing. Thus, it is more accurate to consider a continuous spectrum of mixing conditions, ranging from active mixing to active suppression, than it is to think of mixing simply as good vs. bad, mixing vs. inversion. Nonetheless, as a concession to conventional wisdom, we'll describe inversions and their causes and leave the more elaborate concepts until later.

Inversions, Stagnations, and Episodes

An inversion can occur whenever a portion of the temperature-profile graph slopes to the right of the adiabatic, or neutral, rate (line *A* in Fig. 2–8). It doesn't have to begin at the ground and go all the way up, as in Fig. 2–8; in fact, the Los Angeles inversions that have contributed so much to the notoriety of this condition often occur aloft, above the ground, as in Fig. 2–9. When this type of temperature profile exists, the air below the zig-zag in the line can mix about, but it can't mix above the point of the inversion. Thus, this situation gives rise to the common description of an inversion as a "lid" on mixing; the diagram shows how such a lid, in conjunction with the topography, causes the extra problems in the Los Angeles Basin.

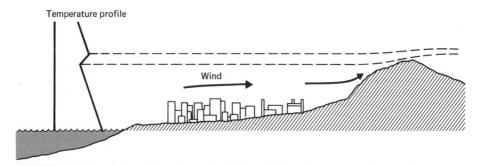

Fig. 2–9. Inversion condition in the Los Angeles Basin. When the inversion is low enough to nearly meet the mountains, the strong wind flows up the "chimney" along the mountain slope and increases smog damage far from the urban areas of the Basin.

The most common type of inversions, however, are ground-based and are of short duration. Caused by the cooling of the earth by radiation overnight, they're called, logically enough, nocturnal radiation inversions. The development of these inversions over time, illustrated in Fig. 2–10, is quite interesting and can be seen fairly easily. At night, the earth radiates heat energy, as do all bodies; on cloudy nights, the clouds bounce the heat energy back; but on clear nights, it escapes to space, causing the surface temperature to decrease. As the earth's surface cools, the air in contact with it also cools, and in turn cools the next layer of air, and so on; thus, the temperature profile slowly curves back under to the left as the night progresses, causing an inversion. When the sun comes up in the morning, the earth's surface is gradually warmed again, as is the lowest layer of air, which warms the next layer, and so on, and the curve swings back to the right, straightening out the bend and letting the air mix again. If the inversion is deep enough, or if the morning's warming is not sufficiently strong, the inversion may persist aloft through the day, but generally this happens only in unusual conditions.

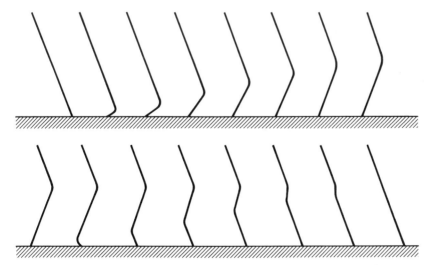

Fig. 2–10. The formation and breakup of a nocturnal radiation inversion. The top line of this sequence of temperature-profile plots represents a period from late afternoon to late evening; the bottom line, a period from sunrise to midmorning.

The nocturnal radiation inversions have several effects on air pollution. Obviously, of course, they make night a bad time to release pollutants, though many sources do so anyway in order to avoid being noticed by their neighbors or customers. Such inversions also cause an interesting, occasional morning phenomenon, called fumigation, discussed in Exercise

22. Finally, and especially in winter, inversions may still be around when the early-morning activity, e.g., rush-hour traffic, begins, causing a tremendous peak in the measured values of some pollutants.

Another, less frequent, type of inversion is caused at the boundary between two air masses, a front. When two air masses of different temperatures meet, the warmer of the two, being slightly less dense, will "ride up" over the cooler, as shown in Fig. 2–11(a); this causes an inverted temperature structure. Because these frontal inversions are fairly transitory, they're not of major significance in air pollution; also, the rain frequently associated with these fronts tends to clean the air.

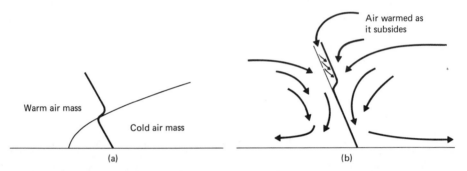

Fig. 2–11. (a) Frontal inversion; (b) subsidence inversion. Both types are caused by the motions of air of various temperatures rather than by changes in the temperature of a given air mass. The frontal inversion occurs when a lighter, warmer air mass rides up over the edge of a heavier, cooler air mass, creating the temperature profile as shown. The subsidence inversion occurs in the center of a high-pressure system, or anticyclone. The lower-level air in such a system slowly spirals outward and is replaced by air sinking down into the center. Under certain circumstances, the subsiding air may warm slightly more than the underlying air, again resulting in an inversion aloft.

The third type of inversion is the subsidence inversion. Though occurring less frequently than the other two types, the subsidence inversion tends to get the most publicity or, more properly, to cause the situations that get the most publicity. In an anticyclone, or high-pressure weather system, the air generally rises at the edges and descends in the center. This descending air is warmed by the thermodynamic forces that increase the pressure as the air comes down, often in such a way as to form an inversion aloft, as shown in Fig. 2–11(b).

Such weather systems have become notorious because they often combine the worst of several conditions. Since the weather associated with a high-pressure system is often rather pleasant and clear, nocturnal conditions are conducive to the formation of radiation inversions. And because of the decreased vertical mixing, such systems are also characterized by the nearly complete stopping of the horizontal wind. In the western United States, these adverse meteorological conditions are created by the large,

North Pacific high-pressure system. In the eastern United States, their occurrence is a little more complicated; the traveling high-pressure systems are smaller and may bump into the North Atlantic high, slow down, and finally stop. This is why such weather conditions are often called stagnations—the moving weather system stagnates over an area, lingering for longer than usual. In the stagnating system, the subsidence produces an inversion, or at least poor mixing conditions, aloft, and radiational cooling likely adds a good radiation inversion at the bottom. If such a situation develops late in the year, the sunlight may be sufficiently lessened so that the radiation inversion does not break up. Thus, the worst stagnations generally occur in late fall or in winter.

So far, we have called these occurrences inversions or stagnations and have described as purely meteorological phenomena. Many times, these conditions occur over open country or wooded areas and cause little harm. When they occur over a populated area, however, where pollutants are being emitted, they can cause massive harm, especially if it is winter and the pollutant emissions are high. The term "episode," as in "killer smog episode," is generally reserved for those stagnations that do occur over urban areas and cause a great deal of ill health and mortality. Fortunately, as we see in Fig. 2–12, the largest urban centers in the East and Midwest are not in the area where stagnations are most frequent.

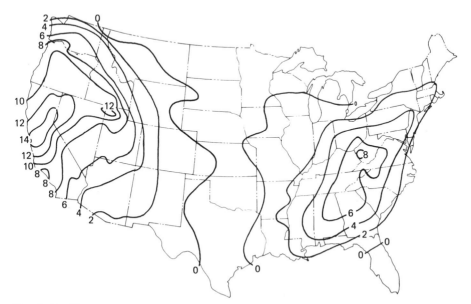

Fig. 2–12. The occurrence of atmospheric stagnations in the United States. Isopleths are in average number of alert days per year. (National Weather Service, High Air Pollution Potential Advisory, or HAPPA.) (G. Holzworth, *Mixing Heights, Wind Speeds, and Potential for Urban Air Pollution in the Contiguous United States,* Washington, D.C.: Department of Health, Education, and Welfare, EPA Publication No. AP–101, January 1972.)

AIR POLLUTION CLIMATOLOGY

Climate is generally defined as the average weather over a long period of time; by extension, therefore, air pollution climatology is the study of the long-term average values of those weather parameters involved in air pollution. We have already seen our first taste of this, the map in Fig. 2–12. Such a summary over a period of years permits one to evaluate the typical long-run frequency of, in this case, stagnations, or whatever other parameters one might gather data for. The other parameters that have primary relevance to air pollution are, of course, the speed and direction of wind and its vertical mixing capacity.

With respect to the other variable of major interest in air pollution—the degree of vertical mixing—the climatological situation is less favorable. What we would most like, of course, is a historical record of measured vertical temperature data, but such data aren't generally available. Meteorologists have therefore contrived more approximate measures of vertical mixing based on what data are available—the limited vertical temperature data, plus data on surface temperature and wind speed, etc. Using such parameters, air pollution meteorologists can evaluate the long-term potential for adverse meteorology as it varies from place to place. Although adverse pollution levels are primarily a function of the amount and type of the pollutants emitted, the meteorology can cause a major difference between areas with comparable emissions. The largest American urban area, New York City, has relatively massive emissions, especially of SO_x, but also has relatively good pollutant dispersal; many people have offered the opinion, in fact, that if the meteorology and topography of New York were as adverse as they are in Los Angeles, the city would be essentially uninhabitable.

In closing, we should perhaps note that the most familiar elements of weather—temperature and precipitation—haven't been discussed extensively here. The effect of temperature is important only indirectly; when it gets colder, we burn more fuels and cause more pollution in order to heat our homes, a topic we'll return to in Chapter 8. Precipitation also has an effect, but unfortunately we can't say a great deal about it. "Washout" by rain and snow is a major mechanism for removing pollutants from the air and thus lessening their long-term buildup in the global atmosphere, and we'll pursue this topic further in Chapter 5. However, since most of this occurs away from our cities, we really know far less about these processes than we should.

EXERCISES

Review Questions

1. List two types of functions of the atmosphere, with at least two specific examples of each.
2. What is the name given to the lowest layer of the atmosphere? How deep is it? What marks its top?
3. Explain why the incoming and outgoing radiation is not in balance at various latitudes. How is the imbalance resolved?
4. Of the radiation reaching the earth at any given point, is more absorbed by the atmosphere or by the earth's surface? What implication does this have for the temperature profile of the atmosphere?
5. Explain briefly the effect of wind speed on the concentration of pollutants in the air and how the effect is caused.
6. List as many as you can of the five "scales of motion" into which meteorologists classify atmospheric motions.
7. What causes the planetary-scale circulations of the atmosphere? Explain briefly how they are generated.
8. How are the semipermanent oceanic "highs" related to air pollution?
9. Distinguish between high- and low-pressure systems with respect to direction of air flow. What type of weather does each typically produce?
10. What major role do the traveling weather systems play in the energy systems of the atmosphere? What significance do they have for air pollution?
11. Draw a sketch indicating the air flow in a land-sea breeze effect and explain briefly how the motion is produced.
12. Answer question 11 for the "valley breeze" effect.
13. What is the dominant force acting in the vertical direction? What causes motions in the vertical direction?
14. What is the adiabatic lapse rate? What is its quantitative value? What is its significance in air pollution meteorology?
15. Draw sketches of three vertical-temperature profile graphs that illustrate three different cases with respect to the adiabatic lapse rate. In each case, what sort of atmospheric mixing would be expected?
16. Explain, using a sketch if desired, the differences in the three types of inversion, as classified by their cause. In each case, are ground-based inversions, inversions aloft, or both, produced?
17. Distinguish among the terms inversion, stagnation, and episode.
18. What climatological data are helpful for understanding air pollution? To what extent are these data available?

Thought Questions

19. Consider the role the atmosphere plays in adjusting the temperature imbalance between the equatorial and polar regions. If there were no atmosphere, what might happen?

20. Temperature differences have been indicated as the basic cause of three of the five "scales of motions" (Table 2–1). What do you think are the causes of microscale motions? Of molecular motions?

21. In order to disperse air pollution, would it be better to locate a pollution source, e.g., a factory, on a hill or in a valley? Is this where they're usually located? If not, can you explain why?

22. Under strong nocturnal-inversion conditions, the effluent from a smokestack may remain in a thin layer at the height it is emitted. In the morning that effluent may be abruptly brought down to ground level, a phenomenon known as fumigation. Use sketches of temperature profiles, such as those in Figs. 2–9 and 2–10, to explain why this occurs.

Problems

23. A typical male adult consumes 2000 Calories of food energy in a day. If he lives at 45° north latitude, what area of the earth's surface would he require to get this same energy from the sun directly (assuming that he could collect and utilize it)?

24. Typically, the range of wind speeds is from 3 miles per hour to perhaps 18 miles per hour, and the range of vertical mixing depths is typically from 200 to 5000 feet. Suppose that a pollution source is emitting enough pollutant to cause unit concentration in the air under conditions of 9-mile-per-hour winds and a mixing depth of 2000 feet. What concentrations would this source cause if the wind speed were varied to the extremes mentioned? If the mixing depth were so varied? Both?

FURTHER READING

In several ways, this chapter does an injustice to a very fascinating subject. For purposes of brevity, the discussion of much of the interesting meteorological material has been omitted, albeit reluctantly. In particular, the discussion has presumed the measurement of all the various parameters without a comment on the instruments by which this is done. Nor have we even tried to consider the roles of clouds and moisture in the weather. To fill these and other gaps, you should refer to one of the several meteorology texts that are available at various levels of discussion. Spar [19] has a good narrative discussion; Miller and Thompson [128] and Day and Sternes [125] give more thorough technical discussions, though both books are quite readable. The former emphasizes the forces acting on the wind; Day and Sternes give a better discussion of the clouds and precipitation aspects of meteorology.

    There are fewer books directly related to air pollution meteorology itself. Battan [1], a meteorologist, gives an elementary discussion of various aspects of air pollution, not just meteorology. Scorer [18] treats almost exclusively the dispersion of smokestack plumes under various meteorological conditions, and his book is lavishly illustrated.

For those of you willing to entertain a more technical approach, Williamson [132] provides an excellent discussion of air pollution meteorology, considering the same topics as in this chapter, but in a much more extensive and thorough manner. Stern [160] includes four chapters on air pollution meteorology at a more specialized level; one of them, the chapter by Robert McCormick, "Air Pollution Climatology," is especially readable. The best available summary of air pollution climatological data is in Holzworth [86].

3

THE POLLUTANTS —
THEIR PROPERTIES
AND
PREVALENCE

Courtesy EPA

With some further discussion about the principal air pollutants, this chapter will conclude our preliminaries. In Chapter 1 we listed the six major pollutants and mentioned briefly what each of them consisted of, with passing comments on their sources and effects. In this chapter, we'll pursue in greater detail the nature and properties of the pollutants and their prevalence in the atmosphere. Our primary purpose here is to try to develop a "feel" for the pollutants, a familiarity that will make our subsequent discussions of effects, measurement, sources, and control more meaningful.

Each pollutant has its own "personality," its own interesting properties. Thus, we'll discuss the physical properties of the particulate matter—the size of the particles and how long they stay in the air—and the chemical properties of the photochemical pollutants—how they react to form the smog. We'll also discuss the prevalence of each of the pollutants in two ways—the total amount of each pollutant emitted and the concentrations in the atmosphere that these emissions produce—and since neither the emission rates nor the ambient concentrations of the pollutants are evenly distributed, either over space or through time, we'll also need to consider geographic and temporal variations.

The pollutants can be logically divided into several groups. Since this is quite useful in providing a mental framework, we'll organize our discussion in terms of these groups. We'll start with the ingredients in classical, or London, smog, particulate matter and sulfur oxides, between which we'll insert a comment on measurement units; next, we'll consider carbon monoxide by itself, and then the three pollutants involved in photochemical, or Los Angeles, smog, followed by a brief discussion of some of the other, minor pollutants.

PARTICULATE MATTER AND SULFUR OXIDES

Sulfur oxides and particulate matter are logically grouped together for two reasons; they generally come from the same sources, primarily fuel combustion sources, and they act synergistically in affecting human health, each pollutant augmenting the effect of the other. And, of course, they are also linked as the two principal ingredients in the classic killer smogs, which is no coincidence and merely follows from the preceding reasons.

Particulate Matter

The particles in the air over an urban area normally exhibit a tremendous variety of sizes, shapes, and chemical composition, ranging from tiny, spherical metal particles from metallurgical fumes to huge, porous conglomerations of sooty carbon, with irregular, flat, cylindrical, or long fibrous particles of almost any nature—soil particles, tiny bits of insect wing or fly ash, pollens, and industrial effluents of all types. Aside from being nongaseous, which defines particulates in the first place,* the most significant property of particulate pollution is the size of the particles.

We are interested in the size of the particles because the size will almost totally determine the way in which the particles behave in the air, how far the wind will carry them, and what effect they will have, either in the lungs of someone breathing the air, or on plants, buildings, and so on. The sizes of particles in the air are quite small, ranging from about 100 microns (about 1/250 of an inch) on down; a spectrum of the sizes of atmospheric particles is illustrated in Fig. 3–1, along with the sizes of some other common items for perspective. The use of the word "size" to describe the diverse batch of particles found in the air needs some clarification. The size attributed to a particle is actually its aerodynamic equivalent diameter, that is, the diameter of a sphere that would have the same aerodynamic settling behavior in the air that the particle has. In other words, because we are interested in the settling behavior of the particle, we use that property to define its size. Since this equivalent size can be determined without ever knowing the true size, shape, and mass of the particle, it is a convenient parameter in practice and so is commonly used. The parameter is often simply called "size," and it's quite appropriate to just think of particles as being "bigger" or "smaller," as we do in Fig. 3–1. In discussing the pollutant particles in terms of their size it is convenient to divide them into three groups, with dividing lines at the sizes 0.1 and 10 microns. The dividing lines are not really that sharp, but generally the particles in these three different size ranges tend to come from different sources and to stay in the air for different lengths of time. In Chapter 1 we mentioned that the particles are divided into two categories—those that settle out rapidly and those that remain suspended in the air for long periods—and these are the size ranges labeled "dustfall" and "suspended particulate matter," as shown in Fig. 3–1.

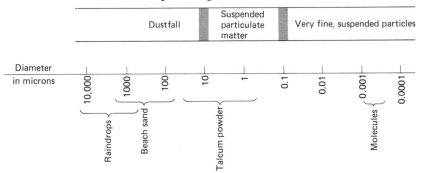

Fig. 3–1. The spectrum of atmospheric particle size.

* There is usually far less liquid than solid material (rain is not included); liquids are included only because they often occur closely mixed with the solids and can't be measured separately.

Dustfall. Particles larger than about ten microns are put into the air primarily by physical processes, such as grinding and abrasion, and as soot and fly ash from fuel combustion; the particles tend to settle back out onto the ground (or windowsill) relatively rapidly. These are the particles gathered in a *dustfall* measurement, which is made by setting out a jar or other container to catch the falling dust and soot. The collected material is then weighed and reported as tons per square mile per month or, in metric units, as grams per square meter per day. Dustfall, or settleable particulate matter, as it is sometimes called, is usually a problem only in the vicinity of the source of the dust, as the particles settle out before the wind can carry them very far.

Dustfall has been of concern for decades; the early public pressures in St. Louis and Pittsburgh were prompted partly by the soiling problems caused by high dustfall levels. Those early smoke-control efforts resulted in very sizeable reductions in this type of particulate pollution, a trend that has been relatively constant for years, as illustrated in Fig. 3–2. Currently, however, it is more or less neglected by the air pollution control establishment in favor of newer, more glamorous pollutants. The biggest factor in this neglect is that dustfall is less of a respiratory health hazard than either

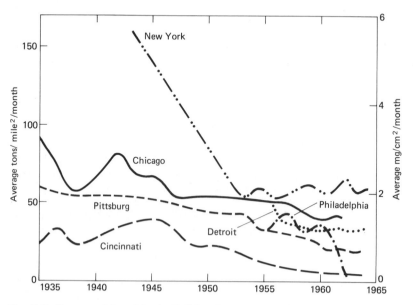

Fig. 3–2. Downward trend in dustfall levels. Note that because measurements are not standardized, comparisons between cities are only approximately valid. The data are from the cities' pollution control agencies. (*Air Pollution— A National Sample,* Public Health Service Publication No. 1562, Department of Health, Education and Welfare, 1966)

the smaller particles or the gases, although it certainly contributes heavily to the economic cost of pollution and to the degradation of many neighborhoods.

Suspended particulate matter. Unlike dustfall, particles smaller than about ten microns in size remain suspended in the air for long periods of time. Being much smaller and lighter, they settle downward only at a much slower rate, so that the turbulent motion of the air is able to keep them aloft more or less permanently. These particles, which comprise the middle-size group in Fig. 3–1, are the most important, at least with respect to air pollution, for two reasons. First, they comprise by far the biggest part of the total weight of particulate matter in the air; and second, they include the sizes of particles that can enter deepest into the lungs and hence cause the most severe effects on health. Included among the particles in this size range are those generated by various industrial processes, some combustion processes—particularly the classical black soot—and particles of the local soil, along with other particles actually produced in the air. Since they don't settle out, the suspended particles must be physically separated from the air in order to be measured. This is usually done by collecting them on filter paper with a "high-volume air sampler" and then weighing the dirty filter; the results are reported as micrograms of particulate matter per cubic meter of air ($\mu g/m^3$).

The *finest particles*, those below 0.1 micron in size, are so small that they can't be filtered out of the air separately; when they are to be studied for research purposes, they usually can't be weighed at all, but rather must be counted. This can generally be done only by specially treating the particles in advance, such as putting an electric charge on them and counting them as ions, or condensing moisture on them to count them as droplets. The cleanest air almost always contains at least several hundred such particles per cubic centimeter, and in polluted urban air this may reach 100,000 per cubic centimeter. Despite these numbers, the particles are so small that they don't amount to much by weight; therefore, and because of the measurement problems, they are generally ignored.

Black smoke. There is one other type of particulate pollution that deserves mention, partly for historical reasons. As defined by the early smoke-control laws, "black smoke" is not really another type of particulate, but rather a different way of looking at particulate pollution. Quite literally, "black smoke" refers to "looking at" particulate pollution, specifically visible, black smoke from smokestacks. Black-smoke pollution is measured not by the weight, amount, or chemical nature of the pollutant, but by its visibility. Black smoke is measured in terms of percent blackness by a smoke inspector, who observes the plume from a smokestack and compares it with the Ringelmann chart shown in Fig. 3–3. Typically, the smoke-control law pro-

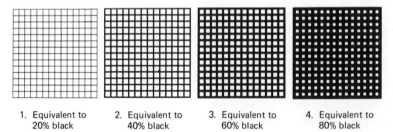

| 1. Equivalent to | 2. Equivalent to | 3. Equivalent to | 4. Equivalent to |
| 20% black | 40% black | 60% black | 80% black |

Fig. 3–3. The Ringelmann chart. Used for grading the blackness of smoke, the Ringelmann chart was proposed in 1898 by Maximilian Ringelmann, a French engineer. It consists of the four shades of gray shown, plus 100% (black) and 0% (white). When held at a distance, the black and white areas blur together and can be conveniently compared with a visible black plume from a smokestack. With training and experience, a professional smoke inspector can judge a plume to within 1/2 Ringlemann number without using the chart. (S. J. Williamson, *Fundamentals of Air Pollution,* Reading, Mass.: Addison-Wesley, 1973, p. 397)

hibits smoke blacker than a specific Ringelmann number, perhaps no. 2, except for one three-minute period per hour. Although frequently regarded in a derogatory way as old-fashioned, the Ringelmann chart and the smoke inspector have been well accepted by the courts for many years as evidence of pollution, and they have helped eliminate a good deal of smoke, as we noted in Chapter 1 and indirectly in Fig. 3–2.

The Prevalence of Particulate Pollution

The prevalence of an air pollutant can be viewed in two distinct ways. One way is by considering the amount of pollutant emitted into the air from the various sources; although this can't be measured easily, it is possible to make reasonable estimates. The amount of particulate matter emitted into the atmosphere amounts to millions of tons each year, as seen in Table 3–1. It is apparent that the bulk of this particulate matter comes from fuel combustion by stationary (nonvehicular) sources, primarily electric-power plants and heating boilers, although industrial processes run a strong second.

Another way of considering prevalence is to look at the concentrations of the pollutant in the environment. Figure 3–2 gave an indication of the levels of one type of pollutant, dustfall. Although dustfall used to be measured fairly widely, such data are not readily available in great detail. The more recent levels shown in Fig. 3–2, about 20 to 40 tons per square mile per month, are typical of dustfall levels in the older, more industrialized parts of a city, whereas values approaching 2000 tons/mi^2 month are found near particularly bad sources. In the outermost suburbs, dustfall would be much less prevalent, perhaps 5 tons/mi^2 month.

TABLE 3–1
Annual emissions of particulate matter (estimates for 1970)

Source category	Emissions, millions of tons per year	Percent of total
Fuel combustion		
Transportation		
Gasoline motor vehicles	0.3	1.1
Diesel, aircraft, trains, vessels	0.3	1.2
Off-highway vehicles	0.1	0.4
Total transportation	0.7	2.7
Stationary sources		
Coal	5.6	21.5
Fuel Oil	0.4	1.5
Natural gas	0.2	0.8
Wood	0.6	2.3
Total stationary source	6.8	26.1
Total fuel combustion	**7.5**	**28.8**
Industrial processes	**13.3**	**51.0**
Agricultural burning	**2.4**	**9.2**
Solid waste disposal	**1.4**	**5.3**
Miscellaneous*	**1.5**	**5.7**
Total	**26.1**	**100.0**

* Includes coal-refuse burning, structural fires, and accidental and intentional forest fires.
Source: J. H. Cavender, D. S. Kircher, and A. J. Hoffman, Nationwide Air Pollutant Emission Trends 1940–1970, EPA Publication No. AP-115, January 1973.

Suspended particulate matter, in contrast, is the most widely measured pollutant; the federal government has an extensive monitoring program, as do most cities and states. The suspended-particulate level in the center of a typical urban area averages about 100 micrograms per cubic meter over the year, with the larger cities typically averaging 150 to 200 $\mu g/m^3$. In the other direction, annual average levels typically decrease from 100 $\mu g/m^3$ in the central business district to perhaps 75 in clean suburbs, 60 in small towns and rural areas within 100 miles or so of urban areas, and down to about 20 $\mu g/m^3$ in relatively remote areas in the West—national parks, etc., as seen in Table 3–2.

Despite the apparent trend shown in Table 3–2 toward higher particulate levels with greater size and urbanization, the dirtiest downtown station is not in New York, Chicago, or Los Angeles, but in Steubenville, Ohio. Actually, this is typical of suspended-particulate pollution; the highest concentrations are not found in the very largest cities, partly because they, unlike the smaller cities, have pollution-control equipment installed on many of their sources. Beyond this, the cities that are usually highest—those, like Steubenville, in the Appalachian region of the Ohio Valley—still burn coal rather than gas for heat and often have particularly unfavorable topography and meteorology as well.

TABLE 3–2
Distribution of particulate pollution levels by city size

	Annual average suspended particulate concentration ($\mu g/m^3$)							
	<20	20–39	40–79	80–119	120–159	160–199	≥200	Total
Urban stations								
Over 3 mill					1	1		2
1–3 mill					2	1		3
0.7–1 mill			1	2	4			7
400–700,000				9	7	2		18
100–400,000			10	54	29	5	1	99
50–100,000			22	44	18	6	3	93
25–50,000			29	24	12	3	3	71
10–25,000			25	28	7	4		64
<10,000		1	12	26	3	2		44
Nonurban stations								
Near urban areas		1	4					5
Intermediate		5	6					11
Remote	4	5						9

Source: Modified from *Air Quality Data from the NASN and Contributing State and Local Networks, 1967 Edition Revised,* Office of Air Programs Publication No. APTD–0741, Environmental Protection Agency, August 1971.

There is, of course, considerable variation of the daily particulate measurements around these annual average concentrations; this is caused by variations from one day to another both in the amount of pollution emitted and in the dispersive capacity of the atmosphere. The maximum daily particulate levels are typically 200 to 300 $\mu g/m^3$ in cities averaging around 100 $\mu g/m^3$, with the dirtier cities having maxima ranging up to 500 and, on rare occasions, over 1000 $\mu g/m^3$.

Suspended particulate levels don't vary as drastically with geography, climate, or season of the year as do some of the gaseous pollutants, however. The northeastern part of the country tends to have greater emissions of particulate matter from industrial and fuel-burning sources, but the West and South have more wind-blown dust and soil and agricultural contributions. The extra fuel used for heating in the winter tends to cause 15 to 20 percent higher particulate levels in the North during the winter, but otherwise there are no major variations with the seasons of the year.

Measurement Units

Although the total amount of particulate matter, as well as other pollutants, emitted into the air is measured in millions of tons, the concentrations in the air are not at all large by everyday standards. A microgram, or millionth of a gram, is quite a small amount of mass, so that even 100 micrograms, distributed through a cubic meter of air, is not much. A large auditorium might have much less than an ounce of suspended particulate matter by weight. Nonetheless, with practice one soon becomes accustomed to thinking in micrograms, once the frame of reference is set; the previous discussion on atmospheric particulate levels probably made some sense, even if the units were unfamiliar. Having now been exposed to one of the common units, let's take a moment to look at some other units before we go on to discuss the gaseous pollutants.

Measurements of gaseous pollutants are normally recorded and reported in units different from those used for particulates; since the air is gaseous, it is natural to express the concentration of gaseous pollutants as a fraction of the whole, much as the percentages of oxygen, nitrogen, etc., were expressed in Table 1–1. Since the pollutant concentrations are small, however, their percentages would be very small; a typical SO_2 concentration would be 0.000003 percent. To avoid this unwieldy number of decimal places, we normally move the decimal point over and have a unit called parts per million, just as "percent" is really "parts per hundred." In other words, parts per million (ppm) is just the number of volumes (say, quarts) of pollutant gas in a million volumes (quarts) of air. As a ratio, "ppm" has no true units, the words appended after the digits merely adjust the decimal point. Thus, 0.000003 percent becomes 0.03 ppm; if the remaining decimal points are inconvenient, one could say 3 pphm, for parts per hundred million, or 30 ppb, parts per billion. These units are also rather small by household standards; if all the pollutant gas were collected together rather than being spread around evenly, one part per million of pollutant gas would occupy one cubic centimeter (the size of a thimble) in each cubic meter, or about two cubic inches in a room $10' \times 12'$.

The primary difficulty with units arises because concentrations of gases can also be expressed in mass per volume units, such as $\mu g/m^3$, if desired, even though they were originally measured as ppm. Making the conversion from ppm to mass units requires calculating the mass of the known volume of gas in a cubic meter of air; this in turn requires knowledge of the temperature and atmospheric pressure at which the ppm measurement was made. Since these data are not usually recorded, it has become common practice to assume some "standard" temperature and pressure, usually 760 mm pressure and 25°C (77°F) for temperature, and make the conversion anyway. This gives only approximate answers, but they are not usually far off. The primary effect of the conversion is to make the gas concentrations seem larger by making them larger numerically, so that they don't seem small and insignificant when set side by side with particulate numbers. The typical particulate concentration will be in the range of 50 to 200 $\mu g/m^3$, while a typical SO_2 concentration in ppm will have a number on it in the range 0.02–0.05. That same range of SO_2 levels in $\mu g/m^3$ (25°C, 760 mm) would be 50 to 130 $\mu g/m^3$, which is comparable to the particulate numbers. In the balance of this chapter and throughout the book, we will express gaseous pollutant concentrations in both types of units.

Sulfur Oxides

Compared to particulate pollution, the various gaseous pollutants will seem quite simple. Sulfur dioxide (SO_2) is historically the most prominent of the gaseous pollutants, having achieved this notoriety as a respiratory irritant; it is the prime suspect in the killer smogs of London, the Meuse Valley, and Donora. Strictly speaking, the pollutant is called sulfur oxides, abbreviated SO_x, and includes not only SO_2, but also sulfur trioxide, SO_3. Sulfuric acid mist and other sulfates are also sulfur oxides, but are not always defined as part of SO_x, because they are particulate in nature and must therefore be measured differently. Nonetheless, we'll include the acid mist and sulfates in our discussion, because they are both important and closely related to the gaseous sulfur oxides. This close relationship occurs because the sulfur compounds change from one form to another in the air. The vast majority of sulfur contamination is emitted in the form of sulfur dioxide, with about 1 to 3 percent of sulfur trioxide mixed in. In the air, the SO_2 reacts with oxygen, ammonia, and other compounds, including the water vapor present in the air, to form sulfuric acid mist, liquid droplets of concentrated acid, as well as various other sulfates. Since SO_3 as such can exist only briefly in the air, the total sulfurous pollution in typical urban atmospheres thus consists principally of gaseous SO_2 plus the acid mist and other sulfates. The acid aerosols and other particulate sulfates formed in this way typically amount to about a tenth of the total suspended particulates; they are particularly significant particles because they are in the size range (less than 1 micron) that is most efficient at causing lung damage and at reducing visibility, that is, at creating visible haze. The latter is exemplified in the dense white plume from the smoke-stack of an oil-burning power plant; such a plume is a visible sign of the process of hot SO_2-laden gases being converted to acid and then cooling and condensing to form a visible mist of extremely small particles.

Total national emissions of sulfur oxides, like those of particulate matter, are measured in the millions of tons—over 30 million tons per year, as seen in Table 3–3. The vast majority of this quantity comes from the combustion of fuel, primarily coal and residual-fuel oil. The majority of the remainder comes from industrial processes, the worst offenders being ore-smelting plants and petroleum refineries. The fuel-combustion emissions are heaviest in the Midwest and Northeast, from Chicago and St.

TABLE 3–3
Annual emissions of sulfur oxides (estimates for 1970)

Source category	Emissions, millions of tons per year	Percent of total
Fuel combustion		
Transportation		
Gasoline motor vehicles	0.2	0.6
Diesel, aircraft, trains, vessels	0.6	1.8
Off-highway vehicles	0.2	0.6
Total transportation	1.0	3.0
Stationary sources		
Coal	22.2	65.4
Fuel Oil	4.2	12.4
Natural gas	—	—
Wood	0.1	0.3
Total stationary source	26.5	78.1
Total fuel combustion	**27.5**	**78.1**
Industrial processes	**6.0**	**17.7**
Agricultural burning	**0.1**	**0.3**
Solid waste disposal	**0.1**	**0.3**
Miscellaneous*	**0.2**	**0.6**
Total	**33.9**	**100.0**

* Includes coal-refuse burning, structural fires, and accidental and intentional forest fires.
Source: J. H. Cavender, D. S. Kircher, and A. J. Hoffman, Nationwide Air Pollutant Emission Trends 1940–1970, EPA Publication No. AP-115, January 1973.

Louis east to Washington and Boston. Not only is this the most urbanized and industrialized part of the country, but it is also the area where coal and oil are most available and hence most commonly used. In contrast, the industrial sources—the refineries and smelters—are located primarily in the West and the South. The smelters have usually located far away from urban areas, not in order to protect the cities, but to be nearer the sites where the ore is mined, though the effect is the same.

Concentrations of sulfur oxides in the air range from over 1 ppm down to essentially zero; in contrast to particulates, there doesn't seem to be much natural background. The vast majority of levels are between 0.0 and 0.1 ppm (0–25 $\mu g/m^3$). A typical annual average in the downtown area of a city in the Northeast is 0.03 ppm, about 80 $\mu g/m^3$; in the South and West, the average is much less because of the warmer climate and the greater use of natural gas as a fuel. Concentrations of sulfur oxides in the air over cities vary much more widely than those for particulates, as seen in Table 3–4. There is also a much greater seasonal variability for SO_x than for particulates; in all but the warmest cities, much of the year's SO_x comes in the winter, as seen in Fig. 3–4. This seasonal variation results from "space heating," the heating of homes, stores, and offices.

TABLE 3–4
Sulfur dioxide and particulate levels in selected cities*

City	Sulfur dioxide	Suspended particulate matter
Charleston, W. Va.	31	182
Chicago	232	187
Cleveland	60	102
Denver	26	175
Detroit	42	141
E. Chicago, Ind.	117	168
Glasboro, N.J.	24	50
Guayanilla, P.R.	8	40
Jersey City	152	115
New York City	364	186
Oklahoma City	11	92
Omaha	20	123
Philadelphia	116	158
Pittsburgh	66	145
St. Louis	87	115
Washington, D.C.	84	118

* Data are 1967 annual average concentrations at downtown sites in each city.
Source: Air Quality Data from the NASN and Contributing State and Local Networks, 1967 Edition Revised, Office of Air Programs Publication No. APTD–0741, Environmental Protection Agency, August 1971.

CARBON MONOXIDE

Carbon monoxide (CO) is the only one of the six major pollutants that is a single, specific chemical compound. Carbon monoxide is a colorless, odorless, tasteless gas; its only interesting property is its ability to reduce the oxygen-carrying capacity of our blood, which of course is the property that makes it a pollutant. Carbon monoxide, a product of the inefficient combustion of carbonaceous fuels, represents a partial oxidation of carbon on its way to becoming CO_2. It is not produced in large quantities by most stationary fuel-burning devices, such as heating or steam-electric boilers, because they are designed and adjusted to be operated as efficiently as possible. Much greater CO emissions result from unplanned combustion, such as building fires, and from solid-waste combustion, which is inefficient because of the nonuniformity of the "fuel" and its high moisture content. Some also comes from various industrial processes, particularly foundries, oil refineries, and paper mills. The principal source of carbon monoxide, however, is gasoline combustion in motor vehicles. Combustion in an auto engine is very inefficient, partly because of the intrinsic properties of the engine, and partly because automobiles are designed to produce speed and power

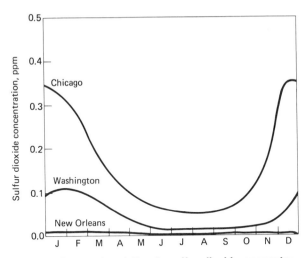

Fig. 3–4. Seasonal variation in sulfur dioxide concentrations. (Data from EPA monitoring program, 1962–1963.)

rather than economy. Cars produce well over half of the nearly 100 million tons of carbon monoxide emitted in a year (Table 3–5), and they account for an even greater proportion in urban areas.

TABLE 3–5
Annual emissions of carbon monoxide (estimates for 1970)

Source category	Emissions, millions of tons per year	Percent of total
Fuel combustion		
Transportation		
Gasoline motor vehicles	95.8	64.3
Diesel, aircraft, trains, vessels	5.6	3.8
Off-highway vehicles	9.5	6.4
Total transportation	110.9	74.5
Stationary sources		
Coal	0.5	0.3
Fuel Oil	0.1	0.1
Natural gas	0.1	0.1
Wood	0.1	0.1
Total stationary source	0.8	0.6
Total fuel combustion	**111.7**	**75.1**
Industrial processes	**11.4**	**7.7**
Agricultural burning	**13.8**	**9.3**
Solid waste disposal	**7.2**	**4.9**
Miscellaneous*	**4.5**	**3.0**
Total	**148.6**	**100.0**

* Includes coal-refuse burning, structural fires, and accidental and intentional forest fires.
Source: J. H. Cavender, D. S. Kircher, and A. J. Hoffman, *Nationwide Air Pollutant Emission Trends 1940–1970,* EPA Publication No. AP-115, January 1973.

This predominance means that the prevalence of CO in the ambient air is determined almost totally by the patterns of motor vehicle traffic rather than by any geographic or climatic differences. The distance from the nearest street and the amount of traffic on that street are the only factors that play a major role in determining average CO levels, although changes in meteorological dispersion have an effect on hour-by-hour changes. The diurnal variation patterns shown in Fig. 3–5 clearly show not only the morning and evening traffic peaks, but also differences on various days of the week, which reflect differences in people's driving habits. Over a longer time period, the average CO levels reflect the overall magnitude of the traffic flow, ranging from less than 3 ppm ($3 mg/m^3$) near suburban streets to over 15 ppm (17 mg/m³) near heavy, downtown traffic. The maximum concentrations are typically three to five times the average. Far higher short-term concentrations (up to 100 or 150 ppm) are typically measured inside automobiles during heavy traffic, as in the rush hour; however, the highest overall exposures are experienced by policemen, cab drivers, and similar workers, rather than by the commuter, who (usually) spends only an hour or so in heavy traffic. This tremendous variation of the concentration caused by traffic patterns makes it essentially impossible to consider any data typical of a very large area, as we did for sulfur dioxide.

You have probably already noticed a much bigger difference between carbon monoxide and sulfur dioxide or the other pollutants—CO concen-

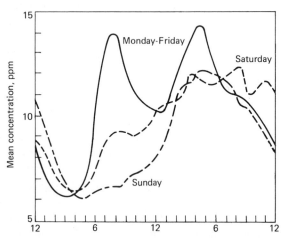

Fig. 3–5. Average diurnal variations in carbon monoxide levels. Note the differences in daily peaks caused by the morning rush-hour traffic and late Saturday night and early Sunday morning entertainment traffic. The data are from downtown Chicago. (*Air Quality Criteria for Carbon Monoxide*, NAPCA Publication No. AP-62, Department of Health, Education and Welfare, March 1970)

trations are measured in whole ppm, ranging in the tens and up to 100 ppm, whereas concentrations of SO_2 are typically measured in hundredths of a part per million. (In mass units, CO is more conveniently expressed in milligrams per cubic meter rather than micrograms, which are used for the others.) Thus, although one ppm of SO_2 is a strikingly high concentration, found only under adverse conditions in major urban areas, one ppm of carbon monoxide is so low as to be suspect, surely so in an urban setting. However, this doesn't automatically make CO of tremendously greater concern as a pollutant; the body can deal with much higher levels of CO than of other pollutants, as we will see subsequently.

THE PHOTOCHEMICAL POLLUTANTS

The last three major pollutants, discussed here as a group, comprise a much more complicated system of substances and chemical reactions than the others. We mentioned in Chapter 1 that photochemical smog results from chemical reactions in the air between oxides of nitrogen and hydrocarbons that produce a resultant product called *total oxidants*. But this $A + B = C$ statement is grossly oversimplified, in fact even wrong, to the extent that it implies that oxidants are totally or primarily made up of NO_x and hydrocarbons. However, such a statement is useful mainly as a reminder that neither NO_x nor hydrocarbons would be a major pollutant were it not for their role in producing photochemical smog. In this section, we will pursue somewhat more carefully the photochemical pollutants and the way in which they react to produce the smog symptoms; even this discussion, however, won't begin to approach a full explanation of everything that takes place, for our understanding of this process is to date incomplete.

The Pollutants

Oxides of nitrogen. In our context this pollutant consists of nitric oxide (NO) and nitrogen dioxide (NO_2); although other combinations of oxygen and nitrogen can exist, these are the only two of interest in air pollution. The oxides of nitrogen are often lumped together for measurement, although when one is interested in the detailed chemistry, they can be measured and studied separately. They are generally grouped together for purposes of discussion because they do not exist independently in the open atmosphere; NO, when exposed to oxygen, slowly oxidizes to form NO_2; in polluted atmospheres, the conversion rate is greatly accelerated. NO_2 is believed to damage plants and is known to be toxic to humans, though not at the concentrations that normally occur in the atmosphere. The only physical property of the oxides of nitrogen that is of much interest in air pollution is their color; though nitric oxide is colorless, NO_2 has an orangish brown color when present in sufficient amounts, and one of the more poetic observers has described an atmosphere heavily polluted with NO_2 as having a "whiskey-brown haze."

Hydrocarbons. There is no clear definition of hydrocarbons as an air pollutant. In chemistry, the hydrocarbons comprise a broad class of organic chemicals, those containing only carbon and hydrogen. However, when the word is used to identify an air pollutant, as it is here, it refers to the subgroup of hydrocarbons that are gaseous at normal ambient temperatures.* These gaseous hydrocarbons have traditionally been lumped together as a pollutant called "total hydrocarbons."

Because they are all different chemicals, however, the various hydrocarbon species do not all join in the photochemical reactions to the same degree; in fact, some don't participate at all. It is therefore useful to make a distinction among these compounds, based on their reactivity, that is, to measure only the "reactive hydrocarbons." This is made difficult, however, by measurement problems; to measure individual hydrocarbons requires laborious and expensive techniques. Consequently, the usual practice has been to just measure all the various hydrocarbon compounds together as a group. This "total hydrocarbons" measurement, although convenient, does not provide a very good measure of the potential of the hydrocarbons for causing smog, however, because it treats all of the hydrocarbons the same, regardless of how reactive they are.

Recently, however, it has become possible to also measure one specific hydrocarbon, methane, fairly readily. Methane constitutes a large percentage of the hydrocarbons in the air, but it does not react at all to form smog. It is now required by the EPA, and hence is rapidly becoming more and more common practice, to measure both total hydrocarbons and methane and to also report the subtracted difference, or the "nonmethane hydrocarbons," as shown in Fig. 3–6. The "nonmethane hydrocarbon" measurement is much more directly related to smog than that for the total hydrocarbons, because it includes all the reactive compounds while eliminating the biggest portion of the nonreactive compounds. Sometimes called a "reactive hydrocarbon" measurement, we'll settle for the more prudent name "nonmethane hydrocarbons" until the former term becomes far more widely adopted and standardized. The National Ambient Air Quality Standard defines hydrocarbon pollution in terms of nonmethane hydrocarbon data, so such data will certainly be used whenever available;

---

* A further caution is also necessary, as there are other hydrocarbon compounds that are of interest in air pollution in a different context. The polynuclear aromatic hydrocarbons are a group of more complicated compounds that are associated with particulate matter; they are of interest because of their association with cancer, and are discussed in the next section.

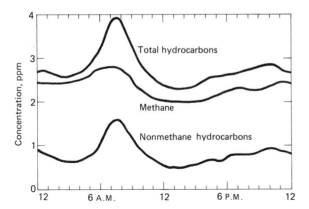

Fig. 3–6. Measurement of nonmethane hydrocarbons.
By subtracting measured methane concentrations from total hydrocarbons, one can determine the concentration of nonmethane hydrocarbons, as in the month's data from Philadelphia shown here. Note that methane constitutes the biggest part of the total, but that the peak concentration at the morning rush hour is caused mostly by increases in the nonmethane portion. For this particular month's data, the diurnal patterns as plotted don't add together exactly, because some of the data were invalid; the loss of either total hydrocarbon or methane data also causes the loss of the nonmethane data. (Data from EPA's Continuous Air Monitoring Program)

however, there is also a large volume of total hydrocarbon data still in use, so we need to be quite careful when speaking of "hydrocarbon pollution."

Photochemical oxidants. This pollutant is unusual in two major respects. First, as we mentioned in Chapter 1, it is a secondary pollutant; the various chemicals included are not emitted from sources, but are formed in the air from other pollutants. Second, photochemical oxidant is unusual because it is defined not by a list of the specific chemicals included, but by the ability of the atmospheric mixture of chemicals to participate in a certain type of chemical reaction. Formally, oxidants are those chemical compounds that can oxidize other substances that cannot be oxidized by the oxygen in the air.* Rather than measuring substances, we are in effect measuring a chemical property of the air. This is necessary because the compounds causing the oxidizing effect are not all known, and those that are known are not easily measured individually. It is known that the vast

---

* Oxidation, a particular type of chemical reaction, derives its name from oxygen; various chemicals are more or less able to perform this type of reaction, and the ones of concern here are those that are the most active, that is, more active than oxygen.

majority of the oxidant is ozone; the nonozone oxidants are fairly complicated organic compounds and are as difficult to measure as are their hydrocarbon precursors. Since the list of the precise compounds included also depends somewhat on the instrument used to measure the oxidant, further definition rapidly gets more complicated than is warranted here. In short, there are a variety of "oxidant" measurement methods in use, and one (chemiluminescence) measures only ozone.

The Photochemistry of Smog

Although the photochemical reactions that involve these three pollutants are complicated, they have been included here for several reasons. First, the complexity of their chemistry is a testimonial to the detective efforts of the chemists who have spent years attempting to decipher it. Second, some understanding of these reactions is necessary in order to judge the best means of reducing the oxidant by controlling its precursors. Finally, the photochemical reactions are a very good illustration of the subtlety so often involved in our relations with the rest of nature.

To describe the formation of photochemical smog, we will first consider a narrative description of the way in which the various pollutants change through the day, and then we'll return for a closer look at the chemical reactions and the role of sunlight and the various chemicals. The narrative, illustrated in Fig. 3–7, begins early in the morning, before there is much human activity. Between 3 and 4 A.M., the atmospheric concentrations of nitrogen dioxide and oxidants are negligible. The nitric oxide and nonmethane hydrocarbon concentrations are somewhat larger and slowly increasing; between about 5 and 6 A.M., they begin to rise more sharply, reflecting the beginning of the early rush-hour traffic, and they continue

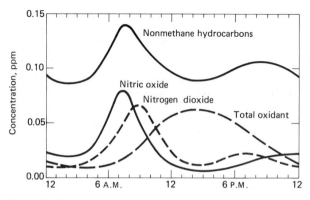

Fig. 3–7. The chronology of photochemical smog formation. The curves of these typical diurnal variation patterns illustrate only the patterns and times; they shouldn't be interpreted quantitatively.

to rise in conjunction with the traffic peak. At about 8 A.M., with the sun now up, the NO levels begin to decrease, while the NO_2 continues to rise. Somewhat later, the NO_2 and hydrocarbon concentrations also peak and then begin to decline, accompanied by the beginning of a gradual increase in oxidant concentrations. The oxidant levels continue increasing for a much longer period of time, coming to a broad peak sometime after noon and then decreasing. Accompanying the rise of the oxidant concentrations are the occurrence of the other characteristic symptoms of photochemical smog—a noticeable haze obscuring distant vision and the reddening and irritation of people's eyes. Then, in the late afternoon and early evening, as the sun goes down, the oxidant and the other symptoms decrease again.

At least five monitoring instruments must be operating in order to get this much description of what is going on. One can well imagine how difficult it was to understand what was happening in the early days, before these instruments were available. In the years since Professor Haagen-Smit's first discovery, it has taken a good deal of study and research, using both atmospheric air pollution data and special laboratory experiments, to define the basic chemical explanation, and our understanding is still not complete.

As suggested by its name, photochemical smog requires light energy. In fact, the entire system of chemical reactions is initiated by the absorption of light energy by the nitrogen dioxide molecules in the air, which then dissociate into NO and free oxygen, O. This starts a cycle of reactions among nitrogen dioxide, nitric oxide, ozone, and the atmospheric oxygen, as seen in Fig. 3–8. In an atmosphere with only NO_x pollution and no reactive hydrocarbons, the conversion of NO_2 and oxygen into ozone and NO is balanced by the conversion of NO back to NO_2, consuming the ozone again, so that the net result of the cycle is no more than a slight warming of the air from the energy of the absorbed light.

If the right hydrocarbons are also present in the atmosphere, however, this balance is destroyed. As illustrated in Fig. 3–9, reactive hydrocarbon molecules in the air are capable of converting the NO back to NO_2, even in the absence of the ozone that normally accomplishes the conversion; this is how the large amount of NO emitted during the morning traffic peak is converted so rapidly into NO_2. More importantly, the hydrocarbons can convert the NO formed by NO_2 dissociation back into NO_2, without converting an equivalent amount of ozone back into oxygen,* which permits the accumulation of ozone that is one of the principal features of photochemical smog.

---

* The hydrocarbon molecules can do this in several ways, that is, via several chemical reactions, not all of which are understood. With most of the hydrocarbons, free radical reactions are involved; these permit each original hydrocarbon molecule to oxidize many more than just one NO molecule to NO_2, because the free radicals react in chain reactions, each step of the reaction producing another

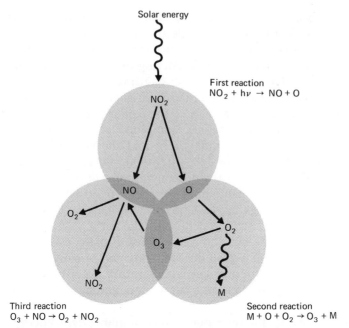

Solar energy

First reaction
$NO_2 + h\nu \rightarrow NO + O$

NO_2

NO   O

O_2

O_2

O_3

M

NO_2

Third reaction
$O_3 + NO \rightarrow O_2 + NO_2$

Second reaction
$M + O + O_2 \rightarrow O_3 + M$

Fig. 3–8. The cycle of chemical reactions initiated by NO_2. In the absence of hydrocarbons, the cycle initiated by NO_2 consists of three reactions. First, NO_2 absorbs solar energy, dissociating into a molecule of NO and a free oxygen atom, which is highly reactive. Second, the free oxygen atom then reacts with an ordinary oxygen molecule (O_2) to form ozone (O_3). Since the ozone formed in this way is unstable, having too much energy to exist for very long, it dissipates this excess energy by colliding with another molecule, transferring the excess as kinetic energy to that other molecule. If another molecule is not handy at the proper time, the ozone molecule will dissociate, leaving the free oxygen atom to try again. When a stable ozone molecule is formed, it can participate in the third reaction, reacting with the NO molecule produced in the first reaction, which forms nitrogen dioxide again. In this way all the molecular species exist in an equilibrium, and the primary result is that the energy absorbed by the NO_2 is transferred to the air as kinetic energy, warming the air.

Some features of the photochemical smog, however, aren't explained by this description. Beyond the rapid conversion of the NO into NO_2 and the subsequent buildup of ozone, there are the more obvious symptoms,

---

free radical to react again. Some of the original free radicals are formed by the absorption of light by the hydrocarbon molecules. The greater proportion, however, are formed by the reaction of the hydrocarbons with the free oxygen atom produced by the NO_2 dissociation. The highly active free oxygen can react with the hydrocarbons to form a variety of intermediate products, which then do most of the converting of NO to NO_2.

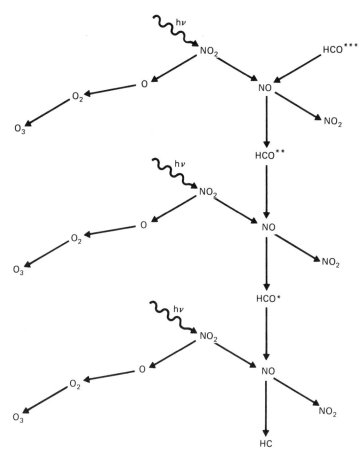

Fig. 3–9. Conversion of NO back into NO₂ in the presence of reactive hydrocarbon molecules. The cycle shown in Fig. 3–8 becomes more complex when hydrocarbons are present, for they add another reaction path that involves a number of unknown reactions. The reactive hydrocarbons can provide an alternate path for the free oxygen atom to react with NO to reestablish the NO₂. However, an oxygen atom utilizing this path can, by means of the complicated hydrocarbon reactions, oxidize more than just one NO atom. This leaves other free oxygen atoms to make ozone, which just accumulates as the daily peak in oxidant levels.

especially the eye irritation caused by the smog mixture. But since an explanation would require a more detailed description of the chemistry involved, we will merely note that in the preceding mechanism, the only ingredient actually making up the ozone is the ordinary oxygen in the air. The hydrocarbons and nitrogen oxides are not consumed; the nitrogen oxides just cycle about, and the hydrocarbons, though modified somewhat, are still considered hydrocarbons.

Actually, the modification of the hydrocarbons is quite significant, and in fact the NO_x are consumed to a slight extent. Although the details of the process are not well understood, some of the hydrocarbons or the intermediate free radicals react with the NO_x to form various nitrogen-bearing organic compounds. These comprise a part, possibly a large part, of the small portion of oxidant that isn't ozone, which accounts for most of the eye-irritating properties of smog. Peroxyacetyl nitrate (PAN) is the most common such oxidant and is the one most often measured or studied. However, measured PAN concentrations usually are not high enough to account for the severity of the eye irritation, so it is normally assumed that there are also other, perhaps yet unidentified, compounds contributing to the smog symptoms.

The Prevalence of Photochemical Pollution

Because the oxidants are secondary pollutants, we cannot discuss the quantity of emissions as we did with the other pollutants, but rather must consider the emissions of the precursor pollutants. And because of the varying intensity of sunlight and other complicating factors, we can't even relate the subsequent oxidant levels to the quantity of hydrocarbon and NO_x emissions very accurately. This difficulty causes serious problems in trying to plan how much precursor reduction is needed to reduce oxidants to acceptable levels.

The quantities of oxides of nitrogen and hydrocarbons emitted are similar to the SO_2 and particulate emissions in magnitude, as seen in Tables 3–6 and 3–7, respectively. Oxides of nitrogen are produced in any combustion operation in which the temperatures are high enough, the NO_x being formed from the nitrogen and oxygen in the air rather than from anything in the fuel. Nitrogen oxides are formed by combustion in automobiles, power plants, industries, homes, and offices; they are the only major pollutants produced in any significant amount by natural gas combustion. Though the nitrogen is generally first oxidized to NO, further oxidation in the stack and in the plume causes most sources to emit mixtures of NO and NO_2, with the relative proportion differing for various sources. In this respect, the automobile tends to emit mostly NO.

Hydrocarbons, too, are emitted primarily from fuel-combustion operations, mostly those in which inefficient combustion permits some fuel to escape unburned or in those using highly volatile fuels that can vaporize and be lost in handling or transfer. The volatility of gasoline and the inefficiency of the internal combustion engine combine to make the automobile the biggest contributor of hydrocarbons, emitting over 15 million of the estimated 32 million tons annually. Most of these man-made emissions are reactive hydrocarbons. Of the nonreactive hydrocarbons in the air, such

TABLE 3–6
Annual emissions of nitrogen oxides (estimates for 1970)

Source category	Emissions, millions of tons per year	Percent of total
Fuel combustion		
Transportation		
Gasoline motor vehicles	7.8	34.2
Diesel, aircraft, trains, vessels	2.0	8.8
Off-highway vehicles	1.9	8.3
Total transportation	11.7	51.3
Stationary sources		
Coal	3.9	17.1
Fuel Oil	1.3	5.7
Natural gas	4.7	20.6
Wood	0.1	0.4
Total stationary source	10.0	43.8
Total fuel combustion	**21.7**	**95.1**
Industrial processes	**0.2**	**0.9**
Agricultural burning	**0.3**	**1.3**
Solid waste disposal	**0.4**	**1.8**
Miscellaneous*	**0.2**	**0.9**
Total	**22.8**	**100.0**

* Includes coal-refuse burning, structural fires, and accidental and intentional forest fires.
Source: J. H. Cavender, D. S. Kircher, and A. J. Hoffman, Nationwide Air Pollutant Emission Trends 1940–1970, EPA Publication No. AP–115, January 1973.

as methane, a large proportion are produced by natural sources, such as decaying vegetation.

The gathering of data on the atmospheric prevalence of the photochemical pollutants is not as widespread as it is for the other pollutants; most of the detailed information is from the Los Angeles Basin, with only a little from a few other cities. In general, the temporal variations at one location are more striking than the geographic differences among various sites (with the exception of Los Angeles). The total hydrocarbon levels typically average 2 to 3 ppm in most places; of this, about 1½ to 2 ppm is methane, about 1.2 ppm background from natural sources, and the balance from man-made sources. In the Los Angeles Basin area, the total hydrocarbon level is typically higher, 4 to 6 ppm, of which 2 to 4 ppm is methane. The seasonal variability of hydrocarbon levels through the year is fairly small, largely because the level of automobile traffic is relatively constant. The variation throughout the day is also modest, partly because the methane levels decrease just when the emissions from traffic are increasing (see Fig. 3–6).

Atmospheric concentrations of the oxides of nitrogen vary a great deal more, largely as a function of the daily cycle of traffic and the seasonal

TABLE 3–7
Annual emissions of hydrocarbons (estimates for 1970)

Source category	Emissions, millions of tons per year	Percent of total
Fuel combustion		
Transportation		
Gasoline motor vehicles	16.6	47.6
Diesel, aircraft, trains, vessels	0.9	2.6
Off-highway vehicles	2.0	5.7
Total transportation	19.5	55.9
Stationary sources		
Coal	0.2	0.6
Fuel Oil	0.1	0.3
Natural gas	0.3	0.8
Wood	—	—
Total stationary source	0.6	1.7
Total fuel combustion	**20.1**	**57.6**
Industrial processes	**9.5**	**27.2**
Agricultural burning	**2.8**	**8.0**
Solid waste disposal	**2.0**	**5.7**
Miscellaneous*	**0.5**	**1.5**
Total	**34.9**	**100.0**

* Includes coal-refuse burning, structural fires, and accidental and intentional forest fires.
Source: J. H. Cavender, D. S. Kircher, and A. J. Hoffman, *Nationwide Air Pollutant Emission Trends 1940–1970,* EPA Publication No. AP–115, January 1973.

pattern of solar radiation. The various diurnal variation plots shown in Fig. 3–10 show both of these relationships. Nitric oxide is a particularly good indicator of the atmospheric dispersion capability in the morning, with the size of the morning NO peak often reflecting the degree of inversion conditions; under a severe inversion, the NO peak can be most dramatic, as illustrated in Fig. 3–11. The data in Figs. 3–10 and 3–11 are from Washington, D.C., but are reasonably typical of most sites, again excepting Los Angeles, where levels are somewhat higher.

The best overall comparison among urban areas, however, is unquestionably that of the oxidant levels produced; because of the time lag and the location of atmospheric mixing, the oxidant concentration is much less affected by the specific location of the monitoring stations and tends to more readily represent levels over an entire urban area. Oxidant levels have the most striking, yet the most consistent and predictable, pattern of variation of any of the pollutants. Because the smog-formation reactions require sunlight, there is usually very little oxidant measured overnight. There is a similar effect through the year; the summer, with abundant sunshine, is much more smoggy than the winter. Both of these patterns are apparent in Fig. 3–12. Because of these patterns, and especially the day-night effect, the use of average concentrations to characterize oxidant levels is rather meaningless; so many near-zero nighttime numbers are averaged in that they mask any real effects in the other data. Thus, it has become customary to characterize the smog on a given day by the maximum hourly average oxidant. A day with a "max hour" of 0.05 ppm is routine, whereas 0.15 ppm is noticeably smoggy. Table 3–8 compares oxidant levels in various urban areas in this manner.

TABLE 3–8
Prevalence of high total oxidant pollution

City or station	Percent of days on which maximum hourly average oxidant level exceeded the stated concentration			Maximum hourly average, ppm
	0.05 ppm	0.10 ppm	0.15 ppm	
Pasadena	75	55	41.1	0.46
Los Angeles	74	49	30.1	0.58
San Diego	71	21	5.6	0.38
Denver	79	18	4.9	0.25
St. Louis	62	10	2.4	0.35
Philadelphia	42	11	2.3	0.21
Sacramento	62	15	2.3	0.26
Cincinnati	52	9	1.6	0.26
Santa Barbara	71	11	1.5	0.25
Washington, D.C.	54	11	1.2	0.21
San Francisco	29	5	0.9	0.18
Chicago	51	5	0.0	0.13

Source: Modified from Air Quality Criteria for Photochemical Oxidants, NAPCA Publication No. AP–63, Department of Health, Education and Welfare, March 1970.

We can conclude from Table 3–8 that photochemical smog is far worse in the Los Angeles area than it is anywhere else. There are two basic reasons for this, the first of which is the city's meteorological situation, which was described in Chapter 2. The other is a function of the nature of the city and the way of life of the people; the city is spread out over a wide area, and there is no rapid transit system. People routinely drive distances that would completely deter most eastern urbanites. Although the smog problem in Los Angeles is obviously the most acute, we must also remember that smog occurs in every other city in which measurements have been made, though these occurrences are far less frequent. The seriousness of the smog in other cities must be considered in light of knowledge about the effects of that smog rather than merely in comparison with the smog in Los Angeles; this topic is still a subject of considerable public debate.

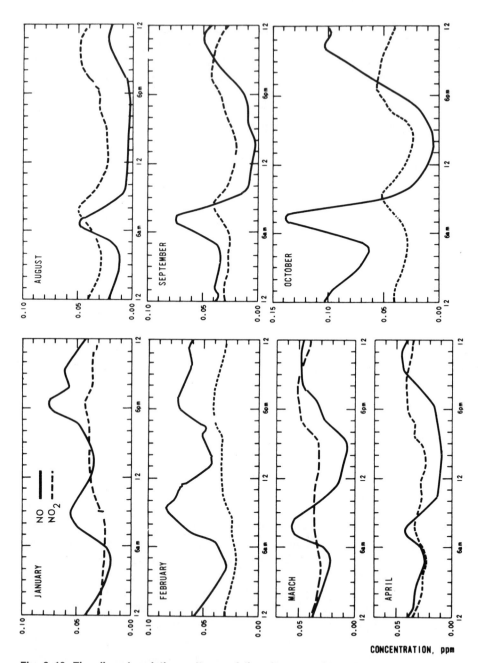

Fig. 3–10. The diurnal variation patterns of the nitrogen oxides. These patterns illustrate several things. The particularly sharp NO peaks in the fall reflect the persistence of the nocturnal inversions into the rush hour, but the lessened sunlight is inadequate to rapidly convert the NO

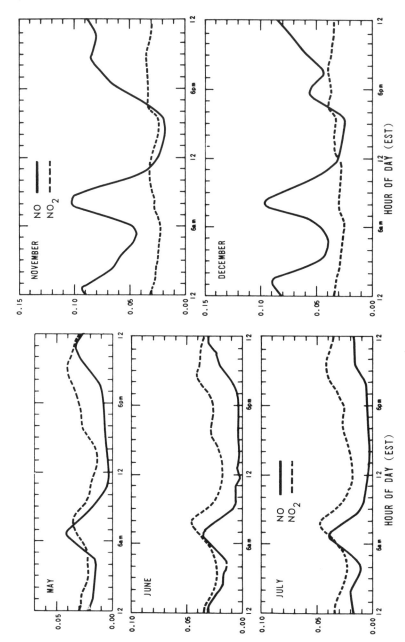

peak into an NO_2 peak. In contrast, the greater sunlight in summer converts NO into NO_2 rapidly, making a distinct NO_2 peak and keeping the
NO levels very low throughout the daylight hours. (*CAMP in Washington, D.C., 1962–1963*, Public Health Service Publication No. 999–AP–23,
Department of Health, Education, and Welfare, September 1966)

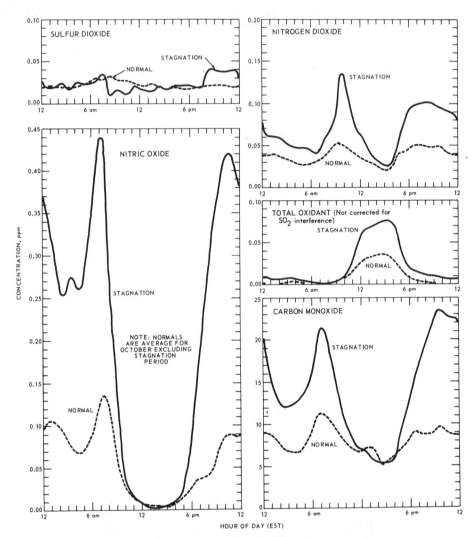

Fig. 3–11. Increases in concentration of gaseous pollutants during a typical stagnation (October 15–19, 1963, in Washington, D.C.). Nitric oxide, which is emitted very near the ground (tail-pipe height), is most dramatically affected. Often, sulfur dioxide is not increased at all, apparently because the fair weather associated with the stagnation reduces the emission of SO_2 from space heating. (*CAMP in Washington, D.C., 1962–1963*, Public Health Service Publication No. 999–AP–23, Department of Health, Education and Welfare, September 1966)

Fig. 3–12. Total oxidant concentration varies with amount of sunlight. The diurnal ▶ variation pattern for each month is maximum in early afternoon, and the size of the afternoon peak increases from next to nothing in January to a maximum in July and then back again. The data are from Philadelphia, but are typical of most cities except Los Angeles, where the levels are higher and the maximum a month later. Here, the highest *average* hourly level is about 0.09 ppm in July; this, of course, includes some days with low oxidant peaks and others with maxima up to about 0.25 ppm. (*CAMP in Philadelphia, 1962–1965*, NAPCA Publication No. APTD 69–14, Department of Health, Education and Welfare, August 1969)

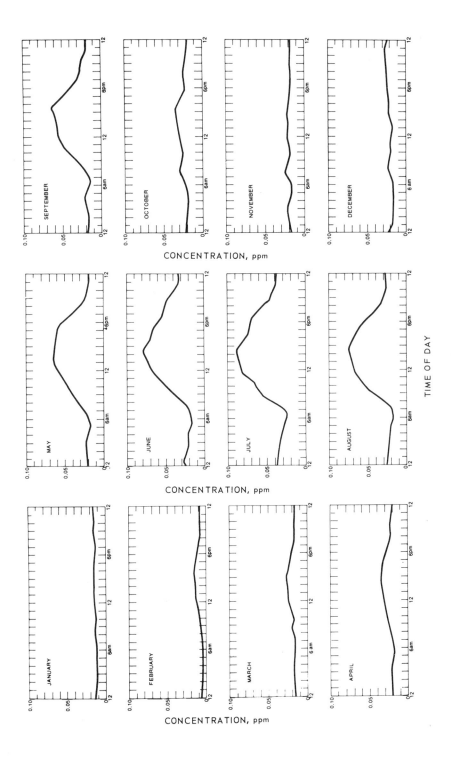

OTHER POLLUTANTS

In addition to the six major pollutants discussed so far, there are a number of other substances of interest as air pollutants. Many substances have been found in the air—some quite widely, others more locally. Strictly speaking, this section should mention only those substances that have adverse effects on our health or welfare. However, as we shall see in Chapters 4 and 5, our knowledge about the effects of many of these substances is nowhere near as precise as we would like it to be, so that such a list of pollutants would be in no way final or definite; consequently, this section includes not only those substances that have definite health effects, but also some others that are particularly widespread or frequently measured, and some that are presently receiving the greatest public attention.

Particulate Pollutants

Many of the substances we lumped together as particulates are significant pollutants on their own. Chemical analysis of the suspended particulate matter from a typical city reveals well over a score of substances routinely present, as listed in Table 3–9. Of the nonmetals, the *sulfate* portion, al-

TABLE 3–9
Partial list of substances in particulate matter*

Substance	Typical concentration ($\mu g/m^3$)
Inorganic compounds	
Nonmetals	
Ammonium (NH^+)	1.2
Nitrate (NO_3^-)	1.8
Sulfate ($SO_4^=$)	10.0
Flouride (F^-)	T (trace)
Metals	
Iron (Fe)	1.6
Lead (Pb)	1.0
Zinc (Zn)	0.7
Copper (Cu)	0.1
Manganese (Mn)	0.1
Arsenic, cadmium, chromium, nickel, tin, titanium, vanadium	< 0.05 each
Beryllium, bismuth, cobalt, molybdenum	T
Organic fraction (benzene-soluble)	6.5
includes benzo-a-pyrene	0.0025
Total suspended particulate matter	100

* The constituents listed above don't even approach 100 $\mu g/m^3$ in total. The remainder, which includes some substances that haven't been identified, comprises mostly known substances that just aren't separately measured, such as silicates and other soil-derived minerals.
Source: Based on National Air Sampling Network data; see [66–73] in bibliography.

ready mentioned as part of the sulfur oxides in the previous section, are formed by the condensation of water or other substances with the SO_2 from a sulfur-bearing plume and are important in producing haze and adverse health effects. *Nitrate* and *ammonium* are routinely measured because of their relevance to atmospheric chemistry. *Fluoride* compounds are well known as dental-health additives to drinking water and toothpastes; at very much higher concentrations, however, they have a detrimental effect on teeth and bones. Fluorides are most generally emitted into the air by phosphate fertilizer plants and are of concern because they accumulate in forage grasses, often poisoning cattle and other grazing animals (see Chapter 5); the economic cost of this is great, to say nothing of the suffering inflicted on the cattle. Except in the immediate vicinity of phosphate fertilizer plants, however, there is very little fluoride in the air; about 90% of the measurements made find no detectable fluoride, that is, 0.05 μg/m^3 or less. Samples gathered have ranged as high as one or two micrograms, but these levels are rare.

Many metals are found in the air, ranging from *iron*—usually, the most prevalent at about 1.5 μg/m^3—down to those found only occasionally and in trace quantities. The most significant of these is *lead*, a toxic metal that comes closest to being the seventh major pollutant. Lead compounds can be emitted into the air in a variety of ways, but the principal one is the use of tetraethyl lead as an antiknock additive to raise the octane rating of gasoline. Lead is of concern as an air pollutant because of its toxicity and its widespread and increasing distribution by motor vehicles. A typical annual average level of lead is about 1 μg/m^3; the highest average urban level is over 3 μg/m^3 (in Los Angeles), and individual daily samples can range up to 8 μg/m^3. Lead averages 10 to 25 μg/m^3 in rush-hour traffic and is even found in low quantities ($<$0.1 μg/m^3) at remote, nonurban stations.

Of the other metals, beryllium, cadmium, and mercury are of special concern because of their toxicity; beryllium and mercury have been singled out as especially hazardous (along with asbestos) by the Environmental Protection Agency. Cadmium and beryllium are routinely measured; *cadmium* averages about 0.02 μg/m^3, with occasional samples ranging up to 0.40 μg/m^3, but there is very rarely any detectable *beryllium* in the air. Very few studies have even tried to measure mercury, but some limited data from Chicago indicate *mercury* levels in the vicinity of 10 nanograms per cubic meter, or 0.01 μg/m^3.*

All of these metal concentrations seem quite small, especially in com-

---

* This same study, using unusual measurement methods, also found the following substances not usually measured: aluminum, bromine, and chlorine, in μg/m^3 quantities, plus smaller amounts of sodium, selenium, cerium, silver, lanthanum, scandium, cesium, and europium, in decreasing amounts down to 0.12 ng/m^3, or 0.00012 μg/m^3 of europium.

parison with the total suspended particulate matter. It is not apparent, however, that these levels are necessarily small relative to the amounts required to produce adverse health effects, although, except for lead, it is believed that they are.

The organic portion of the particulate matter, as is typical of organic chemicals in general, shows a wide variety of compounds, many of which have not been explored for possible pollution significance. For years, the government has measured the total organic particulate pollution as *benzene-soluble organic matter.** It is not of precise interest in and of itself, but is measured because it includes the class of organic carcinogens, and specifically benzo-a-pyrene, as a small portion of the total. The *organic carcinogens* are those polycyclic aromatic hydrocarbon compounds that have been demonstrated to cause cancer in laboratory animals. Largely products of coal combustion, they are relatively widespread, especially in the Northeast. Although they occur in fairly low concentrations, their effect is heightened because they occur together with, and are adsorbed on, black smoke particles. The most carcinogenic, benzo-a-pyrene (Fig. 3–13) has been measured separately, and Table 3–10 shows the concentrations of benzo-a-pyrene in several major cities.

Although the list of chemicals in Table 3–9 is long, there are others that aren't routinely measured, for one reason or another. A very interesting portion of the particulate matter that can't be measured chemically is *asbestos*. Asbestos, a fibrous mineral product, is found in nature and is mined in its natural state for use in a wide variety of products. It is practically indestructible and has a very complicated chemical nature. Actually, several quite similar minerals are lumped together under the term "asbes-

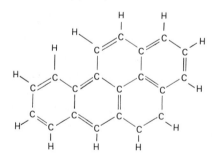

Fig. 3–13. Structure of the 3,4- benzo-a-pyrene molecule. This molecule consists entirely of carbon and hydrogen arranged in five fused benzene rings.

---

* Strictly speaking, this is only that portion of the suspended particulate matter that is soluble in benzene. It is necessary to include "benzene-soluble" in the name, because using a different solvent in the analysis would include somewhat different constituents in the measurement. Benzene was chosen so as to include the benzene-type polycyclic aromatic hydrocarbons that arise from fossil fuel combustion and to exclude the naturally occurring protein-type organic matter, such as pollens and spores.

TABLE 3–10
Typical benzo-a-pyrene concentrations

City	Annual average concentration (nanograms (10^{-9} g) per cubic meter)
Ashland, Ky	10.5
Birmingham, Ala.	18.5
Charleston, W.Va.	3.4
Chattanooga, Tenn.	3.4
Cleveland, Ohio	3.1
Chicago, Ill.	3.3
Detroit, Mich.	4.7
Honolulu, Hawaii	0.16
Houston, Texas	0.89
Indianapolis, Ind.	10.4
Los Angeles, Cal.	2.1
New Orleans, La.	2.3
New York, New York	4.1
Philadelphia, Pa.	3.8
Pittsburgh, Pa.	4.9
St. Louis, Mo.	5.3
San Francisco, Cal.	1.1
Washington, D.C.	2.4
Nonurban	
Acadia National Park, Me.	0.18
Black Hills Forest, S.D.	0.15
Grand Canyon Park, Ariz.	0.29
Yellowstone National Park, Wy.	0.06

Source: Air Quality Data from the NASN and Contributing State and Local Networks, 1966 Edition, NAPCA Publication No. APTD 68–9, Department of Health, Education and Welfare, 1968.

tos"; the most common variety, called chrysotile, is about 40% silica, 40% magnesium oxide, 14% water, with smaller quantities of iron, aluminum oxides, and calcium. Although pollution is likely to result from the mining and processing of asbestos, the more widespread source is the use of the many products ultimately produced from the mineral fibers; these include fabrics, cement, tile, heat insulation products, and friction products, such as the brake linings and clutch plates in automobiles. There is special concern about the use of asbestos cement for heat insulation in building structures, because it is commonly applied by being sprayed on the structures during construction, with the obvious potential for dispersal of stray fibers throughout the urban air. Since there is no satisfactory method for measuring concentrations of asbestos particles in the ambient air, the amount of asbestos pollution is not well known.

Gaseous Pollutants

In contrast to particulates, not many gases, beyond the major ones, are pollutants. Hydrogen fluoride can exist as a gas, but it is so reactive chemically that it reacts with the particulate matter on a hi-vol filter and thus gets measured as particulate fluoride, even though it was gaseous in the atmosphere. Hydrogen sulfide is another gas considered a pollutant whenever it occurs in smellable concentrations, which is seldom.

Actually, all *odorous compounds* can be quite significant problems in air pollution; many of the complaints received by any large-city control agency are likely to concern odorous emissions. As was the case with black smoke, the situation with odors is a little different from that of the ordinary pollutant, since we're concerned with a property of the substance rather than its amount. Unlike black smoke, however, odors haven't been attacked and successfully abated. This is partly because there is no handy device analogous to a Ringelmann chart and partly because the situation has never been so bad or widespread as to cause major public pressures. And of course, odorous compounds comprise a much wider variety than did black-smoke emissions; in fact, many odors today probably result from chemicals that didn't exist in the 1930s. Nonetheless, odors are perhaps the most common problem about which little is being done.

RELATIVE SIGNIFICANCE OF THE POLLUTANTS

Having gone so far as to categorize the pollutants as major and minor, it seems logical to now rank at least the six major ones in order of significance. Such a ranking, if it were realistic, would have definite practical value, permitting priority judgments about the allocation of budget expenditures, for example. It is not possible, however, to rank the pollutants in the most straightforward fashion, that is, by comparing the total damage done by each. It is impossible not only because pollutant prevalence is not well documented, but also because the damaging effects are not well defined and are not readily comparable in many cases, anyway. Failing the most desirable ranking, it is normally considered not really possible to rank them at all.

However, one can't just say that comparisons are impossible and drop the subject, because the general public will in fact develop a ranking whether or not the air pollution "establishment" wishes it. Normally, the public makes an implicit ranking based on the only really comparable figures that exist—the national emissions estimates. Consequently, these tonnage figures are often quoted, usually with emphasis on the importance of one pollutant or one type of source.

These implicit comparisons of tonnages can be quite misleading, however, and it is possible to do better, to provide a relative analysis in terms of not only the quantity of pollutant emitted, but also the levels at which effects may be harmful. The following discussion does such an analysis, which can be followed in Table 3–11. Column 2 of the table summarizes

TABLE 3–11
Relative significance of the major pollutants

Pollutant (1)	Emissions		Standard	Relative emissions	
	10^6 T/year (2)	% of total (3)	$\mu g/m^3$ (4)	10^6/yr/$\mu g/m^3$ (5)	% of total (6)
Sulfur Oxides	33.9	12.7	80	0.424	34.4
Particulates	26.1	9.8	75	0.348	28.2
Carbon Monoxide	148.6	55.8	10,000	0.049	1.2
Hydrocarbons	34.9	13.1	160	0.218	17.7
Oxides of nitrogen	22.8	8.6	100	0.228	18.5
Totals	266.3	100.0		1.233	100.0

the gross national emission estimates from the other tables in this chapter, and column 3 indicates the relative contribution of the various pollutants. The contribution of CO is almost half of the nearly 200 million tons total, indicating that on a mass emission basis, it is certainly the most prominent pollutant; the differences among the other four pollutants are small by comparison. Considering that automobiles contribute about two-thirds of the CO and perhaps half of the hydrocarbons and NO_x, it is easy to see why they are frequently castigated as being our biggest polluters. However, sheer mass of pollutant emission alone is a poor guide to the possible harm it might cause. Column 4 of the table lists the national ambient air quality standards for each of the five pollutants. These are concentrations (in $\mu g/m^3$) that cause an effect on human health (see Chapter 4), but for our purposes here they can be regarded as relative numbers on an arbitrary scale. Dividing column 2 by column 4 gives us column 5, with its unlikely units of millions of tons per year per microgram per cubic meter. The numbers in column 5 are useful only in showing relative significance—each pollutant's mass contribution relative to its harmful level. Much easier to comprehend are the same numbers converted to percentages of the total (column 6). Viewed in this fashion, it appears that SO_x and particulates comprise the biggest share of the total and that carbon monoxide is only a very small part of the total. The reason for the dramatic shift in perspective is, of course, the very large standard for CO in column 4. This level— 10,000 $\mu g/m^3$, or 9 ppm—is much higher than the others, reflecting the fact that humans tolerate a great deal more carbon monoxide than they do sulfur oxides.

The fact that a difference in viewpoint could cause such a drastic shift in conclusions should alert us to be quite careful about such matters as relative significance, regardless of which method we use to look at the question. There is a further caveat also; both of these methods of viewing the major pollutants depend for their intuitive appeal on figures that are percentages of a whole. Such analyses are always quite sensitive to what is included in the whole. That is, if national emission estimates for lead, say, were available and included in Table 3–11, the percentage of all the other pollutants would necessarily go down slightly—but, of course, artificially.

This last comment may suggest that the list of major pollutants is predicated on the existence of emission estimates, and to a large extent this is true; the six "major" pollutants were chosen because of the amount of interest in and study about them, though that in turn is presumably related to their significance in one sense or another. One (correct) implication from this is that when the "major" pollutants of today are largely under control, others will take their place.

EXERCISES

Review Questions

1. How are the major pollutants divided into groups? What is the common thing tying each group together?
2. What is the most significant property of particulate matter? Why?
3. Distinguish between dustfall and suspended particulate matter in terms of the size of the particles and the type of effect caused.
4. Why are particles in the size range from 0.1–10 microns important? How are they measured?
5. What is "black smoke"? How is it measured?
6. What is the typical suspended-particulate concentration expected in the downtown area of a city? What would be the highest and lowest (approximately) expected anywhere?
7. What measurement units are typically used to express atmospheric concentrations of particulate pollution? Of gases? What units are used to express quantities of pollutions emitted?
8. What are the two gases included in the definition of sulfur oxides? Which is the more prevalent?
9. How are the two gases in SO_x related? With what else are they related? How?
10. Approximately how much particulate and sulfur oxide pollution is emitted in the air in the United States annually? From what sources?
11. How is carbon monoxide produced? What sources emit most of it? Why are these sources predominant?
12. What are typical carbon monoxide levels? What factors are most important in determining the level?
13. What chemicals comprise oxides of nitrogen? Total hydrocarbons? Photochemical oxidants?
14. Distinguish among total hydrocarbons, reactive hydrocarbons, and non-methane hydrocarbons.
15. What two characteristics distinguish photochemical oxidants from the other major pollutants?

16. What photochemical reactions would take place in an atmosphere polluted with NO_x but not with reactive hydrocarbons?
17. How does the answer to question 16 change when hydrocarbons are added?
18. Where is photochemical smog most prevalent? Why there?
19. What metals are significant pollutants?
20. What three substances have been singled out by the federal government as especially "hazardous air pollutants"?
21. Why can't we have a precise comparison of the various pollutants based on the magnitude of damage they do?
22. Which pollutant is emitted in the greatest amount? Which has the greatest emissions relative to its effects?

Thought Questions

23. If we consider lead a seventh major pollutant, with which of the three groups would it most logically be included?
24. Where and when would you expect to find the extreme high and low ambient concentrations of: (a) suspended particulate matter; (b) sulfur dioxide; (c) carbon monoxide; (d) photochemical oxidants?
25. Offer an explanation for the differences in the particulate-to-sulfur oxides ratio between New York and Denver or Oklahoma City, as seen in Table 3–4.
26. What would be involved in compiling an emission table for nonmethane hydrocarbons similar to Table 3–6? What else would be needed to do so for "reactive" hydrocarbons?
27. Of the various fractions of suspended particulate matter listed in Table 3–8, which are most important? Why?
28. The federal government is trying out a method of measuring particulate pollution that would classify particles on a finer-size scale than just the division between dustfall and suspended particulate matter. The chief disadvantage of such a method would likely be increased complexity and cost; what would be some of the advantages of having such data? What questions might these data be able to answer?

Discussion Questions

29. Dustfall and black smoke are more obvious to most of the general population than is suspended particulate pollution, yet the latter is probably more injurious to human health. List some reasons for giving priority to the control of one or another of the three. As a citizen, which would you prefer to see controlled? Why? If you were the city air pollution control officer, are there additional factors involved? Would your choice change?
30. What strategy would you apply to controlling photochemical smog, i.e., would you control hydrocarbons, NO_x, or both? What further information might help you make a better decision?
31. The analysis of the relative significance of the major pollutants falls short of the ultimate, because there is no consideration of whether the standards in column 4 of Table 3–10 all cause equally harmful effects. With what

you know about the effects of the pollutants, is this a significant defect? How does one go about comparing the different effects? How does this relate to the choice of which pollutants are major ones?

Problems

32. What would be the amount of pollutant in your classroom if the suspended particulate concentration were 100 $\mu g/m^3$? If the SO_2 concentration were 0.03 ppm?

33. Assume that a smokestack emits 10 tons of sulfur dioxide into the air of a city with an area of 100 miles. If the pollutant is evenly mixed throughout the city and up to a height of 500 meters, where there is an inversion layer, what will the SO_2 concentration be? If 10 percent of the SO_2 is completely converted to sulfuric acid mist, what will the concentration of sulfuric acid be?

34. Assuming that the general emissions of carbon monoxide were evenly distributed throughout the year and across the area of the country, what would the ambient concentration be on a day when the *average* mixing depth was 100 meters? 800 meters? How does this compare with the national air quality standard? How do you account for the difference?

35. Work problem 34 for sulfur oxides, for a summer day with an average mixing height of 1500 meters and emissions at one-third the annual rate, and for a winter day with mixing height of 800 meters and emissions double the annual rate.

36. The midafternoon decrease in NO_2 concentrations seen in Fig. 3–8 reflects the improved atmospheric dispersion in the afternoon, as well as the conversion of NO_2 into nitrogen-bearing oxidants. Assuming that 10 percent of the NO_2 is so converted, estimate the effect of the atmospheric dispersion as a ratio. What would the total oxidant level be if there were no dispersion?

Project Suggestions

37. Using the various tables of emissions by source for the major pollutants, calculate the percent of the "relative significance" contributed by the major source categories, in a manner similar to the calculation of the percent contributions of the major pollutants. How does the result compare with the image of the automobile as the major pollutant source? If computer facilities are available, you could compare a variety of source categories; it would also be interesting to consider the effect of changing the "standards" numbers somewhat.

38. By inquiring of the local air pollution control authorities, find any ambient air quality data gathered in your city. Do these data agree with what you would have guessed after reading this chapter? If a class or other group can all inquire in their own cities, compare the results with Table 3–2.

39. Similarly, inquire about local pollution control laws in one or several cities. Is black smoke mentioned? What level is prohibited? Are more modern specifications of pollution emissions included?

40. If there is a source of visible emissions, i.e., black smoke, nearby, try using the Ringelmann chart. If the source frequently emits smoke, keep records; how does it compare with performance required under the city's law, or under another city's law if none is in effect locally?

FURTHER READING

Two sets of reports provide further information on the pollutants discussed here, as well as on the significance of other substances as air pollutants. The federal government's *Criteria Documents* [23–28] are an integral part of the federal abatement procedure (Chapter 12). Primarily summaries of the effects of the various pollutants, they also include discussions about the properties and prevalence of the pollutants. So far, such documents have been published for the six major pollutants, and other documents are scheduled. The other set of documents, the *Litton Reports* [35–61], covers 27 different substances, presenting for each a literature study of its properties and prevalence and, primarily, its effects on health. Prepared under contract to the government, these are quite similar to the *Criteria Documents*, but they lack any legal status. The various federal *Air Quality Data* reports [62–74] are the best reference source for such data; other data may be available from state or local control officials.

A number of other reports and articles that deal with the nature and behavior of various pollutants are included in the bibliography; especially appropriate are [221] on asbestos, [197] on lead, and [208] on mercury. One of the two versions of survey work on metals [219–220] by Schroeder should be considered. Essentially unique is [76] on the trends in suspended particulate levels. The question of judging the relative significance of the various pollutants is receiving increasing attention; [178] is one additional approach.

4

EFFECTS
ON
HUMAN HEALTH

Owen Franken/Stock, Boston

According to our definition of air pollution, substances are pollutants only if they have deleterious effects on our health, safety, welfare, or property. Since we have labeled a good number of substances as pollutants—some major, others minor—we need to consider the effects that justify this. These effects are the subject of the next two chapters, with effects on our health discussed in this chapter and other effects discussed in Chapter 5. This division, although anthropocentric, is firmly rooted in traditional ways of thinking about pollution. Although we can now recognize that the human situation is not so readily separated from the rest of nature, the direct effects of pollutants on human health have long been considered all-important. This view is now rapidly becoming less predominant, as increasingly large segments of our society become aware of human dependency on other living systems and as more research about these interrelations is planned and conducted.

HEALTH EFFECTS AND HEALTH-EFFECTS RESEARCH

Our knowledge about the effects of air pollution on human health has come primarily from research studies of various types. Historically, those extreme occasions when people were overtly sickened or killed served to warn us that there were probably other, more subtle, effects that we should be deliberately looking for. Consequently, a great deal of research has been carried out over the years, in search of these less obvious effects, and a wide variety has been found, ranging from death, through serious illness, minor illness, and annoyance, down to "body burdens" of a pollutant—the existence of pollutant substances in the body at a level that has no apparent effect at present. This first section considers the general nature of these effects on human health and the types of research on which our knowledge of them rests.

Theoretically, and to a large extent in practice, different effects, at different levels of severity, can be associated with different amounts of exposure to a particular pollutant, with greater exposure causing more severe effect, of course. Thus, one of the obvious goals of health-effects research is to try to define this relationship, which is commonly called a dose-response curve, as a tool for use in planning the amount of pollution control needed. In particular, we want to try to determine the amount of exposure associated with the point of zero effects. It may be that the only way to have zero effects is to have zero pollution; however, we need to know if there is a certain amount of pollutant that can be tolerated without any effect whatsoever. Such a zero-effects exposure is called a threshold level.

There are complications in this picture, however, that generally prevent us from getting the neat definition of a dose-response curve that is possible

in other fields, such as medicinal-drug research. The most serious compli-
cation is that of quantifying the dosage produced by the pollutant exposure. Exposure to pollutants can vary in two different ways: (1) the
amount of pollution being breathed can change, (2) the length of time
spent breathing it can change. Researchers often try to resolve this com-
plication by defining the *dosage* of pollutant as the product of the length
of exposure and the pollutant concentration; for example, 2 ppm of CO
breathed for one hour would result in the same dosage as 1 ppm breathed
for two hours. However, this dosage concept is not very useful when we
consider lengths of exposure greater than a few hours or days. That is,
breathing 0.01 ppm of sulfur dioxide for a year does not produce even
remotely the same effect as breathing 0.12 ppm for a month or 3.65 ppm
for a day. Since the length of exposure time we deal with ranges from a
few minutes to an entire lifetime, we won't make much use of the quantitative dosage concept, but will speak only of generalized exposure-effect
relationships.

Actually, the range of exposure times and types of effects is so great
that for most practical purposes, we usually just speak of two completely
different sets of effects—acute and chronic. Acute effects arise abruptly,
in a few days or weeks of exposure to relatively high pollutant levels.
Chronic effects occur slowly, getting slightly worse year by year; they are
typically associated with long-term exposure to relatively low levels of
pollution. Acute effects are often dramatic, but infrequent enough so that
they usually aren't the biggest concern. Chronic effects are of greater concern not only because they're suffered nearly continuously by many more
people, but also because they're very difficult to study, so that we know
far less about them than we should.

Effects Mechanisms

The second goal of research on health effects is to define the actual physiological mechanism by which the pollutant causes its effect. Part of the
interest in this mechanism is just basic curiosity, but there's more than
that involved; an understanding of the biological mechanisms involved is
also necessary to judge whether or not thresholds exist and to consider
how the results from animal experiments can be extrapolated to humans.

In general, pollutants are labeled, according to the mechanism of their
effect, as being either systemic poisons or nonspecific irritants. The systemic poisons, such as CO and lead, are chemical compounds that can
become involved in and disrupt a specific biochemical mechanism of one
of our bodily systems. The nonspecific irritants, such as SO_2 and particulate matter, remain outside the body's biochemistry, exerting a more generalized effect on an entire group of similar tissues, such as the various

mucous membranes; their damage is the result of the body's reaction to their presence rather than their effect on a specific bodily process.

One other adjective, "toxic," is also used in discussing health effects, e.g., the phrase "toxic effects of" and the word toxicology. Although "toxic" is commonly used as a synonym for "poison," in these phrases it is used more in the sense of harmful, particularly with regard to the pollutants classified as irritants.

Health-Effects Studies

Thus, we have two research goals—the definition of the existence and severity of an effect and the definition of its mechanism of action. How do we go about getting this knowledge? We've already mentioned the first way—by observing acute episodes or accidents. From them, we can gain at least qualitative knowledge and, if proper measurements are made at the time, quantitative evidence also. Another way of learning about health effects is by conducting epidemiological studies; these are also essentially just the observation of health and pollution parameters, but over a longer, less acute period in a more planned, deliberate way. There are two fairly distinct types of epidemiological studies, depending on whether the data on health parameters are gathered from already existing records or by means of special community surveys specifically designed to gain information on the health parameters most likely to be related to pollution. The first type is the more common, depending as it does on inexpensively obtained data that are gathered and compiled for other purposes, such as hospital admissions or health department death records. The disadvantage of such studies is that relevant factors, such as length of residence or smoking habits, cannot always be determined from these available records. Alternatively, studies can be conducted by questionnaire or medical examination or both, eliciting from a sample of the population exactly the information the researcher wants for the study. This permits much better control of extraneous variables, though, of course, it also requires a much higher research expenditure.

Two other ways of gaining information on health effects are through clinical and industrial studies; in these cases the study group consists of a doctor's (or clinic's) patients and the employees of a particular firm, respectively. Such studies are actually just epidemiology studies on special groups, but they are often much better controlled with respect to such extraneous variables as age, sex, socioeconomic status, and exposure to occupational pollution, and they also are characterized by a greater availability of records gathered for other purposes. For example, long-term studies of employee absenteeism have proved of greater value in relating pollution to minor respiratory illness, such as colds and flu, than have studies based on people's memories of occasions when they were sick.

The last major way of learning about health effects, and the one which provides the largest volume of bibliographic material, is through controlled laboratory experimentation. There is a great deal of experimental work carried on in many laboratories, sometimes with humans, but usually with animals, exposing them to pollutants and observing the effects. By using measured dosages, large numbers of subjects, and controlled environmental conditions, these experiments can provide more precise, definite, and repro-ducible information than other methods can. In particular, of course, the use of animals makes it possible to study the fatal effects caused by very high dosages and the internal biologic effects that are revealed only on dissection. The price of these advantages is that such studies are more expensive and are often quite limited in scope.

For our purposes in discussing the results of research studies on effects, we will usually distinguish between only two types of study, experimental and observational. This distinction is whether the experimenter controls the pollutant levels or merely observes them as they occur in nature; by this criterion, all of the study methods mentioned above are observational except the last. As we shall see, both types of studies have contributed to our knowledge of health effects, each in its own way. Observational studies are useful primarily in getting evidence of the existence and magnitude of an effect, but are not very helpful in defining the mechanism of an effect. Animal experiments, largely because they permit dissection, are good for determining mechanisms, but they are generally less helpful in determining the exposure-effect relationship, because there seems to be no reliable way to make quantitative extrapolations to determine at what exposure similar effects might occur in humans.

Typically, both types of evidence play a role in the thorough definition of a pollutant effect. After the effect is first noticed, usually in an extreme case, there is an upsurge in both observational and lab studies, the former looking for less obvious, real-life manifestations, the latter searching for the mechanism and verification of the effect in animals. After a period of such work, the circumstantial evidence from observational studies, plus the demonstration of some effect in animals, with an understanding of its mechanism, is usually sufficient to constitute proof of the existence of the effect even to the die-hards. Then, finally, more sophisticated observational studies can define the effect quantitatively in human populations. It should be emphasized that this final step is only now being done, and even then only for the more thoroughly proved effects of the common pollutants. In the case of some of the more subtle effects, especially the long-term chronic effects, researchers are still very much at the stage of trying to convince the nonbelievers.

In comparison with similar research in related fields, research on the effects of air pollution on health presents two special problems. One is the necessary emphasis on long-term chronic effects. These effects are much more difficult to study than are short-term effects, because one needs to keep a group of subjects together much longer, look for more subtle results, and so on.

The second difficulty arises because a contaminant can assault the respiratory system in several different contexts or environments, which have on occasion been labeled as community, occupational, domestic, and personal air pollution. The first of these is our subject in this book, we mentioned the next two briefly in Chapter 1, and the last, personal air pollution, is just a euphemism for smoking. Since the lungs don't distinguish among the sources of the contaminants they receive, the epidemiologist must; effects from occupational exposure to lead, say, or domestic exposure to carbon monoxide from a defective space heater might be erroneously attributed to community air pollution. Smoking causes by far the most difficulty, however, as occupational and domestic exposures are much less frequent and persistent and affect a smaller number of people. Smoking, of course, is widespread and does have serious effects on respiratory health; they are quite similar in some ways to the effects of pollution and so must be separated if one is to be at all quantitative about the effects. Primarily, this means that observational studies must be "controlled for" the individual's smoking, which is generally done by making comparisons only among people with similar smoking habits. That is, mortality in smokers exposed to pollution is compared only with the mortality of other smokers not exposed, not with the mortality of nonsmokers (see Table 4–3). If this latter comparison were made, the effect of smoking and the effect of exposure to pollution would be added or mixed together, so that neither could be considered separately.

One new and interesting technique is to use school children and their families as a group for observational studies. This minimizes the influence of both occupational and personal pollution exposure; in addition, since attendance records are kept, it is relatively easy to keep track of people who enter and leave the group by moving, thereby making it easier to follow the group for some years. This is the basis for a major federal government study of air pollution health effects, known as CHESS (Community Health and Environmental Surveillance System). The CHESS program involves 33 different neighborhoods in six urban areas and is the source of most of our best quantitative evidence on health effects.

THE HUMAN RESPIRATORY SYSTEM

The air pollutants, of course, all enter the body via the lungs, and most of the effects on our health occur there. Therefore, we will make one more preliminary digression in order to have a brief look at the human respiratory system, emphasizing those aspects particularly relevant to the effect of pollutants.

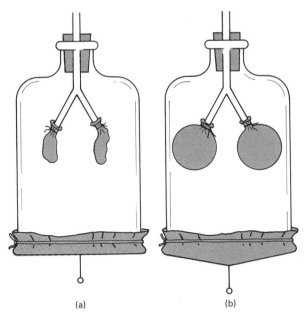

(a)   (b)

Fig. 4–1. The mechanics of breathing. (a) A simple model of a jar with a stretchable diaphragm and two balloons; (b) when the diaphragm is pulled down, the pressure in the jar decreases, and the exterior air pressure forces air through the tubes into the balloons. When released, however, the return to the original condition necessitates elasticity of the balloons and diaphragm, a situation quite analogous to that in human lungs.

The lungs consist of a very large number of tiny air sacs and a great deal of connecting piping. Outside air is brought in and expelled back out by changing the volume of the chest cavity, as shown in Fig. 4–1. The over-all purpose of the respiratory system is to bring the air into close contact with a large number of blood vessels, so that atmospheric oxygen can diffuse into the blood stream and the waste, carbon dioxide, can diffuse out. The major parts of the respiratory system are shown in Fig. 4–2; together, they comprise a system of air passages that get progressively smaller and more numerous. The nasal cavity, pharynx, and trachea comprise the large end of the system, with the other end, the bronchial tubes—the larger ones known as bronchi and the smaller ones, bronchioles. At the end of the bronchioles are the alveoli, individual air sacs arranged in clusters, with each cluster connected to the bronchiole by an alveolar duct. From their beginning at the bottom of the trachea, or windpipe, the bronchi repeatedly branch in two, until ultimately the total number of alveoli is about 600,000,-000, with each alveolus smaller than a pinhead. This extremely fine division makes it possible for the two lungs, with a volume well under one cubic foot,

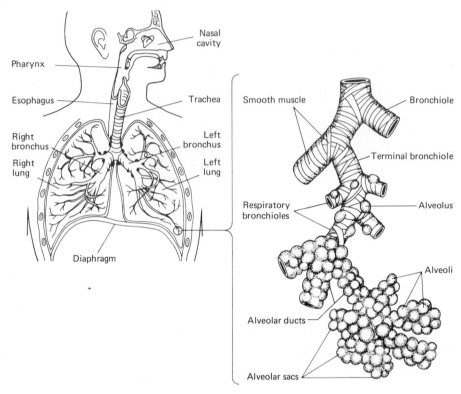

Fig. 4–2. The human respiratory system. (Glen Gordon and William Zoller, *Chemistry in Modern Perspective,* Reading, Mass.: Addison-Wesley, 1975, p. 225)

to have a surface area of over 600 square feet for gas diffusion. It also, of course, makes each tiny, individual alveolus a rather fragile thing.

The inside surfaces of the lung passages are covered with mucus secreted by cells in the epithelium lining the passages, as illustrated in Fig. 4–3. This material has two functions: to moisten and warm the incoming air and to be part of the lungs' protection against foreign particles.

Since the diffusion of oxygen and CO_2 through the alveolar walls requires a moist surface, which must be protected from becoming dried out, the incoming air is moisturized to nearly 100 percent humidity by the mucus along the walls of the nose, sinuses, windpipe, and bronchial tubes. In order to conserve moisture and minimize bodily water consumption, the mucous membranes retrieve much of this moisture back from the air as it is exhaled. The mucous lining also heats or cools the air, as appropriate, to nearly body temperature in order to keep the alveoli from becoming either frozen or fried; the respiratory system can thus survive in air temperatures well over 200°F and well below freezing, a striking adaptive capability.

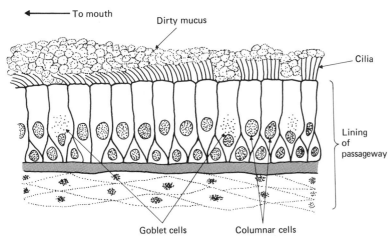

Fig. 4–3. The inside surface of the lung passages. Mucous lining in the bronchial tubes serves to trap and then carry away some of the particles from the air we breathe. Mucus is produced by the goblet cells and is pushed outward by the rhythmic beating of the cilia on the columnar cells. If overstimulated by pollution from sulfur oxides, the goblet cells can produce mucus to the point of overwhelming the cilia; other pollutants, and especially smoking, can also damage the cilia themselves. (*Breathing—What You Need to Know,* New York: National Tuberculosis and Respiratory Disease Association, 1968, p. 16. Reprinted by permission.)

Several of the respiratory system's mechanisms are designed to protect against irritating gases and foreign particles, precisely the types of substances with which it is assaulted by polluted air. The mechanisms for protection from harmful gases are relatively simple and operate only on irritant gases, since the system (obviously) cannot be designed to eliminate gases *per se.* The first mechanism consists merely of sniffing; when faced with a strange breathing situation most animals, including humans, instinctively sniff, and the normal sniff carries just enough air into the nose to reach the olfactory organs and no further; if the air is in fact disagreeable, the animal voluntarily avoids breathing it by merely refraining briefly or by leaving. If this fails, and an unexpected dose of irritant gas is inhaled into the throat, a violent, totally involuntary choking will try to close off the respiratory tract to prevent the intrusion of the gas; an overdose of ammonia is the most common everyday experience along this line. Many other, less common gases, including sulfur dioxide and some of the other pollutants, have this same property, though not in the concentrations at which they are normally found in the air. If the concentration of the gas is too low to irritate, the mucus may still absorb most of it if it is soluble, like SO_2; if it is not, like CO, it can go where it will.

The system for preventing the entry of particles and removing them if they do intrude is more effective, as it can operate against all particles. Hairs in the nasal cavity, by merely acting as a coarse filter, prevent the entry of small insects and very large particles. Through the remainder of the nasal cavity and throat, the air is subjected to many abrupt turns in its path and points of deliberate slowing of the flow, both of which tend to separate the larger particles from the air, driving them into the sticky mucus on the walls. (The same mechanisms also work well for separating the pollutant particles from the air in a smokestack.)

Hence, in the broad channels of the nasal passages, at the abrupt turn at the back of the throat, and at each fork in the bronchi, the larger particles are collected on the walls by the mucus. In this way the particles are kept from reaching the alveoli. The particles, however, can't be left in the mucus indefinitely, but must be eliminated in some fashion. The organs developed for this are the cilia, minute hairlike organs (Fig. 4–3) lining the walls of the bronchial tubes, millions of them per square inch. The cilia are not only numerous, but also organized; they move back and forth like the oars on a boat, in a precise rhythm, about 16 times per second, so that a wave of motion flows along the wall of the passageway. The mucus with its load of particles is moved along by this ciliary beating and flows outward from the respiratory tract in a fairly continuous stream until it reaches the throat, where it and the particles it carries are swallowed or occasionally expelled by a sneeze or cough.

An additional clearance mechanism is active, and probably dominates, in the very finest regions of the lung, near the alveoli. In these areas the special scavenger cells called macrophages, which generally perform the task of attacking foreign substances throughout the body, attack those particles that have escaped the mucus. The macrophages are capable of gathering up particles, rendering them relatively harmless, and to a certain extent transporting them, either out into the larger bronchioles, where they can be carried on out by ciliary-mucus transport, or into the interstices between the alveoli.

Remarkable as these protective systems may seem, they are not by any means totally effective against all the particles that are found in our modern-day air. Some particles are retained in the lungs, particularly at the forks in the bronchial tubes and in the alveoli. Accumulation in the forks occurs because these areas not only are good at collecting particles, but are also weak points in the mucus flow. Because they have an irregular, Y-shaped geometry, the mucus flow through them tends to be irregular; consequently, when the particle concentrations are heavy, the excess loading is felt much more at these points than elsewhere.

Most important, however, is the retention of particles in the alveoli, where the primary business of the lung is carried out and hence where it can be most easily interfered with. Most of the larger particles (greater than 2 microns) do not reach the alveoli, being either screened out or collected and carried out by the mucus at some point higher in the respiratory tract, and this is undoubtedly how nature intended it to be. The smaller particles, however, find their way into the alveoli, where most of them are deposited. The alveoli thus collect the most numerous particles, those around one micron in size, although some of the very smallest particles, of less than half a micron or so, are small enough to act like gas molecules and be carried back out with the exhaled air. It is probably no coincidence that the particles from natural, physical processes, the larger particles, are removed effectively by our lungs' protective system, whereas the smaller particles that ultimately penetrate the defenses are primarily from man-made sources, to which our lungs haven't yet adapted.

The particles retained in the alveoli may be carried back out by the macrophages, or they may be retained, either by a phagocyte or by incorporation into the cells of the alveolar wall or the intersticial spaces between the alveoli. These latter mechanisms may or may not render the retained particles harmless, possibly depending on their chemical nature; much of this is just not well known. The problem with the retention mechanisms, whatever their inactivation potential, is that unlike the cilial-mucus mechanism, the particles are not rapidly eliminated; in being retained, they consume some of the lung's cellular material and space, so that there is a limit to how much particulate matter can be handled this way.

Respiratory Diseases

Several diseases of the respiratory tract are common, everyday words—the flu, the common cold, pneumonia—and most of these are infectious maladies, caused by either bacteria or viruses. Bacterially caused diseases, principally tuberculosis and pneumonia, have been greatly reduced in prevalence and seriousness by modern drugs, sanitation, and public health efforts. Although the viral infections, principally influenza in several varieties and the common cold in even more varieties, are still widespread, the mechanism of control is apparent, and immunization has at least had some impact on the flu. (The bacterial complications of the flu, which formerly made it a major killer, are now readily controlled with drugs.)

In striking contrast to these successes of modern medicine, three respiratory conditions are not decreasing in prevalence (Fig. 4–4)—chronic bronchitis, pulmonary emphysema, and cancer of the lung. Significantly, these diseases are both less well known, at least the first two, and noninfectious, at least so far as we know. Since they are all epidemiologically associated with air pollution, we will dicuss them briefly here and then conclude with definitions of some other minor conditions that arise in later sections.

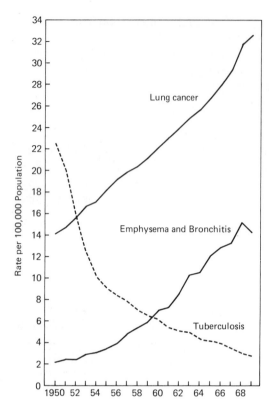

Fig. 4–4. Trends in United States death rates.
Deaths from lung cancer, emphysema, and bronchitis are rising dramatically; the tuberculosis death rate is included for comparison. (Data from *Mortality Trends for Leading Causes of Death: United States, 1950–1969,* DHEW Publication No. (HRA) 74–1853, National Center for Health Statistics, Public Health Service, Rockville, Maryland, March 1974.)

Chronic bronchitis. This chronic condition is one of the most significant cripplers of the middle-aged, though it is not generally directly fatal. The condition results from the oversecretion of mucus in the bronchial lining and is characterized by a chronic cough to get rid of the excess. The condition is worse in cold, damp weather and, in its early stages, often seems to be a typical winter cold and cough. The cough, however, usually then gets worse and stays longer winter after winter, lasting for months and then ultimately year round. Frequently, if the pollutant exposure continues, emphysema is gradually superimposed and becomes the dominant cause of death. Chronic bronchitis is more common in the United Kingdom than in the United States, partly because of methods of death and illness reporting and partly for more substantive reasons. In the United Kingdom, it is responsible for about one-fourth of all illness in men; here, less precise records make it impossible to state firm figures, but chronic bronchitis is considered a major cause of illness, lost work time, and disability.

Pulmonary emphysema. A progressive destructive change in the alveoli, pulmonary emphysema ultimately causes the loss of effective use of much of the lung and leads to death by heart failure. With the destruction of some of the walls of the alveoli, many of the small air sacs are combined into one larger volume, with a resultant loss of surface area for capillaries and gas diffusion. Some of the other walls of the alveoli lose their elasticity, which inhibits exhalation, trapping air in the lungs and forcing a much greater part of the work of exhaling onto the chest muscles. The earliest effect of this destruction is a shortness of breath, probably first noticed on exertion or on rising in the morning, and is usually attributed to smoking or lack of exercise. The shortness of breath, however, progressively worsens until just ordinary breathing is an effort; ultimately, physical activity is impossible, and continued overload causes heart failure.

Lung cancer. Since the mechanisms causing lung cancer, or tumor initiation in general, are unknown at the present, we'll content ourselves here with only a brief, superficial discussion of a very complex subject. Cancer of any location is a growth of cells beyond their normal, biological limit, destroying other tissues in their path, as it were, more or less rapidly in various types. Figure 4–5 shows the typical progress of a common, malignant tumor in the epithelial lining of a bronchial tube (bronchial carcinoma); similar carcinomas originating in the alveoli are much less common, and another type of lung tumor, pleural mesothelioma, is extremely rare. When the bronchial carcinoma shown in Fig. 4–5 breaks through the membrane, it spreads throughout the body, moving particularly rapidly when it enters the lymphatic system or the bloodstream. Similarly, the lungs are frequently the recipients of carcinomas originating in other parts of the body, as all the body's blood routinely passes through the lungs. Such secondary tumors, and the small number (about a tenth) of the primary tumors that are benign, are less serious, their effects usually being limited to obstructing the bronchi. Actually, the earliest outward symptoms of primary bronchial carcinoma is also just bronchial obstruction; the reason it is so routinely fatal is that such obstruction rarely occurs in time to give warning before the tumor has reached metastasis, the stage of rapid spreading throughout the body. The key question, of course, is what causes the cells to begin their unrestrained growth in the first place; the answer apparently lies within the cell, possibly at the molecular level, and is presently one of the major biomedical research frontiers.

Other respiratory diseases. Several other terms relating to lung and respiratory conditions should be described briefly. *Edema* is a condition in which excess fluid accumulates in the bodily tissues; thus, pulmonary

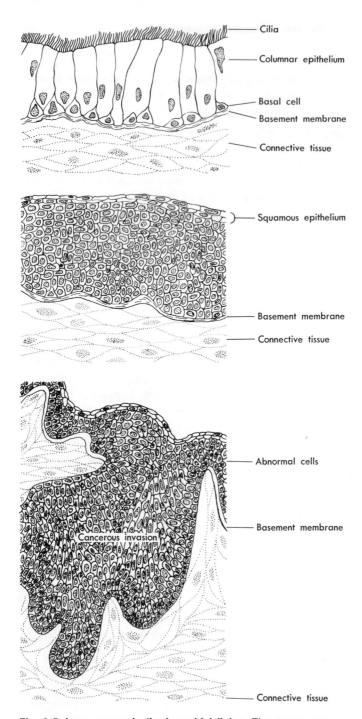

Fig. 4–5. Lung cancer in the bronchial lining. The cancer progresses through various stages until it breaks out of the local area and begins to spread into the rest of the lung tissue and through the lymph system elsewhere. (J. Kimball, *Biology,* 3rd ed., Reading, Mass.: Addison-Wesley, 1974, pp. 244–245)

edema refers to excess fluid in the lung, specifically in the alveoli. Pulmonary *fibrosis* is a thickening, or toughening, of the tissue of the lung, analogous to the formation of scar tissue. The term *pneumoconiosis* applies to the retention of foreign particles in the lung; significant accumulations of certain toxic particles are given specific names, such as silicosis and asbestosis, whereas the more general, less toxic, accumulations that we all have are merely called benign pneumoconioses.

There are several parameters that can be measured that relate to the efficiency of the lung and bronchial tubes as a system of plumbing, such as measures of the speed and volume of the airflow and the resistance to that flow. Generally, these are lumped together under the term *pulmonary function*, or *lung function*. The most common is *airways resistance*, which measures the amount of resistance to airflow in the bronchial system and hence the amount of work needed to breathe a given volume of air.

HEALTH EFFECTS OF PARTICULATE MATTER AND SO₂

Particulate Toxicology

Experimentation on the toxicology of "suspended particulate matter" *per se* is not possible, as it actually consists of so many separate compounds, not all of which are even well identified. Nonetheless, there is observational evidence that as a mixture, urban particulate matter is harmful, and one can recognize three quite distinct ways in which this overall harmful effect might be produced, that is, three mechanisms which can be explored experimentally.

First, of course, some of the particles breathed in are intrinsically toxic. There are a fair number of toxic materials in the air as particles, such as asbestos, beryllium, cadmium, and lead. However, they are generally a relatively small portion of the total amount of particulate matter, so that control of their effects must come from control of their specific sources rather than from control of particulate pollution in general. Accordingly, they're discussed as separate pollutants later in this chapter. Of the larger portions of the particulate matter that might be toxic, black smoke comes first to mind; the toxicology of smoke has been studied fairly extensively. Essentially pure carbon smoke has no acute health effect unless the level of exposure causes the lungs (of experimental animals) to actually clog up with carbon particles. Real-life black smoke is far from pure carbon, however; in particular, it has adsorbed onto the carbon particles various products of organic combustion that are by no means harmless. Many of these organic compounds are carcinogens, and they also are discussed on their own merits later in the chapter.

In addition to black smoke, other specific substances occurring prominently in the collected particulate matter have also been shown to have no acute toxic or irritant effect other than a temporary increase in airways resistance caused by exposure to particle concentrations many times larger than those found in the air. These results clearly illustrate the excellent ability of the normal protective and clearance mechanisms to permit the lung to withstand and recover from short-term assaults by inert, nontoxic particles. Unfortunately for our lungs, however, our present society exposes them to particulate levels in the air beyond what nature has had time to plan for—exposures that are by no means short-term to particles that are by no means completely inert.

The second mechanism by which particulates can exert an overall toxic effect lies in overloading our lungs. First, a heavy dose of inert particles can so overload the clearance mechanism of the lung that the removal of a very few toxic particles is greatly slowed or prevented; the cilia and mucus just can't distinguish between toxic and inert particles. The effect is that a certain amount of toxic material inhaled in a mixture will have a greater effect than if the same amount were inhaled all by itself, so that concentrations of nontoxic particles can be harmful if some toxic substances are also present. Similarly, consistently breathing even moderate levels of nontoxic particles over years and years can overload the protective system—just using it all up or wearing it out.

The last, and probably the most important, of the three methods by which particles can have a harmful effect is by enhancing the effect of harmful gases. The adsorption of gases onto particles can either increase their effect (synergism) or decrease it (antagonism), depending on how far the gases alone would have penetrated into the lungs. This differs among the various pollutant gases. For example, since nitrogen dioxide is not very soluble in the mucus, it normally penetrates deep into the lungs; adsorption on a particle, however, causes it to be removed from the air with the particle, which probably occurs higher up in the lung than the gas alone could have gone, thus lessening the effect. On the other hand, our primary concern is with this type of effect between particulate matter and SO_2. In this case, the effect is strongly positive; particulate matter greatly increases the effect of SO_2 on the lungs.

Effects of Sulfur Oxides

Sulfur dioxide and the associated sulfuric acid aerosol are not systemic poisons, so far as is known, but are irritant substances causing the respiratory system to react to their presence. The primary effect of SO_2 alone at concentrations of a few ppm is to evoke constriction of the bronchi, which is then manifested as increased airways resistance. The effect on airways resistance is not proportional to the time of exposure, however; the bulk of the effect is seen in the first minute or two, with only a slight further increase through 15 minutes and a complete recovery after a similar period without exposure. If the exposure is continuous, without recovery periods, these same relatively low levels ultimately (16 months in rats) produce irreversible degenerative changes and characteristics of accelerated aging.

The mechanism of these effects, both acute and chronic, is the stimulation of the goblet cells in the bronchi to overproduce mucus in their attempt to fend off the insult. The thickened mucus layer increases the resistance to air flow and also tends to overwhelm the cilia. If the exposure is long enough, the body tries to cope by producing extra goblet cells to secrete still more mucus.

The concentrations of SO_2 alone that have been found to increase airways resistance in humans range down to 1 ppm (2620 $\mu g/m^3$ or 2.6 mg/m^3). This level does occur in our larger northern cities for short times. At still lower levels, acute sensory effects occur—the taste threshold for SO_2 is about 0.3 ppm, and the odor threshold is 0.5 ppm. Thus, the range of concentrations that causes overt effects in the laboratory and the range of concentrations in the ambient atmospheres are much closer for pure SO_2 effects than for pure particulate matter effects. Nonetheless, the combined effect of SO_2 and particulates seems to be yet more critical, that is, occurring at even lower levels, which are more routinely seen in the air. The limited experimental work on combined effects was mentioned previously. The increased effect of SO_2 in the presence of particulate matter occurs because pure SO_2 is normally so well absorbed in the upper respiratory tract that adsorption onto particles is the only way it can enter the lower reaches of the lungs. Experimental work is limited, however, by the difficulty of artificially creating realistic particulate pollution; consequently, most of our information on the combined effects of particulates and SO_2 comes from the numerous epidemiologic studies, our next topic.

Observational Evidence of Combined Effects

The most obvious evidence of adverse health effects caused by SO_2 and particulate matter comes from the events that brought pollution to our attention in the first place—the killer smog episodes, which we mentioned in Chapter 1. These unhappy instances provide our most graphic evidence that air pollution can kill and that the effect is largely due to extreme irritation of the respiratory tract caused by the combined occurrence of high concentrations of SO_2 and particulates, especially smoke. The episodes all follow a similar pattern; atmospheric stagnation is superimposed on winter weather when all the home heating is turned on. The SO_2 and particulates (and everything else) accumulate for a period of several days; after about the third day, those persons with already weakened respiratory systems begin to die. Sulfur dioxide concentrations of 0.20–0.25 ppm

(500–650 $\mu g/m^3$) are enough, if combined with particulate levels of about 750 $\mu g/m^3$ or more. Increased mortality is greatest when these levels or higher persist for at least two days after one or two days of rapid increase in concentration. With lower particulate levels, increased mortality does not generally occur until after conditions have persisted for three or four days.

The first two such events occurred in Belgium in 1930 and in Donora, Pa., in 1948; since no measurements of either SO_2 or particulate levels were made, judgment on them is largely circumstantial. Since then, killer smogs have occurred in a number of cities, most severely in London. The London smogs seem to cause greater damage for the same particulate loadings than elsewhere, probably because the moisture in the fog contributes to greater sulfuric acid levels and because a greater proportion of the particulates are black soot, an excellent adsorbent for SO_2.

These episodes, as would be expected, cause an increase in morbidity (illness) as well as mortality; in Donora 43% of the population became ill, and in New York, emergency hospital admissions sometimes tend to rise and fall with pollution levels. The same effect is seen in London, although the effect on morbidity is less pronounced than that on mortality.

These acute episodes, however, are relatively rare and represent only the most extreme conditions. To see how severe the effect of lower concentrations over longer periods might be, a large number of observational studies have been made, attempting to relate various health parameters with SO_2 and particulate levels. Studies looking at day-to-day variations in respiratory or cardiac morbidity or mortality, especially in persons with respiratory illness, generally find a definite relationship with the day-to-day variations in pollution levels, although the effects sometimes seem irregular. One of the problems of these studies is that only the most polluted cities have a population large enough to make them statistically meaningful, and in these cities the pollution levels are rarely low enough to provide any very sharp contrast.

Another approach that has proved useful is to compare mortality and morbidity in groups living in different geographical areas with different pollutant levels. If the different geographical areas are truly distinctly different in air quality, and if smoking effects are eliminated, such studies rather consistently find a relationship between pollutant levels and mortality from lung cancer and bronchitis and often with total respiratory deaths. Similar studies of differences in morbidity, either from records or via questionnaire, generally indicate a positive relation between pollution and bronchitis, colds, influenza, and minor respiratory symptoms, such as sputum production; when measured, various lung-function tests also show such a relationship, and studies of employee absenteeism for respiratory causes add still additional confirmation.

The overall picture of the combined effects of SO₂ and particulates seems rather clear, at least in demonstrating an effect beyond argument and in presenting an understanding of the mechanisms involved. About the only thing more one could ask for would be a quantitative formula for predicting precisely how much effect would occur as a result of a given amount of pollution. Knowledge about the combined effects of SO₂ and particulates has reached the point where such a formula can be estimated reasonably well by standard statistical techniques for any given body of observational data on effects and pollutant levels. Only recently have some of these studies been tried, usually using multiple-regression statistical techniques. These studies are not yet widespread enough to warrant offering any equation as being widely applicable. However, as an example, a study of this type relating mortality in New York City to particulate matter, sulfur dioxide, and temperature provided the equations presented in Table 4–1.

TABLE 4–1
Equations relating mortality to sulfur oxide and particulate pollution

Age	Formula
All ages	R-H deaths = 150.5 + 7.7 × COH + 20.7 SO₂ + 0.7 temp
65+	R-H deaths = 101.8 + 5.3 × COH + 18.9 SO₂ + 0.5 temp
45–64	R-H deaths = 40.8 + 1.9 × COH + 0.9 SO₂ + 0.2 temp
<45	R-H deaths = 8.0 + 0.5 × COH + 0.9 SO₂ + 0.03 temp

Where: R-H deaths = daily mortality from respiratory and heart disease
COH = daily average particulate pollution in standard coefficient of haze units
SO₂ = daily average SO₂ concentration, in parts per million
temp = departure of daily average temperature from 65° in degrees F

Note: The coefficients in these equations don't in themselves reflect the relative importance of the various parameters; remember that SO₂ in ppm will be a much smaller number than TEMP in degrees, and this accounts for part of the differences in the coefficients.
Source: Thomas A. Hodgson, Jr., "Short-Term Effects of Air Pollution on Mortality in New York City," *Environmental Science and Technology* **4** (July 1970): 589–597.

The skeptical reader may well have been nursing along a basic and fundamental question throughout this discussion, which does deserve an answer before we close. Since the data in the studies in this section are all derived from real-life exposures, how do we know that SO₂ and particulates, rather than something else, are to blame? The answer is that in an extremely strict sense, we don't know, but no one in the field challenges it much. We believe it for two reasons: (1) the observed effects are perfectly consistent with the experimentally determined mechanism of action; and (2) in several decades of study, no one has been able to propose a viable alternative, including those persons who would have a financial or other stake in preventing abatement of SO₂ and particulate pollution.

HEALTH EFFECTS OF CARBON MONOXIDE

In Chapter 3 we identified carbon monoxide as the most prevalent of the major pollutants, both in atmospheric concentrations and emission tonnages. It also has the best-understood health effects; the mechanism of injury is well known, and much quantitative information about the dose-response relationship is available. Carbon monoxide harms the body by interfering with oxygen transport from the lungs to the body cells. Normally, oxygen is picked up by hemoglobin molecules in the red blood cells as it diffuses through the alveolar membrane into the lung capillaries (see Fig. 4–6) and is carried in the blood as oxyhemoglobin molecules to the body cells, where it is released and passes through another semipermeable membrane into the cells, while the blood returns to the heart, then the lungs, with a load of waste carbon dioxide. Hemoglobin, however, has a chemical affinity for carbon monoxide 210 times as great as that for oxygen. Consequently, whenever CO is present, it ties up hemoglobin molecules as carboxyhemoglobin (COHb), using up bonding sites that could have carried oxygen and doing so all out of proportion to its relative concentration.*

The equilibrium concentration of carboxyhemoglobin in the blood does not occur immediately on exposure, of course, but rather increases over a period of time. An ultimate equilibrium COHb concentration is reached with exposure to a constant ambient CO level; about 60% of the ultimate equilibrium is reached in two hours, 80% in four hours, and the maximum not until 10 to 12 hours of exposure. If the CO level drops during this time, the blood COHb levels will begin to decrease again; if the CO level increases, they will start up more sharply again. Hence, in real-life exposures with fluctuating CO levels, the blood COHb level is a very dynamic parameter, starting upward when high CO is breathed in, turning downward when the levels fall, and likely never staying precisely constant for any great length of time. Because of this relatively long time to reach equilibrium and the resulting dependence on the pattern of change in exposure, one cannot speak very precisely about CO effects in terms of concentrations and exposure time; therefore, the effects of CO are often stated in terms of a certain level of carboxyhemoglobin in the blood.

As one might expect, the primary effects of CO are on those organs that are most sensitive to a lack of oxygen, notably the brain and central nervous system, and on the heart, which will try to compensate for the decreased oxygen. At very high CO exposures—in the 100s of ppm—headache, drowsiness, and death occur as the brain is deprived of oxygen. At lower exposures—in the range of 50–100 ppm (58–115 mg/m³) for periods

---

* At equilibrium after an exposure of 12 hours or more to CO, the ratio of carboxyhemoglobin to oxyhemoglobin in the blood is about 60,000 times the CO-to-oxygen ratio in the air.

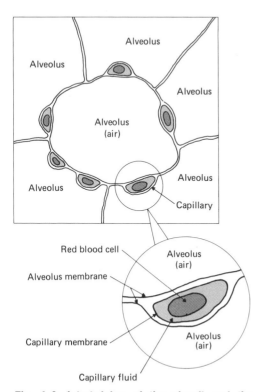

Fig. 4–6. Intertwining of the alveoli and the pulmonary capillaries. Only a thin, semipermeable membrane separates the oxygen in the alveolar air from the blood itself. Oxygen (and carbon monoxide) molecules can diffuse through these membranes and establish a relatively uniform concentration equilibrium. The red blood cells are forced through the capillaries single file; each remains only a few seconds, but the oxygen is able to react with the hemoglobin mulecules and be carried to the body cells. There, carbon dioxide is picked up to be carried in the reverse direction; it is carried largely dissolved in the blood plasma rather than attached to the hemoglobin molecules. (*Breathing—What You Need to Know,* New York: National Tuberculosis and Respiratory Disease Association, 1968, p. 26. Reprinted by permission.)

up to several weeks—one finds animals' blood COHb levels ranging up to 20% and a wide variety of brain and heart damage, as well as blood and electrocardiographic changes.

At carbon monoxide levels lower than 50 ppm, the effects are not drastic and seem to be reversible, so that actual human experimentation is possible; thus, the acute effects occurring at these lower concentrations are beginning to be much better known as interest in air pollution has spurred research in this direction. The effects found at the lowest CO levels involve the brain—effects on time discrimination, mental alertness, response time, and judgment. These effects seem to begin occurring at COHb levels of about 2%, although detailed results from various studies don't all agree. This causes a good deal of debate, as CO levels are presently being experienced in this range, making it by no means a moot point whether the indicated effects are real. The lack of agreement among studies usually arises from differences in the responses used by the experimenters to measure the decrease in performance caused by brain impairment. Because the brain is involved, differences in the psychological bent that subjects bring to the experiment constitute a confusing variable. Thus one study finds a CO effect on time discrimination by studying the subject's ability to accurately compare the lengths of two musical tones, though in an isolated, perhaps boring, environment; another study, conducted in a competitive, relatively exciting atmosphere, finds no CO effect when a hand-reaction test of time discrimination is used.* This kind of methodological difficulty is not unusual in research and will be resolved as experimental work continues. Probably the most difficult question to resolve will be how to handle the fact that a person can possibly overcome the CO effect with extra mental effort. In particular, much of the concern over effects on human judgment, visual performance, etc., arises because of the situation in automobile driving; most people get their highest level of exposure to carbon monoxide (and the highest possible penalty for bad judgment) in this context. Anyone who has ever tried to drive while sleepy will realize what a subtle variable this type of mental alertness really is.

There are other examples of the subtlety that will be needed in the interpretation of these low-level acute effects on mental ability and judgment. The data in Table 4–2 come from an investigation that considered a variety of physiological and psychological tests for possible influence by CO. We first note that many of the psychological tests showed significant relationships, whereas none of the biochemical ones did; this is typical, the mental effects occurring at lower levels than the chemical. But note the differences in some of the psychological tests; in arithmetic and "t-crossing" tests, carbon monoxide had a significant effect on both speed and accuracy, whereas in the "plural-noun underlining" test, speed was significantly lessened, although accuracy was maintained. Despite the differences over details, however, it is clear that some mental effects do occur when blood COHb level reaches about 2.5%, a level typically produced by about 15

---

* This latter test was so insensitive that subjects were still performing it excellently while complaining of severe headaches and sore fingers from the carbon monoxide exposure.

TABLE 4–2
Relationship between blood COHb level and test results

Test	Correlation coefficient*
Physiological tests	
Pulse rate	ns
Systolic blood pressure	ns
Diastolic blood pressure	ns
Respiratory rate	ns
Muscle persistence, left leg	ns
Muscle persistence, right leg	ns
Psychological tests	
No. of responses on letter test	ns
same, errors	0.91
No. of responses on color test	ns
same, errors	0.85
Time, plural-noun underlining	0.81
same, errors	ns
Time, arithmetic test	0.67
same, errors	0.59
Time, t-crossing test	0.80
same, errors	0.54

* The correlation coefficient measures how closely two things are related; values near zero indicate no relationships, whereas values closer to 1 imply a strong positive relationship. The ns means that correlation coefficient was not statistically significant at the $p = 0.001$ level, i.e., there was a good chance that any apparent relationship was merely chance.
Source: J. H. Schulte, "Effects of Mild Carbon Monoxide Intoxication," Archives of Environmental Health 7, 5 (November 1963): 524–530. Copyright 1963, American Medical Association.

ppm carbon monoxide (17 mg/m^3) over eight hours, or about 40 ppm (46 mg/m^3) for two hours, both of which are within the range of typical exposures in major urban areas.

Not many observational studies of carbon monoxide effects have been made, partly because actual experimentation is possible and partly because good data on ambient carbon monoxide levels are not widely available. In Los Angeles County, the one location where carbon monoxide has been monitored extensively for years, studies have been made, and a positive effect of carbon monoxide on heart attack patients was found. The fatality rates for patients with myocardial infarctions correlated significantly with carbon monoxide levels, although the number of such attacks was not. In a different study, a statistical analysis of the type illustrated in Table 4–1, the researchers estimated that the three-fold increase between the lowest and highest (7.3 and 20.2 ppm) carbon monoxide levels found in Los Angeles County would cause an additional 11 deaths per day in the county.

HEALTH EFFECTS OF THE PHOTOCHEMICAL POLLUTANTS

Hydrocarbons and Nitrogen Oxides

Hydrocarbons and the oxides of nitrogen, the precursors of photochemical smog, are of interest because of this role rather than for their intrinsic harmful effects. Of the various hydrocarbons mentioned in Chapter 3, only a few are at all physiologically active. Those that are have adverse effects only at concentrations far higher than any realistic ambient levels; the lowest level having an effect is 100 ppm of benzene, a level at which the mucus membranes become irritated. The photochemical smog mixture also includes some more complicated organic compounds that are formed from the hydrocarbons; some of them are eye and membrane irritants and hence probably account for some of the effect of the smog.

The oxides of nitrogen, also, are not very active biologically, though NO_2 is more so than the hydrocarbons. At exposures well above a few ppm, NO_2 causes lung damage of various types, including bronchial damage reminiscent of that from SO_2, though less severe, and acute pulmonary edema, an effect characteristic of ozone. The precise mechanism is not known; NO_2 has both acid-forming and free radical* properties, which suggests that there may be two distinctly different mechanisms. Observational studies made of intermittent industrial exposures ranging from 10–40 ppm have found only weak evidence for any effect—specifically, the development of pulmonary fibrosis and emphysema. Since atmospheric levels only rarely reach a half ppm (1000 $\mu g/m^3$), there has historically been little concern over the direct health effects of NO_2. This view has recently been questioned by the findings from a major observational study conducted in Chattanooga—decreased ventilatory function and increased respiratory illness in neighborhoods near a factory that manufactures TNT. This unusual situation provided a test area with very low SO_2 levels and NO_2 levels ranging from 0.06 to 0.109 ppm (113–205 $\mu g/m^3$). These NO_2 levels are of the same general magnitude as the higher ambient concentrations experienced in many cities, so that unless further pursuit of these observations fails to confirm the results, we need to consider NO_2 in a new light.

Photochemical Oxidants

The concern about the health effects of photochemical smog is entirely in the effect of the "product" pollutant, the oxidants. The only one of the photochemical oxidants to have been extensively studied toxicologically is

---

* A free radical is an uncharged atom or molecule that has an unpaired electron. For the purposes of this chapter, it is enough to think of it as an especially highly reactive molecule.

ozone, the primary constituent of the resultant "smog." At levels in the 10s of ppm, ozone can kill a variety of experimental animals, generally by acute inflammation, hemorrhage, and edema of the respiratory tract. Concentrations of 5–10 ppm cause similar effects, but without mortality; in general, these effects are more severe on very young animals and on animals that are exercising, but are lessened if the exposure is intermittent. At still lower exposures, lung function is impaired. Levels under 2 ppm can affect animals' pulmonary function, cause chemical changes in the proteins of their lungs, and decrease their resistance to bacterial infections. Long-term exposures about 1 ppm (2 mg/m^3) produce symptoms of bronchitis and emphysema and accelerate the development of tumors.

In humans, experimental studies have considered only the effect on pulmonary function. One study exposed a group of people to 0.5 ppm ozone for three hours daily, six days a week for 12 weeks, and another group to 0.2 ppm for a similar period. These two levels of exposure approximate a smoggy summer in Los Angeles and in other cities, respectively. No pulmonary effect was found with the lower exposure, but at the higher, there was a decrease in lung function (forced expiratory volume) in the last four weeks of the study; the effect was reversed after an additional six weeks. Various sensory effects are also reported in humans exposed to less than 1 ppm ozone—odor and dryness of throat membrane, and near 1.0 ppm, frequent headaches.

The mechanism causing these effects is not known for sure. Only the chronic effects, the bronchitis-emphysema symptoms, fit a hypothesis of a simple irritation mechanism like that of SO_2; the other, acute effects might fit well with a hypothesis of a free radical mechanism. Consequently, research continues, although the known effects are not major ones. In fact, the most significant aspect of this discussion is that one particular effect is not listed. Ozone is not a lachrymator; it doesn't irritate the eye membranes at the concentrations typically found in photochemical smog. Since reddening, watering, and irritation of the eyes is by far the principal acute physical effect of smog, we somehow feel that ozone is not the compound of concern.

Accordingly, we must base our judgment of the health effects of photochemical smog almost totally on observational evidence, gathering data from populations exposed to real, ambient air. Many such studies have been conducted in Los Angeles, where the photochemical smog is acknowledgedly the worst in the country. However, the results have generally been negative. No effect on mortality has been found, no effect on hospital admissions, aggravation of respiratory symptoms, or performance of the general population on lung-function tests. Oxidant levels do seem to correlate with lessened lung function in respiratory patients, and there are positive results showing an impairment of athletic performance and an increase in automobile accidents. The reduction in athletic performance seems to fit with the fact that exercising animals are more severely affected. Because of this effect, school children in Los Angeles are restricted in their physical activities during recess when oxidant levels are above 0.30 ppm. The increase in auto accidents is not a health effect *per se*, though it has an effect on health in a sense. It is probably only indirectly associated with oxidant levels, being more likely caused by lessened visibility on smoggy days or by elevated CO levels.

Finally, there is eye irritation. The early complaints that led to the awareness of air pollution in Los Angeles dealt with eye irritation—reddening and excessive watering—and these symptoms continue to be a primary source of concern. Whenever atmospheric total oxidant levels reach about 0.10 ppm (200 $\mu g/m^3$), symptoms of eye irritation develop, and they increase in severity as oxidant levels rise. The relationship between eye irritation and total oxidant is illustrated in Fig. 4–7; given the subjective nature of "eye irritation," this relationship is very firm and has been consistently verified. Since ozone, which makes up the bulk of total oxidant chemically, does not cause eye irritation, the guilty substance or substances must be in the undefined remainder of the total oxidant. There are a multitude of organic chemicals in the smoggy atmosphere, and some are known to irritate the eyes, although no substance yet identified can account for as much irritation as is observed. Since the organic substances are relatively difficult (and hence costly) to measure, not enough routine, day-in-day-out measurements have been made to firmly label the culprit. Furthermore, the whole smog mixture is known to originate with the photochemical reactions from known pollutants, and therefore there is no reason why control of the pollutant source needs to wait on such identification of specific chemicals; thus, there is less stimulus to find them.

Since we have not included in "health effects" the minor annoyances caused by other pollutants, such as particulate matter in the eyes, some people might question the inclusion of the "eye irritation" caused by photochemical smog. It is, of course, very easy to disparage concern over eye irritation *per se*, especially if one chokes on smoke and SO_2 and worries about emphysema. Eye irritation is included as a health effect in this discussion largely because the people of Los Angeles see it as such. Believing that smog has an adverse effect on their health, Angelenos have always been more aroused over pollution than have people in other areas, where the health effects of pollution would seem to be more serious. There are at least two reasons for this, one of which is that photochemical eye irritation in Los Angeles is very extreme, causing acute discomfort, even though there aren't permanent harmful effects. More important, however, is the adage that "everything is relative"; Los Angeles before the smog was apparently a beautiful, nice place to live, and people are alive who

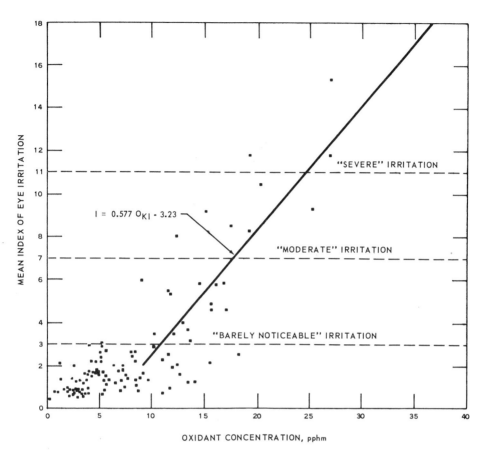

Fig. 4–7. Eye irritation and oxidant levels. The relationship shown here is for Los Angeles. Below 0.10 ppm oxidant, reports of eye irritation are rather random; above that level, they increase markedly, as indicated by the regression line. (N. A. Richardson and W. C. Middleton, "Evaluation of Filters for Removing Irritants from Polluted Air," Los Angeles: Report No. 57–43, University of California, Department of Engineering, June 1957. Reprinted by permission.)

remember that. In contrast, London, New York, Chicago, and other cities have been polluted for generations and were worse (at least visibly) as recently as 20 years ago. No one remembers "how nice and clean" these cities used to be.

HEALTH EFFECTS OF OTHER POLLUTANTS

In this final section, we will briefly consider the health effects or lack thereof for several "other" pollutants. In this context, the distinction between "pollutants" and "substances" is not rigorous—the effects of some of the pollutants discussed in this section are far less well defined than those of the major ones and in some cases their wide prevalence in the air is arguable.

Lead

Lead is one of the best known of the toxic metals to industrial hygienists and public health officials, and with the recent advertisements announcing "lead-free" or "low-lead" gasolines, it is becoming a well-publicized air pollutant as well. Lead is a ubiquitous element in our environment and has been for many centuries; we are exposed to it via our water and food as well as our air. In a pattern that will itself soon seem ubiquitous, high exposures to lead have severe and well-known toxic effects, whereas lower exposures have far less severe and far less well known (in fact often hotly debated) effects.

Today, cases of acute plumbism* are seen relatively rarely, primarily when lead has been ingested rather than inhaled. Eating from lead-glazed earthenware and lead-soldered tin cups may cause this disease, but most cases occur in children who eat chips of leaded paint, a problem that is fast becoming a major public health concern.

Lead is a systemic poison; when acute poisoning occurs, lead is found throughout the body, but the effects are seen mainly as anemia, kidney malfunction, and tissue damage in the brain. The last effect is the most serious, often progressing, with no obvious warning, to severe retardation and death. The specific mechanism for the effect of lead on the blood is believed to be a reduction in the synthesis of heme, a constituent of the red blood cell hemoglobin. This is brought about by an interference with the enzymes involved in the synthesis of the heme; the lead acts by binding up free sulfhydryl (-SH) groups on which the enzymes depend. Since other enzymes throughout the body also depend on having free sulfhydryl groups around to react with, such an enzyme-interference mechanism may well be found responsible for the effects of lead on other tissues, also.

Because lead is so widespread, it is found in the bodies of everyone; the distinction is only in quantity, and the primary unknowns concern the quantitative balance among intake, storage, and excretion. Traditionally, it was thought that the majority of the lead intake was from food and drink; the typical American eats and drinks about 0.3 mg, or 300 μg, of lead per day, of which about 90% is excreted in the feces without ever having been absorbed, while the other 30 μg is absorbed. Respiratory in-

---

* The word derives from the Latin for lead, "plumbum," as does our word plumber. The Romans used lead for plumbing, and it is often noted that lead poisoning might have been responsible for the line of more or less insane emperors.

take, however, has reached the same general range. We breathe in about 40 to 50 μg of lead daily, of which between 25 and 50% is absorbed, so that daily lead intakes of 10 to 20 μg are typical. The greater absorption by the lungs than by the alimentary system is in part the result of differences in the chemical composition of the lead; also, atmospheric lead particles from auto exhaust are of just the size to be very readily retained by the lungs.

Observational studies relating estimated lead exposures to measured levels of lead in the blood have been made on various groups of people, including occupational groups that have higher than typical exposures, such as traffic policemen and employees in vehicular tunnels. Although there is significant variability among the individuals in each group, the averages of the various groups, when considered together, as in Fig. 4–8, fit into a very neat pattern, strongly implying that respiratory exposure is an important part of the total lead burden in the body.

In the process of metabolizing this burden of lead, perhaps 50 μg per day, the body typically maintains a blood level of about 15–25 μg of lead per 100 grams of whole blood. The body response to increases in lead intake seems to be to excrete in the urine as much as possible, then store the remainder, primarily in the bones. If the rate of excess intake is great

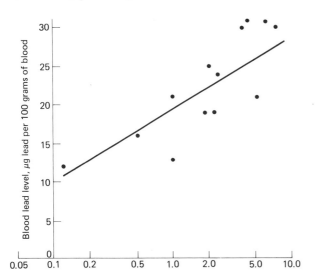

Estimated respiratory exposure, μg lead per cubic meter of air

Fig. 4–8. Relationship between lead in the air and the blood. Note that the horizontal axis is logarithmic; the regression line shown would cross it at about 0.01 μg/m³. (Data from *Survey of Lead in the Atmosphere of Three Urban Communities,* Public Health Service Publication No. 999–AP–12, 1965)

enough to exceed both excretion and bone deposition, levels of lead build up in the soft tissues. It is not known just what levels of lead in the tissues will cause what effect, either acute or chronic, or what the long-term effect of the total body burden of lead may be. Long-time study of acute plumbism has led to the general acceptance of specific lead levels in blood and urine (80 μg per 100 grams of whole blood and 150 μg in a 24-hour urine specimen), below which the level of lead in the body is considered "normal." These levels are based only on the observed absence of clinical symptoms of *acute* lead poisoning, although older studies (and researchers) tend to quote them as levels below which no effects of lead exist at all. Actually, there is no real evidence about how much lead may cause chronic effects over longer periods of time. Blood levels of 30 μg per 100 grams, only slightly above typical levels, are associated with a rise of certain enzyme concentrations in the urine. This is a consequence of the inhibition of heme synthesis already mentioned, but there is no direct evidence as to how harmful this level of inhibition might be. Similar judgments, with even less useful information, apply to the other effects of lead.

Asbestos

Asbestos, the mineral fiber used in heat insulation and friction products, exists in the air as fibrous, solid particles of various sizes. The largest of these particles are removed by the filtering action of the nasal hairs, and most of those particles found in the lungs are less than 50 microns in length. Asbestos has long been recognized as an occupational health hazard, producing in asbestos workers a diffuse fibrosis of the lower lung, a condition appropriately termed asbestosis. The condition is particularly insidious; the only early symptom is shortness of breath, and commonly 20 to 40 years of occupational exposure pass before the condition is recognized, though it can develop in less than 10 years with high concentrations. Once well established, the condition continues progressing, and illness and death can follow many years later, long after exposure has stopped.

Asbestos also causes calcification of the pleura, the lining surrounding the lungs, and is strongly associated with pleural mesothelioma, a form of lung cancer that is nearly unknown outside of asbestos-exposure situations. Persons without any visible effect often carry asbestos in their lungs in the form of "asbestos bodies," particles of asbestos covered with an iron-bearing coating, a result of the lungs' attempts at self-protection.

Most of the available evidence about asbestos effects comes from studies of asbestos workers and general populations near asbestos sources, such as mines and processing plants. The primary concern about asbestos as a general ambient air pollutant arose from the discovery, in the late 1960s, that one-fourth to one-half of the people in the general urban population already have asbestos particles in their lungs. Since asbestos concentrations in the ambient air are nearly impossible to monitor, no one had any idea that exposure to asbestos was so widespread. Considering the great increase in asbestos use over the last few decades, and in particular its use as a spray to fire-proof buildings, there is no positive assurance that today's ambient exposures are strikingly less than the occupational exposures of 30 years ago that caused the effects being seen today. (And, of course, no one wants to "wait and see" for 30 years.) In particular, there is concern about the carcinogenic effects of asbestos; although correlations with length of employment, etc., make us quite certain that asbestosis is quantitatively related to the amount of asbestos breathed, it is far from certain that any more than just one asbestos fiber is needed to somehow provoke a tumor. Once again, we are confronted by our lack of understanding of the basic cellular mechanisms in cancer formation. This risk of cancer, compounded by the uncertainty of the long latency period, has caused the federal government to list asbestos as a "hazardous air pollutant," for which special federal regulatory measures are warranted (see Chapter 11).

Beryllium

One of the most toxic substances currently in industrial use, beryllium, too, has been designated a "hazardous air pollutant." At concentrations in the range from 100 $\mu g/m^3$ on up, acute beryllium poisoning affects many organs, with soluble compounds especially affecting the mucus membranes of the eyes and lungs; there is some controversy about whether or not there are residual effects. A chronic condition is caused at unknown, but presumably lower, levels; although often called berylliosis, like silicosis, the chronic beryllium disease is actually a systemic poisoning affecting almost all organs. The precise mechanism of acute and chronic effects is unknown, although biochemical involvement in enzyme chemistry or immunological mechanism has been suggested. Beryllium is a relatively rare substance in use, and it is not generally found in the ambient air, except near beryllium processing operations; interest in beryllium as an air pollutant has been prompted largely by its use in rocket fuels.

Mercury

Mercury is the third "hazardous air pollutant" designated to date. Metallic mercury and its compounds are enzyme poisons; they are readily adsorbed on inhalation, and are distributed to nearly all organs of the body. Mercury is excreted by the body, but at a relatively slow rate. Precisely which enzyme systems are affected has not been documented, and the situation is complicated by the fact that different mercury compounds cause different effects (methyl mercury being the worst), presumably by acting on different systems. Acute exposures to mercury vapor cause extreme gastro-intestinal symptoms, and with increasing dose, pulmonary ones as well. Of greater concern, chronic poisoning primarily affects the nervous system; although such extreme symptoms as tremors are easily recognized, early symptoms are more of a general nervousness and emotional nature, thus making early diagnosis very difficult.

Inhaling mercury has been a known occupational hazard for centuries.* Quite recently, many people in Japan experienced extensive poisoning from eating fish from industrially polluted waters, and there have been seed-grain poisonings in the United States; these situations have led to considerable concern about mercury as a pollutant in water and food. It is not yet known whether mercury is significant as an air pollutant, primarily because only minimal measurements of general ambient levels have been made. Since the use of mercury is widespread and is increasing, probably both elemental mercury vapor and other compounds are in the air, and the publicity brought by the water-borne "disasters" will no doubt bring further study.

Organic Carcinogens

These are polycyclic organic compounds that have been shown to produce cancer in test animals. Benzo-a-pyrene, a product of coal combustion, is the best known and the most carcinogenic. As early as 1775, soot from coal smoke was suspected of causing cancer; in 1915 coal tar was actually shown to cause skin cancer in mice, and in subsequent years the carcinogenicity of many separate compounds has been studied. In most of the experiments the test material has been painted on or implanted or injected into the animals, rather than their inhaling it, and many studies have used specially bred cancer-susceptible animals. These methods were used because large number of tumors are not readily produced by simple inhalation of the carcinogenic material, although adsorption onto carbon or soot particles increases the incidence. Therefore, these compounds probably are not ter-ribly potent at causing human tumors, either, and in fact the statistical association of measured levels of benzo-a-pyrene with cancer rates is not striking.

Nonetheless, compounds that produce cancer in any way must of neces-sity remain suspect, so long as there is an observed association between polluted atmospheres in general and incidence of cancer; this evidence is found repeatedly, though in one sense it is not unequivocal. There is an unquestioned "urban effect" in cancer incidence rates, as shown in Table 4–3; even after separating out people who smoke, the incidence of lung

---

* The former use of mercury in the processing of felt caused the mental symp-toms that were responsible for the expression "mad as a hatter."

TABLE 4–3
The urban-rural difference in lung cancer deaths (per 100,000 population)

Study group	Smokers			Nonsmokers		
	Urban	Rural	Ratio	Urban	Rural	Ratio
California (men)	101	80	1.26	36	11	3.27
America (men)	52	39	1.33	15	0	∞
England and Wales	89	85	2.23	50	22	2.27
Northern Ireland	—	—	—	38	10	3.80
England	149	69	2.15	23	29	0.79
America (men)	100	50	2.00	16	5	3.20

Source: Lester B. Lave and Eugene P. Seskin, "Air Pollution and Human Health," *Science* **169** (21 August 1970): 723–732. Reprinted by permission. Copyright 1970 by the American Association for the Advancement of Science.

cancer in American urban areas is at least one-third greater than in adjoining rural areas, with generally greater increases in various areas in the United Kingdom. Even after other possible explanations (better medical reporting, relocation to urban areas for better medical care) are controlled as much as possible, the effect remains, and it is generally attributed to air pollution. There are also suggestions of an "urban stress" or other intangible factors related to the general degradation of the physical and psychological environment in urban areas. Evidence for an organic rather than intangible factor is found in the cancer statistics for emigrants from Britain to Canada and Australia; their cancer mortality rate shows a holdover effect lasting 20 years into their new, presumably more tranquil surroundings.

Yet, of course, having concluded that air pollution is probably the source of the urban excess in cancer deaths, we can't readily attribute that effect to any one pollutant with much reliability; there are just too many candidates. Consequently, a truly definitive resolution of the question of air pollution and cancer will probably need to wait until we have a better understanding of tumor-initiating mechanisms.

Arsenic

Arsenic compounds (primarily arsenic trioxide) have an aura of poison about them because of their role in real and fictional homicides—ingestion of only one-tenth of a gram (100,000 micrograms) of arsenic trioxide is fatal. Arsenic trioxide and other compounds exist as particulates in the air, resulting from the smelting of arsenic-contaminated ores, the use of pesticides, and from coal burning. Although they may be inhaled and absorbed into the body, they are irritating enough that one can't really inhale enough to incur systemic poisoning. Irritative effects, mild bronchitis, nasal irritation, and particularly dermatitis are symptoms of exposure to arsenic dust;

a relationship to cancer, especially skin cancer, is sometimes alleged, but has not really been demonstrated. Arsenic absorbed into the body is excreted fairly rapidly, mostly in the urine, but also in hair and nails.

Nickel

Nickel metal *per se* is relatively nontoxic, although metallic nickel fumes have caused respiratory effects in workers, and allergic contact dermatitis is common in both workers and users of nickel-plated articles. Nickel salts, and especially nickel carbonyl, $Ni(CO)_4$, are much more toxic. The salts are toxic if introduced into the blood, but nickel carbonyl is a liquid with a significant vapor pressure and hence can be an inhalant poison. It appears to attack the proteins in the alveoli of the lung, regardless of whether it is introduced by inhalation, intravenously, or by some other method.

Epidemiologically, occupational exposure to nickel in various forms has long been linked to cancer of the lung and sinuses. Although metallic nickel is suspected, the precise carcinogen is not known; it may even be some other co-occuring metal, as it is quite difficult to separate the effects in observational studies. In fact, the carcinogenic effects often attributed to arsenic are more generally believed to be due to nickel, and it has been suggested that the nickel content may be the cause of the carcinogenicity of asbestos.

Whether nickel may be important as an ambient air pollutant is not clear. Minor nickel sources are common—in combustion ash from coal, fuel oil, and from incinerators and gasoline engines. Nickel is useful as a catalyst, and some compounds have been patented as motor fuel additives. Carbon monoxide in contact with metallic nickel can form nickel carbonyl at CO levels of only 100 ppm, levels that can occur in heavy traffic and certainly occur in the exhaust system. The diversity of nickel sources makes for difficult watching, but since nickel is more biologically active than most metals are, it may be wise to watch.

Cadmium

Most *cadmium* compounds, in particular cadmium oxide, are toxic in humans and animals, as demonstrated in occupational situations and studies of laboratory animals. The inhalation of cadmium fumes or cadmium-bearing dusts causes pulmonary emphysema and, in sufficient doses, fibrosis. Systemically, chronic exposure to cadmium causes kidney damage which results in proteinuria, an abnormal protein excretion in the urine, and larger exposures seem to cause gastric and intestinal disorders. There is some evidence for carcinogenicity, but it is not conclusive. Epidemiologically, cadmium at realistic ambient levels has been associated with heart disease, and in the laboratory a definite correlation is seen in both humans and rats, between cadmium levels in the kidneys and hypertension.

Hydrogen Sulfide

Hydrogen sulfide (H_2S), the only gas in our list of "other" pollutants, is extremely toxic at very high concentrations and has been responsible for an "episode" of sorts. On November 21, 1950, in the small town of Poza Rica, Mexico, an industrial accident released large quantities of H_2S at about five o'clock in the morning. At this time, the atmospheric dispersion was very poor, and most of the people were still asleep; 320 were hospitalized and 22 died, chiefly of severe respiratory irritation and damage to the central nervous system. However, this toxicity is not the reason hydrogen sulfide is viewed as a pollutant; it is of concern because even at very low concentrations, it smells horrible—the "rotten egg" smell of chemistry class. Ironically, and sadly for the people of Poza Rica, the gas at toxic levels overwhelms the sense of smell so rapidly that the foul odor is useless as a danger signal.

IS AIR POLLUTION REALLY AS BAD AS THEY SAY?

This question is the one most often asked by someone who has just learned that you are "in the air pollution business." It is impossible to answer this question precisely; not only is "bad" an undefined generality, but "they" is usually a very vague amalgam of news items, magazine articles, and television specials. On the other hand, the question is highly pertinent, and for someone "in the field" to refuse to even try an answer would surely open us to the charge of spending our efforts on self-serving research not relevant to the real problems of real people.

Trying to answer this question brings us first to a summary of this chapter and second to a consideration of the philosophy and perspectives involved in deciding just what "bad" really means. A pollutant-by-pollutant summary of the effects noted in this chapter would be relatively straightforward and could almost be done in tabular form, but something more than just that is needed. For brevity, this chapter has, unfortunately, had to be a rather dry catalog of nothing but facts. This is unfortunate not because the mass of facts precluded supposition, but because it precluded any thoughtful pursuit of the implications of those facts. Consequently, the summary paragraphs that follow try to remedy that deficiency by emphasizing what is *not* known about the *safety* of our air rather than what *is* known about the *harm* it might cause.

In combination at normal atmospheric levels, *particulate matter* and *sulfur oxides* cause progressive destructive damage to the respiratory system, largely by irritating the bronchi and destroying the alveoli. Sufficient exposure over a long enough period of years eventually adds up to a gradually decreasing lung capacity, and ultimately failure, unless another source of death intervenes, as it usually does. There is no firm evidence that any particular level of pollution is absolutely without effect. On the other hand, it is apparent that the effects on most people of moderate exposures to particulates and sulfur oxides are not fatal, incapacitating, or even strikingly noticeable, but are perhaps quite tolerable. Thus, the primary type of research still needed is quantitative, to determine how much damage is caused by how much pollution, so that some balance can be drawn between the damage and the cost of preventing it.

Similarly, *carbon monoxide* has no obvious threshold below which there is no effect at all; even small amounts of CO routinely consume a small part of the oxygen-carrying capacity of our blood. To what extent this causes either permanent harm or temporary incapacity is the area of investigation currently active. Principal concern is over the significance of acute changes in mental function caused by CO levels that are frequently encountered in urban areas, especially in driving situations.

The *oxides of nitrogen* and *hydrocarbons* are believed to cause no noticeable effects at the concentrations normally seen in urban areas, although an effect of NO_2 on respiratory illness is still under active investigation. The two pollutants together, however, cause the formation of *photochemical oxidants* in the air, which have effects of their own. The overall photochemical smog mixture is capable of causing sufficient discomfort and nuisance, particularly irritation of the eyes, to be called an effect on health and can cause increased difficulties for respiratory patients, though it doesn't seem to cause illness or mortality in the general population. The research forefront for these pollutants is not in studying health effects, beyond the NO_2 effect, but in the chemical reactions of the system —the nature and reactivity of the hydrocarbon ingredients.

Many readers will no doubt feel (correctly) that there is a great contrast between these paragraphs and the public discussions one often hears, some of which predict the demise of the human race in 20, 30, or however many years. Depending on personal predilections and viewpoints, some will consider this discussion incredibly complacent, naïve, and perhaps deceitful, while others will feel that at last they have seen some facts in refutation of the wild predictions of self-serving doomsayers. The difference between these extreme viewpoints is, however, only an apparent one, more a difference in tone and viewpoint than in fact. There are at least three major areas in which careful examination of just what is being said in each case turns up much less difference in the two views than at first seems apparent.

First, of course, this chapter has not discussed all the effects of air pollution, but only those generally called health effects. Although the thought of air pollution "killing us" does make us think first of our health, the demise of humanity need not necessarily be by poison—the effects on our physical environment or on the deterioration of the psychological quality of our life may well be just as effective, perhaps more so; these possibilities are pursued in the next chapter. And of course, air pollution is not acting alone; similar problems beset other areas of life as well.

Second, to speak more specifically of tone, one must remember that most of those who make predictions are speaking to the "whole" person in their audience, to the emotions as well as to reason, something that we've not tried to do in this chapter. Thus, when we speak briefly of 11 extra deaths on a day of high carbon monoxide levels or write formulas for the mortality caused by high particulate and sulfur oxide levels, these are abstractions—necessary, but nonetheless cruel, abstractions. The realities of the situation also include the agony of an elderly emphysema patient and the grief of a couple whose newborn infant has been killed.

The third, and perhaps most significant, reason for the apparent difference between this chapter and the predictions of the doomsayers is the difference in viewpoint between the statement of generally accepted, proved facts and the statement of prudent, conservative estimates. In part, this is just a restatement of the classic problem of placing the burden of proof: do we breathe pollutants until they are proved deadly, or do we ban their production until they are proved safe? The food and drug laws, for example, attempt to apply the latter view to our medicines; history has long since applied the former view to our air. But there is more to this third point than just the question of burden of proof; there is also a problem of realizing how much we know or don't know about the situation and of judging which way more knowledge will take us. The best illustration of this point probably lies in a discussion of effects thresholds. The concept of an effects threshold, a pollution level below which no effects occur, must be recognized as really meaning "below which no *observable* effects occur." Such a threshold is influenced not only by the ability of the pollutant to cause an effect, but also by our ability to observe that effect. Consequently, so-called thresholds set in many areas of life are continually being lowered as our ability to detect effects improves. Thus, it is unwise to assume a threshold for an air pollutant unless the pollutant's mechanism of action is well known and makes a threshold seem reasonable.

Rather than trying to find thresholds below which effects don't occur, we should be trying to define levels below which effects are tolerable. These two processes would, of course, be the same if our definition of "tolerable" never changed; it does, however, change, and sometimes drastically. Although we'll return to changing tolerance levels later, we should indicate here that far from being a scientific venture, a society's determination of its own tolerance for pollution (or anything else) is a complicated, sociopolitical function. The United States has formalized such a determination by the adoption of National Ambient Air Quality Standards for the six major pollutants. These numbers, which we met briefly in Chapter 3, are listed in Table 4–4. As an integral part of the present federal-state mechanism for reducing air pollution (see Chapter 11), these standards are those levels of pollution below which human health is "protected." Published only after much research, consultation, and debate

TABLE 4–4
National air quality standards (primary standards, protective of human health)

Pollutant*	Concentration not to be exceeded
Sulfur oxides (as SO₂)	0.03 ppm (80 μg/m³) annual mean 0.14 ppm (365 μg/m³) maximum† daily average
Suspended particulate matter	75 μg/m³ annual mean (geometric) 260 μg/m³ maximum daily average
Carbon monoxide	9 ppm (10 mg/m³) maximum eight-hour average 35 ppm (40 mg/m³) maximum hourly average
Photochemical oxidants (as O₃)	0.08 ppm (160 μg/m³) maximum hourly average
Reactive (nonmethane) hydrocarbons	0.24 (160 μg/m³) maximum 6–9 A.M. average
Nitrogen Oxides (as NO₂)	0.05 ppm (100 μg/m³) annual mean

* Standards for the first four pollutants are nominally based on the health effects discussed in this chapter, with appropriate safety factors; the hydrocarbon and NO_x standards are the levels believed necessary to meet the oxidants standard.
† The "maximum" figures quoted are those levels permitted to be exceeded once per year. If the suspended particulate geometric mean of 75 μg/m³ were to be expressed as the normal arithmetic mean, it would be somewhat higher, perhaps 85 or 90 μg/m³.

among scientists and at public hearings, the standards represent precisely the kind of tolerance standard just discussed.

Before closing, I should return to the question posed at the beginning of this section, lest I, too, be accused of avoiding it. As this last section probably indicates, I personally believe that air pollution *is* as bad as "they" say, at least those who say that *if nothing is done soon*, life in our urban areas 20 years hence will be at best drastically altered, and at worst nonexistent. I don't believe this will come to pass, however, as will become apparent in the final chapters. Things *are* being done, and more will be done; one of the purposes of this book, in fact, is to help move things in the direction of action. Consequently, let this be the end of our negative thinking.

EXERCISES

Review Questions

1. List two major categories of research studies on health effects and two or three subcategories under one of them.
2. What are the advantages and disadvantages of the several types of studies in question 1?
3. Name a situation in which each of the two major types of studies must be used, the other being impossible.
4. In your own words, list several categories for classifying the severity of health effects.

5. Distinguish between chronic and acute effects.
6. Distinguish between irritant effects, systemic poisoning, and toxic effects.
7. Beginning with the nose, name the various major parts of the human respiratory system and their principal functions.
8. How does the respiratory system protect itself against irritant gases?
9. List three ways the respiratory system protects itself against foreign particles; on what size particles is each most effective?
10. Are the mechanisms in questions 8 and 9 always effective? What happens if they are not?
11. Since particulate matter *per se* is not toxic, how does it exert a harmful effect? List three distinct ways.
12. What does sulfur dioxide alone do in the lungs? How does this change if particulate pollution is also present?
13. By what means does breathing carbon monoxide harm the body? What is the lowest exposure known to have an effect? What effect?
14. What are the effects on human health of the oxides of nitrogen and hydrocarbons?
15. What are the effects of the oxidants produced in photochemical smog? How are these effects studied?
16. What is the principal health-related reason for concern about lead in the air? Asbestos?
17. The federal government has identified three "hazardous air pollutants"; in each case, why is it so listed?

Thought Questions

18. In health effects studies involving employees, there is a major source of confusion in the data about absenteeism on the various days of the week; what might be the source of this, and what would you do about it if you were the investigator?
19. Observational studies of the effects of air pollution on health often try to separate the effect of socioeconomic status from the effect of pollution. How can one's socioeconomic status affect one's pollution exposure? How can it affect one's health independent of the pollution exposure?
20. What effects might the extensive use of air conditioning have on the adverse health effects caused by pollution exposure? Would it be the same for all pollutants?
21. Why is the national air quality standard for carbon monoxide partly expressed as an eight-hour average?
22. Suppose a very abrupt reversal of the earth's magnetic field, or some other unlikely event, caused a tremendous increase in the rate of genetic mutations in the human species. Of the wide variety of physiological changes that could occur, what ones would you expect to be favored for continuation in our present polluted environment? That is, what evolutionary changes in our bodies might help us resist the adverse effects of pollution?
23. If black smoke is not strikingly toxic, why has so much effort gone into eliminating it?

24. At present, there is much talk about the possibility that cancer is associated with, or may be caused by, a virus. Can you think of any way of reconciling this possibility with the presumption that various air pollutants cause cancers?

25. Suppose a massive three-year campaign succeeded in eliminating 95% of all air pollutant emissions. Would you expect the health effects of pollution to drop similarly? All health effects? If the effects were not reduced as expected, what would need to be done?

26. Does the health service or other office of your college maintain health or attendance records? What other data would be needed to conduct an observational study of pollution effects among the students?

Discussion Questions

27. To what extent do you think the protection of human health should be the primary goal of air pollution control? Include consideration of the existence of specially susceptible groups in the population, the fact that pollution control costs money, and the fact that there are other effects besides those on health.

28. Of the four types of "inhalant pollution" mentioned at the beginning of the chapter, which do you believe is the worst social problem, and why? Which is the one government should attack most vigorously? Consider how your views might differ if you were a housewife, a labor union leader, a doctor, an industrial executive, a factory worker with young children.

29. It is sometimes argued that we don't need any more research on the health effects of pollution and that we should spend the money now going for research on "doing something about pollution." List the arguments on both sides of this question, and then give your judgment on the question.

30. If you had authority over all funds being spent on health-effects research, to what pollutants and what studies would you give the highest priority? Why?

31. Which of the "other" pollutants concerns you most? Why?

32. Do you think the national air quality standards in Table 4–4 represent the quality of air you consider desirable?

Problems

33. Assume that the 600,000,000 alveoli in an adult are all identical spheres, with surface area totalling 600 square feet. What would be the diameter of a single alveolus? Its volume? Suppose that emphysema destroyed enough of the alveolar walls to reduce the number to 300,000,000 spheres, each with twice the original volume; what would be the effective surface area? If the number were reduced to 100,000,000 what would the effect be?

34. Using the figures in the second paragraph of the section on the effects of carbon monoxide (p. 100), sketch a curve of percent COHb saturation vs. time of exposure to constant CO level. One of several formulas for calculating the saturation level is $\%COHb = 0.16 \times ppm\ CO + 0.5$, where the extra 0.5% is a natural level maintained by the body. Using your sketch and

this formula, calculate and plot the blood COHb levels which would correspond to the estimated CO exposure pattern of your typical daily routine. To keep the arithmetic simple, you can consider each hour's exposure uniform, resulting in a distinct jump in blood COHb at the end of the hour. (See project suggestion 36.)

Project Suggestions

35. By obtaining morbidity data from your school health service, or perhaps mortality data from your local health department, and pollution concentration data either from the local air pollution agency or by measuring some yourself, you can plan and conduct a variety of interesting and useful observational studies.
36. (See Problem 34.) If the use of a computer is possible, a model of blood COHb levels as a function of ambient CO levels can be made much more sophisticated, considering shorter time intervals.
37. Your local Lung Association may have access to equipment for the various lung-function tests. Try to get a demonstration or use of the equipment for a simple study.

FURTHER READING

For further information on the effects *per se* of the various pollutants, the best starting point would be the federal government's *Air Quality Criteria* documents [23–28] for the major pollutants and the "Litton documents" [35–61] for other compounds. Lead, omitted from these series, is discussed in [85] and [96]; the former is general and the latter more technical. Dr. Amdur's survey [88] of the toxicology of sulfate compounds and sulfuric acid mist is excellent. The article by Drs. Shy and Finkley of the CHESS program [222] is a good description of that important health effects study, and [99] is a major technical publication on the results from CHESS concerning sulfur oxides pollution. Other recent work may be found in the current journals, with the *Archives of Environmental Health* [170] probably the most productive and the *Journal of the Air Pollution Control Association* [174] also good.

For reading on the methodology rather than the results of studies on health effects, the research papers themselves are probably the best source; the reference list here includes most of the major studies, and just looking through the journals is worthwhile. Two booklets by the National Tuberculosis and Respiratory Disease Association [12 and 13] provide a good introduction to the respiratory system and respiratory diseases at a level a little more elementary than this book. For a more careful treatment, any standard biology or physiology book could be consulted. For a nonscientific, more human view of pollution and health, try Wise's *Killer Smog* [22], about the 1952 London smog, or Roueche's *Eleven Blue Men* [16], which has a chapter on Donora.

5

ECOLOGIC
AND
ECONOMIC EFFECTS

Courtesy EPA

This second chapter on the effects of air pollution could have been accurately titled "Other Effects," that is, effects other than those on human health. The same point could be made by calling it simply "Ecologic Effects," since ecology refers to our relationship with the environment, and anything that isn't part of us specifically as creatures is part of our environment. As it stands, the title is meant to draw a distinction between effects on things that do and don't belong to us, humans, as a species. Since we share the atmosphere with all other species, it is clearly not ours alone. On the other hand, part of the environment—the part we've built—does belong to us alone and is ours to damage if we must; although many of us would draw a big distinction between damage to downspouting on our house and damage to a centuries-old cathedral, the loss of either affects only the human species.

Air pollutants cause a broad variety of nonhealth effects in a variety of situations. One aspect common to most of them, however, is that they have not yet been studied to the extent that health effects have. A recurring theme in this chapter, even more than in the previous chapter, will be the many things we don't know about the effects of air pollution.

EFFECTS ON THE PHYSICAL ENVIRONMENT

Since the pollution caused by humans goes into the air, one of the most obvious effects of the pollution is simply that it changes the air itself. Does this matter; is it an adverse effect? Anyone who has ever been close to a pollution source will recognize that the air emerging from a smokestack or tailpipe is adversely affected; it's no good for any of the common uses we make of air. But since, of course, the air gets stirred and mixed around, the pollution in it also gets diluted and dissipated, and the air becomes cleaner. But there is a basic point here that must not be overlooked because of its simplicity. Something was put into the air, and just because it was diluted enough to become unnoticeable doesn't mean it isn't still there. It is a fact that the substance may be removed from the air; there are various means by which this can happen, but we can't wisely just assume so. Recently, increasingly sophisticated research studies of various types are looking for, and finding, subtle effects on the atmosphere itself that weren't even thought of a decade or two ago. These effects range from those that occur in cities due to their own pollution, through larger-scale regional effects of partly diluted urban effluents, all the way to possible effects of much smaller pollution levels on a global scale.

The Urban Atmosphere

The modern city or urban area has many effects on the atmosphere over and around it. The most prominent is heard daily, when the TV weatherman predicts temperatures 5–10 degrees cooler in the outer suburbs than downtown, but urban areas also have less sunlight, less wind, more fog and haze, and, of course, more dust in the air than is found in the open country. These are not all the results of air pollution; in fact, most of these differences are the result of an excess of heat energy in the city. This excess produces a "heat island," a dome of air in which the temperature is several degrees higher than in the surroundings. Some of the extra heat is a sort of "thermal pollution" caused by our wasteful use of energy, especially in driving cars and heating poorly insulated buildings; however, the bigger part results from the fact that the vertical building surfaces and the preponderance of concrete and other dense, stonelike materials causes the city to absorb and hold the sun's energy much more efficiently than the "cool, green" countryside. This heat island, though not an effect of air pollution, is perhaps the most consistent of our effects on the atmosphere.

The direct effect of a city on pollution of the air is just the concentration of emissions caused by the concentration of human activity in a relatively small area. When the overall regional winds are light, these emissions tend to remain in a relatively compact area, accumulating noticeably. This dust accumulation has been observed from planes so consistently in recent years that the brownish gray haze layer marking major cities has become as familiar to pilots as the temperature difference is to meteorologists.

To the residents within the city, the most familiar effect is the reduction of visibility due to the particulate matter in the air. Particulate pollution can be involved in reducing visibility in various ways. One is by increasing the frequency or duration of fog. Because the extra particles in the air help moisture condense into fog, a city typically has about double the amount of foggy weather in winter and about a third more in summer. However, because of the higher temperatures, the fog in the city is less likely to become extremely thick and dense. In the United Kingdom, where the climate is typically damp and humid, severe levels of air pollution are frequently associated with damp, penetrating fogs, and, of course, this was the origin of the word "smog."

Years ago in the United States, visibility problems were also caused by smoke, but fog played a much less prominent role than in, say, London; more recently, the kind of reduced visibility most Americans think of is not so much smoke or fog, but a haze, usually in the afternoon, that obscures distant vision. Although it's obvious that the mountain or skyline one's used to seeing has disappeared, the reason is often a bit puzzling. In the coal-burning cities of 25 years ago, and more recently in London, it was obvious that restricted visibility was caused by the black smoke being emitted; one could even filter it out of the air by breathing through a handkerchief. But today, the reason is much less obvious; one doesn't see that much visible smoke emitted, and the haze is most often light gray, bluish white, or even a little yellowish brown, rather than smoky. This haze is caused by more than just visible particulate pollution emitted directly from sources; it also involves very small particles that are formed in the air from gaseous pollutants. These latter particles are among the very smallest in size, less than 1 micron, and they operate to reduce visibility in a different way from that of the large particles.

The large particles that are put directly into the air as, say, smoke, reduce visibility by absorbing the light from an object, preventing it from ever reaching the observer's eye. The very small particles affect visibility by scattering light rather than by absorbing it. They scatter the light from a distant object away from its path toward the observer's eye, and they scatter light ɪrom the background into the path of light from the object toward the eye. This tends to blur the distinction between the object and its background; with enough scattering by enough particles, the two become indistinguishable, and the object disappears. And yet, because the light is mostly just scattered about rather than absorbed, the overall effect is blurriness rather than darkening, and the observer's reaction is generally a blinking and straining of the eyes rather than an urge to turn on the street lights.

There are at least two major atmospheric processes producing this very fine particulate matter—the condensation of sulfate particles from SO_2 plumes and the photochemical smog process, during which some sort of particles, probably nitrates, are formed. Both of these phenomena are worse with high humidity, but rather than fog droplets, they produce particles about 0.3–0.5 microns in size; this is just about the wavelength of light, thus making these particles very efficient at light-scattering. This description is greatly oversimplified, as these gas-particle reactions in the atmosphere are not at all well understood, but are still the subject of much research; nonetheless, the principal point is that there's a great deal more to reducing adverse visibility effects than just stopping the obvious emissions of visible particulate matter.

Considering that visibility does not affect health, there is a surprising amount of research, measured data, and general knowledge about it. However, the reason we know as much as we do about visibility reduction is not due to the government's concern about citizens' seeing the mountains, but rather to concern about commercial pilots' seeing the mountains, as well as the runways and so on. The National Weather Service's airport weather stations routinely record visibility, or visual range, as it may be called, along with other meteorological parameters, and this provides some data that help us illustrate the different trends in the two types of visibility reduction. Table 5–1 compares the proportion of time airport visibility was less than seven miles in various cities for a period in the 1930s and another in the 1950s and 1960s. In general, visibility in cities that had smoke-pollution problems in the 1930s has improved, whereas that in the smaller,

TABLE 5–1
Changes in frequency of low visibilities, 1930s to 1950s

City	1929–1938	1955–1961	Change*
Bakersfield, Calif.	8†	18	+128%
Burbank, Calif.	32	35	+11%
Caribou, Maine	24	18	−24%
Chicago, Ill.	59	37	−37%
Columbia, Missouri	20	11	−45%
Columbus, Ohio	37	28	−24%
Des Moines, Iowa	30	15	−51%
El Paso, Texas	3	2	−44%
Grand Island, Nebraska	15	9	−36%
Greensboro, North Carolina	19	19	+2%
Indianapolis, Indiana	40	25	−39%
Lake Charles, Louisiana	10	13	32%
Medford, Oregon	12	17	+42%
Milwaukee, Wisconsin	36	20	−45%
Moline, Illinois	42	21	−51%
Nashville, Tennessee	25	17	−31%
Oakland, Calif.	17	18	+6%
Peoria, Ill.	37	21	−44%
Richmond, Virginia	27	23	−16%
Sacramento, Calif.	17	18	+6%
Salem, Oregon	23	13	−43%
San Diego, Calif.	87	79	−9%
Seattle, Washington	29	20	−31%
Sioux City, Iowa	10	11	+6%
South Bend, Indiana	38	29	−24%
St. Louis, Missouri	31	17	−47%
Tulsa, Oklahoma	13	8	−41%
Winslow, Arizona	1	1	−15%

* Determined from unrounded frequency data.
† Figures are % of hours with visibility less than seven miles.
Source: Modified from G. C. Holzworth, "Some Effects of Air Pollution In and Near Cities," in *Symposium: Air Over Cities,* Public Health Service, 1962.

cleaner cities, especially those on the West Coast, has been reduced, though the change is not so great.

It is very easy to question the importance of a seven-mile range of visibility, and in fact, it probably is less important to most people than are some other effects. Indeed, for most people the effect of reduced visibility is totally psychological and is therefore difficult to quantify. Consequently, reduced visibility is an effect frequently neglected in scientific discussions of pollutant effects. Yet the psychological impact of frequent haze or smoke can be striking, especially if it's coupled with the black, dirty windowsills that occur with heavier particulates, dustfall. Probably one of the most profound aspects of the nation's overall environmental problem is that the people in the older cities of the Northeast have lived for so long with literally dirty air, in addition to their many other urban problems, that they have very little recognition of the problem and little expectation of any solution. Although it's clearly an exaggeration to say that New York City children never see the sun, it's also clearly true that they implicitly assume that the entire world is pretty much like the piece of it in which they live.

Regional Weather Effects

As it moves outward, beyond the boundaries of the city and the urban area into rural environs, the pollution put in the air by the city is diluted somewhat, and its effects become more subtle, less noticed. Not long ago, say 10 or 15 years, most scientists presumed that there were no such effects, but few of them would blithely say so now. Fairly little is known about the precise effects of widely dispersed pollutants, but it seems that the more we conduct careful scientific studies of the matter, the more effects we find; this area is clearly one of the creative research forefronts of environmental science.

We'll look first at an effect of the city's pollution on precipitation. In the mid-1960s it was discovered that the effluent from the south Chicago–northwest Indiana industrial complex was causing increased precipitation 30 miles downstream in Indiana. Known as the LaPorte anomaly, after the town in Indiana where the extra rain, hail, and thunderstorms are measured, this phenomenon was discovered by climatologist Stanley A. Changnon, Jr., in comparing weather records from LaPorte with similar data at nearby reporting stations. The LaPorte station averages 50 inches of precipitation annually, the surrounding areas 36 inches. In fact, this extra amount of rain had been occurring ever since the end of the Depression and the wartime boom in the steel industry, but no one had ever looked carefully enough. Since then, similar, though smaller effects have been found elsewhere.

The precipitation effect of the urban effluents is apparently produced by a combination of three emissions. The industrial plants produce huge quantities of small particles, known to atmospheric scientists as condensation nuclei because they help moisture condense from the vapor state into rain, fog, hail, etc. The plants also emit large amounts of moisture, which, of course, raises the humidity, and also quantities of heat. Ironically, the 30% increase in rain at LaPorte is greater than the fondest hopes of the scientists deliberately trying to increase rainfall artificially. This situation of urban particulates having an influence on rural areas is not unique to those areas that are close to huge cities, though the situation at LaPorte is clearly more dramatic than at most other sites. Figure 5–1 illustrates

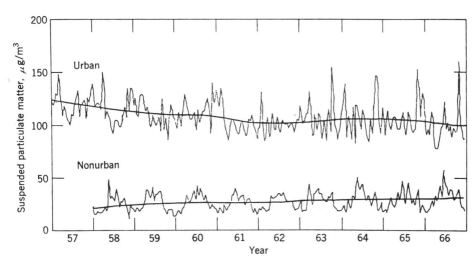

Fig. 5–1. The long-term trend in suspended particulate levels in urban and nonurban areas. The data are averaged over the sampling stations of the National Air Surveillance Networks. The irregular line represents the basic data; the smooth curve is an objectively calculated trend line. The urban stations, which represent center-city areas, are declining, whereas nonurban levels have continually risen. (R. Spirtas and H. J. Levin, "Patterns and Trends in Levels of Suspended Particulate Matter," *JAPCA* **21,** June 1971, p. 331. Reprinted by permission.)

the long-term trend in the levels of suspended particulate matter in non-urban areas, a gradual increase which is easily masked by the large random variations. This sort of data analysis, of course, makes one wonder just how many subtle effects like those in LaPorte are yet to be detected even farther away from the cities.

The Global Balance: Sources and Sinks

In the long run, however, the ease with which the changes to LaPorte's climate were both caused and went unnoticed serves primarily to raise serious questions about what smaller effects may be occurring, yet remain unnoticed, on a much, much wider scale. It is here, on a global scale, that our ignorance is greatest, the research possibilities the most tantalizing, and the prospects most frightening, at least to some people. The earth has always been so huge, the individual person or nation so small, that few seriously considered it reasonable that humans could affect the entire planet at all, for good or ill. But in the last 25 years, within a single generation, the existence of nuclear weaponry, the explosion of the human population, and many similar things have drastically changed this simple view. We are continually getting evidence of our ability to spread things all over the globe—DDT in Antarctic penguins, mercury in the glaciers on Greenland, and so on.

There is no way to treat the subject of global-scale effects on our environment in a neat, organized way; the few known facts just don't yet fit such a structure. Consequently, we'll just discuss briefly the overall concept of global dispersion and sinks and then the major and a couple of minor examples.

The idea of pollutants dispersing globally is one of those simple, obvious concepts that, because of the enormity of its scale, is hard to truly comprehend in all its ramifications. We spoke in Chapter 2 about the wind diluting our effluents, with a fixed amount of pollutant being mixed into varying amounts of air, depending on the wind speed. What happens then, of course, is that the parcels of air containing the pollution become mixed with other parcels of air, the coherent plume from the source disappears, and the concentration of pollutant becomes smaller and smaller. As we'll see in Chapter 8, this has been, and to an extent still is, considered a viable way of eliminating the effects of the effluent; one just goes far enough out into the countryside or builds a smokestack tall enough, so that the pollutant is diluted to an unnoticeably low concentration before it ever gets near anyone or anything it might harm. However, the basic law of the conservation of mass says that pollution can't just quietly disappear; it must either stay in the air or be taken out in some way. If it stays, the overall global concentration must inevitably increase, though for a long time it may still be too low to measure. If the pollution is removed from the air, other questions arise: Where does it go? Is it harmless there?

More often than not, the latter possibility is the case; what we know so far of the fate of the major pollutants seems to indicate that they don't accumulate indefinitely, but rather are removed and deposited somewhere else. "Somewhere" has a name; we describe those parts of the environment where the pollutants ultimately go as "sinks." It is in this context that we earlier described the atmosphere as a distribution system; it functions as a central reservoir, with a large number of sources putting a certain pollutant in and probably a smaller number of sinks taking it out elsewhere.

To illustrate the idea, we'll consider some of the recent changes in our belief about the fate of CO in the atmosphere. CO is not a very reactive chemical, and it was long thought that CO accumulates in the atmosphere, but that the concentration was just too low to measure. Then, better global measurements made it possible to determine that the atmosphere contains only about 500 million tons and that even with emissions estimated at 200 million tons each year, the concentration isn't increasing. This finding set off a renewed search for a CO sink, and interest quickly centered on the oceans, which have the capacity to absorb and hold huge quantities of dissolved gases. Then, experiments demonstrated that the oceans were already oversaturated with CO and actually were a source rather than a sink, giving off more CO rather than absorbing any that came from pollution sources. Apparently, CO from plankton and algae in the ocean is the reason why the seas are sources of CO. Other studies showed that microorganisms in soil acted as a sink, taking in CO and apparently using the energy in the soil by oxidizing it further, to CO_2. More recent research has shown that dying plants are also involved, acting as a source and even producing much more CO than humans' fuel-combustion activities. The entire subject has thus rapidly become quite complex, with CO involved in a cycle of natural processes operating on a scale that makes our contribution seem pretty small. Thus, although CO is still a major urban pollution problem, apparently it's not a global one.

CO_2, Particulates, and the Radiation Balance

In contrast, there is one clear example of global increases in pollutant levels, and we have some idea of their possible effects. The two pollutants involved are carbon dioxide and particulate matter, either or both of which can affect the overall radiation balance of the earth's surface, which in turn could change the average surface temperature.

In seeing how this might happen, let's consider CO_2 first, since both its atmospheric levels and its effects are better known. The average concentration usually given for CO_2 is about 0.03% of the air by volume, or about 300 ppm, and actually the figure varies a good bit from that level. Although CO_2 has an important role in the biosphere, as a part of the carbon cycle, we are interested in CO_2 for its absorption of radiant energy from the sun.

Sunlight, in common with other forms of electromagnetic radiation, is characterized by its basic properties of frequency and wavelength. As illustrated in Fig. 5–2, the important feature is that radiation wavelength is distributed along a spectrum; our ability to both see different colors and tune in different radio and TV stations depends on the differences in the wavelengths of the electromagnetic waves carrying the light or the broadcast signal. The CO_2 effect arises because the earth's energy balance involves different kinds of radiation, and CO_2, like many other substances, absorbs radiation of certain wavelengths well and others not at all. CO_2 lets pass the solar radiation (visible light) coming to the earth and the energy it carries, but it absorbs the infrared energy radiated back out by the earth. Thus, the CO_2 in effect traps some solar energy, helping to warm the earth. A balance is struck between this effect, called the *greenhouse effect*, and the earth's surface temperature, such that an increase in the average CO_2 concentration in the atmosphere increases the average temperature of the earth's surface.

The reason for concern is that the global CO_2 level has been increasing for at least 100 years, primarily as a result of our massive combustion of

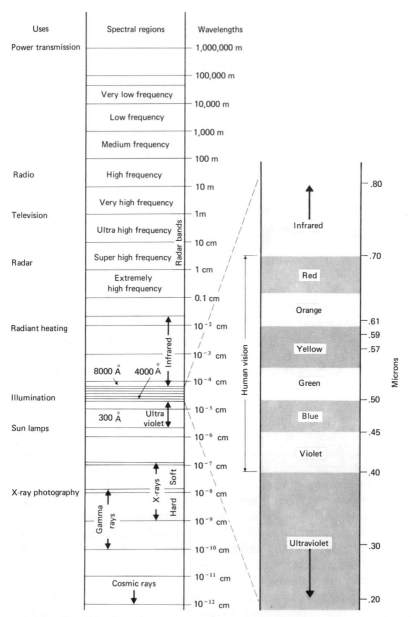

Fig. 5–2. The electromagnetic spectrum. Visible light occurs as a narrow band near the center of this spectrum, with long-wave, low-frequency uses such as radio and TV broadcasting on one side and shorter-wave radiation on the other. The energy of such radiation is proportional to the frequency, that is, higher toward the bottom of the figure; this is why x-rays need to be treated with care and cosmic rays are dangerous, although an atmosphere filled with TV and radio waves is harmless. (S. J. Williamson, *Fundamentals of Air Pollution,* Reading, Mass.: Addison-Wesley, 1973, p. 78)

fossil fuels to provide energy. We have produced CO_2 at a rate faster than the CO_2 sinks can absorb it. The oceans have the capacity to readily absorb the quantities of CO_2 being emitted, but they haven't done so. As evidenced by the measured amount of CO_2 increase in the atmosphere, no more than half the CO_2 has been absorbed, apparently because the surface layers of sea water are nearly saturated with CO_2, and the oceans don't mix enough to stir it on down very fast. Various projections of future fuel use indicate that the CO_2 level, which is presently increasing about one percent a year, could reach over 400 ppm. Theoretical calculations indicate that this could amount to an increase in the average global temperature of about 4°F.

The effect of suspended particles on the radiation balance is more complicated and less well known, partly because particles are such a heterogeneous lot. The particles of concern are again the smallest ones, those less than 1 micron in size; these particles can stay suspended long enough to become fairly evenly distributed throughout the atmosphere. As we saw before, particles can have various effects: they can absorb the sunlight or scatter it in various directions. If the particles in the air either absorb the incoming radiation or scatter it forward toward the earth, the effect is a warming of the atmosphere and the earth.

The third effect, the back-scatter effect, can work in two different ways. The particles can scatter the incoming visible radiation back out into space, tending to cool the earth, but they can also scatter the outgoing infrared radiation back toward the earth, tending to warm it. Here again, the difference in the wavelength of the radiation has an effect—because their size matches the wavelength of the solar radiation, the submicron particles are much better at back-scattering the incoming energy than the outgoing. The overall net effect of the particles, at least as best we know with our present knowledge, is an overall cooling. Thus, the influence of the CO_2 and particulate effects are opposite, and the net change in the average global temperature might be either up or down, depending on the degree to which these two effects cancel each other out.

In addition, other forces may come into play; a slight change in temperature might cause changes in the overall average humidity and cloudiness. When we consider the color pictures of the earth taken by the space program, it is obvious that the light-colored, cloudy areas play the biggest part in reflecting light back; therefore, changes in cloudiness can significantly affect the temperature also. At present, the best guess is that the temperature will rise, but no more than a few degrees, although this is by no means a well-established fact.

One may logically ask: Who cares if the earth's temperature goes up or down a shade? Although many subtle effects might occur, our biggest concern is with the balance between the open ocean and the polar ice caps, especially the huge Greenland glacier, which extends farther away from the poles than other ice sheets do. The precise nature of the forces that control the ocean–ice balance is not known, but a number of studies have indicated that only a surprisingly small change in temperature would be needed to upset the balance. At present, a third of the ice melts during the warm season, only to be replaced when winter comes again. It's estimated that a given piece of ice typically lasts only about ten years. The ice sheet is not at all the massive, stable thing that it might seem, so that changes do seem possible, although we're in no position to predict them precisely.

The consequences of any sizeable change in the glaciers are a little easier to come by, or at least the most obvious ones are. The glaciers tie up a huge amount of water; if only the Greenland ice sheet were to melt, the sea level would rise about 20 feet, flooding most of the world's major cities. No one, of course, expects this to happen very soon, if ever. It is, however, believed that the earth is presently cooler than its geological average and is still in the process of warming up again after the last Ice Age. Perhaps the earth's temperature and the glaciers oscillate quite naturally in a cycle so massive we could never dream of modifying it. Or, perhaps they exist in a delicately struck balance that we could readily destroy.

Other Problems

As an example of a different problem, let's consider the fate of SO_2 in the air. Like carbon and nitrogen, sulfur can assume several different oxidation states and is therefore involved somewhat in biological processes. It is estimated that the SO_2 emitted by humans is at present only about one-fourth the amount naturally produced in the atmosphere from hydrogen sulfide emitted by decaying organic matter. The atmosphere seems able to handle the SO_2 readily enough; it's estimated that the average lifetime of SO_2 in the air is only one to two weeks. The reason why the air handles it so well is that the SO_2 is readily oxidized to particulate sulfates and sulfuric acid. Some of these stay in the air and are distributed fairly widely; 40% of the particles over the north polar regions are sulfates. The majority of the sulfur emissions, however, are removed from the air by precipitation as sulfuric acid. This rapid washout simply means that the long-term effects of the pollution show up not in the air, but in the acidity of the rainfall. In Europe, where the most research has been conducted, the acidity of the rainfall has risen dramatically, as seen in Fig. 5–3. It is not yet clear to what extent this may have ill effects, but the acidity of water is a very fundamental parameter, and it is disturbing that the acidity is increasing in the rivers and lakes of northern Europe.

Another example of letting pollutants disperse through the entire global biosphere, and one which leads us into the next section, is the emerging question of the heavy metals—lead, mercury, cadmium, copper, zinc, and nickel—and their role in the environment. In direct contrast to degradable

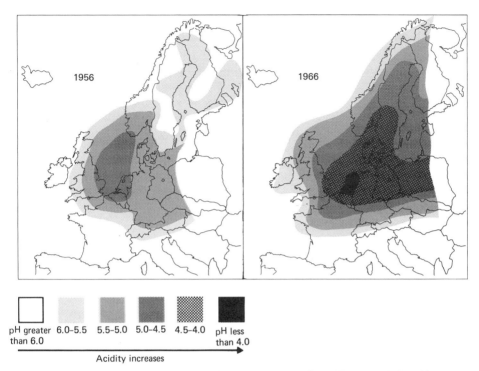

pH greater   6.0–5.5   5.5–5.0   5.0–4.5   4.5–4.0   pH less
than 6.0   than 4.0

Acidity increases

Fig. 5–3. Changes in the acidity of precipitation over northern Europe, 1956–1966. The 1956 map shows no areas of pH less than 4.5, whereas the 1966 map includes an area less than 4.0, in the southern Netherlands and Germany's Rhine valley. (Svante Oden, "Nederbordens forsurning-ett generellt hot mot ekosystemem," in I. Mysterud, ed., *Forurensning og Biologisk Miljovern,* Olso: Universitetsforlaget, 1971, p. 74. Reprinted by permission.)

compounds like SO_2, the metals are basic chemical elements and cannot be changed. An atom of lead dug out of a mine and put into gasoline remains an atom of lead when it emerges from the tailpipe into the environment; it is not changed when it comes to lodge in a person or in a lichen, nor is it changed when the chemicals from the person or the lichen are ultimately returned for re-use. This striking immutability, and our present ignorance of the ways these metals act in the biosphere, lead to worrisome questions. Most of the heavy metals in the world are found in underground mineral deposits, presumably as a result of the geological formation of the earth's crust. What we are doing now, of course, is to dig these ores out of their isolated location, extract the metals, and turn them into products we want; when we're through with the items we made and the metals they contain, or, more accurately, when we're through with our initial involvement with them, we tend to spread them all over the biosphere, with no real idea where they go or what they do.

This is not to say that we have created a major problem. It is not known that the heavy metals have serious effects beyond those on health mentioned in the previous chapter, but neither is it known that they don't. However, we do know that these metals are found everywhere and that they are stored or accumulated by organisms ranging from humans and other mammals to the lichens and mosses. The connecting link that needs to be explored is the ecology of how the other organisms affect the environment we all share and how the metals, which generally affect us adversely, might affect these other organisms. Actually, of course, this is merely an example; we also need to know a great deal more about how all the pollutants affect other organisms.

EFFECTS ON OTHER LIVING THINGS

As we've just suggested, we know a great deal less about how our pollution affects other species than we do about how it affects human health. And what we do know is rather heavily slanted toward those species we cultivate, either as crops or as livestock, for our own economic use.

Animals

To begin with effects on animals, we note first that the health effects seen in humans generally also occur in other animals, at least in other mammals; this, of course, is the basis for using such animals in research on the effects of air pollution. Animals, as well as humans, can be harmed by ambient pollution exposures—records of the killer smog in the Meuse Valley include references to dying animals, and the 1952 London smog thoroughly disrupted a concurrent livestock exhibition. More recently, pathologists in New York City have uncovered widespread lead poisoning of zoo animals that appears to be the result of airborne lead. Generally, however, the epidemiologists have, perhaps understandably, not applied their trade to animal populations.

The one striking exception to this is the study of air pollution effects on livestock. Fluoride compounds (chemical symbol F), and to a lesser extent arsenic compounds (As), cause severe damage to foraging livestock, with the result that much study has been directed at those effects. Animals grazing near pollutant sources eat fluoride or arsenical particulate matter that has been deposited on and collected in the grass surrounding the source. The fluorides cause a deterioration of the bones and teeth, ultimately leading to crippling and tooth loss, a fatal problem for animals that walk around and eat grass. Fluorosis of this degree is found only in the near vicinity of the source, but the major sources are phosphate fertilizer plants, which are understandably located in agricultural areas; aluminum smelters are another, less prevalent, fluoride source. Arsenic poisoning of grazing animals occurs in a similar manner, the arsenical particulates generally coming from ore smelters, which also tend to be in remote areas. It is a less severe problem because the sources are fewer and the symptoms less dramatic.

The problem of damage from both fluoride and arsenic is alleviated by a combination of reducing the emissions and moving the animals elsewhere; neither is generally viewed as a major problem, of the magnitude of SO_2 in urban areas, for instance. Nonetheless, we should note one unusual aspect of these effects—though clearly the result of air pollution, these effects occur via the victims' food, not their respiration. Not only is this an interesting anomaly, it also reminds us that we, as well as the cattle, participate in a complex system in which various species exchange nutrients with one another. Often described as a food chain, this system might be better described as the food cycle, since the flow of nutrients doesn't end with us and the other carnivorous animals, but ultimately returns, through the decay organisms, as shown in Fig. 5–4. The concept of a food cycle is not com-

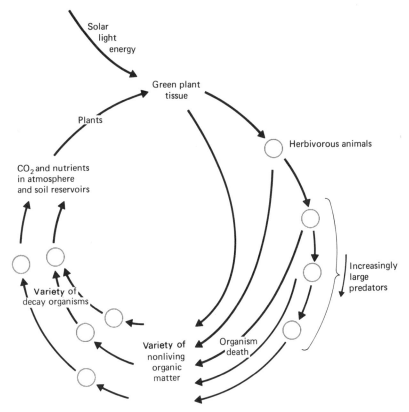

Fig. 5–4. The food cycle. Plants make organic food with energy from sunlight; the food is consumed in a complex series of herbivore-carnivore relationships; with death, the organic matter is broken down again by an even more complex arrangement of decay organisms.

monly considered a topic relevant to air pollution. But here, we have
one clear intervention of air pollution into a food system, and as we study
other species more carefully, we may find others.

Vegetation

In turning to the plant species, we find a wider variety of topics to talk
about; there have been some extreme episodes of plant damage, there is
some research into the mechanisms of pollutant effects, and there's a good
bit of effort in defining the effects quantitatively, especially for economically significant plants, that is, crops. Historically, there have been instances
of pollutant sources in wooded areas totally denuding their surroundings,
killing all forms of plant life. These sources have usually been ore smelters,
which are typically located in rural areas and used to produce prodigious
quantities of sulfur dioxide from the sulfides that were mixed in with the
ore. This type of wholesale destruction is generally now believed to be a
thing of the past; the type of plant damage of concern currently is somewhat less dramatic.

Before pursuing the effects of SO_2 and other pollutants that constitute
the present problem, we should digress briefly to consider the typical structure of a plant's leaf (Fig. 5–5). The leaf has two distinct types of cells—
the relatively tough, inactive epidermal cells that provide protection, and
the softer parenchyma cells, where the leaf's principal business, photosynthesis, takes place. The parenchyma cells are of two structural types—the
elongated palisade cells and the irregular spongy cells. The former, regularly
arranged in a layer, tend to provide strength to the leaf; the spongy cells are
arranged in a loose, irregular manner that creates open spaces through
which air can circulate to the various cells. The air enters these passages
through openings in the epidermis called stomata, which usually occur only
on the underside of the leaf. Each individual stoma is formed by two specially modified cells that can open or close the stoma to regulate air passage
through it.

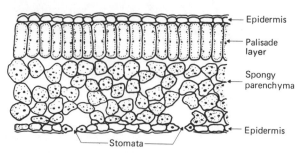

Fig. 5–5. Cross-section of typical leaf.

Most of the biological function of a plant takes place in the leaves. Most important is the photosynthesis of glucose, a simple sugar, from water and atmospheric carbon dioxide. This reaction is made possible by the absorption of solar energy by molecules of chlorophyll in the parenchyma cells. Since this is the only chemical reaction able to do this, green plants are the only living species able to manufacture food energy directly from solar energy; hence, they form the base of the food cycle, providing all the food for all other species, as well as produce oxygen as a "waste product" that can be used by animal species. Plants also carry on biochemical respiration —the reverse of photosynthesis—in order to provide energy for their own cell growth and transpiration, the transport of water from the roots up through the stems and out through the leaves as a means of both cooling the plant and transporting mineral nutrients from the soil. All of these processes involve the movement of air in and out through the passages and stomata of the leaves and, of course, the entrance of whatever pollutant gases are in the air.

Damage to plants is usually categorized as one of three types—growth alteration or one of two types of leaf damage, outright tissue destruction or *chlorosis*, a discoloring of the leaf tissue. Growth alteration can be dramatic, as when herbicidal chemicals, or weed-killers, become air pollutants, but more commonly, growth alteration simply refers to the overall stunting of plant growth. Although some stunting results from interference with specific aspects of plant growth, such as poor flower development or premature leaf drop, most stunting is merely a generalized, overall decrease in plant health. This may be caused by damage to the leaves, which results in decreased production of the materials necessary for plant growth.

Most of the known pollutant effects on plants do involve damage to the plants' leaves. Some pollutants cause plasmolysis and the necrotic collapse of tissue, that is, damage to the cells that causes them to lose water and then to structurally collapse and die, leaving a discolored dead area in the green tissue. A similar-appearing type of damage is chlorosis, a bleaching or fading of the leaf's green color, caused by the loss of chlorophyll; air pollutants can cause chlorosis, but it can also result from attacks by nematodes or viruses or from nutrient deficiencies. In fact, diagnosing pollutant damage in plants is in general tricky and requires a good bit of experience.

Of the various plant-damaging pollutants, the most significant is photochemical oxidant, the smog milieu produced from hydrocarbons and nitrogen oxides. Both ozone and PAN (peroxyacetyl nitrate) readily damage plants, and the combined effect can be very serious; one of the earliest signs of the smog problem was plant damage in the area around the Los Angeles Basin. Agriculture in this region, which is a major citrus-growing area, is suffering very severely from the Los Angeles smog, as is some of the surrounding forested area. In fact, things have become so bad that the highway department has been forced to landscape the Los Angeles freeways with artificial trees; the smog damages the real ones too severely.

Ozone causes a pattern of small spots, or flecks, that first blacken and then turn light as the tissue dies. Only with severe exposure do the spots unite to form large areas of dead tissue. The ozone apparently enters the leaf through the stomata, but for some reason preferentially attacks the palisade layer of cells, so that the damage appears on the top surface of the leaf. In contrast, PAN affects primarily the spongy parenchyma cells closest to the stomata, so that PAN damage, which often has a shiny bronze or silvery color, occurs primarily on the underside of the leaf. The maturity of the leaf cells has a significant effect on their susceptibility to PAN, so that the damage sometimes seems to occur in stripes or bands across the leaf, where cells of a similar age are clustered.

The susceptibility of leaves to ozone and PAN, or to any other pollutant, varies greatly, depending on the particular species of plant, the length of the exposure and time of day, the general health of the plant, and so on; thus, it's quite difficult to characterize the pollutant concentrations at which damage occurs. With some species, ozone damage begins to occur at levels of 0.03 ppm or more for a few hours, a quite typical daily level. PAN damage can occur at levels as low as 0.01 ppm for a few hours or even in a very few minutes, with levels in the vicinity of 0.1 ppm, but these levels generally occur only in fairly severe smogs.

Damage to plant leaves from sulfur dioxide consists of a diffuse chlorosis caused by chronic low-level exposures, with distinct necrotic-tissue damage resulting from more acute exposures, beginning at about 0.3 ppm for eight hours. Sulfur dioxide enters the leaves through the stomata, first attacking the spongy parenchyma cells and then spreading to the palisade layer, thereby extending the damage through the thickness of the leaf. Since the cells nearest the veins of the leaf are less readily affected, a damaged leaf often shows a green network of veins on a discolored, brown background. As with other effects of SO_2, it's not thoroughly clear whether the damage is caused by SO_2 or by accompanying acid aerosols; very likely both are involved. The effect of SO_2 is heightened in the presence of dew, mist, or light rain, which might increase the proportion of H_2SO_4, but it's lessened by heavy rain, which apparently just washes all the pollution away.

The combination of SO_2 and ozone exerts an unusually strong effect and provides us with an excellent example of a synergism, i.e., the combined effect of two pollutants is greater than the sum of the separate effects. As illustrated in Table 5–2, simultaneous exposure to about one-fourth ppm each of ozone and SO_2 caused damage to a significant proportion of the leaf area, although neither had any effect alone. A similar synergism with SO_2 increases the effect of NO_2, which alone and at reasonably realistic levels has no effect on plants.

TABLE 5–2
Synergistic effect of sulfur dioxide and ozone
on tobacco bel W3 plants*

Exposure time	Pollutants, ppm		% of leaf damaged
	O_3	SO_2	
2	0.03	—	0
2	—	0.24	0
2	0.027	0.24	38
4	0.031	—	0
4	—	0.26	0
4	0.028	0.28	75

* Data courtesy of the Agricultural Research Service, U.S. Department of Agriculture.
Source: H. A. Menser and H. E. Heggestad, "Ozone and Sulfur Dioxide Synergism: Injury to Tobacco Plants," *Science* **153** (21 July 1966): 424–425. Reprinted by permission. Copyright 1966 by the American Association for the Advancement of Science.

Fluorides are the only other major known cause of plant damage. Interestingly, leaves are not damaged when fluoride particles are deposited on them, although, as we've seen, cattle do suffer ill-effects from eating those leaves. Fluoride is absorbed into plants only if it's dissolved by dew or rain or if it comes as a gas in the first place, the latter being the more significant. Plant leaves accumulate the fluoride they take in, so that even a plant exposed to very low levels could eventually accumulate sufficient fluoride to cause damage. Fluoride damage results in the destruction of the leaf tissue; characteristically, the effect is seen at the edge of the leaf, although the fluoride may enter through all the stomata, and there is usually a very sharp dividing line between damaged and healthy tissue.

One other pollutant effect on plants, though minor, has an interesting twist. Ethylene, a hydrocarbon, acts as a plant hormone and produces a variety of growth defects. In very high concentrations, other chemicals, perhaps many others, can have striking effects on plants, but none of them presently constitutes any kind of general problem in air pollution.

The Smaller Species

Air pollution may also have an effect on the smaller species of both plants and animals, such as the micro-organisms, mosses, fungi, etc. Not much is known about the effects of air pollution on such species. Ozone, which is used as a germicide in water purification and indoor air sterilization, has a fatal effect on many types of micro-organisms; this effect, however, occurs only at concentrations far above ambient levels. The principal reason for mentioning these small organisms is that they play such an important role in the natural life processes, although their relationship to air pollution is only now beginning to be studied. Many of these organisms take part in the continuous cycle of organic compounds as the principal mechanism for decaying complex substances back into simple chemicals; others contribute by "fixing" atmospheric nitrogen in the soil in a form plants can use and by filling other, similar roles in the overall ecology of the biosphere. These key roles make them worth study, although the large number of different species involved likely makes them one of the less vulnerable links in the system.

Much of the research that has been done consists of field studies measuring the heavy metals found in naturally occurring species. Mosses, lichens, and even trees have been found to collect lead, mercury, etc.; in some cases, these organisms may be important global sinks for such compounds. One interesting study demonstrates that the effects of pollution from New York City has eliminated several species of lichen for a distance of 40 miles out onto Long Island, killing not only the native specimens, but also any that are brought into the area. This type of study of these species is increasing, and an overall picture may emerge in a few years.

ECONOMIC EFFECTS

In contrast to the emphasis on pollution's effects on human health and the more recent interest in ecologic effects, economic effects have received little attention recently. There are decided adverse economic effects, however; various pollutants can cause expensive damage to buildings and other property, they can dirty our homes and mechanical equipment, and in various other ways cause harm that requires economic expenditures to alleviate. These various expenditures are often lumped together, perhaps somewhat poetically, as "the cost of dirty air." We need to distinguish this phrase from the similar, and more current, phrase, "the cost of clean air," which is commonly used to refer to the economic cost of reducing or controlling pollutant emissions.

The phrase "cost of dirty air" arose as a catchy way of making a point about pollution; in the 1950s and early 1960s, estimates of the dollar cost of polluted air were almost always compared with the much smaller dollar amounts spent on cleaning up the pollution and frequently were coupled with pleas for increases in the budget of the government agency making the estimate. But when Congress finally decided to vigorously control pollution, the decision was made largely on the basis of the effects on human health. As a result, studies on the economic effects, and attempts to estimate the dollar cost of these effects, became much less popular. More recently, as estimates are made of the cost of taking pollution-control measures, there is renewed interest in quantifying the costs that are inadvertently paid by letting the air remain dirty.

The fact of these two opposing economic costs would seem to call for a cost-benefit analysis, a quantitative weighing of the two costs against each other to determine the amount of pollution control that will have the lowest overall cost. This kind of rational analysis has much to recommend it, and we'll return to this topic in Chapter 12; for our present purposes, we'll just consider the adverse economic effects—what they are and how they're caused.

Smoke, Soot, and Soiling

One of the earliest recognized economic costs of dirty air was the amount of wasted fuel, the quantities of unburned carbon that showed up as smoke and dustfall; when one spends money for fuel to burn, any waste of its energy value is clearly an economic cost. It was largely this cost, which was very sizeable in the smoky history of St. Louis and Pittsburgh, for example, that made those cities' clean-up campaigns successful. The smoke was reduced primarily by the installation of much more efficient, modern coal-burning equipment, although the shift to gas furnaces in homes and from steam to diesel railway locomotives was also important. However, the industries concerned justified the new furnaces and the new locomotives as much because they saved money as because they cleaned up the air. This is not to say that the industries weren't very pleased to be able to say "yes" to the civic associations, nor that the citizens hadn't reason to be proud of their efforts. However, now that the savings from better fuel economy have long since dropped below the break-even point, the resistance to better pollution control has stiffened considerably.

Despite the smoke reductions, fuel combustion and its pollutants—particulate matter and sulfur oxides—are still among the principal causes of economic loss, though now less through fuel waste than through simple soiling and the deterioration of materials. The first of these, soiling, though a rather obvious effect, is most difficult to study very carefully. Without question, particulate pollution, especially dustfall, gets things dirty, so that they need to be cleaned; it is claimed that in the worst days of Pittsburgh, one had to *literally* wash window curtains daily. This doesn't happen anymore, at least not in any broad sense. The amount of dustfall is far less, homes and buildings are kept closed and air conditioned; and white lace curtains have given way to heavy drapes. Nonetheless, one can't avoid the conclusion that pollution causes some portion of the total cost in dollars and effort we put into keeping our personal environment clean, although these figures are difficult to arrive at. In one of the few good studies done in the mid-1960s, the Public Health Service surveyed Steubenville, Ohio, and Uniontown, Pennsylvania, a nearby city that is similar in most ways, but drastically cleaner; the study found that the annual per capita costs for cleaning, etc., in Steubenville were $85 higher than in Uniontown.

Another, perhaps more obvious, aspect of soiling is its effect on buildings; most of us have seen cities in which all the downtown buildings were black from decades of soot and smoke. As a child, I grew up near Youngstown, Ohio; my principal impression of the city was not that "Youngstown is big" or "Youngstown is busy," but "Youngstown is black." This type of effect is mostly psychological, becoming economic only when a building is cleaned. Similarly, much of the common neighborhood soiling is more important psychologically than it is economically; I am bothered when black soot comes in through the closed windows in my home every winter here in the Boston area, although it costs essentially nothing to wipe off the windowsills.*

Corrosion and Materials Damage

Compared to soiling, the outright deterioration of substances is perhaps a more serious effect of polluted air; at least its effect is more directly economic. Also, deterioration involves more than just particulate pollution; both the sulfur oxides–particulate "London smog" in our eastern and midwestern cities and the photochemical smog, most often found in Los Angeles, are capable of destroying materials exposed to the atmosphere. The former can be highly destructive of metals and various other materials, whereas the oxidizing photochemical smog attacks primarily organic chemical substances.

The effect on metals, caused by both sulfur dioxide and the sulfuric acid it forms, is much worse when they are concentrated by being adsorbed onto particles. In dry air sulfur oxides merely etch the surface of the metal, but this effect is heightened when the humidity is high and the surface is even slightly moist; then, more acid is formed, electrochemical processes become involved in moving the molecules of metal around, and the rate of corrosion is greatly accelerated. The corrosion reactions operate primarily by converting the metal into metallic sulfates. Of course, most metals left unprotected outdoors will corrode a little anyway, reacting with the oxygen in the air to form oxides—iron rusts, copper turns green, etc. The important difference is not in the specific chemistry, but in the rate at which the changes occur; it's surprising how slowly iron rusts in very clean, dry air.

---

* Another anecdote: A prominent federal pollution official, fresh from relatively clean Los Angeles, once testified at a hearing that Washington, D.C., was the third dirtiest city in the country, as evidenced by the curtains in his hotel room. As his agency had just promulgated a list showing Washington to be down around 20, based on objective data, a humorous conflict arose. The man and his boss were invited to a Congressional hearing, at which the man stuck to his opinion; the industry lobbies had a field day with the "drapery index." Ultimately, the publicity probably did more good than harm, but for a while there were some embarrassed bureaucrats.

Of the various metals, the corrosion of iron, i.e., rusting, is clearly the biggest problem, causing extensive economic losses from damage to railway rails, steel buildings and other structures, and so on. This is partly because iron, and the steel we make from it, are the most commonly used metals. Also important, however, is the way in which iron corrosion occurs; the rust on a piece of iron is flaky and falls off, exposing more metal. In contrast, the oxides and sulfates of most of the other, nonferrous, metals remain on the piece of metal, serving as a protective layer that ultimately stops the contact between air and metal. Thus, even with corrosion accelerated by sulfur oxides, the harm is generally less than on iron products. The biggest problem on the nonferrous metals is corrosion of the copper in electrical contacts, which occurs significantly only in polluted atmospheres; the protective coating prevents the copper from flaking away and disappearing, but that same coating makes the electrical flow across the contact erratic. This is a serious problem in the telephone-telegraph industry and a lesser one in the manufacture of computers.

Other pollutants also contribute to the corrosion of metals. Silver, another good electrical conductor, is subject to tarnishing, mostly from hydrogen sulfide (H_2S); it is also silver sulfide that one polishes off the silverware. Zinc, which is used to galvanize iron pails, downspouting, and other implements against natural corrosion, is itself corroded by several pollutants, which act to break down the protective barrier formed against natural oxidation.

Although exterior metals are the most prominent target of SO_x pollution, it attacks other materials also. Buildings and other structures made of concrete, or of carbonate stone such as marble, are subject to greatly increased deterioration in atmospheres polluted with sulfur oxides. The SO_x converts carbonates in the stone to soluble sulfates that gradually dissolve away with the rain. This type of damage becomes an economic factor when one has to pay to replace the structures or when one is forced to build with a more expensive, more resistant stone, e.g., granite or sandstone. But the biggest concern to many people is not the cost of replacing modern buildings, but rather the damage to irreplaceable ancient buildings and stone sculptures. Throughout Europe, the many medieval cathedrals and other smaller works of art are being seriously threatened. Comparisons with old records still in existence reveal that the 150 years since the beginning of the Industrial Revolution have caused more damage than occurred in all the previous centuries.

Sulfur oxides pollution can also affect leather and paper, making the safe storage of valuable books a serious problem for libraries. With both paper and leather, the SO_2 is apparently first absorbed and then converted to sulfuric acid within the material. However, the case of paper illustrates how the effects of civilization and progress can be very subtle. Ancient paper is essentially immune to SO_2 damage, at least in comparison with modern paper; the vulnerability of modern paper is caused by the many metallic impurities from the chemicals used in manufacturing it, impurities which accelerate the conversion of SO_2 to sulfuric acid and which the cruder, more natural, ancient paper lacks.

Similarly, animal fibers, such as wool, are more resistant to SO_2 damage than are most of the synthetic textiles, although cotton, also a natural fiber, is not completely immune. It isn't clear just how much SO_2 damage there is to textiles, as distinguished from the associated soiling and cleaning damage, but it is evident that at least some damage arises from the classic SO_2–sulfuric acid conversion and attack; this damage generally occurs as a loss of tensile strength, which is believed to result from tiny breaks in the individual fibers.

The consideration of textiles is a convenient point to pick up our consideration of photochemical smog, especially ozone, the other principal source of damage to materials. Ozone attacks a wide variety of organic chemicals, a category which includes the synthetic fibers, e.g., nylon and rayon. Persistent stories used to come from Los Angeles about nylon stockings dissolving off the legs of women standing at curbside bus stops, but these stories probably gained currency more for their sex appeal than for their valid information about smog damage. Although ozone can physically damage fabrics, including nylon, a more significant problem is that the dyes used for coloring the fabric tend to fade. These textile dyes are complicated organic chemicals, and they are faded significantly by ozone and somewhat less by nitrogen oxides. The ozone apparently operates by breaking double bonds, one of the types of carbon-carbon bonds that hold organic molecules together.

Another effect of ozone on materials—in fact, one of the first noticeable of all the effects of smog—is the deterioration of rubber, both natural rubber and synthetic "elastomers." The damage occurs as cracks, which destroy the rubber's strength and elasticity. Here, the mechanism is quite clearly the double-bond breaking just mentioned, since synthetic elastomers that don't have double bonds are immune from ozone attack. The deterioration of rubber is a bit of a problem with rubber-insulated electrical wiring, but the major concern is with automobile tires; the rubber is under constant tension, which widens the cracks, exposing more rubber to be damaged. First seen in the 1940s in Los Angeles, where the concentrations of both ozone and the automobile are highest, this problem has been "overcome" in the intervening years by the development of more resistant synthetics, by the development of additives to mix in the rubber, and by the use of protective methods, such as covering tires with a wax coating for storage. All this, of course, costs money, raising the price of tires. In fact, all these effects result in higher prices; for tires, the added cost is about 50¢ per tire.

Totaling the Economic Costs

In addition to the direct cost of soiling and materials damage, there are other "costs of dirty air" that can best be described as the economic aspects of other pollutant effects, such as those on human health. However hard it may be to view human death or misery in economic terms, it is not at all difficult to see the dollar cost of the associated hospitalization, doctors, etc. Similarly, plant damage and harm to animals can be viewed as economic costs when plants or animals are economic property, and these costs can be significant. A California Agriculture Department survey of damage to the 1970 crops in that state found losses totaling over $25 million, much of it occurring as losses in the citrus crop in the Los Angeles Basin.

Note the use of the phrase "viewed as economic costs" rather than, say, "calculated in economic terms." There is a difference between just being able to see that an economic loss exists and being able to estimate it at all well, and this in turn is different from the fact that some effects can easily be put in dollar terms. For instance, in the California study just mentioned, some types of plant damage costs couldn't be included easily. Even though this was one of the more thorough studies ever done, the investigators couldn't include the invisible crop damage, any reduction in the quantity of crop yield, or damage to ornamental landscaping plants; although these are clearly real and obviously economic in nature, the damage can't be estimated well. On the other hand, damage to the forests, which is only indirectly economic, is excluded not because the damage can't be estimated, but because the dollar value of that damage can't be agreed upon.

Thus, even though it takes little imagination to see the economic aspects of pollutant effects, it does take a great deal of imagination and ingenuity to gather the data and make estimates to put together a realistic total cost for the nation. Such an estimate, though inevitably controversial, would be a most helpful figure in judging the appropriateness of control efforts. For a number of years the figure of $65 per capita per year was used; when multiplied by the *urban* population, the total is $4 billion nationally, and if the *total* population is used, the amount is $11 billion. Both figures have been widely published. Although the origin of the $65 figure is hazy, it seems to derive from some 1913 data from Pittsburgh, since adjusted and readjusted for population and inflation, etc., hardly a good, rational basis on which to base policy decisions. Table 5–3 contains a more recent, and likely much better, estimate of total national economic cost, $25 billion a year. Note that the cost of health effects, which were often ignored previously in making these estimates, are over a third of the total. Costs of the effects of vehicle-related pollutants, not even attempted in Table 5–3, have since been estimated by the National Academy of Science as an additional $2.5–10 billion annually.

TABLE 5–3
Projected national costs of air pollution damage in 1977 (in millions of dollars per year)

Type of damage	Particulate matter	Sulfur oxides	Carbon monoxide	Oxidant ($H_x C_x$)	Nitrogen oxides	Total
Health	3,880	5,440	*	*	*	9,320
Residential property	3,330	4,660	*	*	*	7,990
Materials and vegetation	970	3,680	Negligible	1,700	1,250	7,600
Total	8,180	13,780	*	1,700	1,250	24,910

* Estimate not attempted; insufficient information.
Source: 1972 EPA Economic Report to Congress.

As we noted at the beginning of this section, one hears much more about the cost of controlling pollution, usually called "the cost of clean air," than about the economic cost of the pollution. The cost of pollution abatement is in fact, and quite reasonably, a prominent topic of debate. Not only are there questions about the figures themselves, but there is disagreement about the significance of those figures. The pollution control agencies generally seem to be saying "Yes, it'll cost, but not that much, and besides, it's worth it," whereas some industrial groups and their patrons in government agencies are saying "That's a horrible expense; it's going to ruin the country's economy, and we better slow down."

None of the present estimates, of either abatement cost or pollution damage, are good enough to completely end this debate, and it seems clear that the final answers are yet to come. The federal Clean Air Act requires the Environmental Protection Agency to submit to Congress annual reports on the economic aspects of air pollution. In the 1973 report, EPA estimated the abatement costs for 1970–1978 at about $125 billion, or about $14 billion a year. This is of the same general magnitude as the pollution damage costs and in fact compares quite favorably with the $30 billion per year estimate in Table 5–3. The fact that these two costs are roughly comparable does suggest that the nation's pollution control efforts are neither wildly overstringent nor woefully inadequate. A more precise analysis, however, requires a good bit more than just comparing two cost estimates; we'll return to that effort in Chapter 12.

EXERCISES

Review Questions

1. What effects does a large urban area have on its own weather? What is the primary cause?
2. Identify the two kinds of reduced visibility discussed. What causes each?

3. Why are extensive visibility data available?
4. What is the LaPorte anomaly? What causes are suggested?
5. What is meant by dispersion as a method of pollution control?
6. What is an environmental "sink"?
7. Why are increasing global CO_2 concentrations of concern?
8. What effects can suspended particles have on the radiation balance of the earth?
9. What is the ultimate fate of SO_2 emitted into the air?
10. Why is the wide dispersal of heavy-metal waste of particular concern?
11. How are fluoride pollution and livestock related?
12. What is the unique role of green plants in the food cycle?
13. What pollutants can damage the leaves of plants?
14. Distinguish between the phrases "cost of clean air" and "cost of dirty air."
15. List several economic effects of pollutants.
16. What was the economic impact of the major smoke-control campaigns in St. Louis and Pittsburgh in the 1940s?
17. Why is the corrosion of iron the biggest problem in the deterioration of metals?
18. What effect does urban pollution have on stone buildings? What pollutant causes it?

Thought Question

19. It was noted that the time of day influences the susceptibility of plants to damage by gaseous pollutants. Can you explain this effect?

Discussion Questions

20. To what extent should general ecological considerations, such as global climatological effects or the dispersal of heavy metals, affect our national policy toward pollution control? Would you feel differently if you were from an undeveloped country?
21. Suppose that scientists in all the industrialized countries agreed on the need to drastically reduce the global emissions of a certain pollutant. How do you think this could be accomplished? What problems do you foresee? How would it depend on the type of source from which the pollutant comes? Assume that it is technically feasible to control the pollutant, but only at a significant cost.

FURTHER READING

The ecologic and economic effects of pollutants are not well organized and categorized; the series of federal *Criteria Documents* [23–28] mentioned in Chapter 4 contain some information, but relatively little. Two articles by Changnon [186–187] discuss the LaPorte anomaly and similar effects elsewhere; an article by Lear [204] is a good discussion of the nontechnical background. Peterson's *The Climate of Cities* [81] is a good summary and literature review of the pollution and primarily heat island aspects of cities. The reports of two study groups sponsored by MIT are excellent sources on the human impact on the physical environment: *Man's Impact on the Global Environment* [149] is a survey of climatic and ecologic effects, with assessment of our knowledge (little) and recommendations for research. *Inadvertent Climate Modifications* [144] is the report of a more specialized inquiry into the possibility of climate changes caused by humans and includes excellent coverage of climate over geological time, the ice ages, etc. The best technical discussion of the global sources and sinks of the various pollutants is Robinson and Robbins' Chapter 1 in Strauss [164]; the American Chemical Society report [21] has simple discussions of the cyclic balance of carbon, sulfur, and nitrogen in the biosphere.

For more quantitative, technical information about effects on plants and materials, Chapters 12 and 15 of Stern [160] are good. The EPA booklet "Air Pollution Inquiry to Vegetation" by Hindawi [82] has many good color photographs and an elementary discussion. The lead poisoning in zoo animals in New York is discussed by R. J. Bazell [179]; the study of lichens on Long Island by I. M. Brodo [182].

There are few good sources about economic effects; Ridker [157] is a good start. The study of economic costs in Steubenville is by I. Michelson and B. Tourin ("Comparative Method for Studying Cost of Air Pollution," *Public Health Report* 81, 6, June 1966, pp. 505–511). The survey of agricultural damage by the California Agriculture Department is published as *A Survey and Assessment of Air Pollution Damage to California Vegetation in 1970,* EPA Publication No. APTD–0694, June 1971. Ultimately, the best source will probably be the series of annual EPA Economic Reports to Congress [107–111]; the first ones, however, still lack a consistent estimating procedure.

6

MEASURING AIR POLLUTION

EPA-Documerica, Marc St. Gil

INTRODUCTION

Except smoke or haze, which are actually visible, the only way to detect the presence of typical levels of pollutants in the air is by deliberately measuring to find them. This is one of the principal distinctions between our current, broad view of air pollution and the traditional focus on only the most obvious pollution. The practice of actually measuring air pollution is relatively new and dates from the early 1950s. As early as 1897, however, the Ringelmann chart was used in the United States to describe black smoke quantitatively, and in 1912 the Mellon Institute in Pittsburgh conducted a major study involving dustfall measurements. But most of the early air sampling and the development of air sampling methods were done in the context of industrial hygiene—measuring dusts and gases in indoor working environments, where levels are typically much higher.

In the late 1940s, Leslie Silverman, an industrial hygienist at the Harvard School of Public Health, adapted a filter sampler to gather the much larger volume of air needed to measure the lower quantities of particles in the ambient air, and with it launched the practice of measuring invisible pollutants. By the mid-1950s, Silverman's "high-volume" sampler was in common use, and the first program of measuring gaseous pollutants had been begun in Los Angeles County. As interest in air pollution developed through the 1960s and as more money became available, routine programs to sample the ambient air became increasingly more extensive and widespread, bringing knowledge inconceivable 20 years earlier.

However, many people now take the measurement process for granted —we subconsciously think, "Just go measure it" and then direct our concern to other aspects of the problem. Unfortunately, however, this attitude is unwarranted, and therefore one of the purposes of this chapter is to present enough of the complexities of the measurement process so that we can dissociate measurements of air pollutants from some of the simpler measurements we make with a ruler or a bathroom scale. On the other hand, since there is so much to say on the subject of measurement, anyone who ultimately becomes much involved in the study of air pollution will quite likely pursue the complexities at some depth. Consequently, here we'll omit most of the details and concentrate on an overview with just a few examples, hoping to provide not only an understanding of present practice, but also a broad, conceptual framework.

Actually, we'll speak in terms of two frameworks into which we can fit the various measurement methods. One relatively abstract one involves the three basic steps of measurement: gathering an air sample, separating the pollutant, and then measuring its amount. The other framework, a much more visible one, involves the three basic types of measurement devices, or "sensors": static sensors, mechanical devices with pumps and piping and other moving parts, and automatic equipment.

In addition, there are two quite different situations in which the measurement of pollution is generally undertaken. One of these is the measurement of pollutants in the effluent from a pollution source, generally a smokestack, and hence is known as stack sampling. Stack sampling is carried on to provide information on what pollutants and in what quantities are emitted from various sources. The other situation, measuring pollution in the ambient outdoor atmosphere, views pollution from the receptors' point of view—regardless of its source or how long it has been in the air—what amount of pollution we are currently breathing. This provides a measurement known as the ambient pollution level, or in more positive terms, the ambient air quality.

A Conceptual View

Although there are many differences among various measurement methods, there are also important similarities, the most prominent of which is the set of basic measurement steps we mentioned earlier. Three distinct steps in the measurement process can be readily isolated; first, the collection of a measured sample of air from the air mass we're interested in; second, the separation of the pollutant substance from the remainder of the air sample; and third, the measurement of the amount, or quantity, of the pollutant substance. With a few exceptions, all the measurement methods in common use involve these three steps.

The first basic function, collecting the air sample, involves two physical operations—the removal of a sample of the air from its natural locale into a collecting device and the measurement of the size of the sample. The devices generally used in collecting the sample, sometimes called "air movers," are just pumps or fans. The choice of a particular device depends on the amount of air to be moved and the pressure or vacuum against which it's to be moved. The only special requirement is that pollutant samples always be collected on the upstream side of the air mover, so that the air flows through the sampling and analytical equipment first, before passing on out through the pump; this avoids any contamination of the sample by the pump.

In contrast with the simplicity of just moving a sample of air, measuring the amount we've moved is more complex. The volume of air in the sample is generally determined from the rate of air flow, or volume of air flowing per unit time, and the length of time it is flowing. The air flow rate is clearly the more difficult of the two measurements; it is generally determined by placing some constriction in the path of the air, measuring the difference in the air pressure before and after the constriction, and then using this pressure difference to determine the flow rate. Although this procedure sounds complicated, the principles of fluid mechanics on which it's based are well developed, and the procedure is routine. Nonetheless, it does suggest the complexity that is possible, with several measurements and calculations involved before we can begin to consider the pollutant itself.

Before we can measure the pollutant, we must usually separate it from the air sample, although this step is omitted with some automatic instruments. The separation of two substances from each other is accomplished by exploiting some difference in their properties; in the logical extreme, if there's no difference in their properties, they're not really different substances. In practice, of course, the most common separation techniques are based on the most obvious differences, although some of the newer, more complicated automatic instruments are based on some very subtle properties of the chemicals involved. The primary point of emphasizing separation techniques as a discrete step, however, is to note that the philosophy and techniques of separation used here are the same as those used to separate a pollutant from an airstream for purposes of emission control; the only real differences are in the size and cost of the equipment.

The third basic step, measuring the amount of the pollutant after it has been separated from the air sample, involves several techniques, ranging from the simple weighing of particulate pollutants, through various chemical analyses of the gases, to quite sophisticated physical methods used in some of the automatic instruments.

Basic Types of Sensors

The second frame of reference we want to establish before we consider specific measurement methods involves the type of measuring device, or sensor. The equipment and instruments used for measuring pollutants are readily classified into three groups on the basis of the functions they perform and their method of operation. The simplest ones are called static sensors, or static monitors; this group includes, for instance, the dustfall jar described in Chapter 3. The "static" devices have no moving parts and do not require electric power or human supervision. These features, along with their intrinsically low cost, are also their primary advantages. Unlike static equipment, the second group of sensors, mechanized samplers, operate by means of mechanical pumps and therefore require electric power and physical shelter.

Both the static and mechanized samplers, however, perform only the sample-collecting and pollutant-separating functions; the pollutant-analysis step is conducted in a laboratory. The third type of equipment, automatic sample-analyzers, or automatic instruments, can perform the analysis automatically, as well as gather the air sample and separate the pollutant from the air sample. Human operators receive the instrument's analysis in the form of a number or an electric signal.

In the next three sections we'll discuss the principal measurement methods used for the six major pollutants, emphasizing those that EPA has designated as "reference methods." We'll consider static and mechanized equipment together—first for particulates and then for gaseous pollutants—and then discuss automatic instruments. Finally, we'll consider stack sampling. Since the methods of collecting the air sample are similar, our discussion will focus on ways of separating and measuring the pollutants.

MEASURING PARTICULATE POLLUTION IN THE AMBIENT AIR

Separation Techniques

All techniques for separating solid particles from the air are based on the fact that the size and mass of the particles are many times larger than the gas molecules with which they ride. The two most common techniques are filtration, which focuses on the size of the particles, and inertial separation, which is based on the mass of the particles.

Essentially, filtration is the drawing of air through a substance, a filter media, which is constructed so that the smaller gas molecules can pass on through while the particles are caught. Most filter media are made of woven or compressed fibers—cloth, paper, or fiberglass. Unlike a window screen, with its pattern of fibers and holes, most filter media have a jumbled mass of fibers with convoluted, tortuous passages between them, through which the particles must pass if they are to escape.

Inertial devices can be somewhat more complex, but they all operate on the principle that when a stream of air is forced to turn a sharp corner, the lighter gas molecules turn more readily than the heavier particles do. Therefore, the particles are thrown to the outside of the turn, much as a car passenger is when the car goes around a curve.

Sampling Devices

The variety of devices for measuring particulate pollution includes at least one of each of the three basic types—static, mechanical, and automatic, although each measures particles of different sizes. The only static monitor, the dustfall jar, measures only the largest particles, those large enough to fall under the influence of gravity. Thus, the dustfall jar produces a unique measure of pollution and cannot be used as a cheap substitute for a hi-vol. The only automatic sampler-analyzer in common use for particulates also measures only particles in a particular size range, in this case, the smallest.

The vast majority of all particulate sampling is done with mechanized devices that gather the air sample and separate the particulates, leaving them for subsequent analysis. In fact, as we've already noted, most of the data on particulate pollution are gathered by a standard high-volume filter sampler very similar to the one originally developed by Dr. Silverman. This particular arrangement of filter media, filter holder, shelter shape, and so on, has become so standardized as the means of measuring the suspended portion of the particulate matter that it must be essentially considered the definition of "suspended particulate matter." This sampler, universally known as the "hi-vol," is illustrated in Fig. 6–1. The hi-vol consists of an 8-by-10-inch glass fiber filter held horizontally in a shelter of standard size and shape; air is pulled through by a rather powerful (and noisy) vacuum-cleaner-type motor. The hi-vol was first used extensively by the federal occupational health program, before the beginning of the federal air pollution program. The hi-vol was first used around 1950, and in 1953 a routine ambient air sampling program was begun; this program was the forerunner of the present National Air Surveillance

Fig. 6–1. The high-volume air sampler, or "hi-vol." A vacuum cleaner motor pulls air through a filter paper 8 x 10 inches and made of glass fiber; a shelter holds the sampler with the filter on top, forcing the air to come in under the eaves and then down through the filter and out the bottom. (Plain Dealer photo)

Network (NASN). The researchers experimented with the hi-vol and slightly modified it, and it has been in consistent use by the NASN since 1957. It is available commercially and has been widely adopted by state and local pollution control agencies.

The hi-vol is so named because it collects a much larger sample of air than was possible before its development, in order to get reliable measurements in the ambient air, where the particulate matter concentrations are much lower than in indoor industrial environments. The hi-vol is typically operated for 24 hours at a sampling rate of 40 to 60 cubic feet of air per minute; this gives samples of about 70,000 cubic feet, equivalent to 25 to 30 times the volume of a 15-by-20-foot classroom. If the suspended particulate level were 100 $\mu g/m^3$, it would gather about 27 milligrams of particles, or about a thousandth of an ounce.

The hi-vol dominates the outdoor sampling field; whenever a measurement of suspended particulate matter is referred to, it is almost invariably gathered by a hi-vol. This dominance has been made official; the EPA has defined the hi-vol as the "reference method" for setting national air quality standards for suspended particulate matter.

There are, however, some special occasions when the hi-vol, with its glass fiber filter, cannot be used. One such situation occurs when a specific chemical substance within the particulate matter is to be measured. If the substance occurs in high concentrations in the glass fiber filter medium, such sampling cannot be very precise. The usual recourse in this situation is to use a membrane filter medium, a manufactured organic substance with no inorganic chemical contamination. But since the membrane filter has such a very fine pore size, a much more powerful pump is needed to draw even a small flow of air. Therefore, membrane filter samplers often need to be run for longer periods of time, perhaps several days, to collect enough particulate matter for analysis, and it's for this reason that they haven't replaced the glass fiber filters.

Another special situation occurs when the particulate matter is to be separated into various size ranges or size fractions. In this case, of course, a filter can't be used at all, since it gathers all particles indiscriminately in one pile. All of the samplers available to gather fractional samples work on inertial principles. The simplest outdoor-type instrument is a cascade, or sequential, impactor, with five or more stages, each producing a separate sample, as illustrated in Fig. 6–2.

Analysis

Once the suspended particles have been separated from the air, the analysis step—measuring the amount of the particulate matter gathered—consists simply of weighing it. The weighing of the filter would seem to be, and is,

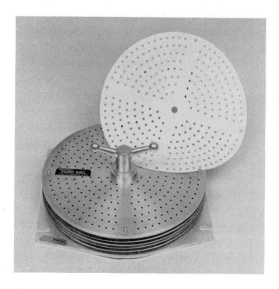

Fig. 6–2. Andersen impactor. (Photograph courtesy Andersen 2000, Inc.)

one of the simplest possible lab determinations, but the procedure does have problems and special aspects. Since the particles can't be removed from the filter, we have to weigh the entire filter; in order to get just the weight of the particulate matter, we must have first weighed the clean filter, so that we can subtract its weight. Finally, we have to number or otherwise label the filters, in order to keep track of the before and after weights.

Both of the weighings can be done on any laboratory balance or scale capable of weighing such small weights accurately, but really good technique requires that some extra precautions be taken. If we fold the clean filter, the crease will cause the air to flow through it unevenly; thus, at least for 8-by-10-inch filters such as a hi-vol uses, it is best to have a balance with a special rack to hold the large, unfolded sheet. There is less concern about folding the dirty filter—that doesn't cause any harm.

The special effort involved in weighing the soiled filter derives from the nature of the particulates collected. Many substances in the air are hygroscopic, that is, they attract moisture from the air to themselves; this means that when the humidity is high, a noticeable amount of water may be added to the weight of the dirty filter, giving an erroneously high measurement of the amount of particulate pollution. This problem can be avoided by keeping the filters in a humidity-controlled weighing room or storage box for a day or two before the final weighing or by not doing any weighing when the relative humidity is more than about 50 or 60%.

Precautions such as this, familiar to the analytical chemist, are easily overlooked by the nonchemist. They are quite necessary, however, since the overall accuracy of our pollutant measuring systems is just not great enough at the present for us to be very careless with any portion of the process. With these precautions, the hi-vol is actually one of the most precise of the common measurement methods. If the hi-vol is run and maintained carefully, the suspended particulate values are reproducible with 3–5 $\mu g/m^3$ in a typical urban atmosphere of over 100 $\mu g/m^3$; this figure is about 3 or 4% precision, which is quite good. In routine, casual use the figure is closer to 10%, which is still fairly good.

MEASURING GASES IN THE AMBIENT AIR

Measuring ambient concentrations of gaseous pollutants is quite different from, and much more complicated than, measuring particulate levels. Separating gaseous pollutants from the other gases in the air requires methods totally different from those used for particulates. Although the size and mass of the molecules of the various gases differ, these differences are not large enough to warrant the engineering of a reasonably cheap and simple separation device based on them. Conceptually, however, it can be done; a gaseous diffusion plant enriches nuclear fuel based on a mass difference of 1% between the two types of uranium, but air pollution doesn't have that kind of priority yet.

Separation Techniques

The two types of separation methods used to separate gases from the air bear the confusingly similar names "adsorption" and "absorption." Adsorption techniques, the less common, are based on the tendency of gases to stick to the surface of solids. Granular, porous solids with a very large surface area, such as activated charcoal and silica gel, can be used to collect gases by adsorption. Although such solids are commonly used for cleaning unwanted gases from an airstream, they're not used much for pollutant measurements, because after the gas has collected on the solid, it isn't easy to remove it again to measure it. Only one area of instrumental application, gas chromatographic techniques for hydrocarbons, makes use of adsorption principles.

The second, and much more common, technique, the absorption of the gas in a liquid, is closely related to the actual chemical measurement of the amount of pollutant; both are ultimately determined by the chemical properties of the pollutant gas. As opposed to physical properties such as size and mass, the chemical properties of a certain chemical compound are those involving its reaction with other chemicals, what products are formed in the reactions, and so on; these chemical properties determine how the pollutant is measured and whether the measurement is done with mechanized sampling equipment or with automatic instruments.

Sampling Methods

Both mechanized samplers and automatic sampler-analyzers are used to collect samples of gaseous pollutants, and often the chemical analysis in the automatic instrument is the same as the lab analysis of the sample collected with the mechanical apparatus. The principal mechanical sampler for gaseous pollutants is a liquid impinger system, which is also known as a bubbler. This instrument is based on the principle of gaseous absorption in a liquid. Air is pulled, or "bubbled," for a fixed length of time through a test tube containing the proper chemicals, and then the test tube is taken to the laboratory for analysis. With the appropriate timing mechanisms, one can collect a sample for a 24-hour period, or collect 12 two-hour samples with an arrangement of 12 bubblers. This latter arrangement is usually called a sequential sampler, as the various bubblers are used one by one in predetermined sequence. Bubbler equipment is largely the same for any pollutant, the difference being the various absorbing reagents as defined by the appropriate chemistry.

Another mechanized sampling technique that is sometimes appropriate is known by the somewhat inelegant name "bag sampling." Bag sampling is just using a pump to gather a sample of air into a large plastic bag or into some bottlelike container and then taking it back to a laboratory for analysis. This technique is mentioned here primarily because the removal of the air sample from the air mass being tested is such a clear-cut, obvious operation. Bag sampling is used most frequently to gather air samples in places where the operation of mechanical sampling equipment would be difficult, e.g., collecting CO samples from the inside of a car moving in traffic or from a crowded, downtown street corner. This technique is also used to gather research samples for the analysis of gaseous pollutants like the complicated hydrocarbons involved in photochemical smog, which requires delicate equipment that couldn't be used outdoors.

Wet Chemical Analysis

The more difficult part of measuring gaseous pollutants is analyzing the sample that has been gathered. There are two broad types of methods, based on the gases' chemical and physical properties, respectively. Some automatic instruments utilize the physical properties—not simple size and weight, but much more subtle properties, such as the ability of the gas to absorb infrared radiation or microwaves. Most gaseous pollutant analysis, however, is still done with the chemical methods.

The chemical methods used to analyze for gaseous pollutants are often called "wet chemical" methods because the reactions among the chemicals, called reagents, take place in a beaker, test tube, or flask of water. The pollutants are first dissolved in the water in a bubbler containing one of the chemical reagents. After the bubblers have been returned from the field, other reagent chemicals are added, depending on the particular chemical scheme.

The ultimate purpose of any analysis scheme is to form a new chemical compound that can be separated from the water or otherwise distinguished in some way. The simplest example is the formation of a new compound that doesn't stay dissolved in the water, but rather settles out as a solid substance, a precipitate, which can be separated and weighed to determine the amount of pollutant originally present. This technique, called gravimetric because gravity separates the precipitate from the water, is very common in analytical chemistry. It is not very commonly used for the analysis of air pollutants, however, because the very small amounts of pollutant chemical normally present make weighing rather delicate and imprecise. Rather, most of the wet chemical methods are based on producing a compound that can be measured directly in the water. The most common method is colorimetry, the sensing of the pollutant amount as an intensity of color in the water. Such an analysis requires the use of chemical reagents that will react with the pollutant to form a colored compound in proportion to the amount of pollutant present, as well as a reference or standard for determining the amount of pollutant from the intensity of color.

Sulfur dioxide. A variety of methods of chemical analysis exists, and we'll present a brief discussion of some of the methods commonly used for the major gaseous pollutants. Of the gaseous pollutants, sulfur dioxide has been studied the most, and consequently several chemical methods have been developed for analyzing it. The federal "reference method" for SO_2 is the modified West-Gaeke method, named after the men who developed it. It is a colorimetric method, and just as an example, we'll specify the chemicals involved. In the West-Gaeke method, the bubbler used to absorb the SO_2 from the air is filled with sodium tetrachloromercurate. This compound reacts with SO_2 to form dichlorosulfitromercurate ions, which stay in solution in the water until the sample is returned to the lab. There, formaldehyde and pararosaniline dye are added, and they react to form pararosaniline methylsulfonic acid, which has a red-purple color that can be measured in a colorimeter and compared to data produced by known amounts of SO_2. The "modified" in the name of the method refers to some minor improvements over the basic method; they make it more complicated, and so we'll ignore them here, but they do provide a vehicle for introducing and distinguishing between two other concepts related to analytical methods: specificity and interferences.

The West-Gaeke method is said to be "specific for SO_2," meaning that it will react only to SO_2 and not, for instance, to sulfur trioxide (SO_3). This is of interest because not all analytical methods are precisely specific for the compounds intended, and it does seem important to know just what one is measuring. As an example, we'll consider the other major method historically used for SO_2, the conductometric method. It is based on the fact that SO_2 dissolves in water to form an acid; such an acid is ionized in the water, and the ions increase the ability of the water to pass an electric current. The sensing method, then, is to measure the change in the amount of electric current when SO_2 is absorbed. This method is not specific for SO_2, however; it will react to anything in the air that will ionize in water. There are a number of gases that fit this description, but since SO_2 is usually the only one found in any great quantity, the method at least approximately represents SO_2.

The other concept—interferences—is slightly different. A chemical method is said to have interferences, or to suffer from interferences, if some extraneous substance is able to take part in the reaction and thereby cause an erroneous result. In the West-Gaeke method, ozone and NO_2 can interfere by destroying some of the colored dye, so that the amount of SO_2 appears to be less than it really is; this is called a negative interference. In other situations, a positive interference can occur, with some substance adding to the results, thereby giving a falsely high determination. Much of the superiority of one wet chemical method over another is a matter of the degree of interferences and the ease with which they are overcome. The modifications of the West-Gaeke method mentioned above were made in order to control such interferences.

Nitrogen oxides. In measuring the other major gases, mechanized sampling and wet chemistry are much less common; instead, there is a far greater reliance on automatic instruments. There are two chemical methods in use for nitrogen dioxide. Both of them are colorimetric, and both are named after the men who developed them. The Griess-Saltzman method is used if the color sample can be measured very shortly after the reagent has been added, either in a very few hours in a laboratory or in a few minutes in an automatic instrument. If the sample is to be gathered over a 24-hour period, will be mailed to a central lab, or for some other reason cannot be analyzed rapidly, the color formed by the Griess-Saltzman reagent will fade badly; in such cases it is better to use the Jacobs-Hochheiser method. This method uses a different set of reagents to preserve the sample for a length of time and then analyzes it by a similar colorimetric reaction.

Although these two methods have been around for a long time, neither is completely satisfactory for mechanized sampling. NO_2 does not dissolve readily in water; when it does, two different ions, nitrite and nitrate, are formed in only partially known proportions. Thus, in calculating the results, one must adjust the values by empirical "fudge" factors, which results in inaccuracies. All told, bubbler sampling for NO_2 leaves much to be desired. In fact, in 1972 EPA was forced to publicly suspend for a year its entire NO_2 abatement program; the assumptions about the percent of the NO_2 absorbed were found to be seriously wrong, and years of data had to be re-evaluated.

At the present there are no measurement methods for nitric oxide, NO, as such; all the measurements are made by first converting (oxidizing) NO to NO_2 and then measuring the NO_2 by one of the methods described above. This introduces another nontrivial chemical reaction, the oxidation step, which just adds to the complexity of the analysis; consequently, very little mechanized sampling for NO is ever done.

Photochemical oxidant. Although photochemical oxidant can be measured with bubblers and lab chemistry, it rarely is. The reagent used to measure the oxidant is important, because the very definition of oxidant depends on it. Oxidants are those substances that will oxidize a certain substance, the reagent, under certain conditions. The use of potassium iodide, KI, as reagent is the most common; when the KI reagent is exposed to the oxidant in the air, some of the iodide is converted into molecular iodine, with its characteristic color; the color is then measured with a colorimeter. There are other ways of sensing the amount of iodine produced, and there are other reagents that can be used, but all of the methods have drawbacks. There are substances in the air, notably SO_2, that interfere by pushing the reactions backward. In addition, the methods don't agree with one another, not only because they measure different things, but also because they just don't work well by themselves. The need for better wet chemistry techniques is probably the greatest here.

Carbon monoxide and hydrocarbons. The other two major gaseous pollutants, carbon monoxide and hydrocarbons, are not measured at all by wet chemical techniques; no procedures have been developed, and it seems unlikely that any will be. CO and hydrocarbons are generally measured with automatic instruments, but both can also be measured by the simplest techniques, bag sampling and lab analysis, if necessary. The lab analysis of CO gathered in bags is done by infrared absorption; the analysis of hydrocarbons, by gas chromatography. Both of these methods are also used in automatic instruments; in fact, the lab analysis is often done on the same type of automatic instruments that are used for ambient monitoring.

Static Sensors

The static sensors available for sulfur oxides are based on contacting the SO_x containing air with lead peroxide and measuring the amount of lead sulfate formed. The results are reported as the amount of sulfate per area of exposed surface, often called a sulfation index, and are interpreted as an approximate indicator of overall sulfur pollution, including some particulate sulfate which adheres to the surface. There are two types of sensors, the traditional "lead candles," in which the lead peroxide paste is smeared on a piece of gauze on a glass tube, and the newer "lead plates," which are much easier to use. The latter type is illustrated in Fig. 6–3.

These types of sensors are often used because they are relatively cheap; they require no mechanical equipment, electric power, or supervision. They must be considered, however, along with the dustfall jar, as measuring an effect of pollution rather than actual pollutant concentrations. Because there is no specific volume of air to which they can be referred, the resulting numbers become more a property of the site, the physical location, than of the air. That is, a sulfation measurement does not indicate how much SO_x is present in a certain parcel of air, but rather how much was found at a specific location from whatever air happened to be passing along. How-

Fig. 6–3. Lead plate. (Photograph courtesy Doerfer Laboratories)

ever, we should draw a distinction between dustfall and sulfation measurements. Although the dustfall jar measures a distinct size range of particulate pollution not otherwise measured, the lead candle really offers no more than an approximation to other information, and its use can be justified only on grounds of cost.

There are no static sensors for other gaseous pollutants, although static devices are sometimes used to monitor pollutant effects. These devices include various types of small metal plates to measure corrosion, etc. They are useful tools, but as with dustfall, are fully useful only when differences can be compared among identical sensing units. This type of effect measurement would be more useful if a standardized form could be established, but this is unlikely to happen, as the sensors are relatively unglamorous.

AUTOMATIC SAMPLER-ANALYZERS

The most complicated, expensive type of ambient air sampling equipment is the automatic sampler-analyzer, so named because it performs both the sampling and analysis steps automatically, without direct human intervention. There are a great number and variety of such instruments; they draw in their own sample, perform the analysis, and then output the result as an electric current to a strip-chart recorder or some computer-compatible datalogging device, or sometimes both. Automatic instruments are available for measuring all the major pollutants, and little else. There are wet chemical instruments for NO_x, SO_2, and oxidants that are in wide use; instruments based on other sensing systems are used for CO and hydrocarbons.

These automatic sampler-analyzers are often called "continuous instruments" because they can operate without ever stopping; that is, in fact, a reasonably accurate description of how they are usually used. Here, however, we will use the term "continuous," as opposed to "intermittent," to refer to the way the equipment is scheduled to operate, rather than to the equipment itself. Automatic sampler-analyzers may be, and are, operated intermittently, and mechanized equipment, e.g., hi-vols and bubblers, may be, and are, scheduled to gather data continuously. We will use the phrase "automatic instruments" here.

Each automatic instrument consists of a box containing a number of pumps, pipes, and other components organized to perform the desired functions. Because the nature and appearance of the components vary greatly, the instruments often appear wildly complicated and vastly dissimilar. Actually, the visible aspects of the instruments are usually the least significant with respect to their function; more important are the operating parameters, such as speed of response and amount of drift, which depend on the design of the system, and general durability, which depends on the quality of the components.

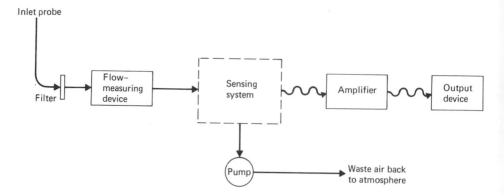

Fig. 6–4. Schematic diagram of an automatic instrument.

Despite these differences, there is much basic similarity among these instruments. Figure 6–4 is a schematic sketch of a typical automatic instrument. The air sample is drawn in through an inlet probe (a tube sticking outside the shelter) and then through a flow-measuring device, with possibly a filter in between. The flow measurement is made in order to determine the amount of air sampled; this quantity is usually selected in advance and then held constant. The filter is designed to keep particulate pollution from damaging the other parts of the system.

The sensing system is shown in Fig. 6–4 as a dashed box because it is not a single, fixed component, but varies widely depending on what pollutant the instrument is designed for and what sensing technique it is based on. Many methods of measuring the various pollutants can be worked into an automatic sensing system, with varying degrees of engineering problems. The only requirement is that the system produce an electrical signal in proportion to the pollutant concentration in the incoming airstream. The wavy arrows in Fig. 6–4 indicate that this electrical signal goes through an amplifier to an output device. The amplifier is used to increase the size of the faint electric signal until it's strong enough to operate the output device, which must move a pen, punch holes in a paper tape, record on magnetic tape, or quite often a combination of these.

Wet Chemical Instruments

Let us return now to the sensing system. The earliest instruments, as well as most of those still in use, use wet chemical analytical techniques—more or less the same ones used for bubbler sampling. Most of these instruments have many features in common, as illustrated schematically in Fig. 6–5. In wet chemical systems, liquid pumps pump the reagent(s) to a contact

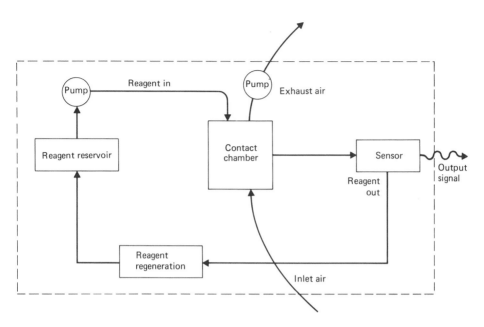

Fig. 6–5. Schematic flow diagram of wet chemical sensing system.

chamber, where the air and the chemicals are mixed, as in a bubbler; the air is drawn on out, and the reagent flows on to a sensor, which measures the change produced by the pollutant—the amount of color produced, the increase in electric conductivity, etc. The contact chamber is the heart of this type of instrument; conceptually, the contact chamber is like a bubbler tube, but with the liquid flowing continuously, as well as the air. Usually, the contact chamber is a length of glass or plastic tubing; often, it's coiled like a spring to squeeze a longer tube, which allows longer air-liquid contact, into a smaller space.

Nitrogen oxides. The wet chemical instruments for oxides of nitrogen utilize the Griess-Saltzman colorimetric method, since the color is produced within 15–20 minutes of sampling and then analyzed immediately. Such instruments can be used for NO, NO_2, or both combined—NO_x—although the basic instrument measures only NO_2, as that is what reacts with the Griess-Saltzman reagent. If the air is first passed through a step to oxidize the NO, the instrument will measure both as though they were NO_2, giving data on total NO_x. To measure NO alone, one must use two instruments. One way is to measure both NO_2 and total NO_x and then subtract the results to get NO; another way is to have one instrument remove and measure the NO_2, oxidize the NO that is left to NO_2, and then send the air through the other instrument to measure the NO_2 again. Either method, of course, suffers from the additional uncertainties caused by the subtraction or the extra oxidation.

Sulfur dioxide. There are several automatic instruments for monitoring sulfur dioxide; the most common, because they've been around the longest, are based on the conductometric principle. The chemistry of the conductometric method is well suited to automatic instruments, but since it is not specific for SO_2, the measure is only approximate at best. More recently, an instrument based on the reference method, West-Gaeke, has been developed and is rapidly becoming common.

Oxidants. A number of wet chemical instruments are available for analyzing either ozone or total oxidants. The most commonly used are instruments based on the potassium iodide method mentioned previously. Most of the other instruments were sold and used as ozone instruments until subsequent research and experience showed that they weren't specific for ozone. Nonetheless, until very recently, almost all of the data gathered were obtained with one of these wet chemical instruments and hence are really total oxidant data. More recently, however, new instruments that are highly specific for ozone have been developed, and one of these has been designated as the EPA reference method.

The reason for using ozone-specific instruments, knowing that they fail to include such other oxidants as PAN, is primarily a matter of interferences. Any method that makes use of the oxidizing properties of the oxidants to measure them will suffer interference from reducing agents in the air, chemicals that reverse the oxidation reaction in the instrument to give erroneously low readings. The principal culprit in this regard is SO_2, which is widespread enough to cause serious problems. The interference caused by SO_2 can be partly avoided by trying to chemically treat the incoming air to remove the SO_2, but this in turn causes a new interference problem involving NO, and the overall result is a series of empirical fudge factors. Therefore, the availability of an ozone-specific method that doesn't depend on oxidation begins to look quite attractive.

The point of this experience, however, has wider applicability than to just oxidant measurement. Nothing is gained by adapting a wet chemical method subject to some interferences or other analytical difficulties to an expensive, fancy, automatic instrument; the problem of interference will remain, and the volume of data produced won't allow one to make even approximate mental allowances for the interference. Therefore, the automatic instruments adapted from older wet chemical methods are in several instances being replaced by more sophisticated instruments, those based on the physical rather than chemical properties of the specific molecules of interest.

Physical Methods

In discussing these physically based instruments, we'll focus on the sensing system, the core of the instrument (see Fig. 6–5). Such instruments, of course, also have all the other components, and in fact often require more elaborate electronics and perhaps switching mechanisms to permit them to monitor more than one pollutant. Physically based instruments are therefore usually more expensive than wet chemical instruments.

The instrument that led us into this discussion initially was the ozone-specific instrument that EPA has designated the reference method for oxidants. This instrument is based on a chemiluminescent mechanism, the ability of certain gases to give off minute amounts of light when stimulated by another gaseous reagent. The ozone-specific instrument is based on the reaction between ozone and ethylene, whereas the reaction of atmospheric NO with ozone as a reagent forms the basis for a chemiluminescent NO instrument.

There are also a variety of other physical techniques under development or in trial use. Some of these techniques promise significant improvement in overall monitoring capabilities, and many represent "fallout" from space-age research into materials and remote-sensing mechanisms. Here, however, we will discuss at some length only the techniques that pick up the last two major pollutants—infrared spectroscopy as used for monitoring CO and gas chromatography as used for hydrocarbons.

IR spectroscopy and carbon monoxide. The word spectroscopy refers to measuring things by dispersing them in a spectrum or by observing them at their particular point in a spectrum or range of some property. In optical spectroscopy the spectrum is of electromagnetic radiation (Fig. 5–4) or a part of it, usually near the range of visible light. Infrared spectroscopy is the most common type of spectroscopy, although ultraviolet instruments are available, and techniques based on the microwave portion of the spectrum are being developed.

All of these spectroscopy techniques derive from the fact that molecules of various gases, including the pollutants, can absorb radiation selectively, that is, absorb only radiation of certain wavelengths that are characteristic of the gas. The instruments compare the amount of the characteristic radiation absorbed by an air sample to that absorbed by some clean reference air and calculate the concentration of the gas in question. Some instrument techniques, called dispersive, break the spectrum up and send only one narrow band of wavelengths through the sample to the detector; by changing the wavelength used, such an instrument can be adjusted to monitor several gases that have different absorption bands. More common, however, are the nondispersive instruments that send a fairly broad spectrum of wavelengths through the sample; the detector on nondispersive instruments is designed to measure the pollutant of interest, so they are typically limited to one pollutant.

Actually, the only truly common spectroscopic technique is the nondispersive infrared (NDIR) measurement of carbon monoxide; the NDIR method, the federal reference method for CO, is essentially the only method in significant use. The method involves sending infrared light through two tubes—a sample cell and a reference cell—to a detector at the other end. The detector has two compartments, each filled with a very high concentration of CO, which absorbs most of the infrared radiation that comes through the two cells. The amount of infrared radiation coming through the sample cell, however, has been lessened by the amount absorbed by the CO in the sample; therefore, the two halves of the detector receive different amounts of radiation. The cell receiving more radiation is warmed more, which in turn increases the pressure, and it is this pressure difference that is measured.

The conceptual neatness of this oversimplified discussion shouldn't deceive us, however. Though in common use, the NDIR CO instruments can have serious problems with interferences. Both CO_2 and water vapor absorb IR radiation at wavelengths close to that absorbed by CO, and this causes trouble. Typically, the sample is drawn through a drying agent to remove the water, and the CO_2 effect is minimized by narrowing the band width of the infrared source to more precisely concentrate on the CO absorption wavelengths. Despite these problems, however, the CO instruments are probably better than the wet chemical instruments for some of the other pollutants.

Hydrocarbons and methane. Hydrocarbons, the last major pollutant, are measured only by automatic instruments, those using a method called flame ionization detection, or FID, which is the federal reference method. The instrument has a small flame of burning hydrogen, into which the air stream is introduced. In these circumstances, the burning of an organic hydrocarbon molecule in the flame produces an ion for each carbon atom burned, and the total of the ions can be directly measured as an electric current. Such an instrument thus measures all hydrocarbons indiscriminately and produces data on what we have called "total hydrocarbons." Total-hydrocarbon instruments have been operated since the 1950s and early 1960s by the Los Angeles County District and federal government and more recently by most of the larger control agencies. As we noted in Chapter 3, the preferred practice since the late 1960s has been to also monitor methane, the simplest specific hydrocarbon; one then subtracts the methane from the total measurement to get "nonmethane hydrocarbons," a measurement that is more useful for describing the potential of the hydrocarbon levels to produce photochemical smog.

In discussing the measurement of methane, however, we will be invading the outskirts of a measurement technique called gas chromatography; although FID isn't really a gas chromatographic method, it is close, and the method for measuring methane is even closer. Beyond this, since gas chromatography is used extensively in more research-oriented programs which distinguish among the various hydrocarbons and is being proposed as a sophisticated instrumentation method for pollutant monitoring, it's worth a short digression.

Chromatography refers to the process of separating closely related substances by their differing rates of diffusion through some medium. The name "chromatography" comes from the fact that when substances of different colors are separated, they form a rainbowlike display, with parallel bands of the different colors. Gas chromatography is one of a variety of techniques only loosely related to the original situations in which color was involved. Here, a sample (of air, in our case) is put into a stream of "carrier" gas, which is being drawn into the instrument through a long tube filled with an absorbent substance called a "packed column." Because of their different physical properties, different substances have different rates of diffusion through the column, so that some come out the other end first, and others follow in a certain order. As used in many applications, the gas flow out of the column is then passed through a detector, either a flame ionization detector or one of several others, which measures the quantity of hydrocarbon coming past at a given instant. Thus, over the period of time required for the entire sample to pass through the column, the detector measures a concentration peak as each of the different hydrocarbons comes through in turn. Since the different substances always come through in the same length of time, depending on the column packing and the carrier gas, each peak can be identified; the concentration can be determined from the size of the peak, using the area under it rather than just its height.

This type of chromatographic analysis of an air sample is the backbone of research into the various chemical reactions involved in photochemical smog, for instance. Although atmospheric levels of CO and SO_2 can be measured by such techniques, they rarely are, partly because the instruments are so delicate that field operation is difficult and partly because the time lag, or cycle time, makes it impossible to run such an instrument in a truly continuous way.

The way in which this type of technique does arise in measuring air quality is in the technique for measuring methane, which is accomplished by a regular FID hydrocarbon instrument with an adsorptive column on the sample inlet. This column is filled with activated charcoal that has been saturated with methane so that its capacity to adsorb methane is used up, though it is still able to capture other hydrocarbons. Thus, when placed on the front of the instrument, the charcoal adsorbs the others and lets only the methane pass on into the instrument, which then measures it just as though it were a normal atmospheric mixture of hydrocarbons and produces a methane measurement. Later, one can subtract the methane value from the total hydrocarbon value to obtain the concentration of nonmethane hydrocarbons.

Particulate matter. Throughout this section we have used the phrase automatic instrument as though it applied only to gaseous pollutants, and this is very nearly true. The federal reference method for suspended particulate matter is the hi-vol sampler, and that's how most sampling is done. There are two ways, however, that one can monitor particulates automatically; one can use a spot-tape sampler or a new, sophisticated instrument.

The tape sampler, which operates with a roll of filter paper tape, pulls a sample air stream through one area of the tape for a period of time and then advances the tape to a new area, creating a series of circular, dirty spots on the tape. The instrument is generally run for two hours at a spot before it is advanced, thus producing 12 two-hour average numbers a day. The provision of short-term data and the automatic nature of the data collection are the tape sampler's primary advantages. However, since the spot on the filter paper contains such a relatively small mass of particulate matter, an analysis can't be made by weighing, and the tape sampler can't provide mass-per-volume-of-air data. Rather, the analysis is made by measuring the transmission of light through the soiled spot and comparing it to the transmission through an adjacent clean area. The data are then expressed as a "coefficient of haze," or COH data. Because the measurement depends on light, the surface area of the collected particles is more important than their mass; thus, COH data tend to reflect primarily the smaller particles that are gathered, since they have a larger area for their mass than do larger particles. COH data therefore don't correlate well with hi-vol data.

Although not yet in routine use, there is a sophisticated new instrument that makes automatic measurements of particulate mass concentrations. This instrument operates in a manner analogous to that of the tape sampler, gathering a sample for a fixed, short period of time, measuring it, and moving on. Rather than measuring the amount of light absorbed, however, this new device measures the absorption of beta radiation from an internal radioactive source. Since the beta absorption is proportional to the mass of the particles collected, rather than to their size, shape, or color, the data correlate well with hi-vol measurements.

Utilization of Automatic Instruments

One of the most important reasons for using automatic instruments is that no other method is available for measuring and analyzing some pollutants. In addition, they give us much more data, over a shorter time period, and can be run without a chemistry laboratory. On the other hand, automatic instruments require electronics technicians and similar personnel to act as repairmen, calibrators, and maintenance providers, and one can't get much true information out of their data without a computerized data-processing system. Automatic instruments are of relatively recent vintage, and they are not up to the reliability levels of the space program; most of them need a shakedown period, relatively careful watching, and frequent maintenance. Thus, the need for chemists and a laboratory is replaced by the need for other personnel and equipment.

Almost all pollution control agencies use some automatic instruments, and the largest agencies have extensive systems of a dozen or more stations, each with automatic instruments for several pollutants. Some stations telemeter or automatically transmit the data to a central headquarters, where there is a central processing computer and perhaps some form of visual data display.

MEASURING POLLUTANTS AT THEIR SOURCE

Although most air pollution measurements are made in the ambient air, it is also important to be able to measure the amount of a pollutant coming out of a source. Since measuring pollution at its source ultimately comes down to measuring the pollutant concentration from an individual stack rather than from the entire plant, it is generally known by the phrase stack sampling.

There are several reasons why one might wish to measure pollutants in the effluent from the stack. The polluter may wish to study his production process to learn about his own pollution as a prelude to controlling it, or he may want to evaluate some pollutant control device by measuring the emissions with and without it. A governmental pollution control agency might wish to conduct stack sampling to either gather research information about the manufacturing process in question or verify that an emission standard, a legal limit on the emissions, is not being exceeded.

The collection of a sample of gases from a stack seems conceptually simple; we need only put in a piece of tubing or probe of some type and draw out the gases with a vacuum pump. This is, in fact, more or less what is done; however, complications and difficulties abound. First, gaining access to the stack can be difficult. Then, one needs to know the details of the operations of the source in order to choose the appropriate time of the day and week for sampling. Largely, however, the complexity arises from the

fact that conditions inside the stack are so very different from those outside, where the equipment and the people are. Stack gases are generally hot,
200° to 1500°F, and are usually moving very fast, thousands of feet per
minute. These conditions, especially the high temperature, cause difficulties
in collecting the sample and require a number of extra measurements, such
as the volume of gas flow and the moisture content, in order to permit expressing the results as a total mass of pollutant rather than as a concentration. Actually, in comparison to measurements of the ambient air quality,
the greatly increased complexity in getting the sample turns out to be the
biggest difference. Because of the higher concentrations of pollutant gases
found in a stack sample, the separation and analysis steps are much simpler,
and no special difficulties arise when ordinary wet chemical techniques are
used.

EXERCISES

Review Questions

1. When did air quality measurement begin to become common? What had
   been done before that?
2. What three basic steps of measurement were discussed?
3. Where should the air pump be put relative to the sampling equipment?
   Why?
4. Distinguish among the three types of measuring equipment described.
5. Identify two separation principles used for particulate matter. On what
   properties of the particles are they based?
6. What type of particulate sampling is most common? Why?
7. Under what circumstances would you need to use membrane filters?
8. What precautions should you take in weighing a soiled filter? A clean
   filter?
9. Identify the two general techniques used in separating gases from the air.
   Which is commonly used for measuring pollutants?
10. Describe the mechanized sampling equipment most commonly used for
    measuring gaseous pollutants.
11. What is "bag sampling"? When would you do it?
12. Describe in general terms the analysis scheme involved in colorimetric
    analysis methods.
13. What does the West-Gaeke method measure? In what type sampling equip-
    ment is it used?
14. Briefly explain the concepts of specificity and interference.
15. Why are there two different colorimetric methods for NO_2 in common use?
16. Describe the static sensors available for gaseous pollutants.
17. Distinguish between automatic and continuous sampling.
18. Considering an automatic instrument in a schematic sense, what is a sen-
    sing mechanism? What else must it have?

19. What is involved in a wet chemical sensing mechanism?
20. How is SO_2 related to the wet chemical sampling for photochemical oxidant?
21. What is a chemiluminescence instrument? What does it measure?
22. What is the standard method for CO based on? Sketch briefly how the instrument operates.
23. What does FID stand for? How does it operate?
24. When would an air pollution scientist need to use gas chromatographic measurement methods?
25. Outline the scheme used for obtaining methane measurements.
26. Describe the automatic instruments used for measuring suspended particulate matter.
27. Why might we want measurements of the amount of pollutants in stack gases?
28. What are the aspects of stack sampling that make gathering the sample the most difficult step?

Thought Questions

29. The use of the West-Gaeke wet-chemical procedure has been seen as a possible (small) water pollution problem. Can you figure out why?
30. Because of the close relationship between vehicular traffic and CO, it is difficult to decide on an appropriate location on a CO sensor—how near the roadway, etc. Why is the location of hydrocarbon sensors not considered a similar problem?
31. Can you offer a reason why having good wet chemical methods for bubbler sampling in addition to continuous automatic instruments is of more significance for oxidant than for other pollutants?
32. Consider a spot-tape sampler for particulate matter, recalling that particle size is important. It is possible to measure the dirty spots by the reflectance of light, producing data known as RUDS, Reflectance Units of Dirt Shade. If this were done, what other property of the collected particles would become important? How would this exaggerate the difference between the measured levels in the center city and rural areas?
33. In stack sampling for particulates, it is considered desirable to adjust the rate of flow through the sampling train so that the velocity of flow into the sampling probe is the same as the velocity of gas flow in the stack. This is known as isokinetic sampling. What happens if it isn't done?

Project Suggestions

34. There is of course a variety of projects possible utilizing air monitoring equipment if there is any available. One project involved directly with the mechanics of sampling involves consideration of hi-vol sampling times less than 24 hours. How well do two 12-hour values correlate with the standardized 24-hour value? Is airflow a factor? (Reduce airflow by reducing the power to the motor.)

FURTHER READING

In general, the more detailed discussions of both stack sampling and ambient measurement techniques are scattered through the technical journals; *Environmental Science and Technology* [173] is the best for specifically pollution-oriented measurement methods. The federal Criteria Documents for the major pollutants [23–28] discuss measurement methods and have good reference lists. Title 40 of the Code of Federal Regulations [122] collects EPA's various rules and regulations, including official sampling methods. The chapter by Morgan, Tabor, and Thompson in Mamantov and Shults [148] provides a brief history of ambient monitoring, with emphasis on the federal program. An article by Maugh [207] provides a good account of the shift in the basis used for continuous instruments from chemical to physical processes. For those of you who are interested in the engineering details of stack sampling, Stern [160] has several chapters.

7
MONITORING NETWORKS AND DATA ANALYSIS

Los Angeles Pollution Control District

Although the sampling methods and equipment described in Chapter 6 can be used to make isolated measurements or short-term studies of pollutant levels, most of the data on air quality are actually gathered as part of long-term, systematic, routine measurement efforts. These ongoing studies are usually called monitoring programs, and the array of sampling sites and equipment are known as monitoring networks. Almost every air pollution control agency operates a program of monitoring ambient air quality, as a part of its overall effort to maintain current information on the quality of the air in the area over which it has jurisdiction.

MONITORING NETWORKS

The extent of these monitoring efforts varies, primarily with the size and development of the geographical area in question. These areas range from small cities with one hi-vol and an SO_2 bubbler in the center of town, to major urban areas with a dozen or more sophisticated stations, each with automatic instruments for all the major gaseous pollutants. Most monitoring programs are similar—all require a field staff to gather the samples, exchange hi-vol filters, etc., laboratory capacity to analyze them, people to maintain and repair the equipment, and someone to handle the data. A small system of a few hi-vols and bubblers might be operated by one field man, a chemist, and a secretary, each mixing in other duties as well; a very large automated system would require several station operators, electronic technicians, instrumental chemists, computer systems analysts, and statisticians.

Beyond this obvious effect of size and wealth, the precise nature of the monitoring efforts of various pollution control agencies also depends somewhat on the nature of the urban area—its topography, the distribution of population, the nature and distribution of sources. The overall monitoring effort should be coherent, with the emphasis on systematic monitoring, to provide useful information rather than just data. The monitoring system should provide a number of different types of information. It should help identify the areas of highest pollution, provide an indication of the pollutant concentrations and their seasonal and long-term variations in the various geographical areas, and should also include some monitoring in relatively unpolluted areas in order to guard against unexpected increases there. In accomplishing these various goals, within cost constraints, an agency has various choices to make—how many samplers to have, the mix of the three basic types, where to put them, and how often to run them.

Most networks are a mixture of the three types of instruments which we defined earlier—static, mechanized, and automatic—simply because each type provides something that the others do not. Any network beyond the very smallest should include at least one automatic instrument or sequential sampler for sulfur dioxide and possibly for particulates, in order to get information on the short-term fluctuations of pollutant levels; this information can generally be provided only by automatic instruments. Nearly all networks include a few hi-vol samplers for particulates; mechanized sampling for gases is less common. The static monitoring devices are less consistently used; they've been abandoned as old-fashioned by some agencies and newly adopted by others as a cheap way to extend sampling activities over a broader area than might otherwise be possible.

A good, balanced network will have the three types of instruments geographically mixed, with the less expensive instruments interspersed among a smaller number of more expensive installations. For example, a "primary station" might have automatic, mechanized, and static equipment all together, for each 25 to 50 square miles or each 50,000–75,000 people. Additional sites, with mechanized samplers and dustfall jars, could fill in gaps between primary stations and could document levels in locations where industrial and residential areas meet, and sulfation index sites could extend into the outer suburbs and rural areas, to determine how far the influence of the urban area extends.

These ideas are typical of the kind of thinking that goes into choosing the sites for a monitoring network. The other principal decisions involved in network design concern the frequency of operation of the samplers and are typically a compromise between the desire for as much information as possible and the limitations on resources available to devote to analysis of the samples. Because no extra effort is required for sample analysis, the automatic instruments are generally expected to operate continuously, except for downtime for calibration and maintenance. The static devices are commonly operated for a month at a time and are generally run continuously, that is, for the 12 months in the year. Mechanical sampling equipment, however, the hi-vols and the gas bubblers, can be operated largely at will. Almost invariably, they are operated for 24-hour periods, but since they require lab analysis, the further question of how many 24-hour samples becomes important; is daily sampling at one site a better use of the lab capacity than every-other-day sampling at two sites? Usually, the answer to this question is "more sites with less frequent sampling at each." The question of just how often is necessary to get a good measure of the typical pollution levels at a site is determined by the variability of the pollutant levels at the site and is approached as a statistical question. Every three days or every six days is a good choice.

DATA PROCESSING

The purpose of gathering data in a monitoring program is, of course, to subsequently make worthwhile use of it. Between the gathering and the use of the data, however, lie several essential steps that go by various labels: data processing, data handling, validation, storage and retrieval, data analysis, interpretation, and so on. For our purposes here, we will distinguish between data processing—the clerical and validation procedures and the data-storage system—and data analysis—the summarization and interpretation of the data after they have been processed and stored, but before all the available information has been extracted.

There is much more to these operations than often meets the eye; in an extensive air quality monitoring program, data processing may well prove to be the primary source of problems. Yet there is very little discussion of data processing in the literature of the air pollution field; it has just never been of much interest, because in the old days there was little data and hence little need.

In the abstract, the purpose of data processing is to move the result of a sample, in whatever form it may be, from the laboratory or field sensor, or wherever it may have originated, to a position or status of storage, ready for subsequent analysis, and to perform in the process any necessary calculations, labeling, and other clerical operations, removing or correcting any erroneous data without, of course, adding other errors. Despite the length of this definition, the data-processing operation is conceptually simple; it becomes a problem primarily because of the very large volumes of data often involved.

For purposes of discussion, let us divide data-processing systems into three categories. The first, which we will call manual, consists of those systems which do not make use of a computer. Systems in the second group, called semiautomatic, make use of a computer but still involve a great deal of manual intervention, that is, a number of key steps performed by humans are intermixed with computer processing. The third type, automatic systems, consists of those data-processing systems that are totally computerized; manual effort is needed only to maintain and modify the computer system.

A manual system is useful only for handling small amounts of data from intermittent sampling operations. Because the volume of data is small and is often handled by only one person, such a data-processing system usually causes few problems. An automatic system is possible only for automatic instruments, which generate an electric output signal suitable for *telemetering*, that is, for automatic transmission along telephone wires to a central computer. Such processing systems are complex and expensive and are therefore limited to the larger automatic monitoring networks in the larger cities.

The vast majority of data, whether intermittent samples from hi-vols or continuous data from automatic instruments, is processed by some blend of manual and computerized functions, that is, a semiautomatic system. Although there is a great variety of semiautomatic data-processing systems, there are also many common elements. The continuous instrumentation feeding into such a system is typically not directly connected to the computer; the data are transported manually and, after some manual checking, are then entered into the computer for further processing and storage. The processing of the data fr~·¬ intermittent sampling operations is not likely to be computerized, excepι for ultimate data storage, unless the monitoring is extremely extensive.

Input Data Forms and Formats

Our use of the phrase "input data" refers to the interface between the sensor or sampler and the data-handling system, regardless of its physical form. In automatic instruments, the data usually pass from the instrument to the data-handling system in some type of storage format—computer cards, magnetic recording tape, or punched paper tape. With mechanical sampling equipment or static sensors, the format for the input data is almost invariably a piece of paper, a "record card" or "record form." The record card for each individual sample, perhaps a monthly sulfation plate determination or a daily hi-vol measurement, generally accompanies the sampling equipment or apparatus through the laboratory during advance preparation, out to the field and back, then through the lab again, and ultimately to the front end of the data-processing system.

Any record card that contains the required information is satisfactory, so long as the person receiving the data at the end knows what information is what, etc. If possible, it should be easy to keypunch from. Even if the data-processing system is presently a manual one, such systems almost always ultimately expand to involve a computer.

Clerical Processing Operations

In manual and semiautomatic systems, most especially the latter, the processing of the data requires several operations which can only be described as clerical; these operations, however, are generally necessary to ensure the smooth flow of data. The exact nature and location of these steps in the processing stream vary widely, depending on the overall design of each system. For example, if a number of field personnel gather samples and return them to the office, the samples generally need to be logged in at one central location, so that the location of the various samples and their record forms can be identified, and the actual gathering of each sample according to the preplanned schedule can be later verified. If the forms so require, a clerk can add code numbers and identifying information, and the clerk should also make sure that the field personnel have filled in the forms completely. In the case of data on magnetic tape from automatic instruments, the clerk may need to match the beginning of each tape with the end of the previous one, check the operators' logs for completeness, etc.

These clerical functions become problems in a data-processing system not because the work is difficult, but precisely because it is a boring, routine task. As such, it is often overlooked as insignificant by the planners of the system and disliked intensely by those who need to perform it. However, these functions require particular accuracy and care, as errors made in these steps usually cannot be detected later. The only solution to these problems is to design the forms, the computer program, and the entire system to require as little clerical work as possible.

Data Storage and Retrieval

Earlier, we said that the goal of data-processing systems is to get the data to a "position or status of storage," ready for analysis; we will now consider this "position or status" as a clear-cut function. The simple purpose of what has come to be called "data storage and retrieval" is to store the data in a safe, convenient place. In manual data systems, the need for this function is so intuitive as to remain essentially unrecognized and unnamed, although all manual systems *do* make an effort to keep their data in a convenient file, where it will be readily available for use. In addition to storing the actual data, one must also store important auxiliary information, such as site location, analysis method, etc., as well as the meaning of any special symbols used by the data recorder.

Data storage and retrieval as a specific function worthy of a name emerged with the widespread use of computers and the development of computerized data-storage systems. Data storage on a computer-readable medium, such as magnetic tape, is quite different from storage in a file. There is a large body of technical knowledge about the safe storage of data in computerized systems, about making choices between magnetic tape and disk storage, about arriving at decisions of record format, and so on, but these are the province of the computer-systems analyst and are beyond our purpose here. Rather, we will mention only two areas in which such choices are not dictated solely by computer technology: the arrangement of the data (see Problem 16) and the assigning of codes that identify the data.

Assigning identifying codes is simply a matter of choosing numbers to represent the various pollutants, stations, analysis methods, etc. However, a few precautions are necessary. In particular, it is probably true that "anything that *can* change, will"; this adage suggests not only that one must leave room for expanding the numbering system, but also that one be very careful to label every conceivable type of information. Do not assume that only one instrument or analysis method will be used at one site for one period of time, and do not assume that one will never want to operate two identical instruments side by side. One may be tempted to assume, for example, that since suspended particulate matter is essentially defined as a pollutant by the hi-vol sampler that collects the sample, the need for separate codes for the pollutant and for the sampler is minimal. Although this assumption may be correct now, one would be unwise to assume that one will never want to operate another, almost identical method, perhaps comparing two hi-vols from different manufacturers, for example.

In addition, we want also to briefly mention the numerical coding system that the federal air quality program has developed and which is being widely adopted by other agencies. This coding structure consists of codes for stations or monitoring sites, instruments and analytical methods, and pollutants. The code for the station or site consists of nine digits—a two-digit state code, a four-digit city or county code, and a three-digit site code within the city or county. The code for the pollutant is one of a complex system of five-digit codes that permits the coding of almost any conceivable chemical substance or related parameter. The instrument-method code is a two-digit code that is hierarchically arranged with the pollutant code to form a seven-digit pollutant-method code, i.e., there are 99 instrument-method possibilities for each five-digit pollutant.

The air quality staff of EPA developed these codes for the computer storage of their own air quality data, using them in a data-handling system called SAROAD (Storage and Retrieval of Aerometric Data); the codes are, of course, known as "SAROAD codes." Using the SAROAD system, the EPA also maintains a data bank for the permanent storage of the air quality and other aerometric data reported by state and local control agencies. Such a central data bank provides a variety of benefits. EPA doesn't need to continually ask other agencies for their data; conversely, the other agencies are not continually bothered by these requests. And although the data bank cannot completely substitute for an agency's own data-processing system, the EPA does provide certain summaries and special analyses of contributed data to the nonfederal agency. The primary benefit, however, accrues to the entire air pollution control field by virtue of the ready accessibility of the data for researchers and data analysts. In this day and age, when computerized data systems are required for the handling of even modest amounts of data, the existence of one central system, where data from various agencies are available in a common computer format, literally makes possible much research and analysis that otherwise could not be undertaken.

Data Validation

So far in our discussion of data processing, we've made no mention of data validation, although, chronologically speaking, we've seen our data all the way through to ultimate storage. This is not inappropriate, because data validation is not really a distinct step in the chronological flow of data, but rather occurs as many small steps throughout the system. Data validation may be defined as the attempt to detect and correct errors that have entered the data in previous steps. It is not generally a major aspect of manual data-processing operations, partly because the volume of data is small, and, more importantly, because it is usually watched over by the same individual through the entire process.

Data validation is of much greater significance with semiautomatic data systems, which involve a complex of steps requiring both human and computer operation. The variety of errors that occurs in such systems is amazing—major laboratory or field operational errors, data entry or copying errors made by field or clerical personnel, bad data from malfunctioning instrumentation. All of these are likely to proceed through the processing beyond the point at which they were made, to be caught and fixed at some later point, or else to be not fixed at all, leaving a number which is not what it ought to have been. The only way a validation system could catch the majority of these errors would be to require each operation to be double-checked. Such a system, however, would be expensive, and many field operations simply can't be repeated for the sake of checking.

What, then, do we do to "validate" our data? For clarity of discussion, let us divide the errors we are looking for into two groups, even though they are really just the opposite ends of a continuum. First, there are small errors in data near the middle; these errors, which are quite close to the true value, are detectable only if we know the true value, since they don't seem "out of line." Second, there are bigger errors, which are detectable because they produce "data" which deviate a great deal from what we expected.

The first group is the more difficult. Because we can never really know what the "true value" is, we must essentially give up any hope of a system capable of detecting, for example, a 28 in the midst of the data which should really be a 31; there is no way of even knowing it is an error if the true value is not known. This type of error can be largely prevented if the sampling, analysis, and data-processing procedures are designed to minimize the chance for error and if spot checks of each operation are made to avoid systematic errors; then we can assume that the few remaining random errors of small magnitude will generally "average out."

Somewhat more susceptible to validation efforts are large-scale errors, those that produce numbers that are "outlying" in some sense—extremely large, extremely small, or perhaps extremely different from the surrounding figures. Since we don't have any known true value against which to judge an unusual number, we can only judge it against what we expect the data to be. This, then, is a basic dilemma, any resolution of which is necessarily a compromise. Since we can't know the "correct" value against which to compare our data for correctness, we are forced to compare it only against our expectations, which are not completely correct either (else why gather more data?). Thus, we must recognize that we will not be able to detect those errors that happen to agree with our expectations and that we will no doubt detect and correct some "errors" that were really true and valid events which happened to deviate greatly from our expectations.

The question remains as to how we decide what "deviates from our expectations." Most commonly, an upper limit is set, above which all data are marked by the computer as possibly in error; for particulate data and some gases, a lower limit should also be set, and for continuous data recorded as hourly averages or less, a criterion of change between adjacent data values is appropriate. These boundary limits, beyond which data are singled out, may be based on the past data for that pollutant and that station, etc., setting aside a fixed percentage of the data, or the limits may be standard for the entire system. Although using past data to establish outer boundaries is a more rational way of doing this operation, devising standard limits is the far more common practice. The specific choice of cut-off numbers is a function of the general run of data and the amount of data that can be further verified.

Having selected certain data for further investigation, the field and laboratory personnel (for data from mechanized sampling equipment) or the instrumentation staff (for data from automatic instrumentation) then go back to the record cards, strip charts, or other records to either supply the correct value, if in fact an error has been detected, or to offer an explanation of why the value, though extreme, is probably correct. This second look by the sampling personnel is more often rewarding in the case of continuous instruments, because the automatically recorded data have probably been processed from the instrument to the first, preliminary computer tabulation with little human scrutiny. In the case of intermittent data, the laboratory personnel have probably used their experience to verify the numbers, at least subconsciously, while they were recording the data, so that second looks are less frequently fruitful with these data.

A system of this type, in which computer flagging of extremes is combined with manual verification of the flagged values, will catch most of the blatant instrument errors, laboratory errors, and clerical misrecordings. Since we have already abandoned any hope of detecting small errors in the bulk of the data once they have occurred (as opposed to preventing them), we are left between these two extremes with the question of what to do with those flagged values which, after having been checked, do not appear to be in error, but which by our reasoning (or by that behind the limits in the computer program) seem to be "out of line." In these cases, a data analyst can learn a great deal by studying the data, especially in conjunction with meteorological data. When we talk of further study, however, we leave the

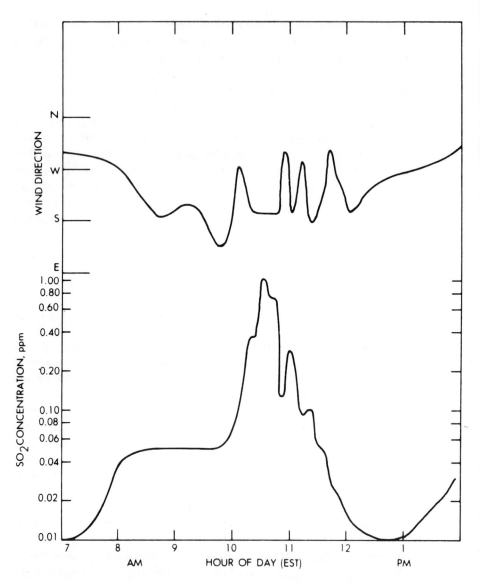

Fig. 7–1. Sulfur dioxide levels on August 22, 1963, at the Cincinnati CAMP station. In one type of data validation, peripheral data, such as the wind direction data here, are used in connection with the pollutant data. The 0.99 ppm values might have been re-jected if the wind direction had not confirmed the influence of the plume from a nearby power plant to the south-southwest.

realm of commonly practiced data-processing operations; when faced with the situation just described, most existing data-processing systems would retain the data as valid and proceed to drop the matter.

If at all possible, however, the study of the flagged values should not stop here. The desirability of pursuing these seemingly extraneous values further lies not just in finding a basis for keeping or rejecting a few specific numbers, but also in the fact that these extreme, unusual data values are the ones that offer the most promise of gaining new information and understanding. For example, if suspiciously high sulfur dioxide concentrations are clustered overnight in the winter, meteorology data may reveal a very cold, clear night; such information helps us judge the effect of a certain degree of space heating during an overnight radiation inversion. In a striking case of unusually high sulfur dioxide values in the middle of August, when the bulk of data was running near zero (see Fig. 7–1), the wind was found to be coming directly from a power plant near the station; the high values were thus a measure of the extremely high concentration possible in the plume of a source as it strikes the ground. The data of these two examples would generally be considered valid, having been based on a reasonable explanation, although the second might well have been deleted as erroneous if wind direction data had not been used.

Although one need not hesitate to leave such extreme values in the midst of a mass of continuous data, a similar case involving intermittent sampling data poses a more difficult decision. Here, the data may be too few to "average out" the effect of an extreme value, and one must be guided by the intended use of the data in deciding how strict to be. For example, for years the North Dakota nonurban station operated by the EPA's National Air Surveillance Network averaged about 26 $\mu g/m^3$ suspended particulates; then, in the spring of 1963 a single value over 1000 $\mu g/m^3$ was recorded, the highest level ever measured by the National Air Sampling Network to that time. An extensive, careful study determined that this value was the result of a dust storm, which had similar, though less extreme, effects at stations throughout the northern plains area on that date. Although this explanation contributes to our knowledge of the possible extremes of nature and certainly offers much satisfaction for successful detective work, it leaves us with the problem of what to do for an annual average for that station for 1963. We certainly don't want to totally abandon such an interesting number, but keeping it in the data will distort any analytical work, in part because it is present as 1/25 of our sample rather than as 1/365th of the year. Looking at Fig. 7–2, we would probably argue further that if we are measuring nonurban data in order to assess the extent of degradation by urban pollution, we don't want such a number in there at all. The NASN in this case had no real problem; since their only intent at

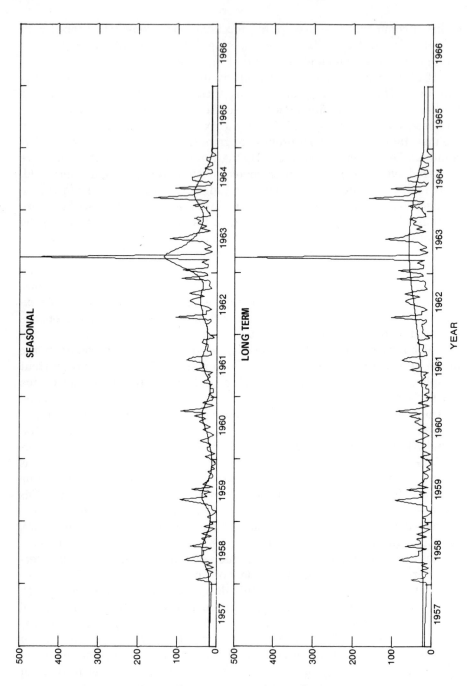

◀ **Fig. 7–2. Trends in particulate pollution at the NASN's Ward County, North Dakota, non-urban site.** This diagram includes the 1000 μg/m^3 sample discussed in the text. The jagged curve in each graph is the same, a plot of the raw data, 26 samples each year; note that the extreme value is well above the limits of the graph. The smoothed curves are representations of the seasonal cycle and the long-term trend, calculated by finite-difference formulas. (R. Spirtas and H. J. Levin, *Characteristics of Particulate Patterns 1957–1966*, NAPCA Publication No. AP–61, Public Health Service, March 1970)

the time was to report the data, this particular phenomenon was merely prominently noted in the text.

There is a genuine problem, however, in what to do with such a number in data gathered for the specific purpose of comparison with other stations or with other years. Obviously, the answer will be different in each instance, based on the precise needs of any given data analysis; however, a new approach developed in the field of statistics, the use of "resistant" measures of the center of our data, seems to offer great promise.

By now we have got the data analyst fairly well involved in our data validation process. The line between the validation and analysis of data is in fact fairly hazy. The data analyst, who sees a great deal of data in a variety of summary formats, can frequently detect errors not detectable by an "extreme-searching" procedure such as we described earlier. Most typically, an analyst would be able to detect an erroneous value which, because of instrument malfunction, say, is unusually high for a particular time of day or particular season of the year, but is not high enough to exceed the limits set by the computer program, which are based on high levels expected at other times or seasons. The previous example of extremely high level of SO$_2$ during the summer is such a case; another might be a week of carbon monoxide data that consistently peaks at 4 A.M. rather than at the time of the morning rush hour, which the analyst would probably recognize as an error in the time synchronization of the instrumentation. There are several kinds of errors a data analyst may catch; his job is in general to figure out why the data does what it does, and one possibility is always that it is in error.

DATA ANALYSIS

Air quality data can be analyzed on various levels and with various general or specialized objectives. Here, we will discuss briefly the simpler types of data analysis currently practiced by agencies gathering data and will mention a few of the more sophisticated analyses that will probably be used in the future.

The simplest type of data analysis, perhaps more properly called merely data summarization, consists of calculating simple averages and condensing or rearranging the data into some form that is easy and convenient to

Fig. 7–3. A typical monthly summary of hourly averages from automatic instrumentation. ▶
Collected at EPA's station in Cincinnati, these data from August 1963 include the data
plotted in Fig. 7–1. Note that the data are printed in pphm, so that decimal points don't
need to be used. The summary rows and columns give daily averages at the right, a
diurnal variation pattern at the bottom, and the monthly average, 0.009 ppm in this case,
in the corner. Also of interest are the periods of missing data, probably the result of instrument malfunction or maintenance.

visualize and understand. The precise form of this summarization will vary,
depending on the data analyst's or agency's preferences and experience. At
least one such basic summary must be prepared as an integral part of any
data-processing system, however, to form the "retrieval" part of data
storage and retrieval function. Typically, the basic summary for continuous
data is one month's worth of hourly averages on a single computer page
(see Fig. 7–3); this is convenient for the computer and has been found to
be manageable for the humans, although monthly sheets do make a fat pile
quickly.

Whatever the nature of this basic summary, it should lend itself to use
over only shorter periods of time, in the sense that we don't want to have to
wait for an entire year before looking at the data, and we might not want to
wait for an entire month before looking at a summary like Fig. 7–3. In fact,
in the extreme, analyses of this type are routinely performed by some completely automatic monitoring systems, which continuously display current
data summaries.

In contrast to this type of basic summarization, there are several more
complicated summaries or simple analyses that must be based on data for
an entire season or year or similar logical period. Most common among
these are diurnal variation patterns, frequency distributions, and pollutant
roses. The simplest of these analyses, the diurnal variation pattern, is appropriate for any data of less than 24-hour duration, but is used primarily
with continuous sampling data. Basically, this type of analysis is just a
collection of averages, one for each time period within the daily cycle;
plotted as in the figures in Chapter 3, such patterns convey an effective understanding of the way pollutant concentrations vary through the day.
Since the pattern of human activity through the day is well known, these
analyses also provide an intuitive view of that cause-and-effect relationship.

A frequency distribution is a way of summarizing how often concentrations of specified magnitudes occur. A fairly common statistical tool, the
frequency distribution is most often applied to situations requiring a condensation of a huge volume of data, e.g., continuous SO_2 data. In the air
quality field, however, the use of frequency distributions began with the
NASN data, with only 26 samples per year (see Fig. 7–4). In Fig. 7–4 the
frequency distribution is used partly to condense the data into a conve-

Month	Week	AM 12	1	2	3	4	5	6	7	8	9	10	11	PM 12	1	2	3	4	5	6	7	8	9	10	11	Daily mean	No. of hours	5-min max.
1	Thu	0	0	0	0	1	1	1	1	1	0	0	0	0	0	0	0	0	0	0	0	0	0	0	0	0.2	24	2
2	Fri	0	0	0	0	0	0	0	0	1	3	4	1	0	0	1	1	3	5	0	0	0	0	0	0	0.8	24	22
3	Sat	0	0	0	2	4	3	3	3	3	1	0	0	0	0	0	0	0	0	0	0	0	0	0	0	0.8	24	6
4	Sun	0	0	0	0	0	0	0	0	0	1	0	0	0	0	0	0	0	0	0	0	0	0	0	0	0.0	24	1
5	Mon	0	0	1	0	0	0	1	2	2			0	0	0	0	0	0	0	0	0	0	1	0	1	0.3	22	2
6	Tue	0	0	0	0	0	0	0	1	5	1	2	3	3	1	0	1	0	0	0	0	0	0	0	0	0.7	24	14
7	Wed	0	0	2	0	0	0	0	0	0	0		0	0	0	0	0	0	0	0	0	0	0	0	0	0.1	23	13
8	Thu	0	0	0	0	0	0	0	1	0	0	0	0	0	0	0	0	0	0	0	0	0	0	0	0	0.0	16	1
9	Fri																											
10	Sat																											
11	Sun	0	0	0	0	0	0	0	1	5	5	3	1	0	1	3	2	0	0	0	0	0	1	1	1	1.0	24	16
12	Mon	0	0	0	0	0	0	1	3	7		3	3	3	1	0	0	3	4	1	0	1	2	2	2	1.5	23	18
13	Tue	1	0	0	0	1	2	1	0	0	0	0	0	0	0	0	0	0	0	0	0	0	0	0	0	0.2	24	5
14	Wed	0	0	0	0	0	0	1	0	0	0	0	0	0	0	0	0	0	0	0	0	0	0	0	0	0.0	24	1
15	Thu	0	0	0	0	1	0	1	2	1	1	0	1	0	0	0	0	0	0	0	0	0	0	0	0	0.3	24	2
16	Fri	0	0	0	0	0	0	0	3	9	5	0	0	1	2	1	0	5	5	3	0	1	1	0	0	1.6	24	39
17	Sat	1	2	4	4	3	1	4	1	1	1	1	1	1	1	0	0	0	0	0	0	0	0	0	0	1.7	15	12
18	Sun																											
19	Mon	0	1	6	10	2	2	1	0	0	0		0	0	0	0	4	3	2	1	1	1	1	0	0	1.7	21	15
20	Tue	0	0	0	0	0	0	0	0	0		0	0	0	0	0	0	0	0	0	0	0	0	0	0	0.0	24	2
21	Wed	0	0	0	0	0	2	1	1	4	6	5	2	4	3	5	0	0	1	0	0	0	0	1	0	1.2	24	24
22	Thu	0	0	0	0	0	2	1	1	5	5	42	10	1	2	0	1	1	1	1	0	0	0	0	0	3.1	24	99
23	Fri	0	0	0	0	0	1	0	1	2	10	5	0	0	0	2	0	0	1	0	0	0	0	0	0	0.8	24	16
24	Sat	0	0	0	0	0	1	0	0	0	0	1	3	2	3	0	3	2	1	0	0	0	0	0	0	0.7	24	6
25	Sun	0	0	0	0	0	1	0	0	0	0	0	0	0	0	0	0	0	0	0	0	0	0	1	1	0.1	24	1
26	Mon	1	0	0	0	1	2	1	2	2	5	2	1	0	0	0	0	0	4	0	0	0	1	1	1	0.8	23	21
27	Tue	1	1	2	1	2	2	2	3	3	4		1	2	2	1	1	1	1	1	1	1	1	12	1	1.6	19	5
28	Wed	1	1	1	1	0	1	3	2	3	1	1	9	0	0	0	0	4	17	9	6	1	0	0	9	3.9	24	35
29	Thu	10	2	1	0	0	1	1	2	1	2	1	1	0	0	0	0	0	0	0	0	0	0	0	1	1.0	24	13
30	Fri	0	0	0	0	0	1	1	3	3		1	0	0	0	0	0	0	0	0	0	0	0	0	0	0.4	24	3
31	Sat	1	1	1	1	1	1	1	2	2	1	1	0	0	0	0	3	0	0	0	0	0	0	0	0	0.6	24	20
Monthly mean		1		1	1	1	1	1		2	2	3	1	1	1	1	1	1	2	1	0	0	0	1	1	0.9		
No. of days		27	28	28	28	28	28	28	28	28	24	24	27	27	27	25	26	27	26	26	26	26	27	27	26		642	
Max. hrly mean		10	2	6	10	4	3	4	3	9	10	42	10	4	3	5	4	5	17	9	6	1	2	12	9			

Location: Region, State or Station	Years	Number of Samples	Min	\[Micrograms Per Cubic Meter — Frequency Distribution—Percent\]									Max	Arith Mean	Geo Mean	Std Geo Dev
				10	20	30	40	50	60	70	80	90				
TOLEDO	57	26	48	64	70	81	90	107	133	145	166	180	311	124	110	1.63
	59	24	52	56	62	70	83	90	115	127	143	170	193	104	97	1.50
	57 59	50	48	58	66	76	86	107	121	137	155	176	311	115	104	1.57
YOUNGSTOWN	57	26	63	76	96	127	137	151	197	214	254	302	406	180	160	1.66
	58	26	79	87	112	127	135	147	159	168	180	214	391	158	147	1.44
	59	26	65	90	99	110	116	124	143	158	180	203	277	138	130	1.42
	60	26	58	64	85	101	112	127	145	166	214	241	371	148	132	1.63
	61	26	60	70	81	93	100	117	139	151	227	254	298	142	126	1.62
	57 61	130	58	77	92	107	121	136	150	174	208	254	406	153	138	1.56
OKLAHOMA **OKLAHOMA CITY**	58	25	38	54	61	66	68	71	73	76	82	90	98	71	69	1.25
	60	23	42	50	66	71	76	82	86	90	99	117	173	84	80	1.36
	61	25	45	61	70	81	85	92	95	99	102	107	128	88	86	1.28
	58 61	73	38	54	65	69	73	79	85	90	97	105	173	81	78	1.31
TULSA	57	20	22	42	47	50	54	72	83	99	127	143	268	87	75	1.75
	59	21	38	40	45	59	68	78	82	86	90	117	146	76	71	1.44
	61	23	20	23	43	48	54	62	66	69	73	90	114	62	56	1.53
	57 61	64	20	40	45	51	61	68	73	82	90	123	268	74	66	1.59
OREGON **EUGENE**	61	22	23	38	45	59	70	80	87	99	139	161	158	87	77	1.71
MEDFORD	61.	22	45	50	64	84	90	107	117	127	180	227	249	123	109	1.66
PORTLAND	57	26	32	38	45	59	67	76	107	120	139	151	315	99	82	1.83
	58	25	26	27	38	61	90	96	99	105	139	180	334	99	81	1.94
	59	26	21	42	50	61	67	76	84	90	127	180	208	91	78	1.76
	60	24	21	30	43	50	57	60	63	76	99	127	185	70	62	1.68
	61	26	30	38	50	57	61	68	96	107	122	151	186	87	76	1.66
	57 61	127	21	35	46	56	63	73	90	103	125	163	334	89	76	1.78
PENNSYLVANIA **ALLENTOWN**	59	26	42	54	72	83	90	107	133	145	170	214	298	122	108	1.66
	61	25	60	90	97	107	117	132	141	157	168	234	261	135	127	1.43
	59 61	51	42	67	82	94	105	124	138	151	169	224	298	129	117	1.56
BETHLEHEM	61	25	84	101	110	118	124	139	151	168	180	214	254	146	141	1.33
ERIE	61	22	41	59	76	90	96	101	107	117	158	173	197	108	101	1.47
HARRISBURG	58	25	46	54	64	87	94	107	139	191	214	244	292	135	117	1.75
	60	25	50	54	64	78	83	90	95	102	107	143	189	92	87	1.39
	58 60	50	46	52	64	80	87	95	102	127	151	214	292	113	101	1.62
JOHNSTOWN	59	22	65	94	103	115	123	151	180	254	302	359	424	198	172	1.71
	61	22	70	90	99	114	127	143	157	168	191	214	452	166	148	1.59
	59 61	44	65	92	103	112	125	145	163	191	254	359	452	182	160	1.65
PHILADELPHIA	57	24	86	132	146	161	189	206	221	241	254	290	323	205	196	1.38
	58	23	61	90	117	127	151	166	175	189	206	302	349	170	157	1.52
	59	25	54	76	90	127	156	170	180	222	238	302	411	179	159	1.66
	60	25	70	90	107	119	127	145	166	197	214	254	342	160	147	1.52
	61	26	86	110	115	122	127	141	180	194	214	302	345	173	160	1.47
	57 61	123	54	90	116	128	145	166	185	207	234	288	411	177	163	1.52
PITTSBURGH	57	23	78	85	101	127	156	170	180	203	234	427	534	203	176	1.72
	58	26	85	96	107	127	133	142	151	170	214	278	344	167	155	1.48
	59	24	83	99	127	139	158	173	214	376	410	604	977	276	218	1.96
	60	24	43	76	84	90	120	139	166	203	227	302	475	166	143	1.74
	61	26	61	68	76	100	107	133	151	161	175	214	297	137	126	1.53
	57 61	123	43	82	99	116	135	151	168	190	236	359	977	189	160	1.73
READING	58	25	56	76	83	93	100	117	139	170	191	278	404	142	125	1.63
	60	25	34	64	76	90	99	110	117	127	170	203	242	120	108	1.60
	58 60	50	34	67	80	90	99	110	122	156	180	208	404	131	117	1.62

Fig. 7–4. Frequency distributions of NASN sampling results. This table, from a 1957–1961 NASN summary report, gives a frequency distribution of particulate data and some other statistics in a one-line summary for each year's data. The plot on p. 193 is the 1957 data for Youngstown, Ohio, the fourth line in the table. The scales of the graph are unusual: the particulate scale is logarithmic, and the percent scale is spaced according to the probabilities of a standard normal distribution. This "log-normal paper" will make the graph come out as a straight line if the logarithm of the concentration is normally distributed, as the Youngstown data is. It's interesting to note that the average particulate level in Youngstown, a dirty, steel mill city, decreased from 1957 to 1961, although it didn't last past 1962.

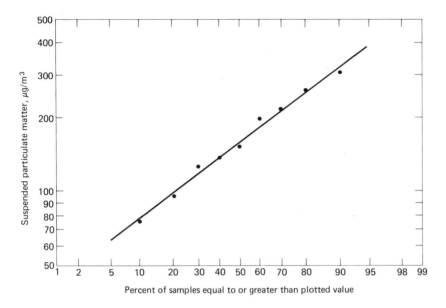

Percent of samples equal to or greater than plotted value

nient, one-line summary and partly because the deciles are intuitively appealing. With continuous data, a useful frequency distribution can be prepared (by hand easily enough) for as little as a month's data; with longer-term, intermittent data, at least 20–25 samples are desirable.

The "pollutant rose" analysis categorizes the data by wind data, in much the same way that diurnal variation patterns group the data by time of day. The pollutant rose is less common, primarily because wind data are often not available in the computer system, and it is a fairly inconvenient analysis to do by hand. The analysis is made by grouping the data according to the prevailing direction of the wind; once separated, the data in each group are averaged. For example, if the wind data were divided into 16 compass points, the analysis would produce 16 average concentrations. Most pollutant roses are made from hourly averages of continuous data, along with hourly wind data; pollutant roses can also be used with 24-hour data, if the "resultant wind" direction for the day is used as a "prevailing" direction to categorize the day. The graphical display of this type of analysis is almost always in the form of a compass-type figure resembling a wind rose (hence the name), as shown in Fig. 7–5. Such displays point to (both in a figurative, or if on a map, in a literal, fashion) the sources producing higher pollutant concentrations at a particular sampling site.

Although much more could be said about the analysis of air quality data, particularly in the application of the wide variety of statistical tools that are available from various other fields of specialization. Finite-difference formulae have proved to be valuable for trend detection (Fig. 7–3). Many other time-series techniques also exist, but they are used only on air

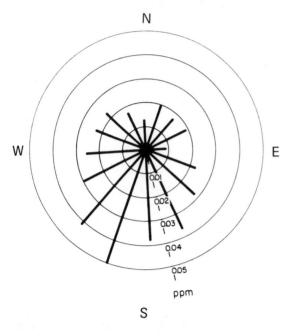

Fig. 7–5. Sulfur dioxide pollutant rose. This analysis, from EPA's Cincinnati CAMP site, shows concentrations for 1962–1963. The figure points obviously to the SSW, where there was a small power plant. When winds were from that direction, pollutant levels averaged 0.05 ppm, double the overall average.

quality data. Problems that require such sophisticated tools for solution just haven't yet arisen in quantity, and air quality data analysts are still busy using the simpler techniques on simpler problems.

EXERCISES

Review Questions

1. How does an air quality monitoring program differ from simply measuring ambient pollutant levels?
2. What sorts of information should a good air quality monitoring program provide?
3. What choices are usually available in deciding the operating schedule for the sampling equipment?
4. Why is air quality data processing a relatively new subject area?
5. Distinguish between data processing and data analysis.
6. Distinguish among the three types of data processing systems defined. Which is most common?

7. What can be done to minimize clerical errors?
8. What is a data storage and retrieval system?
9. What role does SAROAD have in data processing?
10. What one general technique is usually used to validate data?
11. Why should a data analyst be part of the data-validation process?
12. What is a diurnal variation pattern? A frequency distribution? A pollutant rose analysis?

Thought Questions

13. In selecting an operating schedule for a hi-vol sampler, why would you want to avoid sampling every seventh day, or every fourteenth day?
14. Frequently, hi-vol filters are kept in storage and analyzed for constituent substances at a later date, either because that gives the most efficient use of lab resources or because concern over a new pollutant arouses interest in what its levels were previously. What special concerns might be raised by such retrospective chemical analyses, in designing a data system, and especially in data analysis?

Discussion Questions

15. It is frequently noted that planning an effective data-processing and analysis program requires a knowledge of the uses to which the data are to be put. Yet rarely can pollution control officials define these uses precisely enough to be of much use for such planning, largely because they haven't consciously thought about it on just those terms. Try to think of some *precise* uses (consulting Chapter 11 may help) and discuss how they would influence the design of a data system.

Problems

16. If one operates an air quality monitoring network with two or more sampling sites, each measuring two or more pollutants, several different hierarchical arrangements of date, station, and pollutant labels might be used. Dates could be the highest order, within which stations could be arranged in order, with the different pollutants under each station. Alternatively, all data for the first station could come first, with the pollutants in order, and the data arranged by date within each pollutant. List the six possibilities for a network with two stations and three pollutants. The most appropriate choice among these for use in storing data on computer tape, for instance, depends on the use to which the data will be put. Which would seem best for the "current working tape," to which data will be continually added through the year? Which for the most recent completely validated data? Which for the storage of a long history of data? In the latter two cases, consider what types of statistical analysis might be most likely.
17. With a large body of data, say a year's worth of hourly average SO_2 values, cumulative frequency distributions can be plotted in two ways. One can determine the concentration corresponding to certain percent points, e.g.,

1%, 5%, 10%, and plot them, or one can determine the percent of the total data at, say, 0.03 ppm or less, plot that value at 0.035 on the scale, and so on. Construct a frequency distribution by each method for a body of data and compare them. Which do you feel is preferable? Why?

Project Suggestion

18. If a computer is available and if there is an air quality monitoring project planned in your area, design the data forms and the validation procedures. Write computer programs to present the data in an attractive, usable display, or to calculate some of the standard analyses. If there is no class project planned, inquire of the local pollution control agency; many smaller agencies might appreciate computer programming assistance in dealing with their data.

FURTHER READING

There is little general reference material on the overall subject of this chapter, but there are some worthwhile references on specific topics. The network-design aspects of air quality monitoring are discussed by Morgan and Ozalins in [150] and by Morgan and Keitz in [148]; the latter is a good discussion of the relationship between the network and an agency's data needs.

There is a great deal of material on data processing in general, especially computerized data processing, but there has been very little published on air quality data processing. What there is also emphasizes computer processing. An older reference from 1967 [155] includes several papers on the topic of computerized data handling in air and water pollution control. These references are mostly prospective, emphasizing plans for, rather than experience with, such data systems, but they also include papers on Chicago's automated data system and the early stages of the federal SAROAD system. Among the other published information on the federal SAROAD system are two good discussions by the originators of the system, [211] and [212]. Other EPA documents [89–91] provide codes and other technical information. Anyone interested in using the data in the system should direct inquiries to the Monitoring and Data Analysis Division, EPA, Research Triangle Park, North Carolina 27711.

The best sources for reading on the analysis of pollution data are those reports that actually analyze data, such as the federal data publications. There is no good, comprehensive, single source, largely because extensive data-gathering is quite recent, and extensive data analysis is just not common yet. Statistical techniques useful in analyzing data with possible outlines are discussed by Mosteller and Rourke [129].

8
POLLUTION
FROM
STATIONARY SOURCES

EPA-Documerica, David Hiser

This is the first of two chapters concerned with the sources of air pollution and their control. We'll discuss human activities that emit pollutants, as well as how those emissions are (or could be) reduced or eliminated. In this chapter, our topic is stationary pollution sources, as opposed to mobile or motor vehicle sources. In contrast with the homogeneity of motor vehicles, stationary pollutant sources are quite a varied lot, ranging from individual homes and the neighborhood restaurant to the largest electric power generating stations and industrial plants.

Table 8–1 is a condensation of the emission estimates from several tables in Chapter 3. It's apparent that stationary sources account for almost all of the particulate and SO_x pollution, half of the NO_x, and significant portions of the others, CO and hydrocarbons. The biggest share of the emissions from stationary sources comes from combustion, or fuel-burning, sources. Since fuel use is fundamental to any human society, especially an industrial one, we'll consider these sources in some depth. We'll also consider, but in much less detail, the disposal of solid waste and some of the various industrial processes. First, however, we'll briefly consider the various methods of controlling pollutant emissions.

TABLE 8–1
Estimated nationwide emissions for 1970 (in millions of tons per year)

Source category	Particulate matter	Sulfur oxides	Carbon monoxide	Hydro-carbons	Nitrogen oxides
Stationary sources					
Fuel combustion	6.8	0.1	7.2	2.0	0.4
Solid-waste disposal	1.4	26.5	0.8	0.6	10.0
Industrial processes	13.3	6.0	11.4	9.5*	0.2
Miscellaneous†	3.9	0.3	18.3	5.3	0.5
	25.4	32.9	37.7	15.4	11.1
Transportation sources	0.7	1.0	110.9	19.5	11.7
Total	26.1	33.9	148.6	34.9	22.8

* Includes solvent evaporation and gasoline marketing.
† Includes coal-refuse banks, agricultural burning, forest fires, and structural fires.
Source: James H. Cavender, David S. Kircher, and Alan J. Hoffman, *Nationwide Air Pollutant Emission Trends 1940–1970,* Publication No. AP-115, Environmental Protection Agency, 1973.

BASIC APPROACHES TO EMISSION CONTROL

There are three broad, conceptual approaches to the problem of reducing pollutant emissions—preventive techniques, effluent dispersal, and effluent cleaning. The first, *preventive techniques,* needs to be emphasized, since such measures are often overlooked. For example, one way to prevent or reduce the formation of pollution is to change or eliminate the pollution-causing process. This is feasible in more cases than one might at first think; many things are done a certain way because of decisions made years ago, when technology was different and the pollution potential of the process was of little concern. Although it's psychologically hard to reassess major decisions, many minor improvements of this type have been made, and thinking about some of the bigger problems has shifted, e.g., changing the fuels used for electric-power generation and increasing the use of sanitary landfills for solid-waste disposal.

Other cases of preventive changes can be made in plant design and operating practices. In many cases, just covering 'storage containers can eliminate the loss of some of the stored material, thereby reducing the pollution and saving a little in the process. Operating practices are slightly different, in the sense that they involve human actions rather than the design of equipment. The ways in which boilers, incinerators, and similar equipment are used often have a major influence on the amount of pollution they emit. Sizeable pollution reductions can sometimes be obtained by examining the exact working procedures, making improvements, and inducing employees to follow them. This last factor is very important; it is very difficult, for example, for a janitor in an apartment house to accept the fact that it's important how and when he throws the trash into the incinerator, especially if he's told by the owners' lawyer, who never saw an incinerator before. Many operating procedures can have an effect on pollution emissions, as can maintenance standards (repairing leaky valves) and work scheduling (overloaded equipment frequently emits excess pollution). All of these minor changes, of course, come under the general heading of "good housekeeping," and in general, one should always try to exhaust the gains from this type of improvement before making major changes.

We should note that these actions are more relevant to the larger industrial polluter than to the individual. There are very few ways in which an individual can reduce pollution, and even when preventive measures are applicable, the individual rarely has a choice about the matter. In between, however, are the smaller and medium-size commercial and institutional concerns; and these facilities often have many opportunities for making improvement, through fairly simple preventive techniques.

Tall-Stack Dispersion

When feasible preventive measures have been exhausted, large pollutant sources will probably try to disperse the pollution effluent as widely as possible. At one time it was considered acceptable for a source to reduce its pollutant damage by building a taller smokestack, so that the plume would be carried farther away and diluted to a greater degree before it came back down to ground level and caused damage. A great deal of effort has gone into studying the diffusion of plumes in the wind, much of it from scientists and engineers concerned about the dispersal of radioactivity from hypothetical nuclear reactor accidents. The results are what we call diffusion equations, algebraic formulations (based on stack height, rate of emission, wind speed, and atmospheric stability) that permit the calculation of estimates of the pollution concentration at various points. Figure 8–1 presents such a formula, along with an illustrative sketch. By calculating backwards, one can also use this equation to find a stack height associated with a specified ground-level pollutant concentration; in this way the diffusion equations have served design engineers well for a number of years. Over these years, the maximum height of stacks has increased from 100–150 feet to

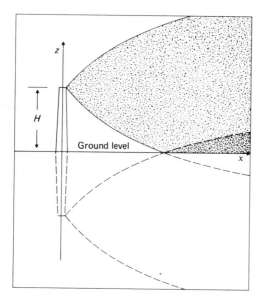

$$\chi = \frac{Q}{2\pi \bar{u}\sigma_y \sigma_z}\, e^{-(y^2/2\sigma_y^2)}\left[e^{-[(z-H)^2/2\sigma_z^2]} + e^{-[(z+H)^2/2\sigma_z^2]}\right]$$

Fig. 8–1. Meteorological diffusion equation. This formula is used to estimate the concentration X occurring at a distance x from a source emitting a quantity of pollutant Q at height H. The average wind speed is represented by $\bar{u}$, and σ_y and σ_z are parameters reflecting the extent of transverse and vertical spread of the plume that are determined from stability considerations. The second term in the square brackets represents the pollutant reflected from the ground surface, as illustrated in the sketch. (S. J. Williamson, *Fundamentals of Air Pollution*, Reading, Mass.: Addison-Wesley, 1973, p. 220)

about 600–800 feet on new, large power plants; 1000-foot stacks do exist, and more are planned. This is no small change; while from a distance a tall stack may seem a big paper-towel tube, up close they are an incredibly massive, and incredibly expensive, piece of concrete and brickwork and represent a real effort to keep down pollution levels.

Despite the attempt to reduce pollution levels by building taller stacks, such efforts are increasingly regarded as short-sighted. First, the gains in dilution occur as a result of letting the wind and atmospheric stability average out over a period of time. At a given moment, one can still have fairly high pollutant levels if the wind is unfavorable; with taller stacks, these adverse situations are less likely, but can still occur. With the tallest stacks that insert their pollution into the upper parts of the atmosphere, plumes may travel along for hundreds of miles on winds in a stable layer of air; forest damage in Sweden, for example, has been attributed to SO_2 from huge power plants in the United Kingdom.

The second problem with very tall stacks is more fundamental. Recognizing that the earth's atmosphere has some limit, we must consider overall global pollution; from this perspective, it makes relatively little difference where or how the pollutant enters the air. For both these reasons, tall stacks are no longer considered the best answer to controlling very large pollutant sources, although much of the electric power industry disagrees with this conclusion. The use of dispersion to keep ambient levels within the desired limits will undoubtedly continue to be a viable alternative in at least some circumstances.

Effluent Cleaning

When most people think of air pollution control, they usually think not of prevention or dispersion, but of some device or piece of equipment that cleans the effluent, i.e., removes the pollution, and in fact adding pollution control devices is the method most commonly used. As we sketched briefly in Chapter 6, a wide variety of types of devices, based on a variety of separation methods, are used to clean pollutants from source effluents.

For particulates, the separation methods employed are inertial, relying on the particles' mass, and filtration, relying primarily on the particles' size. The simple inertial techniques are used for the largest particles—sawdust, metal chips, and so on; the most common device is a cyclone (Fig. 8–2), whereby air is pulled into a spiral motion throwing the particulate matter to the outside. Basically simple in design, cyclones have long been used and are seen fairly frequently on rooftops. A number of complicated modifications have been made to this type of device in an effort to improve the efficiency of collection or the durability of the instrument. One such modification is to introduce water to help trap the particles, for

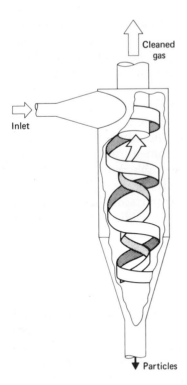

Cleaned
gas

Inlet

Particles

Fig. 8–2. Cyclone particle separator. Upon entering the inlet, air is forced to flow in a spiral pattern, which creates continuous force on particles or droplets, moving them toward the walls. (S. J. Williamson, *Fundamentals of Air Pollution,* Reading, Mass.: Addison-Wesley, 1973, p. 277)

instance. Even at their best, however, cyclones are not very good for small particles, e.g., those less than two to three microns.

The only filtration device in common use is the baghouse, or fabric filter system (Fig. 8–3), which operates on the same principle as a household vacuum cleaner. A baghouse consists of a number of long, thin bags hanging in an enclosure, arranged so that the air flows into the open end of the bag at the bottom, out through the fabric sides of the bag, and then out the top of the shelter. Dirty bags are cleaned by shaking them periodically, the particles shaken off falling into a hopper below for collection and removal. Baghouses are quite efficient at collecting small particles; their use is limited primarily by the availability of fabrics that can be used in hot temperatures and corrosive gases and because it's hard to predict just what efficiency a specific installation might get.

Two other devices for removing particulate matter, especially small particles, from stack gases are wet scrubbers and electrostatic precipitators. These might be classed as augmented inertial methods, as they operate by modifying the small particles to increase their collectibility and then collecting the particles by inertial methods. A wet scrubber is a device to mix some liquid, usually water, with the gases; the water droplets or

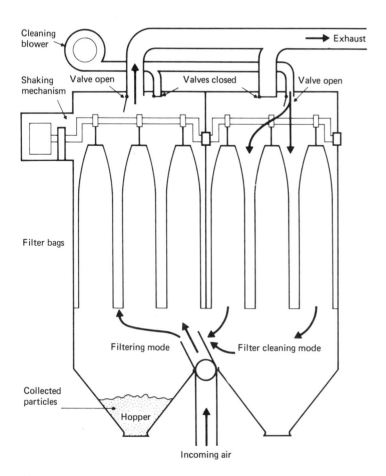

Fig. 8–3. High-efficiency fabric filter, or baghouse. This device is used for collecting small particles when environmental conditions are not too severe. This sketch shows a model that can provide a reverse flow of air during the filter-cleaning cycle. (S. J. Williamson, *Fundamentals of Air Pollution,* Reading, Mass.: Addison-Wesley, 1973, p. 276)

mist entrap the very small particles, in effect making them much larger for easier removal in a cyclone.

The most important factor in a wet scrubber is the thoroughness with which the water is mixed into the air; the more tumultuous the mixing, the finer the mist and the more efficient the removal of the particulate matter. As a result, there are a very large number of engineering variations, all attempting to provide the most energetic mixing for the money. The simplest variation is a spray tower; water sprays down while the gas flows upward. Most such spray towers have some form of baffle plates or are

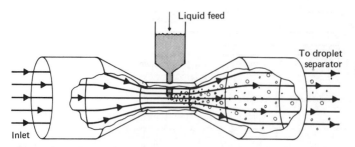

Fig. 8–4. A Venturi scrubber. Liquid is added to the flowing gas stream just before it undergoes expansion as it leaves the narrowed throat; the resultant energetic mixing of the liquid and air promotes effective collection of the particles by the liquid droplets. (S. J. Williamson, *Fundamentals of Air Pollution,* Reading, Mass.: Addison-Wesley, 1973, p. 279)

packed with irregularly shaped material, in order to maximize mixing of the air and water. Thus, the water droplets, together with the collected particles, are collected at the bottom by gravity.

Much higher collection efficiencies can be achieved with a Venturi scrubber (Fig. 8–4). A Venturi tube is a narrowed section of a pipe or duct in which the narrowing causes the flowing gas to attain a very high velocity and undergo an abrupt decrease in pressure. Water is injected into a Venturi scrubber at just the right point as the stack gas flows through the narrow section, resulting in a very energetic mixing and dispersion into droplets; the gas-droplet mixture then typically goes to a cyclone separator, where the large droplets, with their captured small particles, can be easily removed. In all types of wet scrubbers, some thought must be given to disposing of the dirty water in a manner that avoids creating water pollution.

Electrostatic precipitators are the most complicated, the most expensive, and yet the most commonly used high-efficiency control device, essentially because of their ability to control very small particles. They do this by giving the particle a property it didn't have before, an electrical charge, and then using that charge to collect the particles. Precipitators have a high-voltage DC power source, which produces a corona discharge, an arc, through which the gases and particles must pass. The negative ions in the arc quickly give a negative charge to any particle passing by, drawing the particle to the positive electrode, where it is deposited. The positive electrode plates are then cleaned by periodically rapping them with a mechanical hammer, shaking the particles loose to fall into a hopper below. Two configurations are common—sets of parallel collecting plates with discharge wires between them or cylindrical collecting tubes with the discharge wires at the center. Either configuration can be repeated many times over to give the desired capacity, and both the spacing between them and the voltage of the arc can be adjusted to effect the various changes in the performance of the precipitator.

This last statement is actually typical of all the separation methods; various ratios of dimensions, air and water flow rates, and so on, can be changed in order to design a specific collection device to suit the specific characteristics of a particular effluent. Further necessary flexibility is gained by using different devices in sequence; a common arrangement, for instance, is a cyclone to collect the largest particles, followed by a bag-house or other high-efficiency device to separate the smaller particles.

The similarity of inertial and electrostatic devices, relying on gravitational and electrical forces, respectively, to push the particles toward a desired location, suggests the possibility of using other forces in an analogous way. In fact, both thermal and sonic forces, associated with heat and sound, can be used to move particles. Although these forces aren't yet used in any operational equipment for air pollution control, an everyday example of thermal precipitation can be seen in the dirty spots on a wall or ceiling immediately adjacent to a hot pipe or radiator.

Gaseous Pollutant Removal

Turning now to methods of separating gaseous pollutants from an effluent stack gas stream, we find fewer overall methods and fewer specific processes, partly because this is still a new area for research and partly because gaseous pollutant removal is more difficult. Among the overall methods are adsorption and absorption techniques, as well as combustion, the burning of combustible pollutants to prevent their escape. Although combustion is not really a separation method, but rather an add-on pollution control device, we'll mention it briefly. Carbon monoxide and the various hydrocarbons will oxidize to carbon dioxide and water under the proper circumstances; this will probably become a principal means of controlling their emission from motor vehicle engines. In stationary sources, the only significant use of combustion is in controlling hydrocarbon and other organics from such small pollutant sources as restaurants and dry cleaners. Adsorption methods also see very limited use in controlling pollution from stationary sources. Activated charcoal is used to adsorb organics from small sources, and there is research on charcoal adsorption of sulfur dioxide.

By far the most common method of cleaning gases from stationary source effluents is chemical absorption; variations arise in the different chemicals used and in the way they are introduced into the pollution-causing process. Actually, the only gaseous pollutant usually controlled by any means is sulfur dioxide. Control methods for sulfur dioxide involve bringing the stack gas into contact with another chemical, which results in a substance that can be removed easily. Usually, the stack gas is caused to react with a water slurry of lime or limestone that is put into the stack gas in a scrubber. There's a variety of SO_2 control methods, but they differ only in detail, and none of them is yet regarded as clearly better than the others. We'll return to the topic of SO_2 control later, when we talk about pollution from combustion sources.

Controlling emissions of the other gases is rarely undertaken at present. In addition to SO_2, NO_x is the only other of the six major pollutants to come from stationary sources in any significant quantity. Present indications are that if NO_x from stationary sources will need to be controlled, the methods will have to be preventive, as chemical methods do not seem to be feasible at present. Thus, our list of control methods for stationary source pollution comprises little more than the various methods of separating particles of various sizes and the various chemical means of absorbing sulfur dioxide. This, of course, is consistent with the presumption in Chapter 1 and the data in Table 8–1, namely, that SO_2 and particulates are generally stationary-source problems, whereas the other four major pollutants are primarily motor vehicle problems.

Recycling and Reuse

Before leaving the topic of generalized approaches to pollution control, we should mention one other approach, recycling. Actually, recycling waste products for further use is perhaps just another type of process modification, but the topic warrants some specific discussion, both for its philosophical implications and its present popularity as a public issue. Most people think of recycling in the context of municipal refuse or solid waste— the garbage and trash from our homes and small businesses. Although it's probably true that reclaiming materials from municipal trash is the most challenging and potentially most rewarding recycling possibility, the same philosophy is equally applicable in other, more typically industrial, situations.

The philosophy underlying pressures for increased recycling springs from the realization that our planet and its resources are finite; indeed, the massive economic growth since 1940 has brought us noticeably closer to those limits. Only recently have significant numbers of people come to realize that we've already made more than a trivial dent in that stockpile of resources and that maybe we should try to determine just how big a portion is already gone and how much is left. This viewpoint was at the core of much of the environmental movement of the late 1960s; here, we're interested only in the fact that interest in reclaiming waste materials, cleaning and purifying the water and air we use, etc., will undoubtedly increase.

FUEL COMBUSTION

Turning now to a discussion of the specific human activities that cause pollution, we find that the principal source is the burning of fuels to produce energy for our various needs. Even with the burning of fuels for our transportation needs excluded, the use of fuels to satisfy our need for heat and electrical energy is the principal source of sulfur dioxide and a major source of particulate pollution. This most significant role is not so strange when we consider life in a broad, ecological sense; the methods of getting, transforming, transporting, and using energy are at the basic core of life itself.

There are three major categories of stationary-source fuel combustion. The first of these is miscellaneous domestic and commercial use—space heating (the heating of our living and working spaces during the cold season), plus burning fuel for cooking and heating hot water. The other two categories are industrial or manufacturing fuel use and electric-power generation. These categories may overlap; for example, industrial space heating is generally included with other industrial use rather than with

TABLE 8–2
Emissions from stationary fuel combustion sources (in millions of tons per year)

	Sulfur oxides	Particulate matter	Carbon monoxide	Hydro-carbons	Nitrogen oxides
Electric-power plants					
Coal	17.7	3.6	0.2	—	3.4
Oil	1.7	0.1	—	—	0.6
Gas	—	—	—	0.1	0.7
Total	19.4	3.7	0.2	0.1	4.7
Industrial					
Coal	4.1	1.9	0.1	—	0.5
Oil	0.8	0.1	—	—	0.3
Gas	—	0.1	—	0.2	3.7
Total	4.9	2.1	0.1	0.2	4.5
Other (heating, etc.)					
Coal	0.4	0.1	0.2	0.2	—
Oil	1.7	0.2	0.1	0.1	0.4
Gas	—	0.1	0.1	—	0.3
Other fuels*	0.1	0.6	0.1	—	0.1
Total	2.2	1.0	0.5	0.3	0.8
Total	26.5	6.8	0.8	0.6	10.0

* Primarily wood, but also kerosene, LPG, etc.; also includes the industrial use of these fuels.
Source: James H. Cavender, David S. Kircher, and Alan J. Hoffman, *Nationwide Air Pollutant Emission Trends 1940–1970*, Publication No. AP-115, Environmental Protection Agency, 1973.

domestic space heating. Electric-power plants could, conceivably, be viewed as just a different type of industrial fuel use, but they are sufficiently different from the others and constitute a large enough proportion of the total to warrant keeping them separate.

Table 8–2 lists the emissions from these three categories of fuel combustion sources classified according to the fuel used. It's apparent that power plants are the biggest of the three categories and that stationary fuel use in general presents little problem with CO and hydrocarbons; what emissions there are come primarily from the use of wood as a fuel in the Pacific Northwest. Not so apparent from this tabulation is the fact that over 80% of the SO_2 and nearly 90% of the particulates from these sources come from the use of coal rather than from oil or gas. This tremendous difference leads us to discuss the various fuels, a topic that will become increasingly important as the development of a national energy policy makes questions about the use of coal vs. gas a matter for the public media. After discussing fuels, we'll consider the equipment used to burn them and the control of pollution from these sources; then, we'll turn to the other principal stationary pollution sources—the disposal of solid waste and losses from industrial processes.

Fossil Fuels

Coal, oil, and gas, known collectively as fossil fuels, were formed (by nature) from the fossilized remains of prehistorical vegetation. Typically, the remains of the ancient forests were decayed by bacteria in bogs of what we now call peat and over the ages were gradually transformed by heat and pressure into first lignite, then subbituminous, bituminous, and finally anthracite, the various grades of coal. Under somewhat different circumstances, in lake bottom sediments rather than bogs, similar geological forces produced the deposits of oil and natural gas, which typically occur together. Actually, fossil fuels are very nearly the only fuels that are burned; wood is sometimes used in forested areas, and manufactured gas is burned in some cases, but in general one's choices are limited to the various types or grades of coal, oil, and gas. In fact, since the only alternative energy sources—nuclear power and hydroelectric power—are relatively minor, the fossil fuels are by far the predominant source of our energy.

Coal. The most common of the three fossil fuels in terms of availability, coal is, however, no longer common in everyday life in many parts of the country. The primary advantages of coal are its widespread availability and low cost; for several centuries, it was the only fuel available other

TABLE 8–3
Typical characteristics and composition (in %) of coals and related fuels

	Moisture	Carbonaceous		Ash	Energy content (1000 BTU/lb)
		Volatile	Fixed		
Coke	1	2	87	10	13
Anthracite coal	3	5	82	10	15
Bituminous coal	5	30	60	5	14
Subbituminous coal	15	35	45	5	13
Lignite	35	30	30	5	10
Peat	55	23	20	2	4

than wood and was used for every purpose. Now that other fuels have become available, the choice of coal or another fuel has become a matter of balancing good and bad features, and in recent years these have included air pollution considerations.

Coal comes in different grades that are defined by their properties, as tabulated in Table 8–3. These differences—primarily the balance of moisture and ash content, and fixed and volatile carbonaceous matter—affect both the uses to which the different grades are typically put and also the pollution potential involved in their use. The moisture content of a fuel, for example, is a detriment; not only does water not burn to give energy, but it also consumes energy in the process of forming steam. The volatile matter is the portion of the organics in the coal that is emitted as vapors when the coal is heated; the fixed carbon is the part that remains. The ash content is a measure of the inorganic, noncombustible material in the coal. The energy content of the coal is, crudely, the energy in the carbonaceous matter less the energy needed to vaporize the moisture content. Since there is a great deal of variability in the different deposits of each type of coal, the figures in Table 8–3 are only approximations and are presented primarily to indicate the pattern of the properties among the grades of coal.

The properties of coal that have a bearing on air pollution are the ash content, the volatility, and mostly the sulfur content. The ash content is related to the amount of particulate emissions when the coal is burned. As shown in the table, however, the ash content varies much less with the rank of the coal than do the other parameters; the difference from one coal deposit to another is more likely to be important. The volatility of the coal is related to smoke formation and the emission of the benzo-a-pyrene type of organic material, in each case the higher volatility being less desirable. In the case of smoke, however, the concern arises only with the smaller, inefficient fuel-burning installations; in a major power plant, by contrast, even high-volatile fuel can be burned smokelessly. The sulfur content of coals is important because it relates directly to the amount of SO_2 emitted when the coal is burned; like the ash content, however, the sulfur content is more a function of the precise coal bed in question than of the type of coal. Sulfur content ranges from nearly zero to several percent, some occurring as inorganic pyrites and some bound in organic compounds. We'll return to this topic shortly, after we pursue the various types of coals a little further.

The various grades of coal don't occur together, and the geographical location of the various fields is an important aspect in determining their use. The map in Fig. 8–5 shows the principal coal deposits in the United States. Peat is the decayed material from swampy bogs that ultimately becomes coal. The peat that was not buried deep enough to change has some fuel value, though not much, largely because of its high moisture content. The United States has a great deal of peat, mostly in Minnesota, but it is used for gardening and agricultural purposes, not for fuels. Peat is used for fuel in some countries that don't have adequate supplies of higher-grade fuels.

Lignite, the lowest-grade coal, is not widely used, and the same is true for subbituminous coal, the next higher grade. Both lignite and subbituminous coal tend to dry out and crumble if they're stored too long in the open air; therefore, transporting them any distance is relatively expensive. Yet as we see from Fig. 8–5, long-distance transport is needed to bring coal from the major lignite and subbituminous coal deposits, located in the mountains and plains areas, to the major industrial and population centers. Therefore, these lower-grade coals have typically been used only in small quantities by local users.

Bituminous coal, in contrast, has been and continues to be used in huge quantities. The two major bituminous coal areas are Appalachia and an area in Illinois; the five states of West Virginia, Kentucky, Pennsylvania, Illinois, and Ohio produce over three-fourths of all our coal, with almost half of it coming from West Virginia and Kentucky. Bituminous coal, which has a higher heating value than the lower grades, is relatively dry and doesn't crumble; it is the type of coal that is familiar to the average person.

Anthracite coal is much harder and drier than bituminous coal; it occurs only in relatively small amounts, however, mostly in northeastern Pennsylvania. The use of anthracite is further limited because it's hard to burn and has to be carefully washed and sorted by size, which makes it

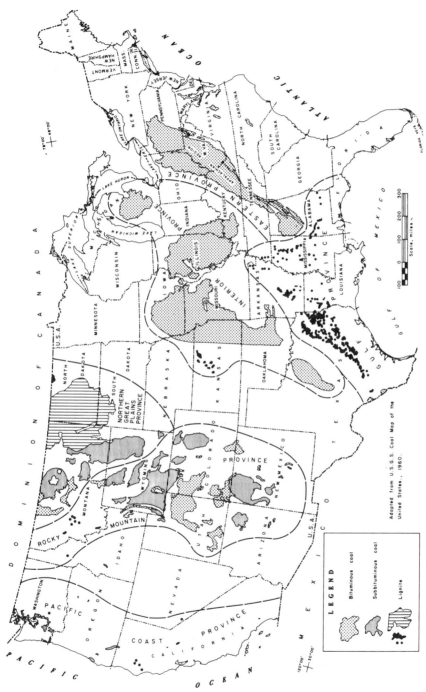

Fig. 8–5. Location of major coal fields in coterminous United States.

expensive. Anthracite is used primarily for space heating and in the making of coke.

Coke is not used as a fuel in the normal sense, but is used extensively in the iron and steel industry. Coke is not mined, but is manufactured from anthracite and some bituminous coals by heating them to drive off the volatile materials, leaving a grey, porous material that is almost all carbon.

TABLE 8–4
Distribution of coal reserves by sulfur content (in %, weighted by energy value)

| | East of Mississippi River | | | West of Mississippi River | | | |
	Low	Med.	High	Low	Med.	High	Total
Anthracite	1			*	*		1
Bituminous	5	12	14	9	1	7	48
Subbituminous	*			28			28
Lignite	2			21			23
Totals	8	12	14	58	1	7	100

* Known, but less than .5%.
Source: Senate Public Works Committee Staff, *Some Environmental Implications of National Fuels Policy,* December 1970.

The sulfur content of the various grades of coal (Table 8–4) is important in considering the effects of fuel-use patterns on air pollution. The table categorizes available coal reserves of the various types by sulfur content (low, medium, and high) and by location (east or west of the Mississippi). Approximately two-thirds of our coal has a low sulfur content (1% or less), and at first this might seem to be good. However, most of these deposits are of the subbituminous and lignite varieties and are located west of the Mississippi; most of the coal we use is the higher-sulfur bituminous coal found east of the Mississippi. Efforts to control air pollution have put enough of an economic premium on low-sulfur coal to warrant shipping it cross-country. In addition, since it's easier to transmit electricity along high-voltage power lines than it is to ship lignite in covered railroad cars, there's been pressure to move power stations closer to areas of low-sulfur coal. Since the residents of the Great Plains coal fields are opposed to that idea, and since nobody is in favor of strip-mining, the stage is set for a major battle over coal resources and energy needs.

Fuel oil. Like gasoline, motor oil, and a variety of other chemicals, fuel oil is a petroleum product. Crude oil, or petroleum as it comes from the ground, is a complex mixture of hydrocarbons and other liquid organics which are separated into different products by a variety of oil-refining methods. The properties of the various grades of fuel oil are thus determined not by nature, but by the parameters of the refinery operation. There are loose industry standards for grades 1 through 6, but these are usually condensed into two categories—distillate oil and residual oil—for considering air pollution. Distillate fuel oil (grades 1 and 2) has essentially no ash and has sulfur limits of 0.05% for grade 1 and 1% for grade 2. A relatively minor source of pollution, distillate oil is used in small to medium-sized oil-burning units, primarily for domestic and commercial space heating.

Residual fuel oil, by contrast, is used by power plants and larger fuel users and is a significant source of SO_2 emissions. It is a heavy, thick, gunky stuff that must be thinned out by heating before it will even flow into a burner. Although it is a relatively cheap energy source, its high sulfur content is a major drawback. The word "residual" is literal; residual oil is what remains after the lighter-weight fractions of the petroleum have been refined away. The refining process removes the sulfur from the gasoline and distillate oil, but the residual oil retains whatever sulfur content was in the original crude oil, often up to several percent. Crude oils from the various oil fields around the world vary considerably in the amount of sulfur they contain, and as pressure on fuel users to reduce pollution has increased, low-sulfur oil has come to be a valuable commodity.

Natural gas. The most recently developed of our fossil fuels, natural gas is the least polluting and by far the most convenient to use. Widespread conversion to gas as a fuel would be an ideal solution to many of our air pollution problems were it not for the fact that gas is the least commonly available of all our fossil fuels. Consisting mostly of methane, natural gas also contains other light-weight gaseous hydrocarbons; some deposits of natural gas also have some sulfur, but it is easily and routinely removed.

Before the widespread use of natural gas, other fuel gases were in use, the most important of which was producer gas, an industrial product derived from coal with air and steam. The combustible components in producer gas were CO, hydrogen, and methane, but it also contained a fair amount of incombustible nitrogen. Because of its CO content, producer gas was dangerous, and desperate heroines committed suicide by putting their heads in gas ovens; with modern natural gas, that doesn't work so well.

Other fossil fuels. The recent abrupt increases in the price of imported crude oil has brought to public attention other fossil fuels, the two most prominent of which—tar sands and oil shale—are petroleumlike hydrocarbons in deposits that are particularly difficult and expensive to extract. When the price of crude oil was $3–$5 a barrel, no one could afford to tap these other deposits, except for experimental research and development. In 1973, however, when the price of imported crude oil rose to well over $10 a barrel, this economic restraint disappeared.

Tar sands are deposits of sand saturated with tar and oil, which can be extracted in commercial quantities by processing huge amounts of sand. The known tar sand deposits are in western Canada. Oil shale is simply shale, a sedimentary rock, that has a small amount of oil trapped in its structure. The oil is extracted by mining the shale, crushing it, cooking out the hydrocarbons, and, of course, disposing of the residue. The oil shale deposits in Colorado, Utah, and Wyoming are estimated to contain more recoverable petroleum than all the known crude oil deposits in the world, perhaps 600 billion barrels. Since the first, relatively small-scale development sites were leased by the Interior Department in 1974, any significant production of oil is a few years away.

Fuel-Burning Devices

The variety of devices or equipment for fuel combustion ranges from the simple fireplace, through the domestic furnace, on up to the largest, most efficient boilers in the newest steam-electric power plants. Here, we'll focus primarily on coal-burning equipment, however, because coal is our biggest problem. We'll talk about the factors that affect smoke production and other aspects of combustion efficiency or inefficiency, and we'll then relate these factors to the fact that combustion of oil and gas is much easier and cleaner than is the combustion of coal.

The hand-fired coal furnace. The basic elements of a fuel-burning furnace are the firebox, or combustion chamber, within which the fire burns, and the grate, on which the fuel (a solid fuel, now) rests while it burns. The grate serves to keep the fuel off the floor so that air can circulate. Figure 8–6 shows the operation of a simple, hand-fired coal furnace, the type used for domestic space heating. The operating parameters of most concern are the flows of air and fuel into and out of the combustion chamber. Adjustable openings above and below the grate control the air; the bottom opening is also used for shoveling out the ashes. One fires the furnace by shoveling coal into the grate. The bottom door (draft) can be opened to let more air in, and this makes the coal burn faster. The burning coal gives off organic gases and CO, and these, too, burn. If the fire burns too rapidly, the flow of air can be reduced by closing the draft door, or cool air can be let in above the fire by opening the upper door (damper). As the coal burns, the ash falls through the grate.

Crucial to the efficiency of this operation is that enough oxygen from the air get in contact with the hydrogen and carbon in the hot coal to permit the chemical oxidation reactions to go to their ultimate chemical

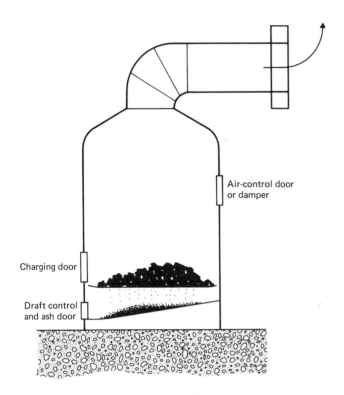

Fig. 8–6. Hand-fired domestic coal·furnace.

end point, sending up the flue only CO_2 from the carbon and water (H_2O) from the hydrogen. To this end, we can control the amount of fuel we put in and to some extent the air flow, though both need to be related to our need for a certain amount of heat. Inside the furnace, the crucial factors are typically expressed in a short-cut memory device—"T, T, T, and O" (time, temperature, turbulance, and oxygen). *Time* means that the combustibles have to be in the furnace long enough for the combustion reactions to be completed; *temperature* means that the combustibles must be hot enough for the combustion reactions to proceed; *turbulence* means that the fuel and air should be well mixed; *oxygen*, of course, means that enough oxygen must be present for the chemical reactions to occur.

To see how these factors affect the design of a furnace, we'll discuss what happens when the T, T, T, and O conditions are not satisfied. For example, trouble arises when the combustibles don't stay hot enough long enough to burn. When the coal is heated, it gives off volatile organic vapors, which must be burned in order to get the energy they contain. Since the poor air flow on the surface of the coal results in inefficient combustion, much of the carbon will be initially oxidized only to CO, which must then be further oxidized. Both the CO and the organic vapors are typically oxidized further in the space above the coal bed; in fact, much of the actual chemical oxidation takes place there, in the hot gases of the flames above the coals. Insufficient oxygen in the flames causes the oxidation process to falter; if the upward flow of gases is too rapid, they may cool too quickly, leaving insufficient time for the reactions to be completed. This is especially true if the furnace is too small; the gases strike the relatively cooler sides of the firebox before there's been time for combustion to finish. Thus, smoke is typically formed when hot, organic gases, especially from coal with high volatile content, strike the top of the firebox and cool, having been only partly oxidized, leaving the un-burned carbon to emerge as smoke. If there is insufficient turbulent mix-ing, even an adequate supply of oxygen cannot reach the combustibles.

A number of these problems are aggravated simultaneously when a new charge of fuel is put in. The new fuel is cold, which lowers temper-atures and provides cold surfaces, and its bulk reduces the air flow. The low fire provides a relatively low draft and hence low oxygen flow. Par-ticles are often shaken loose into the exhaust gas when the new coal disturbs the previous bed. In fact, given the need for a periodic infusion of fuel into a hand-fired unit, it is impossible to keep all the parameters even near optimum under such a wide variety of conditions, thus making hand-fired units big polluters. Thus, one of the first improvements we make with a furnace is to provide a smooth, continuous flow of fuel rather than intermittent hand firing. The devices that do this are called mechanical stokers; they put coal onto the grate in a slow, continuous manner, with the stoking rate adjustable according to heating demand. There are stokers for small, domestic furnaces, but they are more commonly used in the larger, more complex commercial and industrial fuel-burning installations. Figure 8–7 shows a common type of stoker for large boilers, a traveling-grate spreader-stoker; the coal, spread continuously from a hopper to a continuously moving grate, then travels through the combustion zone on the grate, with the incombustibles being dumped in an ash pit at the other end.

Pulverized-coal units. The next logical step in obtaining more efficient combustion is to use pulverized coal, which is the most common method in large, new units. In this method, the coal is pulverized to a fairly fine powder and then blown by huge fans into the furnace, along with the air for combustion. This is a far cry from the simple hand-fired furnace, in which the air is pulled in by the natural updraft over the fire, but the results are a far cry from the efficiencies of a small furnace too. The finely divided coal powder is very well mixed with the air, resulting in very high combustion efficiencies. The chief drawback in using pulverized coal is

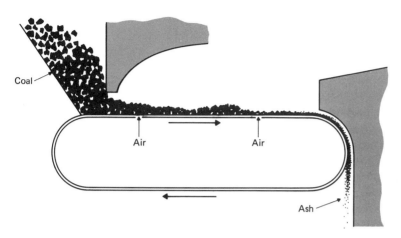

Fig. 8–7. Traveling-grate spreader-stoker. The stoker shown here is for medium-size coal-burning installations. Such equipment permits smooth, uniform combustion, which results in much greater efficiency and hence lower emissions. (W. L. Faith, *Air Pollution Control,* New York: Wiley, 1959, Fig. 3.4. Reprinted by permission of John Wiley & Sons, Inc.)

that a greater portion of the incombustible ash is carried up the flue with the air rather than falling into the ash pit at the bottom of the furnace. Because of this large amount of fly ash, as it's called, electrostatic precipitators must be used for the efficient collection of quite small particles.

The gains in efficiency resulting from burning pulverized coal serve as a good introduction to a discussion of the equipment used for burning oil or gas. Greater mixing of the fuel and air, the principal advantage of pulverizing the coal, is even more readily attained with oil and gas. Liquid oil can be sprayed into the combustion air, and gas, of course, mixes easily with air. Thus, the combustion units designed for the various fuels differ mainly in the devices used for mixing and feeding the fuel. In large power plants, these devices comprise a relatively small portion of the overall equipment and cost, as compared to the huge draft fans and the heat exchange tubing systems in which the water actually boils, to say nothing of the huge, precisely made electric generator that the steam drives. Thus, for many such installations it is well within the range of feasibility to have dual sets of burners for different fuels and to change from one to another in response to seasonal variations in economics and pollution control requirements.

Controlling Particulate Emissions

Because the small, hand-fired domestic furnace is operated intermittently, it is extremely difficult to design this type of furnace for efficient operation. Typically, the methods of control have included requiring the use of low-volatile and low-sulfur coals, or even eliminating the furnace. In London and other industrial areas of Britain, the principal source of the extreme smogs since the days of John Evelyn has been the ubiquitous coal-burning open fireplace used for home heating. In the aftermath of the 1952 killer smog, the government finally initiated a control program aimed at eliminating these emissions, at least in London, by either eliminating the fireplaces or requiring the burning of such high-grade fuels as coke or anthracite. In the United States, domestic space heating is not the biggest problem, since few homes are now heated by coal fireplaces or furnaces. With the advent of natural gas in the 1950s, coal furnaces have largely disappeared, at least in the urban areas.

With larger fuel-burning equipment, in which the fuel is fed into the furnace in a smooth, continuous process, more can be done to control particulate emissions. First, within the limits of the design of the equipment, the combustion can be made as efficient as possible by adjusting the flow rates of the fuel and air and perhaps also adjusting the quality of the fuel used. On smaller or older units, these operating adjustments have typically been the only measures taken. If the best possible operation still produces too much black smoke or particulate matter, the equipment is usually replaced whenever it becomes economical to do so. The alternative is to install a particulate collection device; however, until very recently, when regulatory efforts became more stringent, no one wanted to do that. Thus, progress toward eliminating black smoke was made by replacing old, inefficient equipment. Although replacing such outmoded equipment might have been undertaken for economic reasons, it is also likely that the pressure of public opinion helped promote the early replacement of much marginal equipment.

To control particulates beyond the heaviest particles and the smoke, however, it becomes necessary to add control devices. Since the fly ash from large units fired by pulverized coal is so light, high-efficiency particle collectors are needed, and increasingly the same is true for the smaller power plants and the larger industrial installations. The principal remaining questions about particulate controls concern the efficiencies of control devices vs. their cost. The trade-off is between upgrading the control equipment on an older boiler or waiting until it's more economically feasible to replace it with a bigger, more efficient installation. Although the problems of particulate emissions from fuel-combustion installations have not yet been eliminated, they have decreased. Now, a larger share of the particulate emissions comes from process losses, those losses of material from the industrial process itself, rather than from the production of heat and energy.

Controlling Sulfur Dioxide

Fuel combustion is still a serious pollution problem, however. Conspicuously absent in the discussion so far has been the major problem of SO_2 emissions produced by the oxidation of the sulfur in the fuel. Although the problem has been recognized for decades, there has never been any inexpensive way of reducing the SO_2 emissions, so consequently there has never been any serious control effort. In the late 1960s, when pressure to control emissions increased, a number of cities and states passed regulations limiting the sulfur content of fuels for use in combustion installations. This can be a very effective control measure. Washington, D.C., was fortunate, in that many of the biggest combustion installations belong to the federal General Services Administration. Figure 8–8 shows the dramatic decrease in SO_2 levels that occurred when the GSA switched to lower-sulfur fuel.

Such fuel-sulfur regulations typically provide that higher-sulfur fuel can be burned if effluent-cleaning devices to reduce the SO_2 emissions from the stack by an equivalent amount are installed. This gives the source operator a choice of which control technique to use. When the regulations first went into effect, no thoroughly proven SO_2 scrubbing devices were available, and therefore most users opted for switching to low-sulfur fuel, including many who switched from coal to oil. This, of course, led to

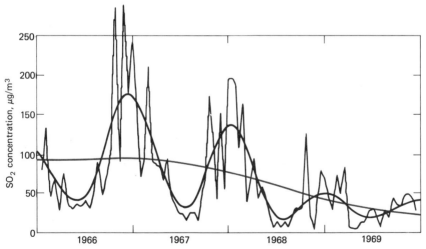

Fig. 8–8. Decrease in sulfur dioxide levels in Washington, D.C. Both the seasonal and long-term trends are plotted. Note the distinct lowering of the winter peaks over the three winters as the General Services Administration changed to lower-sulfur fuels in heating installations.

competitive bidding and much higher prices for the limited amounts of low-sulfur coal and oils available.

The higher costs should, according to economic theory, spur the development and use of flue gas desulfurization processes, primarily the chemical scrubbing processes described earlier. This did happen to some extent, but nonetheless the use of stack-gas cleaning systems has been disappointingly sparse. Major sources resist using these processes, contending that the feasibility of scrubbing has still not been demonstrated, although there are a number of such systems in operation. In essence, the large sources are unwilling to try the processes for the very reason that they are still untried on very large sources.

The result of this resistance, of course, is continued reliance on burning low-sulfur fuels without stack-gas cleaning, thus making much of our coal and residual oil supply unusable. This, in turn, has contributed to the increased demand for the remaining fuel supplies and hence to the "energy crisis." During the winter of 1973–1974, air pollution restrictions on the sulfur content of fuel for major users, e.g., power plants, were in fact relaxed so that they could burn high-sulfur oil and reduce the shortage of higher-quality domestic heating oils.

The fuel-sulfur regulations have also increased the desirability of designing large units so that they are capable of switching to sulfurless gas as a fuel, and this is increasingly common. Some power plants routinely switch seasonally, perhaps burning gas except in the winter, when domestic gas customers get priority. More commonly, plants in urban areas often have plans to switch to lower-sulfur fuels for short periods when adverse weather conditions may cause serious pollution episodes. These are basically short-term solutions, however. For the long run, the only solutions available are removal of the SO_2 from the stack gases or removal of the sulfur from the fuel before it's burned. At the present, the most well-developed options are the stack-gas cleaning processes; although these processes have not been perfected, they are being installed on major power plants. There are many different types of processes being used, and no one variety is best in all circumstances. Actually, since SO_2 sources also vary widely, there likely won't be one best type of process, but rather several, each for certain circumstances. Here, we'll categorize only the major types of processes.

All the methods involve absorbing SO_2 with another chemical; some processes use dry absorbents, but most use wet methods—either reagents dissolved in water, as in a bubbler, or insoluble absorbents simply mixed with water to form a slurry. The absorbent can be either thrown away (in an environmentally protective manner, we hope) or else run through some additional chemistry to regenerate the absorbent and get the sulfur into a saleable form, usually sulfuric acid or elemental sulfur. Although the regenerative approach may appear to be the more attractive, there is a problem; if even a moderate proportion of the sulfur now going up stacks were reclaimed, there would be so much sulfur on the market that no one would be able to sell it at an attractive price.

Most of the chemicals used as dry absorbents are metal oxides, and these processes don't seem too promising. In the wet processes, the absorbent chemicals are usually either an alkali, such as sodium or ammonium, or else calcium or magnesium. The single most common absorbent chemical, and the one that has been the most thoroughly researched, is calcium, usually in the form of lime or limestone. There are a dozen or so lime or limestone scrubbing projects in operation, and a similar number are planned or under construction; most are on power plants, though a few are on ore smelters or sulfuric acid manufacturing plants. Most are throwaway rather than regenerative plants, and one of the major problems is what to do with the waste sludge; another serious problem is the formation of calcium deposits on the equipment. In general, there is a good deal more engineering to do, not just on limestone scrubbing, but on all stack-cleaning methods.

Fuel Desulfurization

The possibility of removing sulfur from fuels is also a very viable alternative and is especially attractive because it creates low-sulfur fuels for fuel-burning sources that are unable to remove sulfur from stack gases economically. As we've already noted, sulfurous components of natural gas are routinely removed. Removal of sulfur from residual oil is also practiced, but economics plays a bigger role here. Because gasoline is more profitable, refiners of the relatively low-sulfur crude oils from the United States produce relatively little residual oil; with their less advanced technology, foreign refineries produce more and cheaper residual oil, although some of it has a high sulfur content. Thus, most of our residual fuel oil is imported and becomes a factor in national policies relating to the balance of payments, etc. Most of the oil used in the urban Northeast comes from Venezuela, and recently a desulfurization plant was built there by the American oil company that imports the oil. The cost of this extra processing increases the cost of the residual oil by 20% to 35%.

The major role of desulfurization, however, could be in making the huge deposits of bituminous and subbituminous coal available in a low-sulfur form. The Department of the Interior has been conducting a research and development program toward this end, and the energy crisis has accelerated efforts. The "cleanability" of coal depends in part on the form in which the sulfur occurs—whether as inorganic sulfides, called pyritic sulfur, or bound into the organic matter, called organic sulfur—

and this distinction should be kept in mind as various coal-cleaning processes are proposed.

Because our natural gas reserves are low, conversion of high-sulfur coal to gas is an attractive possibility for reducing SO_2 pollution and getting better use from our energy reserves. A number of *coal gasification* processes are in use or under development; they are more sophisticated than the old producer gas process, producing a better-quality gas and removing both types of sulfur as well. The production and use of such man-made gas will be increasingly common as natural gas supplies dwindle and prices increase.

There are also various ways of solvent-refining, or chemically treating crushed coal with a solvent, that are designed to remove sulfur and make a liquid product; some of these liquefication processes remove both types of sulfur, others only the inorganic sulfides.

Alternative Combustion Techniques

A radically different approach, in which the common concept of combustion in air is set aside, is a combustion process in which pulverized coal, limestone, and air are injected into a bed of molten iron. The combustibles in the coal are partially oxidized to CO within the molten iron; the gaseous CO comes off the top of the mass of iron and is efficiently burned further in a conventional way. The sulfur in the coal, however, is retained in the iron and forms a slag with the limestone; the slag is then collected off the top of the pool of iron. This method will probably not become widespread in the near future, but it does indicate that creative thinking about process changes can be fruitful.

Alternatives to Fossil Fuels

Among the longer-range alternatives are a number of suggestions for using something other than the fossil fuels to satisfy our energy needs. Closest to substantial realization is atomic power; there are a number of uranium-fuel fission plants in operation, and it is projected that such plants will meet an increasing share of the demand for power. Such plants generate heat from the nuclear reactions of radioactive uranium by converting a small amount of the uranium's mass directly into energy. The potential of this energy source is great, even though uranium reserves are relatively small. Presently, the atomic power industry is behind schedule in meeting projections, in part because of delays caused by various private groups' insistence on environmental safeguards that the industry hadn't planned on.

Two other nuclear power processes are under development and may become significant in the future. Breeder reactors are similar to present systems, but use plutonium rather than uranium as the fissionable fuel. Plutonium-based systems, however, can also convert nonfissionable types, or isotopes, of uranium into fissionable fuel, thus "breeding" more fuel and greatly extending the capacity of our uranium reserves. The Atomic Energy Commission expects to have the first breeder reactor providing power by 1980.

The other new process is the development of fusion reactors, much talked about but clearly far in the future. Both fusion and fission are reactions that involve the nucleus of the atom and the conversion of mass into energy, but the physics of the reactions are fundamentally different. The difference is analogous to that between the hydrogen and atomic bombs; atomic fission reactions split very large uranium atoms (weight 235) into smaller pieces, whereas thermonuclear fusion reactions fuse two very small atoms of the deuterium isotope of hydrogen (weight 2) into a larger helium atom. Since fusion reactors would probably use sea water to supply the deuterium needed, their ultimate potential is essentially unlimited; on the other hand, since containing and controlling fusion reactions, which occur at temperatures over 100 million degrees, is proving to be an extremely difficult problem, fusion power is clearly a long way off. However, one way to make quicker use of "fusion energy" would be to make direct use of the energy from the sun, which is produced by fusion reactions. This would entail collecting sunlight by one of the various means that can convert it directly to electricity; although this is a reasonable possibility, its extensive use is limited by the large space required for solar collectors and by its dependence on the vagaries of climate and weather.

Limited by geography are such other natural-energy sources as hydroelectric and tidal power sources. For centuries, humans have used the power potential of waterfalls, either natural ones like Niagara or huge man-made projects, the most recent of which is the Aswan High Dam and Lake Nasser. In the United States, most of the useful sites for hydro power have been more or less exhausted. There have long been proposals to obtain energy from the power of the tides, letting them lift water up at high tide and then generating electricity as the water flows back out at low tide. The cyclic nature of the tides is a bit of a problem, but the biggest problem is that the only sites where the tides are high enough to work in this way are not located where there is great need for electric power; these sites are all on Maine's rocky coast or in Alaska.

A more promising source of natural energy is geothermal energy, the basic flow of heat out from the molten core of the earth. This energy source can be directly tapped at a fair number of geologically appropriate locations. Usually, these are sites where the heat flow up through the rocks meets underground water in such a way as to create steam under pressure, e.g., the geysers in Yellowstone National Park. In theory, it sounds simple to tap this energy source; one simply drills wells to capture the steam and uses it to run the generating turbines. In fact, the process is simple, though in practice engineering problems arise because of the heavy mineral content in the steam, etc. Currently, one geothermal steam plant is operating in California, and others are expected to be built wherever appropriate sites become available, mostly in the West. On a national basis, however, geothermal energy will make only a small contribution to our supply of energy.

Since none of these alternative sources seems capable of producing enough energy to meet our future demands, the only other alternative to continued massive reliance on fossil fuels would be to decrease the future demand. Although many people feel that this would be ecologically desirable, even necessary, it is also clear that such a stance will be difficult politically, since it would impinge on what many people consider essential parts of their high standard of living. Clearly, however, some things *can* be done to reduce energy demand without lowering our standard of living; perhaps, we just haven't thought of some of these measures or, as is more likely, we simply haven't tried to make them work. As an example of the latter, our building codes, mortgage-lending practices, and just plain habit all encourage the construction of poorly insulated buildings, with the consequent waste of heating energy year after year after year.

SOLID-WASTE DISPOSAL

Another area that exemplifies our society's general wastefulness is our generation of solid waste. The problem caused by the garbage, refuse, and trash we generate is often called "the third pollution," and it does in fact have some parallels with air and water pollution. "The solid-waste problem," however, generally refers to problems of recycling, the recovery of resources, and the tremendous costs of disposal. However, we will pursue only the air pollution aspects of the solid-waste problem. The significance of solid-waste disposal to air pollution is roughly comparable to a single industrial process; however, with respect to the nature of its process operations, solid-waste disposal is much more like a fuel-combustion source.

Historically, solid waste has been either dumped or burned, or perhaps first dumped and then burned. More recently, relatively careful burning in an incinerator has been common; still more recently, sanitary landfills have also been used. Clearly, the worst disposal method with respect to air pollution and other considerations is the burning of solid waste in open dumps. Combustible material in dumps used to be burned in order to save space, but the high moisture content and very poor combustion conditions led to horrendous smoke and odor problems; now, this practice is becoming less common in urban areas. If space is available, ordinary dumps do not cause an air pollution problem, but sanitary land-filling is a better solution. Sanitary landfills are deliberate, carefully planned dumping sites where the refuse is distributed evenly, compacted, and covered over with soil; properly used landfills cause no unpleasant neighborhood nuisance and can be used for recreation when they're filled up.

The only major air pollution problem comes from the incineration of solid waste, either in small units of home or apartment-house scale, or in large, municipal incinerators. The incineration of solid waste is quite similar to the combustion of fossil fuels, except that the "fuel" to be burned is wet, has a low energy content, a very high ash and incombustible content, and can be very nonhomogeneous and hard to handle. Nonetheless, solid waste does burn, which greatly reduces its volume. In fact, one of the main reasons for burning solid waste is to reduce the quantity that needs to be dumped. The basic requirements for good combustion are the same as those for burning fossil fuels—adequate T, T, T, and O. As with the case of fossil fuels, it's the smaller, older incinerators that cause the most air pollution.

One of the biggest problems is the flue-fed apartment-house incinerator, and in some urban areas its use has been banned. These small, single-chamber incinerators are much like a small, hand-fired furnace. Trash and garbage are dropped into the firebox from a disposal chute on each floor of the apartment building. Often, the disposal chute also serves as the exhaust flue from the incinerator, although it may also be a separate chute dropping into the firebox. In either case, the falling trash disturbs the combustion, shaking up ashes and particulates and cooling and wetting the already burning material on the grate. A better solution is to have the disposal chute lead to a storage bin and have the custodian charge the incinerators properly.

An even better alternative is to have some sort of afterburner on the incinerator. Solid-waste combustion produces a large amount of volatile matter in fairly high temperature cool stack gases. Using an afterburner to burn these gases reduces emissions considerably.

Another approach to the same problem is to use multiple-chamber incinerators. A single-chamber incinerator is a simple firebox, the kind the custodian throws the trash into from the storage bin. A multiple-chamber incinerator, by contrast, contains one or more additional, insulated chambers into which the stack gases can go after they leave the firebox. These chambers keep the gases hot longer before they go up the stack, thus helping to facilitate the combustion of the remaining volatile matter.

Table 8–5 lists emission factors (not total emissions) for various types of incinerators; it's apparent that the multiple-chamber incinerator emits about half or less of the particulate, CO, and hydrocarbon emissions of the single-chamber type. A similar comparison shows us that flue-feeding an

TABLE 8–5
Emission factors for solid-waste incineration (in pounds of pollutant per ton of solid waste)

Type of incinerator	Particulate matter	Carbon monoxide	Hydro-carbons	Nitrogen oxides	Sulfur oxides
Municipal					
Uncontrolled	30*				
Settling chamber and water spray	20				
Cyclone, etc.	10	35	1.5	2	1.5
Wet scrubber	4				
Electrostatic precipitator	2				
Fabric filter	0.5				
Industrial-Commercial					
Single chamber	15	20	15	2	1.5
Flue-fed	30	20	15	3	0.5
Flue-fed with after-burner	6	10	3	10	0.5
Multiple chamber	7	10	3	3	1.5
Small domestic					
Without burner	35	300	100	1	0.5
With primary burner	7	0	2	2	0.5

* The range of this figure for various installations is from 8 to 70 pounds per ton, and the other figures are similarly approximate.
Source: Compilation of Air Pollutant Emission Factors, 2d ed., Publication No. AP-42, Environmental Protection Agency, 1973.

incinerator doesn't produce more gaseous pollutants, but doubles the emission of particulates.

Actually, the flue-fed incinerator is a major problem mainly because of its widespread use. If we compare the emission factors listed in Table 8–5, we can see that some other incineration methods also do badly—specifically, uncontrolled municipal incinerators or small, domestic incinerators with no primary burners. The municipal incinerator is a problem for more or less the same reasons the flue-fed incinerator is—uneven charging of the nonhomogeneous waste. Overall, however, they're less of a problem, because all such incinerators have at least a minimum of settling chambers and water spray by way of emission controls. The reason the smaller single-house domestic incinerator is bad is that the amount of waste is not sufficient to provide enough energy to maintain good combustion; note that combustion improves tremendously with the addition of a primary burner, that is, a continuous flame applied to the waste, rather than just lighting it and letting it try to burn on its own.

This latter is typically the case with solid waste; it is just not possible to burn normal refuse really efficiently without adding some extra energy.

Major municipal incinerators do this by installing pumps which provide extra air; some users burn some extra fuel, which is of greater help in providing the extra energy. The extra energy, of course, costs money, although in a large unit this cost can be offset by the steam produced. The most common approach to emission control is to work on the design of the incinerators, large or small, and to try to optimize the balance between the cost of fancier equipment or additional energy and the cost of removing particulates from the stack gases afterward. Although the various particulate control techniques work well enough on incinerators, very few of them have high-efficiency control equipment, mostly because they're owned by impoverished local government units.

An increasingly common alternative is to try to combine other types of processes, with or without incineration, to form a more complex, but more flexible, array of choices. Partial sorting of trash can reduce the incombustible portions; the waste can be shredded and composted if the cellulose content from paper is not too high; or, finely shredded waste can be combined with pulverized coal for boiler fuel.

INDUSTRIAL PROCESS SOURCES

Although "industry" commonly seems the chief villain in environmental scenarios, this is partly because industry consumes tremendous amounts of fuels for energy. Pollutant emissions from the industrial processes themselves are less striking, though clearly significant; they amount to about a fifth of the total SO_x emissions, over half of the man-made particulate emissions, and a major share of many of the "other" pollutants. To speak so blithely of our entire industrial plant as a single category is really an unfair oversimplification, although a necessary one. It is unfair, in a sense, because some of our bigger industries produce no process emissions, while sizable emissions can come from those industries we often think of as minor. It's necessary, however, to treat them in a rather catch-all manner because of the variety of their processes and their emissions.

Some estimates of process emissions from various industrial categories are tabulated in Table 8–6. The EPA selected these industries in order to analyze the economic impact of the federal Clean Air Act; the figures in Table 8–6 represent estimates for 1967, the year the major relevant portion of the law was passed, and therefore may differ from the figures in Table 8–1 or the data in Chapter 3. Table 8–6 should, however, give a reasonably accurate idea of the degree to which various industries contribute to the process-loss portion of the pollution burden. The table shows that particulates are the biggest process-loss problem and that the biggest contributors to pollution are the iron and steel, grain handling, and cement industries.

TABLE 8–6
Industrial process loss emissions (estimates for 1967 in thousands of tons per year)

Industry	Particulate matter	Sulfur oxides	Carbon monoxide	Hydro-carbons	Nitrogen oxides
Asphalt batching	243				
Cement	813				
Coal cleaning	225				
Grain handling	1269				
Grey iron foundries	217		3200		
Iron and steel	2310		*	*	
Kraft pulping	380				
Lime	393				
Nitric acid					145
Petroleum	185	2310	9300	1191	
Phosphate	260				
Primary nonferrous Al	32				
Cu	243	2580			
Pb	34	185			
Zn	57	446			
Secondary nonferrous	24				
Sulfuric acid	25	600			

* Indicates significant emissions not estimated.
Source: The Economics of Clean Air, Annual Report of EPA Administrator to Congress, Senate Document 92–67, March 1972.

Iron and Steel Industry

Hundreds of firms are involved in various aspects of turning iron ore into finished products. Aside from their rise of energy, the pollution potential of most finishing and fabricating operations, e.g., rolling mills, is small. Here, we're concerned primarily with the "steel mills," which produce basic iron and steel from iron ore, coal, and limestone. This process requires two distinct steps; first, iron is smelted from the ore in a blast furnace, and then it is refined into the various types of steel by a number of different processes. However, two relatively minor processes at a steel mill—ore sintering and coke production—have the most impact on air pollution, and both are involved in the preparation of ingredients for the blast furnace.

When it arrives at the steel mill, iron ore is a granular material containing a fair amount of relatively fine particles, which are wasted if they're used directly in the blast furnace. Therefore, the ore, along with other waste dust from the mill, is put through a sintering plant, which heats the material and fuses much of the fine dust into larger, heavier particles. The particulate emissions that arise from the handling of the material are typically processed through cyclones or other dust control equipment, but improvements are needed in the degree of dust control.

Coke production is a major source of pollution in the iron and steel business. Coke, the carbonized material that remains when the volatile matter in coking coal is driven off by heating, is analogous to charcoal, which is made from wood in a similar manner. Coke is the material put into the blast furnace to react with the iron ore. Coke is made by heating coal in an oven; enough air is permitted in the oven to burn only enough coal to heat, but not burn, the rest. When coal first replaced wood in the making of iron, coke was made in dome-shaped brick ovens called beehive ovens. After the coal was heated in the oven, the hot coke was quenched (cooled) with water, removed, and carried away. The volatile organic products driven off the heated coal were wastes, emitted into the air as pollutants. Now, beehive ovens have been almost completely replaced with by-product coke ovens, which reclaim the valuable organic chemicals. The only emissions from the square, highly mechanized by-product ovens occur when the doors are open to charge coal in or take coke out, but these emissions still comprise a considerable amount of pollution. Some of the newer coke ovens are further controlled by completely enclosing them and collecting all the air around them; since the older ovens can't be so modified, however, further emission reductions cannot be made until all of these older ovens have been replaced.

Perhaps surprisingly, the heart of the iron-making operation, the blast furnace, is not a major pollution problem. In the blast furnace, iron ore, coke, and limestone are heated with tremendous blasts of hot air; the ore, which is iron oxide, reacts ultimately with the carbon in the coke to release the iron and to form carbon monoxide. The limestone forms a molten slag containing much of the mineral impurities from the ore; on cooling, it can be used instead of gravel in paving roads. The tremendous volume of exhaust air is heavily laden with waste particulate matter; fortunately, however, it also contains much carbon monoxide. The mills need to use the energy value of the CO in their furnaces, and in order to use it safely, they must first clean the particles thoroughly. Therefore, economic factors have eliminated the biggest potential source of pollution.

The last principal step in making steel is to refine the iron into the various types of steel. Several methods can be used, but all involve either further heating the iron or melting it again if it was cooled; this is done in combination with other ingredients to eliminate the remaining carbon and sometimes to alloy in other desired metals. All the methods—the electric arc furnace, the basic oxygen process, and the older Bessemer converter and open-hearth process—produce particulate emissions, a large portion of which are iron oxides. The processes usually have some form of particulate control, but except for the open hearth, they all involve huge vessels of molten steel that tilt and move about, thus making it difficult to gather the effluent gases into a duct for treatment. Since the overall efficiency of particulate collection from the sintering and steel-making processes is estimated at about 55%, there is sizable room for improvement, though it is not obvious how that will occur.

Grain Handling and Cement Industries

Though cereal grain and portland cement are completely dissimilar products, the origin of their particulate pollution problems is quite similar—the transportation, storage, and processing of their principal products—and, in contrast with the iron and steel industry, relatively simple. The processing of wheat, corn, oats, and other cereals into products begins, of course, at the farm. Typically, the grain is first brought from the farm to storage elevators located in rural areas; the elevators have loading and unloading facilities. After temporary storage in these *country elevators*, the grain is shipped to a *terminal elevator* operated by either a grain processor or a wholesaler. The grain is then cleaned and dried and ultimately transferred to the user, e.g., a flour mill. Flour mills and other final processors are well controlled and do not experience much particulate loss; the bulk of the emissions comes from the loading-unloading and cleaning-drying operations at the elevators and consists of eroded pieces of grain and adhered soil from the fields. Typically located in rural areas, grain operations, especially the country elevators, have generally been free from pollution considerations. Consequently, industrywide dust collection is only about 28%, and a fairly sizable control program, most likely relying on baghouses, would be necessary to improve this figure.

In contrast, the collection of particulate matter in the cement industry is generally over 90%. The figure for this industry is so much higher because cement processes are carried out in more congested areas and also because the dust recovered is either saleable cement or raw ingredients. Portland cement, the grey powder that is mixed with water, sand, and gravel to make concrete, can be made from a variety of mineral ingredients, most commonly limestone rock. The processing is a sequence of several particulate-producing operations. The raw materials must be quarried, crushed, and blended together. After the mixture has been roasted in a kiln to fuse the ingredients, the resulting lumps, or clinkers, are ground to the final powder form and bagged. Although the 90% control sounds good, the total amount of particulate matter is huge, and most plants will probably be required to install high-efficiency collectors, either baghouses or electrostatic precipitators, on some of their operations.

Other Materials-handling Devices

There are several other industrial categories that also involve using a dry material, with the attendant particulate emissions. These include *asphalt batching*, the making of asphaltic concrete, or "blacktop," by mixing asphaltic tar with gravel or slag, and *coal cleaning*, the processing of coal at the mine to remove dirt, sort it into sizes, etc. This latter process is not the "coal cleaning" sometimes used to describe coal desulfurization proposals, although some inorganic sulfur may be removed. Other industries in this category are the *lime* and *phosphate* industries. Lime, a mineral product produced by crushing and roasting limestone, is used for a variety of chemical purposes. Similarly, the crushing and processing of phosphate rock are the first stages in the production of a variety of phosphorus and phosphate products, many of which are used as agricultural fertilizers.

Another category of industry that produces particulate emissions is the group dealing with *nonferrous metals*—the smelters, the processing plants that extract crude metal from mineral ores. As the ores are mined, transported, and stored, particulate matter is emitted; these emissions are relatively well controlled, however, and smelters aren't considered a major particulate problem. They are, however, a major source of SO_2 pollution, and the reason lies in the basic nature of the smelting process. The ores of copper, lead, and zinc are not just soil with pieces of metal mixed in, as the popular version of gold mining might suggest; rather, they are minerals containing chemically combined metal. Unfortunately, the element the metals are combined with is frequently sulfur. The smelting of the ore thus consists of various operations of roasting, melting, cooking, and otherwise extracting the metal from the ore, and the production of prodigious amounts of SO_2 is more or less unavoidable. Since so much more copper than lead or zinc is smelted, copper smelting produces more emissions; in addition, much more ore is needed to get copper than is needed for either of the other two metals.

The smelting industry has been a major SO_2 source for decades; as we've noted, early smelters caused a great deal of plant damage, and such considerations have continued. The industry does control some of the SO_2, however; if the SO_2 in the exhaust gases is concentrated enough, sulfuric acid recovery plants are economical. The controls most likely to be required to reduce emissions from lead and zinc smelters are the building of some additional acid recovery plants that aren't economical. In the copper smelters, however, the amount of copper sulfide in the ore is so low (averaging less than 1%) that the flow of SO_2 is too dilute to chemically recover sulfuric acid. Many of the 16 copper smelters in the United States, which average 40 years old, will probably have to install major new process changes to keep the level of SO_2 emissions down, and this will likely be a major economic difficulty for the industry.

Primary aluminum, in contrast to the other metals, is produced from its principal ore, aluminum oxide or bauxite, in a totally different way; it is electrolytically reduced in a bath of molten cryolite, an aluminum-fluoride mineral. The particulate emissions, though not large, consist of very fine particles and are quite difficult to collect; in addition, the process emits fluorides and consumes tremendous quantities of electricity.

Finally, we note that the *secondary nonferrous* producers are a rather small source of particulate emissions. The many small firms in this sector of the metallurgical industry reprocess reclaimed metals, such as the lead in old automobile batteries.

Other Industries

Two chemical industries are included in the list in Table 8–6—*sulfuric* and *nitric acid* plants. In each case, the emissions from these plants represent the losses of some of the chemicals involved in their products, and controlling these emissions will require improved chemical engineering. The nitric acid plants, many of which are owned by the government for military ordnance purposes, are among the very few noncombustion sources of NO_x; the sulfuric acid industry is unusual because its product is thoroughly mixed up in the pollution control process, and SO_2-scrubbing processes may well become a principal source of sulfuric acid.

Both the kraft-pulping industry and the petroleum industry are also chemical in nature. The *kraft-pulping* process, one aspect of the pulp and paper industry, is a chemical process for separating the two principal components of wood—cellulose, from which paper and other products are made, and lignin, which is burned for fuel at the pulping mill. The SO_2 emissions result from the chemical process and for economic reasons are already pretty well controlled. Kraft mills, and the pulp and paper industry in general, have long been regarded as severe polluters, but this was largely a matter of water pollution and odors; in recent years, however, the industry has compiled a very commendable record of pollution abatement and control efforts.

Like the steel industry, the *petroleum* industry consists of a variety of operations, each with different emission characteristics. The variety of chemical processes involved in refining petroleum lead to emissions of hydrocarbons, that is, the evaporation of petroleum products, at many places throughout the plants; the SO_2 emissions result from the process of removing sulfur from the oils. One of the major refinery operations is catalytic cracking, which takes place in a "cat cracker," and refers to the breaking of large hydrocarbon molecules into smaller ones, assisted by the presence of catalytic chemicals. Cracking is an important operation, as it increases the percentage of the crude oil turned into highly profitable gasoline; in regenerating the catalyst for reuse, however, large amounts of CO are emitted. The technology needed to control emissions from refineries has long been available, having been developed initially to reduce hydrocarbons in Los Angeles; the amount of petroleum saved by pollution control is generally expected to more than pay for the control measures.

The last industry we will consider, *grey iron foundries*, is unusual because foundries are likely to be harder hit economically by pollution-control regulations than any other industry. A foundry is a plant that remelts pig iron (not steel) and casts it into pieces of various shapes used in machine parts, etc. The iron is melted in various types of furnaces, but the most common type is a tall, cylindrical furnace called a cupola, where coke is burned in direct contact with the metal to be melted. The burning coke causes carbon monoxide emissions; particulate emissions consist of coke dust, dirt from scrap metal, and metal fumes, small particles of metal that evaporate as vapors from the molten metal and then condense back into particles.

Cupola emissions are hard to control, largely because the exhaust air is so hot; if fabric filters are used, for instance, extra-capacity high-temperature filter bags and additional equipment to reduce the gas temperature are needed. The most common control devices are afterburners to burn the CO and high-energy wet scrubbers to control the particulates. The unusual problem arises because this exceptionally high control effort is falling on a relatively weak industry which consists mostly of many small, marginally economic firms. By contrast, the smelting industry, for instance, although faced with an expenditure of similar magnitude, consists of a dozen or so huge corporations that are better able to afford these expenditures and that have strong lobbies in Washington.

SUMMARY

To attempt to summarize industrial-process pollution in any coherent way is as difficult as trying to quickly summarize any other aspect of our complex, industrial economy. The interrelationships among various aspects sometimes defy any analysis. In this chapter we have tried to provide a sampler from which only a few particular facts or ideas may seem worth keeping or pursuing further. In the context of all stationary source emissions, we should keep in mind both the perspective of the emissions listed in Table 8–6 and some idea of the relative complexity and magnitude of the necessary control effort.

EXERCISES

Review Questions

1. What three conceptual approaches to pollution control were listed?
2. What is a diffusion equation? Of what use would it be in designing a power plant?
3. List four distinct control devices used for particulates from stationary sources and explain briefly how each operates.

4. What techniques are used for controlling gaseous pollutants? What pollutants are controlled?
5. What are the principal pollutant emissions from fuel-combustion sources?
6. List the three categories of fuel-combustion sources; which is the biggest?
7. Why are coal, oil, and gas called fossil fuels?
8. List the several grades of coal.
9. Why does increased moisture content reduce the energy value of a fuel?
10. How do the ash content of a fuel and the proportion of volatile matter relate to air pollution?
11. What major differences are there between the coals east and west of the Mississippi?
12. Distinguish among crude oil, distillate oil, and residual oil. Which causes the worst air pollution problem?
13. Why is natural gas not the solution to our clean-fuel problems?
14. In building a fire in a fireplace or furnace, why is it necessary to keep the fuel up off the floor on a grate?
15. Explain the mnemonic device "T, T, T, and O."
16. Why is it important to maintain high temperatures in the air space above the fuel on the grate?
17. How does a stoker lessen the pollution emitted from a furnace as compared to hand firing?
18. How is pulverized coal burned? What advantage does its use offer? Disadvantage?
19. Why is it desirable to have a large fuel-burning installation designed so that different types of fuel can be burned?
20. What is the best way to eliminate the emissions from small, hand-fired furnaces?
21. What control devices are typically used on large coal-burning installations?
22. List the three major approaches to reducing SO_2 emissions from fuel-burning plants.
23. List several possible energy sources that don't involve fossil fuels.
24. What ways of disposing of solid waste do not cause air pollution? Are they otherwise acceptable?
25. Why is solid waste difficult to burn efficiently?
26. Distinguish among flue-fed, multiple-chamber, and single-chamber incinerators.
27. What kind of incinerators typically have some pollution control equipment? What pollutant is controlled?
28. Distinguish between process loss and fuel-combustion emissions.
29. List the major pollution-producing operations in the iron and steel industry. Why is the blast furnace not one of them?
30. What is similar about the emissions from the grain-handling, cement, lime, and other industries?
31. What is the principal pollutant emitted from nonferrous ore smelters? From the petroleum industry?
32. Why were grey iron foundries singled out for special mention?

Thought Questions

33. It was noted that thermal and sonic forces could be used to separate particles from the air. Would you expect these techniques to work best for large or small particles?
34. The Ohio River has a sizable number of major power plants along its shores, though there are no waterfalls. Can you explain why?
35. If you are out camping and don't have a grate on which to build a fire, what do you do? What happens when you stir up the fire with a stick?
36. In Table 8–5, why is the NO_x emission factor higher for multiple-chamber than for single-chamber incinerators?

FURTHER READING

There is a wealth of available material if you are interested in reading further about these topics. Air pollution was at first considered a topic on engineering, and there is much for the person with enough chemistry, physics, and interest to pursue it. Lund [147], Noll and Duncan [152], and Volume III of Stern [162] contain a great deal of material, as does the APCA *Journal* [174].

An article by Slack [224] and a Federal Task Force Report [95] provide good discussions of the spectrum of SO_2 control techniques. The bibliography includes several more technical discussions of wet scrubbing [198, 215] and electrostatic precipitation [214], the techniques most commonly used for combustion sources. Other articles provide technical discussions of control techniques for industrial process sources [181, 183, 216].

Information on the extraction, distribution, and use of fuels is often found in technical encyclopedias and similar references; the Bureau of Mines' *Minerals Yearbook* [124] is also an excellent source. There is a vast literature on energy sources and the "energy crisis" in general. Two congressional studies of energy and the environment are good references [105] and [106]; more technical issues, very well presented for the layman, are included in volumes by *Scientific American* [138], Hammond, *et al.* [143], and Fisher [140]. The entire April 19, 1974, issue of *Science* was devoted to fuel and energy articles. A 1970 article by Squires [226] presents a good summary of alternatives for using coal in nonpolluting ways.

9

POLLUTION
FROM
MOBILE SOURCES

Tony Spina, Courtesy EPA

In recent years, the public news media have given wide coverage to pollution from mobile sources, principally automobiles. Motor vehicles produce by far the largest share of the principal air pollutants in terms of mass emitted, though not necessarily in terms of significance, as we saw in Chapter 3. Pollution from mobile sources includes nearly all the carbon monoxide and about half of the hydrocarbons and oxides of nitrogen.

The attack against automobile pollution has been much more coherent and visible than the attack against pollution from stationary sources, in large part because it is far easier, politically, to organize such an attack. It is also easier for the media to keep track of it, because there is only the federal government dealing with the few major manufacturers of motor vehicles, rather than states and cities dealing with thousands upon thousands of legal entities that operate stationary pollution sources.

VEHICULAR EMISSIONS

In discussing pollution from motor vehicles, we should begin with some understanding of how they operate; in particular, we'll be saying a great deal about the type of engine presently used in our automobiles and pickup trucks. This engine, which is more or less the same in all cars, is generally called the conventional internal-combustion engine (the conventional ICE). The conventional ICE operates on gasoline and takes in air as a source of oxygen to burn the gasoline; it transforms the chemical energy of the gasoline into the mechanical energy needed to drive the car. Gasoline is a mixture of hydrocarbons, other organics, and additives. The original source of the energy contained in gasoline was the sun; this energy, stored as hydrocarbon molecules in green plants, was ultimately converted to petroleum when the plants died.

The conventional automobile engine is described as an internal-combustion engine because the combustion of fuel takes place inside the cylinders, where the pistons are moving to provide the mechanical energy. The thermodynamic processes by which this engine operates are collectively called a four-stroke Otto cycle, after the man who developed the engine and its thermodynamic cycle; four-stroke refers to the four distinct motions of the piston in one repetition of the cycle. As illustrated in Fig. 9–1, these four motions are: (1) the intake stroke, when the air-fuel mixture is drawn into the cylinder; (2) the compression stroke, when the piston compresses the air-fuel mixture and the spark plug fires; (3) the power, or expansion, stroke, when the exploding mixture expands, forcing the piston down and providing the power of the engine; and (4) the exhaust stroke, when the piston pushes the remnants of the exploded gas mixture back out of the cylinder. Following the exhaust stroke, the exhaust valve shuts, the intake valve opens, and the cycle begins again. Because the piston in any one

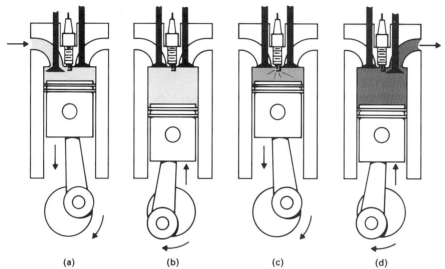

Fig. 9–1. The four-stroke Otto cycle. The conventional internal-combustion engine consists of four strokes: (a) intake stroke; (b) compression stroke; (c) expansion, or power, stroke; (d) exhaust stroke.

cylinder is producing power only periodically, the several cylinders in the engine are arranged to operate in a staggered fashion, so that the resultant motion is smoother.

Pollution from Conventional Automobiles

Three parts of the engine have a direct bearing on air pollution: the carburetor, the exhaust system, and the crankcase. The carburetor, a metering device that mixes the fuel with the incoming air, permits the air-fuel mixture to flow through the intake manifold to the intake valves. Its principal purpose is to adjust the amount of fuel that is mixed with a certain amount of air, so that the resulting mixture will have the proper balance of air and gasoline. If the mixture is too rich in gasoline, there won't be enough air to sustain combustion; if it's too lean, there won't be enough gasoline to ignite. The carburetor maintains the proper air-fuel ratio and also retains a small reservoir of fuel in the engine compartment, from which it can quickly mix in an additional amount of fuel when the accelerator is pressed rapidly for quick acceleration.

The exhaust system is just a set of pipes, beginning with the exhaust manifold, which carries the exhaust gases from the exhaust valves out to the open air. To reduce the noise involved in this procedure, cars have mufflers and long tailpipes.

The simplest pollution-related part of the engine is the crankcase, where the reciprocating motion of the pistons is transferred to a rotating crank connected to the drive shaft and the wheels. The crankcase is simply the cover, or case, on the bottom of the engine within which the crank turns and where the oil stays that is not being spread around the inside of the engine.

Of the three sources of pollutants within the car, the pollution associated with the crankcase is the easiest to control. Although the pistons are made to fit in the cylinders as tightly as possible, some gases are blown past them by the force of the explosion during the compression and power strokes of the engine; these gases, which are mostly hydrocarbons from unburned gasoline, just go into the crankcase. In the older cars, which do not have pollution controls, the crankcase was merely vented out to the atmosphere, so that such "blowby" hydrocarbons just blew out under the car into the air.

The fuel system—the carburetor and gasoline tank—also constitutes a source of hydrocarbon emissions, in this case, evaporation losses that occur when gasoline evaporates into the air and becomes hydrocarbon pollution. Most of these evaporative losses occur either when the gas tank is filled or immediately after the car has been driven, a period known as the "hot soak period." When gasoline is being pumped into a tank, the space above the gasoline remaining in the bottom of the tank is generally full of evaporated gasoline vapors; that is why one doesn't use a lighted match to look in the gasoline tank. But as the gasoline is pumped in and the level of the liquid rises, these vapors are simply pushed out into the air. During the "hot soak period," when the engine is still hot, the small amount of gasoline remaining in the carburetor simply evaporates in the heat.

These two types of emissions—crankcase blowby emissions and fuel-system evaporative emissions—are not the major problem, however; together, they account for about a third of the hydrocarbon emissions from the typical automobile. The other two-thirds, as well as all of the carbon monoxide and nitrogen oxides emissions, come from the exhaust system, that is, out of the cylinders, through the exhaust valves and manifold, through the muffler, and out the tailpipe. The exhaust system is not only the major source of all the pollution, but is also at this time the least completely controllable and so constitutes nearly the entire problem.

The various pollutants in the exhaust result from different processes within the engine. The hydrocarbon and CO in the exhaust are among the chemical products of the fuel-combustion process. Under ideal conditions all the hydrocarbons in the gasoline would be completely burned to produce carbon dioxide and water; however, combustion in the automobile engine is usually anything but ideal, and some of the fuel is incompletely oxidized. The carbon monoxide is just partially oxidized carbon, that is, carbon that was not completely oxidized to CO_2, and many of the hydrocarbon species are the result of complicated reactions among hydrocarbon molecules that are not completely burned. The hydrocarbon portion of the exhaust also includes some of the gasoline which went through the entire process untouched. Thus, anything that would tend to increase the efficiency of combustion in the engine would tend to reduce the amount of CO and hydrocarbons emitted.

The other major gaseous pollutant emitted by automobiles, nitrogen oxides, is not a product of incomplete combustion. In fact, nitrogen oxides are not formed from the fuel at all, but result from the chemical combination of the oxygen and nitrogen in the air. Nonetheless, they are related to the efficiency of combustion. The oxidation of nitrogen requires high temperatures and is increased as the temperature increases. Consequently, if we try to reduce CO and hydrocarbon emissions by improving the engine's combustion efficiency, the engine gets hotter, and the emissions of NO_x increase. This dilemma is all the more difficult because it arises not from the design of the engine or the nature of the gasoline, but from very basic principles of chemistry.

Beyond the gaseous pollutants, automobiles also emit particulates. If the combustion is very poor, totally unburned carbon may be emitted as black smoke; more routinely, the particulates are products of the combustion of the inorganic additives. This is what happens to the lead antiknock additives, and automobiles are the principal source of particulate lead in urban areas.

Pollution from Other Vehicles

Before we consider automobile pollution more quantitatively, let's take a brief look at some other types of vehicle engines and the pollution they produce. The other types of engines used in motor vehicles are the commonly used diesel and the gas turbine engines and the two-stroke gasoline engine, commonly used in motorscooters, power lawn mowers, etc. This type of engine, in which the oil is put in with the gasoline, isn't viewed as much of an air pollution problem; there are relatively few two-stroke gasoline engines, and they are used only occasionally.

The diesel engine is the other power plant in common use for surface vehicles. In addition to using a different type of fuel, the diesel engine, unlike the gasoline engine, doesn't have a spark plug to ignite the fuel-air mixture. Rather, it operates by greatly compressing the air in the cylinder until it becomes very hot and then injecting the fuel into the heated air, where it ignites spontaneously. The principal advantage of a diesel engine is more economical operation; the fuel is much less expensive because it requires less fancy refining. There are also, however, several disadvantages.

Because of the high compression ratio, the diesel engine must be much stronger and hence heavier than a gasoline engine; in addition, its fuel injection system makes it more costly. Thus, the diesel engine is used principally in large trucks and buses, whose weight and initial cost are less important than the longer-term savings in operating costs, and is very rarely used in passenger cars or light trucks. Mostly because of the amount of noticeable smoke and odor they emit, diesel engines are widely believed to be heavy polluters. Actually, however, a diesel's emissions of CO and hydrocarbons are quite low compared to those from an automobile; the high compression and high temperature in the diesel produce very efficient combustion which, of course, also contributes to its economical performance. As with the gasoline engine, however, these same conditions produce fairly high levels of nitrogen oxides emissions.

The gas turbine, more commonly known as a jet engine, and is presently used only in aircraft. However, it is also a candidate to replace the gasoline engine in autos; in that context, the phrase gas turbine is more commonly used. Illustrated in Fig. 9–2, the gas turbine works on the same thermodynamic principle as a gasoline or diesel engine, but with a different mechanical arrangement. Air is taken in at the front of the engine and compressed to a high pressure and temperature; then, fuel is mixed with the air as it enters the combustion chamber, where it explodes, causing the exhaust gases to rapidly expand out the back and turn a turbine as they go. In a jet aircraft engine, the turbine is used only to drive the compressor; the bulk of the energy remains in the jet of hot exhaust gases, which provide the engine's forward thrust as they rush out the back. For an automobile the design is changed so that a maximum amount of energy is transmitted to the turbine and then to the axle and wheels, with a minimum amount being wasted in the exhaust. In its present use in airplanes, the turbine engine

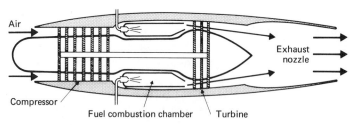

Fig. 9–2. Gas turbine engines. Schematic cross-section of an aircraft jet shows a small turbine, which drives the air compressor. In contrast, the automotive turbine has a large turbine to drive the vehicle, as well as air preheaters, which extract extra heat from the combustion gases before exhausting them. (S. J. Williamson, *Fundamentals of Air Pollution,* Reading, Mass.: Addison-Wesley, 1973, p. 321)

causes significant CO and some hydrocarbon pollution, which can be a significant problem near airports. However, the turbine engine has intrinsically lower NO_x emissions, since it operates at lower temperatures than do gasoline and diesel engines.

Emission Quantities

Although it's relatively simple to determine the kind of pollutants that come from the various types of vehicles, it is much more difficult to determine the precise *amount* of pollution emitted. We are interested in getting two emission quantities—the amount from a single car and the total from the use of all the cars in a given area, and it is surprisingly difficult to get really good estimates of either.

Not only is it difficult to measure the emissions from a car, but the amount of pollutant varies with different factors. There is a wide variety of cars and engines, as well as a variety of conditions, or modes, of engine operation. The emissions of various car models and engines can easily be averaged together to produce a value for a "typical" car. It is not easy, however, to decide what the "typical" operation of the car is, and the level of emissions varies greatly, depending on whether the car is cruising on a freeway or idling in a traffic jam. These differences are shown quantitatively in Table 9–1. In use, a car will typically accelerate, decelerate, cruise smoothly along, and periodically idle at a traffic light. Since these four modes of operation comprise a different proportion of each trip made, we must make some assumptions, i.e., choose a "typical" trip, in order to arrive at a figure for the average amount of pollution per mile driven. This brings us to what automotive test engineers call a "standard test cycle," a defined sequence of operating conditions covering the range of engine-operating conditions and

TABLE 9–1
Relative emission rates for various engine-operating modes

Mode	Exhaust flow volume	Pollutant concentrations H_xC_x	CO	NO_x
Idle	Very low	High	High	Very low
Cruise				
Low-speed	Low	Low	Low	Low
High-speed	High	Very low	Very low	Moderate
Accelerate				
Moderate	High	Low	Low	High
Heavy	Very high	Moderate	High	Moderate
Decelerate	Very low	Very high	High	Very low

Source: Control Techniques for CO, NO_x, and HC from Mobile Sources, HEW Publication No. AP–66, March 1970.

designed to simulate average driving patterns. Obviously, the choice of a test cycle must be somewhat arbitrary, and yet the estimated emission quantities may well change drastically with a different test cycle. Therefore, the test cycle is standardized, and the same cycle is always used. Actually, one has to design an entire standard emissions test procedure, including the sampling procedures and instrumentation used and a test facility where a car can be run through the test cycle inside on a dynamometer rather than on a test track or city street. The federal standard test procedure has been modified twice since 1966; the current version involves several pages of detailed instructions.

TABLE 9–2
Emission from light-duty motor vehicles (1973)

Emission	Amount (grams per mile)
Carbon monoxide	89.0
Hydrocarbons	
Exhaust	9.2
Evaporative	5.8
Nitrogen oxides	4.8
Sulfur oxides	0.20
Particulates	
Exhaust	0.38
Tire wear	0.20

Source: Compilation of Air Pollution Emission Factors, 2d Ed., EPA Publication AP-42, July 1973.

The emissions listed in Table 9–2, based on the present standard test procedure, are the 1973 emission values averaged over the entire national population of light-duty vehicles. These numbers become meaningful only when they are used to estimate the total emissions from all the vehicles in the nation.

Table 9–3 lists the EPA's estimates of the total annual emissions of the various pollutants from gasoline vehicles (which includes trucks) and other categories of motor vehicles. It's easy to see why "mobile source" and "motor vehicle" have come to be almost synonymous with "automobile"; there are presently about 100 million automobiles in the country, but fewer than 8 million diesel-powered large trucks and buses. Of course, in some cases other types of mobile sources may be significant problems; the many aircraft at large airports are major pollution problems, train stations and railroad yards were a major source of smoke in Pittsburgh before dieselization, and ship engines are a difficult problem in port cities. But in general it

TABLE 9–3
Pollutants from mobile sources (estimated nationwide emissions, 1970, millions of tons)

Type of vehicle	Particulate matter	Sulfur oxides	Carbon monoxide	Hydro-carbons	Nitrogen oxides
Gasoline	0.2	0.3	95.8	16.6	7.8
Diesel	0.1	0.1	0.8	0.1	1.3
Aircraft	0.1	0.1	3.0	0.4	0.4
Railroads	0.1	—	0.1	0.1	0.1
Vessels	0.3	0.1	1.7	0.3	0.2
Nonhighway*	0.2	0.1	9.5	2.0	1.9
Total	1.0	0.7	110.9	19.5	11.7

* Includes farm tractors, construction equipment, lawn mowers, etc.
Source: James H. Cavender, David S. Kircher, and Alan J. Hoffman, *Nationwide Air Pollutant Emission Trends 1940–1970*, Publication No. AP-115, Environmental Protection Agency, 1973.

is the automobile that the federal government is pursuing most vigorously, and the automobile is at the center of publicity, public interest, and controversy.

The impact of automobiles varies with geography, however. In urban areas autos are obviously a much more important factor than in rural areas, but there are also differences among metropolitan areas and within a given one. On a national average, a typical car is driven about 11,000 miles a year, but this figure is much higher in sprawling, freeway-strewn Los Angeles than in congested New York or Chicago, which have extensive public transportation systems.

Estimating emission quantities from a population of vehicles is a difficult proposition, for even given an accurate estimate of the emissions per mile for the average vehicle, it is very difficult to estimate the mileage driven. However, since good data on gasoline sales are usually available (because gasoline is taxed), these data, along with an estimate of average miles per gallon, have traditionally been used to estimate the total number of vehicle-miles driven in a particular area. More recently, estimates of emission quantities in urban areas have been based on vehicle-mile data compiled from traffic counts and other transportation planning data. No matter what method is used, however, errors and uncertainties in estimation, make it unwise to put heavy quantitative significance on these estimates, although such data can indicate the approximate magnitude of the problem. Fortunately, standardization helps us again; consistent estimates are more important than very precise estimates. In other words, we don't care too much whether 110 million tons is really 100 or 125 million tons; what we really care about is whether the number is trending upward or downward.

CONTROLLING CONVENTIONAL IC ENGINES

Efforts to reduce the pollution from motor vehicles began with, and is still mostly limited to, reducing the emissions of the gasoline-fueled internal combustion engine. Other approaches, probably far more significant in the long run, are still being developed, and we'll discuss them later in the chapter. Here, we'll begin a chronological narrative about the automobile, considering both the history of regulatory restriction on pollution emissions and efforts to meet them.

Early Control Efforts

Motor vehicle control efforts began in 1959, when California enacted a law regarding exhaust emissions; this was supplemented by a 1960 law relating to crankcase emissions, and a 1963 law pertaining to smoke from diesels. These early California laws were contingency laws; they provided for emission standards, that is, maximum permissible emission levels, that were to become legally effective one year after the development of control methods, so that cars would be able to meet them. This approach was a rather ingenious response to a difficult situation; the automobile had been recognized for some time as the cause of the Los Angeles smog, but the County Air Pollution Control District could do little about it; only the automobile manufacturers had the expertise to solve the problem. Since no city or county, even Los Angeles County, could have much impact on the huge corporations in Detroit, the state government—perhaps with politically mixed motives, but with clearly desirable goals—assumed for itself total authority over the problem of vehicular pollution.

The early California laws created the California State Motor Vehicle Pollution Control Board and resulted in the establishment of emission standards for exhaust pollutants and crankcase emissions, and the development of testing procedures for emissions. An exhaust emission control device submitted to the Board would be tested, and if it passed it would be certified as capable of meeting the standards. Then, one year after at least two different devices had been certified, the installation of an approved device would become mandatory on all new cars. The prospect of selling huge numbers of exhaust control devices sent many independent inventors and manufacturers scurrying to develop them, but the major auto manufacturers refused to take seriously the idea that a single state, even the biggest car-buying state in the nation, would dare challenge them.

In 1960 the federal government got in the act with Congressional passage of the Schenck Act (Public Law 86–493), which required a two-year study of automobile pollution. At the same time, the first tangible pollution control was begun in California—the automobile industry began putting onto the 1961-model cars sold in California a device intended to control the "blowby," or crankcase emissions of hydrocarbons. This "positive crankcase ventilation," or PCV, ventilates the crankcase gases back into the engine rather than just lets them out into the air. Physically, the control system is nothing more than a hose or pipe from the crankcase back up to the air filter and carburetor. When the engine is idling, however, the extra air coming into the carburetor from the crankcase causes trouble; therefore, a valve in the hose closes it off under idling conditions. A year later, under the threat of a federal law and bad publicity, the auto industry "volunteered" to put crankcase systems on all cars nationwide, beginning with the 1963 models, when they would become mandatory in California anyway.

Although progress was slow for another two years, public consciousness of the problem was clearly developing nationally. After receiving the report of the Schenck Act study, which found serious national health implications from automobile pollution, Congress in 1963 put emphasis on motor vehicle pollution in the federal law, and a standardized test cycle of various driving modes was developed and put into use in California. The significant break-through came in 1964, when the California Motor Vehicle Pollution Control Board approved a number of exhaust pollution control devices; exhaust control became mandatory on the 1966-model cars to be sold the following year. By this time it was apparent that California wasn't going to back down, and the air pollution community settled back to await the first really serious controls on cars.

Faced with this *fait accompli* in California, similar stirrings in New York State, and the nightmare possibility of having to keep track of 50 different sets of state standards, the auto industry quickly became advocates of federal regulation, lending their support to some pending federal legislation that called for uniform national standards set that would pre-empt any state standards. This amendment passed in 1965, but vigorous efforts by the California congressmen and senators managed to gain an exemption, permitting California's rules to continue in effect. The quickly promulgated federal standards, identical to California's for standard engines, though more lenient for smaller engines, were to take effect with the 1968-model cars rather than with the 1966 models. Thus began a series of dual standards, with California's separate and generally stricter (or earlier) than the federal standards, a pattern which has continued to the present.

Keeping track of the standards is often confusing, not only because of the dual system, but also because the federal government has scrupulously respected the auto industry's desired lead time, so that the standards are promulgated at least two years ahead of the model year for which they become effective. To simplify our discussion, we've labeled the standards first-generation, second-generation, etc., and have tabulated them in Table 9–4. We will now turn to a discussion of the means of controlling the emissions so that the cars can meet the standards.

TABLE 9–4
Federal exhaust emission standards

Model year	Carbon monoxide Test method			Hydrocarbons Test method			Oxides of nitrogen	Particulate matter
	1968	1972	1973	1968	1972	1973		
Uncontrolled:	79	124	87	12.2	16.3	8.7	4.0	0.3
1968–1969	35*	72		3.4	8.2			
1970–1971	23	47		2.2	4.6			
1972–1974		39	28		3.4	3.0	3.1 (1973)	
1975		21	15		1.7	1.5	3.1	
1975–1976		4.7	3.4		0.46	0.41	0.4 (1977)	
HEW proposed 1975–1976 standards	11			0.5			0.9	0.1
HEW 1980 Goals	4.7			0.25			0.4	0.03

* Italicized values are the legally issued standards; other figures are calculated equivalent values.

Controlling exhaust emissions

The major focus in controlling motor vehicle pollution is to control the exhaust emissions, for they include the bulk of the hydrocarbons, as well as all the CO and NO$_x$. As we discussed in Chapter 8, there are two broad approaches to controlling emissions. Devices put into the exhaust system can remove, alter, or destroy the pollutants; alternatively, preventive measures can be taken, e.g., trying to change the operation or design of the engine so as to reduce or eliminate the pollutants. Although much of the early research was directed toward various types of mufflers and afterburner systems, it wasn't immediately successful, and attention quickly turned to engine design changes, especially ways to improve combustion efficiency so as to reduce the emissions of CO and hydrocarbons.

There are many aspects of engine design that influence combustion efficiency, and we entertain no hope of even mentioning them all, for the IC engine is a very complicated machine. We'll consider at any length only the one parameter that has the greatest effect on the emission rates of the various pollutants, the air-fuel ratio, the number of pounds of air used to burn each pound of fuel. According to chemical theory, approximately 15 pounds of air are needed to provide enough oxygen for the complete combustion of a pound of gasoline. This theoretical chemical balance, or stoichiometric point, does not have to be achieved precisely in order for the engine to run; in fact, the ratio must vary somewhat during different modes of operation. The amount of air the engine uses is pretty much fixed by its speed, so that the amount of fuel is the only thing that can be adjusted, and this is a function of the carburetor.

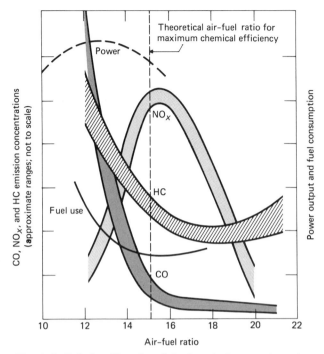

Fig. 9–3. Relationship of pollutant emissions and engine-operating characteristics to air-fuel ratio. (*Control Techniques for CO, NO$_x$ and HC from Mobile Sources,* HEW Publication No. AP–66, March 1970)

Our troubles arise, however, because the optimum value of the various factors can't all be achieved at the same air-fuel ratio. As we see in Fig. 9–3, the best fuel economy results with the most efficient combustion, as does the minimum CO and hydrocarbon emissions, and occurs when the air-fuel ratio is just a little above 15. As the amount of fuel is increased, the ratio goes down, and maximum power comes with an air-fuel ratio between 12 and 13; at this ratio, however, emissions of carbon monoxide and hydrocarbons are quite high, since there isn't enough oxygen to completely burn all the fuel. On the other hand, if the air-fuel ratio is increased above the stoichiometric point by decreasing the fuel, there is plenty of air, so that combustion is efficient, the CO and hydrocarbon emissions remain low, and the fuel economy is good, but the power output decreases.

Therefore, automotive engineers have had to design the engines and the carburetor so that the air-fuel ratio varies between 12 and 16, depending on whether one needs power to accelerate or wants economy while cruising at a steady speed. A few years ago, before pollutant emissions were considered important, most cars were designed to operate toward the low side, favoring power (performance) over fuel economy, although a mechanic could adjust it "lean" if a driver preferred saving the money to screeching away from traffic lights. Since the 1968 models (1966 in California), engines have generally been designed to operate with the ratio near 15 in order to minimize the CO and hydrocarbon emissions. In fact, all of the major automobile manufacturers met the first-generation exhaust standards by making such relatively simple, "economizing" design changes. This was a clear victory for preventative control philosophy, although a major defeat for the independent inventors whose control devices originally triggered the California law.

We should pursue one other aspect of Fig. 9–3 before we continue. Although it isn't really involved with the first-generation exhaust emission standards, the major problem in designing low-pollution internal combustion engines lies in the curve of nitrogen oxides emissions. Near the chemically ideal air-fuel ratio, where CO and hydrocarbon emissions are low, the formation of nitrogen oxides is at a maximum. This is not surprising, given the way in which these oxides are formed; the increased combustion efficiency that reduces the CO and hydrocarbons also raises the temperature of combustion, which causes the increased NO_x formation. Thus, the simultaneous control of all three pollutants is much more difficult than controlling only the two; in fact, many researchers feel that it's nearly impossible. It was largely because of this difficulty that the first-generation standards didn't include any limit on NO_x, although at that time there were also some serious questions about whether lowering NO_x levels was necessary to lower smog levels.

We should also caution that this simplified discussion of exhaust emissions in terms of the air-fuel ratio does not imply that changing the ratio or making other changes in the engine are trivial matters. Quite the contrary. The first-generation standards were met readily enough in large part because they weren't very stringent. Increasingly strict emission limits, however, require very tight control over the combustion process, e.g., precise timing of the spark plug firing, and this precision is very difficult to achieve, particularly since the engine must operate under such a wide range of conditions and the various parts must be able to withstand a certain amount of abuse and poor maintenance.

In June 1968 HEW adopted second-generation CO and hydrocarbon standards, to become effective with 1970-model cars and requiring about a one-third further reduction below the earlier standards. These new standards also included an important change in the way they were expressed; the permitted emissions were specified in grams of pollutant per mile of travel rather than as parts per million, a volume ratio. This is important because of differences in the amount of exhaust among different cars; if the ppm concentration of pollutant in the exhaust is the same, a larger volume of exhaust will amount to a greater overall pollutant emission. Thus, if all cars were permitted the same exhaust concentration level expressed as parts per million, as was the case with the 1966 California standards, this would permit more pollution by the larger car and can thus be viewed as unfair to the small car. Therefore, the first federal standards for 1968 permitted higher ppm concentrations for smaller cars, and the second-generation, 1970 standards are expressed in grams of pollutant per mile of travel, regardless of the car's size.

The second-generation standards were generally met by further carburetor modifications, some changes in the ignition timing (the time at which the spark plug fires in relation to the position of the piston), and changes that made the engine idle faster. This last change was needed because at idle, the very low fuel flow doesn't burn very efficiently; the change, however, caused a noticeable difference in the way cars operate and a decrease in fuel economy.

Federal standards for the 1971 model year also required the installation of controls to reduce evaporative hydrocarbons emissions, and in 1972 a further reduction was required. This control is accomplished largely by plumbing additions—the installation of tubes, pipes, and adsorbent charcoal—so that the evaporated gasoline vapors are caught and retained until the engine is operated again, when they are drawn back into the fuel system.

A much more significant change in the 1971 cars was the beginning of NO_x control in California. Before 1971, there had been no NO_x standards, and NO_x emissions had in fact increased slightly as a byproduct of reducing CO and hydrocarbons to meet the earlier standards. California petitioned the federal government for permission to impose stricter controls, and under California's legal exemption, permission was granted. At this time, federal standards for NO_x were tentatively scheduled to become effective on 1973 cars, and federal personnel were quite happy to have a test run, as it were. The NO_x standards were expected to be met by recirculating part of the exhaust gases back into the engine, mixing them with the incoming air. This procedure lowers the temperature at which combustion takes place and reduces NO_x formation. However, it also has a slight negative influence on CO and hydrocarbon emissions, although when the standards were promulgated, it was assumed that all three standards could be met.

Congress Takes a Stand

Before many of the 1971 cars had been sold and tried out, however, two separate events in late 1970 effectively disrupted the orderly progression of regulatory planning. First, actual road tests on 1970 cars seemed to show that they weren't meeting the second-generation standards, even though prototype cars had passed the federal tests. Therefore, discussion shifted to the details of the testing and certification procedures and the desirability of production-line testing. Much more important, however, Congress took a bold hand in December 1970 by actually setting standards for the future by law.

As the situation existed in early 1970, it was anticipated that total national emissions of CO would be reduced by about 70–75% between 1967 and 1984. But it was also anticipated that these levels would then begin to go back up again (see Fig. 9–4), as the gains from phasing out older, uncontrolled cars stopped and the growth in the number of cars took over again. A similar phenomenon in total hydrocarbons emissions was also expected. At that time, the Department of Health, Education and Welfare had proposed some tightening of the standards for 1975 models and had announced long-term goals for 1980 cars that they felt to be the most stringent that would ever be necessary (see Table 9–4). These 1980 "goals" were in fact much more stringent, amounting to what most people felt would be a "pollution-free" car. But with the "ultimate" goal not to be required until 1980, it would be the early 1990s before the gradual turnover of cars would bring emissions down to a minimum. Many private citizens' groups and elements in Congress felt that to wait until 1990 was too long and the question of when tight controls should come developed into one of

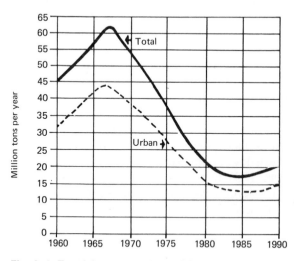

Fig. 9–4. Trend in motor vehicle CO emissions as anticipated in 1970. Note that the tonnage figures vary considerably from those cited elsewhere herein; this is because they're expressed in terms of an old standard-measurement method. (*Environmental Quality—1970*, First Annual CEQ Report [100], based on data from HEW)

the major issues in the congressional debate over the 1970 amendments to the Clean Air Act. In November 1970 the HEW Secretary legally adopted the third-generation standards for 1972–1974 cars, but postponed adopting the proposed 1975 standards pending possible congressional action.

The ultimate result in Congress was a requirement that the 1975 standards for CO and hydrocarbon emissions be set at a value at least 90% lower than those applicable to 1970 cars and that the 1976 NO_x standards be set at least 90% lower than the 1971 uncontrolled emissions. In effect, this made the 1980 goals the standards for the 1975–1976 cars. On June 29, 1971, the EPA administrator announced these standards, along with the first federal NO_x standards for 1973 models. Since then, the debate has continued, primarily over the technical feasibility of meeting the standards by 1975. The law gave the EPA authority to delay them for one year if it found that the automobile industry had made a serious effort to develop the technology, but failed. After public hearings, the administrator acted in April 1973 to delay the application of the standards until the 1976-model year. Congress has since permitted two more annual extensions, and the President and EPA have recommended a further extension until 1980.

Emission Control for 1975–1976

Efforts to control emissions from the IC engine through the 1974 models consisted of design changes—lower compression ratios, leaner air-fuel mixtures, modified ignition systems, and special devices to adjust the carburetor when the engine idles—aimed at improving combustion to reduce CO and HC emissions. Whereas the simplest of these modifications can be described as optimizing the original engine, the more complicated have involved new, more complex controls requiring significant amounts of new engineering and noticeable increases in the complexity of an already complex device. In order to meet the standards for 1975–1976, further such changes are usually needed. But in addition, most cars require an additional device, external to the engine, usually the replacement of the present muffler with a catalytic converter installed in the exhaust pipe.

What is needed is something to further oxidize the incompletely burned CO and hydrocarbons to CO_2 and water; the catalytic muffler accomplishes this extra oxidation by exposing the exhaust gases to a catalyst, a chemical substance that by its presence promotes the oxidation reaction. With a suitable catalyst, this method has no serious competition, except for one problem—lead. The antiknock lead compounds in gasoline "poison" the catalyst materials; a catalyst that works well for several thousand miles with unleaded fuel might cease functioning in a few hours with leaded gasoline. Since the particulate lead in the exhaust is also a pollutant, it makes sense to eliminate the lead; but since it's there for a reason, its removal has other repercussions, some of which have involved making minor changes in the design of the engine. EPA does have the power to set such standards and in 1974 embarked on a planned schedule for the phasing out of leaded gasoline. The oil companies don't like eliminating the lead, since they'll have to change their refineries somewhat, but at present it is national policy and will need to remain so if catalytic mufflers are to continue in use.

Faced with the enormity and complexity of the emission-control program, as well as the fact that at some point in the future the growth in the numbers of cars will again catch up and emissions will again begin to climb, many people and groups, including some in Congress and the executive branch, feel that the time has come to abandon the internal-combustion engine. The ICE has brought us unprecedented mobility, but at a cost to our health and well-being that we can no longer afford to pay, and therefore it must be replaced. This school of thought will surely continue and increase its advocacy in the next few years of decision-making, and so we'll now turn to a brief consideration of some of the alternatives to the internal-combustion engine.

ALTERNATIVES TO THE CONVENTIONAL IC ENGINE

Gaseous Hydrocarbon Fuel

Among the alternatives to cleaning up the conventional IC engine are variations of that type of engine. One of the simplest alternatives is to equip an ordinary IC engine with the plumbing necessary for it to run on a different fuel. Such fuels, unlike conventional, liquid gasoline, are all gaseous hydrocarbons, e.g., the natural gas used in cities, the liquefied petroleum gas (LPG, or bottled gas) that is often used in rural areas, or even the bottled propane used in portable camping equipment. Since conventional gasoline is evaporated and used in the engine as a gas anyway, the use of a gaseous fuel doesn't require much modification to the engine itself, although the fuel tank and carburetion systems must be changed. Existing IC engines can be converted to accommodate natural gas for $200–$300; LPG requires a pressurized tank and costs $600–$700. The advantage of these fuels is mainly smoother, more efficient combustion; this reduces CO and HC emissions significantly, although some other modifications may be needed to keep NO_x emissions down. Because of their economy, the use of these alternative fuels is favored by fleet operators, and a fair number of vehicles run on these fuels are actually in use. The primary short-run disadvantage is the lack of "gas" stations that sell gaseous fuels; therefore, the use of vehicles run on these fuels is generally limited to those making only short trips from a central garage. A more serious problem, however, is that there is just not enough of such fuels. Natural gas is the least abundant of our fossil fuels, and it is conceivable that our supplies could be depleted by the end of the century. Although many people believe that this shortage is artificial, caused by the oil companies who also produce gas, there are no serious proposals at present to encourage widespread use of these gaseous fuels.

Stratified-Charge Engine

To date, the most promising IC engine is the "stratified-charge" engine; one such engine, made by the Honda Motor Company of Japan, has already met the emission standards for 1976. The "stratified-charge" engine comprises a major modification of the conventional IC engine. The engine cylinders are redesigned so that when the gasoline "charge" is drawn in, the air-fuel ratio is different in various parts of the cylinder, i.e., "stratified." Only near the spark plug does the air-fuel mixture really need to be in the ignitable range; elsewhere, it can be higher (more air, less fuel) in order to provide extra oxygen for improved combustion. This cannot be accomplished in the conventional engine, because the carburetor mixes the air and fuel outside the engine, and a uniform mixture is drawn into the cylinder. In order to get stratification, one needs modified air intake and fuel injection systems, in addition to changing the design of the cylinder. Despite these modifications, however, the "stratified-charge" engine could be kept similar to the conventional engine in other respects, which makes this alternative attractive.

Wankel Engine

The Wankel engine, in contrast, is a totally different mechanical device, although it still works on the four-stroke Otto cycle. The basic difference, illustrated in Fig. 9–5, is that the Wankel engine is rotary rather than reciprocating, with a triangular rotor revolving in a figure-eight-shaped housing, forming a moving combustion chamber as it rotates. The Wankel engine is fairly dirty, producing higher hydrocarbon and CO emissions than do conventional engines. However, the Wankel engine is much lower in NO_x emissions, which are harder to control, and has a high temperature exhaust, which means that the CO and hydrocarbon can be cleaned up with a thermal reactor to complete the combustion, which eliminates the need for an oxidizing catalytic muffler. It also has some mechanical advantages; its smooth operation and high engine speeds permit adequate power from an engine that is physically much smaller than the conventional ICE.

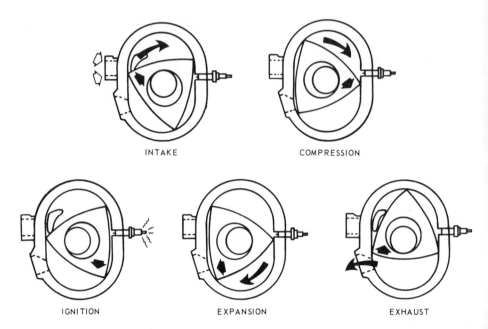

Fig. 9–5. The Wankel engine. The triangular rotor moves in a figure-eight-shaped housing, forming a moving combustion chamber, and follows the same four-stroke Otto cycle as in the conventional IC engine.

The engine's major problems are engineering ones, the biggest of which is that the seals on the point of the rotor are the only barrier between the various chambers in the engine. The seals wear out too fast and must frequently be replaced; in fact, "blowby" past the seals is the reason for the fairly high level of hydrocarbon emissions. The manufacturers feel, however, that this problem has now been solved. The Wankel has been given more attention by the auto industry than most other alternatives; both GM and Ford have paid for rights to build Wankels, and a Japanese firm is already selling Mazda cars with Wankel engines in the United States. The Wankel also has the feature, attractive to many people, of reversing the seemingly inexorable trend toward more and more complexity in the engine design, but also the disadvantage of poor fuel economy.

Alternative Power Plants

There are several alternative power plants that operate on a different principle from the internal combustion engine. Two of these alternatives—the gas turbine and the steam, or Rankine-cycle, engine—presently seem to be viable competitors for future use in cars.

The automotive gas turbine operates on the same basic principle as its aircraft counterpart, except that the automotive turbine is designed to get the power out to the wheels mechanically rather than have it blown out in a powerful jet exhaust. If the IC engine is replaced, the gas turbine is viewed as the most likely replacement, largely because the major manufacturers have some experience with this alternative. In addition, it has the advantage of simplicity and can be run on such cheap fuels as kerosene or diesel fuel. Because the fuel is burned at a more or less constant rate instead of in rapid explosions, a turbine obtains good combustion efficiency and thus low CO and hydrocarbon emissions and at a temperature low enough to hold down NO_x emissions. The problems with an automotive turbine include complicated air intake and exhaust systems, and the need for a sizable transmission to reduce the very high engine speeds.

The Rankine-cycle engine uses water or some other fluid to convert the chemical energy of the fuel into the mechanical energy of moving parts. Heat from the combustion of the fuel vaporizes the fluid into high-pressure vapor, which is then used either to push pistons back and forth as in an internal combustion engine or to spin a turbine wheel as in a turbine engine or a steam-electric generating plant. Even though some Rankine-cycle engines use fluid such as freon (the common refrigerant) rather than water, the engines are generally called steam engines anyway, and we'll refer to them in this way. The steam engine burns fuel continuously, under uniform conditions and at relatively low temperatures, so that both high efficiency and low emissions including fairly low NO_x emissions, are obtained. There are a number of successfully operating steam-driven vehicles, cars, and buses that already meet the 1975–1976 standards.

Although there are some engineering problems yet to be solved, the major barrier to wider use of steam engines is an unusual combination of history and industrial politics. Unlike any of the other alternatives, steam engines were in fairly wide use in the earliest cars on the road, but were replaced by the gasoline IC engine for a number of good and valid reasons. Consequently, any mention of a "steam car" tends to generate snickers, guffaws, and visions of drivers with funny hats and goggles and long scarves trailing in the wind; ever since, the major auto companies have been unable to think seriously about steam engines.

The trouble with this view is that the modern Rankine engine is a totally different machine. Instead of containing a large boiler full of water that needs continual refilling, today's steam engines have only a slender, coiled tube filled with a small amount of fluid that evaporates and condenses over and again, all within a completely closed system. There is no huge amount of steam to explode in an accident, no hissing and spitting as the spent steam is wasted out into the air. These new engines have been developed exclusively by independent manufacturers; the major auto manufacturers in Detroit have shown no serious interest in the work. In fact, in 1969 General Motors put together, as a publicity gimmick, a Rankine-engine car designed to the engineering specifications of a heating boiler in a factory basement; it wheezed and sputtered, belched smoke, and effectively generated publicity all right—publicity against a car with a steam engine. It's basically because of this attitude that the steam engine is ranked well behind the gas turbine as a possible alternative engine.

OTHER ALTERNATIVES

Thus far we've considered two ways of eliminating at least some of the pollution from automobiles—the current approach of modifying the engine to reduce emissions or making a complex change to a different type of engine, the approach that will probably be necessary if the first fails. Underlying these two approaches is a major assumption, namely, that we have to have cars. Although no one seriously proposes the complete elimination of all motor vehicles, it is an unquestioned fact that our heavy reliance on the automobile as a means of transportation, at least in urban areas, is very wasteful—wasteful of resources needed to build and power the cars, wasteful of land needed for roads and parking spaces. This situation has arisen, of course, out of unquestioned habit; the use of the automobile became an accepted part of our national life and remained unquestioned. For most of this century, the opponents of the auto were a small group indeed.

More recently, however, the increase in the number of cars has emphasized the disadvantages of this pattern, with its choked streets, high parking costs, and new highways ruining existing neighborhoods, along with such less obvious effects as the noise and heat from the cars. Such considerations parallel the concern about rising levels of air pollution. Recall that under the 1970 standards, the total national emissions would decrease to a minimum in the mid-1980s and then begin to rise again. The new, stringent standards for 1975–1976 lower and postpone the minimum, but they can't prevent the subsequent rise.

How, then, can we make a decision about where to stop? How much control will ultimately be needed? In fact, on what basis do we try to make such a decision? Our problem is that emission figures alone—grams per mile and percent reductions—are related only indirectly to the effects of the pollution. Since it is the *effects* that concern us, we need to consider the ambient air quality levels and the effects they cause in order to judge whether our emission controls are stringent enough.

The existing standards for ambient air quality are based on health effects, and there is a legal mechanism by which the states need to develop emission control measures to implement the standards, that is, to reduce pollutant levels to the standards. These standards and the legal mechanism, which are considered in Chapter 11, exist under a totally different part of the federal law from the motor vehicle emission control program that we've described so far. After developing control programs for SO_2 and particulates, the EPA and the states turned their attention to the ambient air quality standards for pollutants from motor vehicles. In order to do so, extensive calculations had to be made to estimate the effect of the federal emission standards in the future and the resultant pollutant levels compared with the air quality standards. Many people were surprised to discover that even with the new, stringent 1975–1976 emission standards, many urban areas could not meet the air quality standards by 1975, as was required by the law, or even by 1977, the limit of the maximum permissible two-year extension. Thus, the states were required to develop other measures to control the pollutant emissions from transportation sources still further, something that no one had any experience with and very few knew how to approach.

Transportation Control Plans

There are a variety of possible approaches to consider, some with relatively short-range effectiveness, others with longer-term impact. The most obvious way to get immediate emission reductions beyond those provided by the new-car emission standards program is to require the installation of some type of control devices on the older cars that were originally equipped with less effective controls. If 1972–1975 vehicles were required to install devices equivalent to those on 1976-model cars, for example, the effect on aggregate emissions would be sizable. Such *retrofit devices* on pre-1972 cars, however, would be less effective, because there are fewer of them. Such retrofit is also costly and hence unpopular, but it is nonetheless the most effective control measure there is for a short-term period—three to five years.

The only other way to significantly reduce the emissions from the vehicles themselves is with a periodic inspection and maintenance program, with emission testing and required maintenance if emissions are too high. Depending on the stringency of the program, reductions in overall emissions of between 12%–15% may be realized. This is a relatively popular control measure, and many states are adding the testing of exhaust emissions to their annual or semiannual safety inspection programs.

These retrofit and inspection-maintenance programs can, of course, be viewed as merely realizing the full potential of the federal emission standards program. Once the present population of relatively uncontrolled cars has gone on to the junkyard, however, there will be little further gain, and the growth in vehicular numbers will again take over. To deal with this problem, there are a number of intermediate- and long-range strategies that can be considered, though it is by no means well known how effective they may be. One strategy is to attempt to improve the flow of traffic; since higher speeds generally mean lower CO and hydrocarbon emissions, and especially since idling engines produce high emissions, any improvement in the average speed of traffic or any elimination of bottle-necks and traffic jams will tend to reduce pollution levels. This possibility is favored by transportation planners, because it puts the political weight of air pollution control behind the sorts of things that they have been urging all along. Generally, however, the total air quality improvement from such efforts will be small, and it therefore becomes necessary to con-sider the direct objective of reducing automobile usage—reducing the total number of vehicle-miles of travel, as the transportation planners put it, or vehicle-miles of pollutant production, as we might put it to emphasize a different aspect. So far, the suggestions typically fall into one of two categories that might be called "mass transit" and "less transit."

The mass transit possibilities involve various ways of increasing the use of public mass transit and decreasing the use of private automobiles, especially for rush-hour commuter trips to and from the center-city busi-ness district. This possibility involves two related problems—first, provid-ing improved transit service; second, inducing people to use it; neither improvement alone seems to work. At present, only five of our major cities have rapid rail transit systems (New York, Chicago, Boston, Phila-delphia, and Cleveland), and two more (San Francisco and Washington, D.C.) are in the process of building such systems. Since building a rapid transit system is a long, major, expensive undertaking, most cities will probably settle for metropolitan bus systems. In addition to the problem of providing transit, however, is the problem of providing transit *service*, e.g., clean, safe buses, trains, and stations and fast, convenient scheduling. This aspect is, of course, closely related to inducing the automobile owner to ride the mass transit; without these amenities, the mass transit user will continue to be the poorer individual who has no economic choice.

But beyond providing these amenities, experience shows the necessity of applying gentle pressure on the auto commuter as well. These pressures can be economic, e.g., taxes on downtown parking spaces, or procedural, e.g., a priority system that permits only certain cars to come into town on a given day, perhaps only cars with even-numbered license plates on even-numbered days, for instance. The ultimate pressure, of course, is re-stricting the amount of gasoline available with a rationing program of some type. Most of these control measures, collectively known as *vehicle-use restraints*, have not yet been tried out, except in minor experimental instances. During the summer and fall of 1973, many states adopted these measures as official policy, not because they really wanted to, but because they had to do something, and no one had better alternatives. In general, the mass public in the urban areas affected reacted violently against even the slightest infringement on their "right" to drive whenever and wherever they pleased, despite major public information campaigns by government agencies. It was quite clear that the average American's "love affair" with the automobile was still going strong. Interestingly enough, "the energy crisis" a few months later resulted in serious, nationwide consideration of these same measures.

For the longer-term future—10 to 20 years at least—there are some possibilities involving "less transit," ways to let us carry on our daily lives with less transportation than we now use. It is obvious that the extent to which we move about is a function of where we are and where we need to or want to go; therefore, changes in land-use patterns have striking repercussions on traffic. Build a new highway, and more people are enticed to drive to work; build a park near a residential area, and people may not feel the need to drive to another one. Reciprocally, if we clean up a factory, we may be able to develop residential neighborhoods nearby so that the employees will be able to walk to work. This sort of thinking quickly gets us into questions about our broader environment, our economic and status goals for ourselves and our children, and so on. Far from being melodramatic, these concerns merely reflect the degree to which the automobile has become an intrinsic part of our lives.

EXERCISES

Review Questions

1. Why is the general public more aware of the effort to control pollution from vehicles than of the stationary-source control effort?
2. Describe the sequence of events in the four-stroke Otto cycle.
3. What is the air-fuel ratio?
4. What is crankcase blowby pollution? How is it dealt with?
5. Describe two situations in which evaporative hydrocarbon emissions occur.
6. How is each of the three major gaseous pollutants formed in the engine? How are they emitted?
7. Why is it more difficult to control all three pollutants than to control only CO and hydrocarbons?
8. Why is the diesel engine so much more common in heavy-duty trucks and buses than in light-duty vehicles?
9. How do the pollution emissions from the diesel compare with those from the conventional ICE?
10. What is the principal difference between a jet aircraft engine and an automotive turbine engine?
11. Why is it difficult to determine the average quantity of emissions from an automobile?

12. Explain the role of a standard emissions test procedure, including a standard test cycle.
13. Describe the way in which vehicular pollutant controls first became effective in California.
14. Explain how the early CO and hydrocarbon standards were met. What is the role of the air-fuel ratio?
15. Why is the difference between expressing standards in ppm and in grams per mile important?
16. Why did emission standards become a congressional issue in 1970? What was the result?
17. What kind of CO and hydrocarbon control device is expected to be necessary for the 1976-model cars?
18. What are the short-term limitations on massive switching of cars to gaseous fuels? Long-term limitation?
19. How does a "stratified-charge" engine differ from the conventional ICE?
20. What is the principal pollution-control advantage of a Wankel engine?
21. Why does a Rankine-cycle engine have lower pollutant emissions?
22. Why is the Rankine engine not the front-runner in the competition to replace the conventional ICE?
23. Distinguish between the "mass transit" and "less transit" options. What is their common objective?

Thought Questions

24. In a world filled with acronyms, it's easy to confuse PVC and PCV. The latter is positive crankcase ventilation; what is PVC? (Its only relation to air pollution is that it makes hydrochloric acid when burned in incinerators.)
25. The amount of air used by an engine is fixed largely by its speed; bigger, more powerful engines have larger exhaust volumes. Can you explain why in terms of one of the design parameters of the engine?
26. In testing engines for compliance with emissions standards, the government can test either advance models, called prototypes, or each engine as it comes off the assembly line. The problem with testing prototypes is that the auto firm's mechanics can fuss over it, tune it up, and in general show it at its very best; the problem with testing every car off the assembly line is the major expense involved. Can you suggest a good, third alternative?
27. It is relatively easy to see why the rotary Wankel engine runs more smoothly than the reciprocating conventional engine; can you explain why it is also much more powerful for its size?
28. One obvious way to reduce vehicle use is to encourage the use of car pools; since the average occupancy of autos in rush hour is only slightly above 1.0, it would seem highly profitable. Yet when tried, efforts to encourage car pooling have very frequently failed. Can you explain why? (There is no firmly known single correct answer for this one.)

Discussion Questions

29. Do you feel that it is fair or unfair to require large cars to meet the same emission standards as small ones? On what basis have you decided?

30. In the compliance-testing framework of question 26, there is typically a distribution of values for a car of a certain model, with some above and some below the average for that model. Do you feel that all cars should meet the standard, or should the requirement be that the average must be below the standard?

31. There is a body of opinion that Congress ought not step into the detailed regulatory process, as they did with the motor vehicle standards in 1970. On the other hand, it is true that regulatory agencies of the government have a strong tendency to make peace with the industries they regulate. Discuss this problem, distinguishing if possible between agencies like the EPA and others whose full-time purpose is regulatory in nature.

32. Who do you feel should bear the blame for the several years of poorly operating cars that we will have? What should have been done differently?

33. Some people believe that NO_x control should be abandoned or postponed for a number of years, since it's the most difficult pollutant to control for possibly the least benefit. Discuss this, presenting the likely arguments on both sides. What would you conclude? If you agree that this effort should be abandoned, do you think you could sell this notion to the environmental groups?

34. A few decades ago, most city dwellers lived within walking distance of where they worked. This, of course, is no longer true. Discuss the reasons for this change, whether we should try to reverse it, and what we should do if we decide to try.

Project Suggestions

35. Since cars are usually widely available, there are a variety of demonstration ideas that could be pursued if students have sufficient mechanical interest. Simply looking at the carburetor, etc., is a useful exercise.

36. A different type of lecture topic could be the explanation of the differences in Table 9–1, i.e., an explanation of what is happening in the engine when we decelerate, etc.

FURTHER READING

There is a great deal of material on the topic of motor vehicle pollution, but much of it is on the mechanical-engineering aspects of controlling vehicles, and much of this material is now out of date. Gibney's paper [193] is a good discussion of control hardware, especially catalytic mufflers. The federal Control Techniques Document for CO, NO_x, and Hydrocarbons [32] is quite good, though no longer completely up to date on alternative vehicles. Good sources for the latter are the Senate Hearing Document "Alternatives to the Gasoline-

Powered Internal Combustion Engine" [112] and an article by Crossland [190]. One of the best overall summaries of the entire motor vehicle pollution problem is the RECAT Committee Report [123], which includes a number of federal policy papers as appendixes; it is a particularly good source of arguments about lessening NO_x control requirements. Hayes' article [199] is another good discussion of the arguments for relaxation of the standards based on cost and fuel economy considerations. A series of annual EPA reports to Congress on the motor vehicle problem exists; the current title, since the 1970 amendments, is "Development of Systems to Attain Established Motor Vehicle and Engine Emissions Standards," the first in the series being Senate Document 92–39 [113].

10

THE LEGAL BASIS
FOR
AIR POLLUTION
CONTROL

Newark, N.J. Chamber of Commerce, Courtesy EPA

Our society generally prides itself on being governed "by laws, not men," and hence the control of air pollution must of necessity have its fundamental basis in law. There are other important legal aspects of air pollution control, most notably the development and enforcement of emission regulations by control agencies, but our concern here is with the basic legal principles governing our society's control of pollution-causing behavior. The details of the procedural mechanisms used are covered in the next two chapters; these mechanisms are variable and sometimes subject to rapid change, but they must always rest fairly solidly on one of several more basic legal foundations.

TRADITIONAL COMMON-LAW REMEDIES

For centuries, one of the fundamental principles of Anglo-Saxon tradition has been that harm suffered by one person at the hands of another can be remedied at law. This concept, which of course fits with most people's sense of fairness, is firmly embodied in what is called common law, as distinguished from written laws. The *common law* is a vast body of legal precedents, the accumulated results of cases over the last several centuries, here and in England, to which the courts refer in arriving at their current decisions.

As it has evolved over the years, the common law has in one sense become quite firm, yet in a more important sense has remained remarkably flexible. It is firm in that the various actions that require regulation by society, including the actions that cause harm to others, have been classified into categories, with quite precise definitions of what constitutes an action in a certain category. On the other hand, the common law retains an amazing capacity to change with the times or, more accurately, to change with people's basic sense of fairness, as that sense changes with time. This flexibility has contributed greatly to the success of our legal system, as it has permitted accommodation to necessary change; at the same time, the desire to find legal precedent in past cases has prevented overly rapid, possibly frivolous, changes.

There are three categories of the common law into which pollution suits generally fit: trespass, negligence, and nuisance. Probably because of their antiquity, the legal meaning of each of these categories is not much different from its meaning in ordinary language. The intentional emitting of pollutants onto another person's property constitutes a *trespass*, whereas the merely careless polluter is guilty of *negligence;* both of these actions can be the basis of a suit pleading injury and requesting monetary damages in compensation. Since negligence is hard to prove, however, and intentional trespass even harder, the majority of air pollution suits are based on allegations that the defendant polluter is operating a *nuisance.* An additional advantage of using this type of complaint as the basis for suit is that one may ask the court to not only award monetary damages, but also enjoin, or prohibit, further operation of the source of the pollution. Historically, such suits, brought by private individuals concerning a private nuisance, have been the most frequent common law actions and the type that is most often at least partly successful.

Essentially, a *private nuisance* is the interference of one person (including corporations) with another's use or enjoyment of his property. In the adversary language of law, the injured party is the plaintiff, the alleged polluter the defendant. To succeed, a nuisance action requires proof of damage to the plaintiff caused by the actions of the defendant, as well as a demonstration that the actions of the defendant are unreasonable, that is, not necessary, etc. Both of these requirements pose formidable problems to the widespread reduction of air pollution by this legal means. The first, the requirement of legal proof of damage, places a costly and perhaps technically difficult burden on the plaintiff that effectively prohibits the bringing of private nuisance actions except in the most extreme situations. The second, the necessity to demonstrate that the defendant's action is not reasonably necessary for the orderly conduct of life in society, unavoidably leaves a great deal of discretion in the hands of the court. Almost any polluting activity has some useful aspect to it. Since industrial activities in particular are generally considered socially useful—providing employment, contributing to the GNP, etc.—there is always at least this basis for sustaining the "right" of an industry to pollute the air. At best, it's a difficult weighing of the ultimate public good.

Since past decisions are the basis for present law, perhaps the best way to illustrate these points is to look at a past decision. The issues raised by a common law nuisance suit and the frustrations both of bringing such an action and of judging it are all contained in a 1930 case, as summarized by the judge in the process of rendering his opinion.

> This is a bill by property owners in the vicinity of the Wickwire-Spencer Company's steel works in Clinton, Mass., to enjoin the defendants from maintaining a nuisance by the emission of obnoxious fumes and odors from a galvanizing plant forming part of said works ...

> The plaintiffs are the owners in fee of various residential properties situated on the north side of Sterling Street, Clinton, opposite the steel works and the galvanizing plant in question. All these houses were built before the galvanizing plant was established on its present location in 1915. The DeBlois house is a three-decker apartment house; of the others some are single houses, and some have more than one tenement. They are all of wood construction, and none of them appeared to be in what I should call good condition for such proper-

ties. The assessed value of the De Blois property, which is the nearest to the galvanizing plant, is $3,575: ... The aggregate assessment on all the plaintiffs' property is $22,925. There is no evidence that the presence of the galvanizing plant has diminished their value, nor that they would be more valuable if the steel works were permanently closed down.

The plant of the Wickwire-Spencer Company is assessed for $1,100,000. It employs several hundred persons and has a monthly pay roll running from $60,000 to $90,000. About 60 per cent of its total is galvanized. If a galvanizing plant cannot be operated in connection with the works, the testimony is that they will have to be shut down ...

In a concentrated form the fumes would be highly disagreeable and possibly dangerous to life if breathed for a substantial time. They never occur in this form in the defendants' plant. There is only about 1 per cent of them in the air directly over the molten metal under the hood. As they rise they are much diluted by the air drawn up with them through the ventilating shafts and are still further diluted as they drift with the wind. ... As I saw them on a pleasant day with a light breeze, they appeared like a very thin bluish smoke, visible for a certain distance as they drifted with the wind away from the stack, and thereafter invisible in the air. They could be smelt slightly after they had ceased to be visible. ...

As to the intensity of the fumes at the plaintiffs' houses, and the effect of the fumes on persons, on vegetable life, and on buildings, the testimony was much in conflict. The plaintiffs and their witnesses testified that at times the fumes were very disagreeable; that they caused acute illness; that they killed trees and other growing things; and that they injured the paint and nails on the exterior of the houses, and injured or destroyed interior furnishings. Mr. Lawson, a civil engineer, who had been connected with the Clinton superintendent of streets' office, and Mr. Hamilton, who had formerly been chairman of the Clinton board of health, both testified that on occasions they had observed fumes drifting across Sterling street onto the plaintiffs' property; that the fumes were plainly visible and had a disagreeable odor and made one cough. ...

The defendants' contention is that the fumes were so diluted by the time they reached the plaintiffs' houses as never to be seriously disagreeable there. Professor Gill of the Massachusetts Institute of Technology testified to pretty careful tests of the air, which he had made in the neighborhood of the plant on more than one occasion, which showed only minute traces of acid even where the fumes were sufficiently concentrated to be visible. He said that the fumes consisted principally of chlorine gas, which in extremely dilute form is not un-wholesome; that it would never give paint a brown stain—of which the plaintiffs complained—nor have any effect on the paint at all; that as to persons, chlorine in such dilution as it reached the plaintiffs' houses would not be unhealthy; that he at no time found fumes nearly as strong as are permitted under the English Factory Act. . . .

The testimony coming from the plaintiffs and their families taken as a whole was greatly exaggerated and unreliable. I believe, however, that occasionally in close, damp weather with a light air from the south, the fumes from the galvanizing plant drift across the properties of certain of the plaintiffs in a very annoying concentration. I think this is true only of the houses which may be regarded as directly opposite the galvanizing plant, i.e., the houses of De Blois, Steward, Shanbaum, and Calcia. The houses of the other plaintiffs are farther away and so screened by trees that I do not believe they ever get the fumes in a concentration which constitutes a legal nuisance. The occa-sions referred to are not frequent, but they do occur, and the fumes are then quite sufficient to wake the average person out of a sound sleep and make him or her decidedly uncomfortable. I am not satis-fied that the fumes discolor or injure the exterior of the houses or the interior furnishings. Nor am I satisfied that they cause serious illness. While several of the plaintiffs testified to having been made seriously ill by them, no physician was called to corroborate this testimony, nor was there any evidence of experts that the fumes might cause such illnesses as the plaintiffs described. Moreover, the state board of health, which investigated this question on the complaint of some of the plaintiffs, found that the fumes were not dangerous to health. The plaintiffs also contend that the fumes killed shade and fruit trees around their houses. There are several dead trees around the De Blois house, and other trees in the immediate vicinity appear to be injuri-ously affected by something. Farther up Sterling street, near the Daley house, the trees and other growing things showed no signs of being injured. It appeared in evidence that there had been a leak from the gas main on that street and farther down trees had been killed from that cause. On one tree which appeared to be in an unhealthy condition I noticed many marks of borers. It is not easy to say what kills a tree; they were exposed to these fumes only on infrequent occasions; and on all the evidence I am not satisfied that the fumes seriously injured trees, shrubs, or growing plants.

The test by which the question of nuisance is to be determined is well stated in Strachan v. Beacon Oil Co., 251 Mass. 479, 146 N. E. 787, 790; "It is a matter of common knowledge that in thickly settled manufacturing communities, the atmosphere is inevitably impregnated with disagreeable odors and impurities. This is one of the annoyances and inconveniences which every one in such a neighborhood must endure. Mere discomfort caused by such conditions without injury to life or health cannot be ruled as *matter of law* (italics mine) to constitute a nuisance. Each case must depend upon its own facts and no rule can be formulated which will be applicable to all cases." ... On the question of fact whether the smell, smoke, or fumes of manufacturing establishments were of such character as to constitute nuisances, the decisions indicate great liberality towards industrial establishments. In Tuttle v. Church, supra, Judge Colt found that a fish-rendering plant was not a nuisance; in the Strachan Case, supra, the master found that an oil works was not; In Fay v. Whitman, 100 Mass. 76, a jury found that a slaughterhouse was not; in Wade v. Miller, ... a master found that a hen yard in a village was not. In the Strachan case, supra, it was said that mere discomfort without injury to life or health could not be ruled as a matter of law to constitute a nuisance, though apparently it might have been so found as a matter of fact.

Just where the line should be drawn between on the one side, the interests of a community in its industrial establishments which give occupation to its inhabitants and revenue in the form of taxes and in other ways, and, on the other side, individuals who are annoyed or rendered uncomfortable by the operation of such establishments, is, as the cases say, not easy to define. The question whether the defendants have done everything reasonably practicable to avoid the cause of offense is important. Reasonable care must be used to prevent annoyance and injury to other persons beyond what the fair necessities of the business require. In the present case there is no convincing evidence that the defendants have done everything commercially practicable to control the fumes. It is suggested by the plaintiffs that the fumes could, at not unreasonable expense, be turned into a tall chimney belonging to the defendants near the galvanizing plant and discharged high in the air, so that they would float across the intervening land to the plaintiffs' houses in such concentrations as under present conditions occasionally occur. The defendants have made no satisfactory answer to this suggestion. While, as above stated, I am not satisfied that the fumes have caused physical illness, nor injured the plaintiffs' buildings or growing trees and plants, I do believe that at times they cause physical discomfort and inconvenience to an extent beyond what the plaintiffs ought reasonably to be expected to endure, unless everything commercially possible has been done to mitigate them. In other words, the property owner has the right to reasonably pure air; it devolves upon the person contaminating it to justify his action by showing the business necessity for so doing; in this case such justification has not been made out. While there are cases in which the contamination is so serious in its effects on persons or property that no business necessity justifies it, the present case is not of this extreme character. The contamination here is justifiable if unavoidable; but the necessity is not proved. On the facts as above stated I find and rule that the defendants are maintaining a nuisance.

I am, however, very clear that in view of the infrequent occasions on which the plaintiffs suffer from the nuisance, and on account of the great and disproportionate injury to the defendants and to the community which would be caused by an injunction preventing the operation of the steel works, no injunction ought to be granted. The inconvenience and temporary discomfort of the plaintiffs during the few occasions each year when the fumes are oppressive are greatly overbalanced by the benefits which the community receives from the presence of the plant. . . .

While the plaintiffs are not entitled to, and do not press for, an injunction against the operation of the galvanizing plant, they are entitled to have the defendants make reasonable efforts to abate the nuisance. If the defendants do not forthwith take all steps reasonably within their power to do so, the plaintiffs may move for a mandatory injunction compelling such action.

As to damages, they should be assessed in this proceeding. . . . The damages of the plaintiffs who are entitled to them, . . . appear on the present evidence not to be large in amount and perhaps can be adjusted by the parties. . . .

Case to stand for further hearing in accordance with this opinion.*

Several interesting and illustrative points can be noted in this case. The typical elements of a nuisance suit are all there—confused testimony on the effects of the pollution, with the industry having the expert witnesses; the economic factors, i.e., the relative valuation of the property, the condition of the houses, the size of the payroll. Even the simple, intuitive criterion of who was there first is obscured by the fact that the steel mill, although it was located on the property before the houses were constructed, didn't add the offending galvanizing plant until afterward. Other interesting aspects of this case are the reference to the English law and

---

* *DeBlois* v. *Bowers, Federal Reporter, 2nd series* 44:621 (District Court, District of Massachusetts, 1930).

the suggestion by the plaintiffs of a specific control measure (tall-stack dilution) they felt would be an acceptable solution.

The result of the case is also typical of the nuisance suit—monetary damages but no outright injunction. The judge, however, did acknowledge the "right of the property owners to reasonably pure air" and made an explicit statement of the "line-drawing" dilemma he faced. Although it is, of course, difficult to second-guess, the biggest factor in the plaintiffs' success appears to have been that in this instance, as is so often the case, the offending steel mill had not done as much as possible to minimize the effects of the galvanizing plant. In fact, the judge said that he would later compel some action if necessary.

Overall, however, nuisance actions such as this provide little success in reducing pollutant levels. The injunctive remedy, which might prohibit future pollution releases, is generally too drastic for a judge to invoke, so that victories for the plaintiff generally result only in monetary damages. In addition, of course, the costs involved prohibit the bringing of enough such individual suits to significantly hurt a major firm financially. But beyond these practical concerns, there is a more fundamental reason why the private nuisance suit cannot be expected to cope with the modern needs for air pollution control. The common law is not addressed to the complex problems that presently exist in our large industrial cities, where many pollution sources emit their effluents into the common air mass from which everyone breathes. In such a situation, any single source likely contributes only a small portion of the overall pollution, and only a tiny portion of the overall damage is suffered by any one potential plaintiff. The private nuisance provisions of the common law arose to deal with the circumstance of clear and obvious damage caused by one readily identifiable source on one gravely assaulted receptor and hence are of little practical use in the modern urban area.

The pollution of the air which we all breathe surely constitutes a serious nuisance to the general public, if not to each private plaintiff, and in fact there is just such a concept in the common law—that of *public nuisance.* Legally, however, a public nuisance is quite different from a private nuisance, the biggest difference being that an individual citizen cannot sue for relief of a public nuisance, however bad it might be. Generally, under the common law, if all the public suffers more or less equally, only the government can go to court.

GOVERNMENTAL CONTROL PROGRAMS

Since only the government can bring action against a public nuisance, private suits have been largely supplanted, until very recently, by official control programs at various levels of government. There are many aspects to government control programs, and in this section we will discuss the legal underpinnings of such programs. In Chapters 11 and 12 we will turn to the actual mechanisms of operating such programs.

Smoke Ordinances

The earliest governmental involvement in the legalities of air pollution control came as city councils in major cities legislated a declaration that dense, black smoke constituted a public nuisance. The first American cities to enact such laws were Chicago and Cincinnati, in 1881, and by 1912 most of the large cities had smoke control laws. In 1916 the United States Supreme Court ruled that this approach to the control of smoke pollution was constitutional and legally valid. In the case of *Northwestern Laundry* v. *City of Des Moines*, Mr. Justice Day spoke for the Court:

> ... So far as the Federal Constitution is concerned, we have no doubt the State may, by itself or through authorized municipalities, declare the emission of dense smoke in cities or populous neighborhoods a nuisance and subject to restraint as such; and that the harshness of such legislation, or its effect on business interests, short of a merely arbitrary enactment, were not valid constitutional objections. Nor is there any valid Federal constitutional objection in the fact that the regulation may require the discontinuance of the use of property, or subject the occupant to large expense in complying with the terms of the law or other ordinance.*

From this early time until the 1950s and 1960s, most governmental efforts to control pollution were limited to controlling dense, black smoke, under the auspices of these municipal ordinances. Although the earliest of these laws tended to merely label dense smoke a nuisance and prohibit it, more advanced technology and new knowledge about combustion transformed the smoke control laws into precise engineering regulations. These laws and their enforcement, along with the economic incentives to less wasteful fuel-burning practices, made possible the dramatic "clean-up" campaigns in St. Louis, Pittsburgh, and elsewhere. It is important to understand, however, that these successful efforts were directed against only one type of pollution, that which was most visible and obvious to the public and that which it was most feasible to control economically. Under most of the municipal smoke ordinances, control of other types of pollution was left resting somewhat precariously on the private nuisance action.

The Police Power

Concurrent with the increasing sophistication of the smoke ordinances and the more recent concern about less obvious pollution has come a shift in the legal foundation upon which government air pollution programs are based.

---

* *Northwestern Laundry* v. *City of Des Moines*, 239 U.S. 486, 36 S. Ct. 206 (1916).

Perhaps because the more subtle types of pollution don't seem to fit within the everyday meaning of "nuisance," most modern pollution control laws are phrased so as to rest on the intrinsic "police power" of the state rather than on the public nuisance concept. The police power, which is also a concept intrinsic to the common law, is simply the inherent right of the people to act, through the government, to protect their own life, health, property, and individual welfare. The police power also includes efforts to provide for public order, peace, and safety, and it can legally be exercised even though there may be some consequent unavoidable restrictions on some individual actions and some uses of property. Although the phrase "police power" sounds a bit ominous, few would question the necessity for a civilized society to have at least some power over the actions of individuals within it for the good of the whole group. The primary restrictions on the exercise of this police power by the states are the provisions in the state, and especially the federal, constitutions which define the limits of governmental power and the rights of individuals.

A law or ordinance based on the police power of the state to protect the public health can have a much broader scope than a nuisance law. It may require preventive action rather than merely the assessment of damages after the pollution has occurred; that is, a conviction does not require proof that pollution occurred, but only proof that some provision of the law was violated, which is much easier to obtain. In addition, the penalties for violation can include criminal jail sentences as well as monetary penalties.

To attack such a law, the polluter must argue that the exercise of the police power by the legislature is beyond the scope permitted by the Constitution. Such arguments against air pollution control legislation have been based on two notions. First, it has been argued that such ordinances deny "equal protection under the law" as guaranteed by the Fourteenth Amendment in arbitrarily requiring more or different compliance from one type or size of source than from another. The courts, however, have consistently held that this is not a denial of equal protection, so long as the distinctions among various pollutant sources have some rational basis and are not in fact purely arbitrary. That is, the ordinance may constitutionally require controls by power plants burning coal but not by residences burning coal, on the reasonable basis that very large sources constitute the larger portion of the problem and have to be dealt with first.

On a more basic level, air pollution laws have been attacked as violating the Fourteenth Amendment by restricting property, or the right to make profit from property, without due process of law. The interpretation as to whether passage of any given act constitutes "due process of law" is in effect an evaluation of whether it is an appropriate or inappropriate use of the police power. At present, it is generally accepted that air pollution control legislation *is* an appropriate use of the police power; in 1960 the United

States Supreme Court, in upholding the Detroit Municipal Smoke Abatement Ordinance, declared, "The ordinance was enacted for the manifest purpose of promoting the health and welfare of the city's inhabitants. Legislation designed to free from pollution the very air that people breathe clearly falls within the exercise of even the most traditional concept of what is compendiously known as the police power." *

Modern State Laws

In conjunction with the shift away from nuisance laws toward more comprehensive public health laws, there has also been a shift of primary legal responsibility from local municipal governments to state and federal governments. This has been primarily a social-political phenomenon, and we'll return to it in subsequent chapters. Since this shift has also affected the legal basis under which the government control programs operate, however, we'll give a brief summary here.

The common law police power upon which the municipal smoke control ordinances rested has always been a state authority, delegated to the local governments in accordance with state laws and the state constitutions. Until after World War II, however, authority to control air pollution was exercised by the cities only as a derivative of their general authority to protect the public health and welfare. In 1947 the first state law specifically dealing with air pollution was enacted by the California legislature. That first California law did little more than explicitly delegate to the counties authority that other states delegated implicitly, but it began a general trend toward state involvement in what had been a strictly local concern.

Through the 1950s and early 1960s, more and more state governments enacted laws either establishing state-level programs or more directly regulating the existing urban programs. Through this period, the federal government was trying to encourage the development of broad, public-health-based programs, and they had more luck with the new state programs than with the somewhat entrenched urban programs. Since 1967 federal legislation has effectively required every state to have a state-level program, but this has not prohibited the continuation of local programs; as recently as 1973, such local agencies still accounted for about half the total budget and staff of all nonfederal programs. Nonetheless, the state law has clearly become the legal backbone of the national control effort; the federal law operates primarily by requiring the states to take action, and the local programs, of course, still operate at the pleasure of the state legislatures.

Let us consider, then, the important legal aspects of a modern state air pollution control law. There are, of course, many elements involved in mak-

---

* *Huron Portland Cement Company* v. *City of Detroit*, 362 U.S. 4401, 80 S. Ct. 813 (1960).

ing a law effective; here, we will single out for discussion only four that particularly follow from our discussion in this chapter—the legal definition of air pollution employed, the statement of general public policy involved, the specification of specific responsibilities and authorities, and the establishment of the administrative structure within which the functions are to be executed.

The legal definition of air pollution actually need not be much more complicated than the intuitive definition we offered in Chapter 1, e.g., "Air pollution is the presence in the outdoor atmosphere of one or more air contaminants such as smoke, dusts, fumes, gases, vapors, odors, or other noxious substances, in sufficient quantity and of such characteristics and duration as are or tend to be injurious to human, plant, or animal life or to property or which unreasonably interfere with the enjoyment of life and property." To be noted in this definition is the key phrase "are or *tend to be* injurious"; this phrase permits action of a preventive nature before pollution levels reach the point at which damage actually occurs. Although the definition should be broad enough to permit action against any serious pollution problem, it cannot be too vague; if a potential violator is not put on "fair notice" concerning what actions are prohibited, the law may be judged invalid.

Major pieces of legislation frequently include a statement of the public policy that the legislature intends the law to establish, perhaps in the form of the facts or judgments of the legislature that led them to adopt a particular law. Although of legal significance only if vague provisions in the law itself are called into question, such a policy statement can have very important quasi-legal implications; it sets the tone for future public consideration of the matter, and it may in fact set the tone in which the current law is administered by defining publicly how strongly the legislature feels. Because the general public may be in a poor position to interpret the more detailed, technical provisions of the law, one frequently finds that the initial statement of policy is the most quoted portion of the law and the basis on which most citizens form their opinion of the law and the legislature that passed it. For example, consider the differences in tone between a state statute designed to ". . . restore, maintain, and enhance the purity of the air in the state in order to protect health, welfare, property, and the quality of life and to assure that no air contaminants are discharged into the atmosphere without being given the degree of treatment or control necessary to prevent pollution" * and another statute intended to: ". . . safeguard the air resources of the state from pollution by controlling or abating air pollution consistent with the protection of health, general welfare and physical prop-

---

* Illinois Public Act 76–2429, Title II—Air Pollution, Section 8.

erty of the people, operation of existing industries and the economic development of the state." *

Caution must, of course, be applied to judging a law by its "cover," as it were, as detailed provisions don't automatically implement high-sounding phrases. So long as there are knowledgeable observers watching, however, the tone of such statements will generally be indicative; the two quotations above are from acts which more than carry out the condemning and condoning tones, respectively.

It has also been suggested that inasmuch as the policy statement in a legislative enactment reflects the basis upon which the legislature has chosen to act, it may affect the constitutionality of the law with respect to the due process clause of the federal Constitution. The reasoning is that although "the protection of public health and welfare" clearly falls within the police power, "the promotion of the rational use of our air resources" or perhaps "the protection of the productive capacity of our industrial establishment" may not be sufficiently necessary to the public safety as to permit the uncompensated taking of private property. Regardless of how the courts might rule if the question ever arose, the point is certainly illustrative of the legal subtleties that may be involved in the precise phrasing of laws and regulations.

The third element needing special note relates to the myriad of functions which pollution control agencies perform. These functions are discussed in detail in the next chapter; the important point here is that the law must permit all those functions which need to be carried out by either local governmental or special units created under the state law or by state administrative agencies. This concern arises because existing state laws (and all too often existing state constitutions) usually specify in great detail the powers and functions of the municipalities, counties, or administrative agencies that might be called upon to administer an air pollution control law. It is best that provision for carrying out all the necessary functions be made in very broad, general language, so as to avoid litigation based on the omission of this or that trivial power from a long, detailed list, litigation that could be used as a mechanism to delay the enforcement of the law.

The last aspect of state laws mentioned, the specification of the administrative structure within which the legislature intends the law to be carried out, is usually the major part of the law, both in size and significance. Although it would seem possible for a legislature to choose to leave functional organization to the executive branch of government, almost every state law specifies the manner in which control actions are to be carried out. This is done partly because the mechanisms specified usually involve quasi-judicial

---

* Clean Air Act of Texas, 1967.

hearing boards outside the executive branch and partly because questions of delegations of power to smaller units of government, a politically delicate question in most states, are involved. This second aspect, the determination of which level of government has what responsibility for implementing the act, is discussed more thoroughly later. Here we need note only that any level of government can carry out effective control programs if it has the necessary powers and the necessary desire to do so.

Regulatory Boards and Commissions

Legislative action creating independent boards or commissions to perform some of the regulatory functions of controlling pollution deserves special mention. Commonly, these boards, which usually meet periodically rather than full-time, have the authority to promulgate rules and regulations and to hear and adjudicate appeals. Thus, they have a combination of administrative and judicial powers, although, of course, they are always subsidiary to the court system. Although the role of these boards and commissions is increasingly being questioned, most of the states, including most of those with new laws, have them.

The original reason for creating such boards has become somewhat clouded with time, but was apparently based, at least publicly, on two general premises. The first of these was that having a multimember board apart from the administrative agency would diffuse responsibility for implementing the law and thereby minimize the possibility of arbitrary action on the part of one individual. The second premise was that in this manner one would get the broad variety of technical expertise necessary to administer the law in an equitable fashion. This was particularly important in the past, when the agency administering the law was unlikely to have expertise in the details of combustion operations needed for administration of a smoke control law, for example.

The primary argument against having such boards is that so often they have in fact prevented any effective control of pollution. In the quest of expertise, the members of these boards are frequently representatives of major polluting industries. At best, these representatives can be said to believe in a slow, gradual implementation of any law; at worst, they have deliberately prevented any effective enforcement. Over the years, most boards have had a distinct tendency to be unresponsive to the general public and highly responsive to the technical arguments and economic hardships presented by the polluting industries.

These evils of the system can, of course, be controlled through the power to appoint members to the board, which customarily lies with the governor. With the recent upsurge of public interest and more detailed awareness of the situation, the memberships of these boards has begun to change in most states, just as a political response to the wishes of the public. At the same time, however, the reasons for having the boards have become less significant as the agencies administering the law have become larger, better staffed, and much more subject to public scrutiny. Whether they are ultimately eliminated, or whether they simply become more responsive to the public viewpoint, it would seem that the boards' power to thwart effective pollution control will continue to diminish.

CITIZEN SUITS: THE CHANGING LAW

We have seen that private remedies based on the intrinsic right of an individual to protection and safety have not proved effective in controlling air pollution; therefore, the trend for at least a half century has been toward control of air pollution by government regulatory programs. For some time, however, there has been an increasing body of public opinion (to which I subscribe) that feels that government is doing less than it should. The reasons offered for this failure of public agencies, which vary widely with one's social philosophy and degree of cynicism, are discussed elsewhere. Relevant to our discussion here are the most recent developments in the basic common law, which were sparked largely by this dissatisfaction over government inaction.

In the last few years there has been a great deal of news about environmental litigation, and in fact there has been a major return of the citizen, individually and in groups, to the courts in an attempt to get something done. Citizen frustration, the climate of public opinion, fresh ideas from young, creative lawyers—many factors are combining to make this an exciting period, one characterized by the emergence of a new legal specialty—environmental law.

Nuisance Suits Again

Even the private nuisance suit, which we said had largely been supplanted, is now making a comeback. This type of suit is still only appropriate in relatively extreme cases, when a source causes clear damage to an individual. But in these situations, such suits are quite often more successful than used to be the case, largely because public opinion and better scientific evidence have changed the way in which the courts balance the plaintiff's rights against the public interest in the defendant's activities. In addition, the increasingly common measurement of pollution levels means that suits can now be directed against pollution that isn't necessarily offensive to the senses, but that can be detected only by analytical measurements. In one of the more striking examples, a Houston woman sued a lead company, alleging that lead pollution had caused mental retardation and kidney illness in her six children; she accepted an out-of-court settlement of $175,000 in damages. This is certainly a victory of sorts; although $175,000 isn't much compensation for six ruined lives, it's a great deal more than most pollution victims ever get and is probably enough to get the company to start thinking about reducing or eliminating the emissions.

There are also other reasons why the private nuisance suit has become more successful—there are many more lawyers, mostly young, interested in handling environmental cases, and there are more people willing to believe, or maybe just hope, that it's worth the trouble to bring suit. In addition, of course, the pollution is often worse now than it used to be. Basically, however, although the private nuisance action is currently much more likely to help the individual pollution victim than it was formerly, it still isn't a really effective instrument for reducing the public nuisance, the overall pollution burden carried by society in general.

Legal Standing

The reasoning behind the common law rule that a private individual can't sue to abate a public nuisance is actually sensible, at least in theory. The theory is that government is a mechanism organized by a group of individuals for the purpose of protecting their collective rights; thus, in a very fundamental sense, the people *are* the government. Therefore, an individual who asserts the right to sue to abate a public nuisance is in effect asserting that he is a better guardian of the public interest than is the public itself, an intrinsically undemocratic assertion. As a very practical matter, however, most people recognize that the government is *not* identical with the public and that the government and its officials can and do have interests and motives quite apart from those of the people. As a partial recognition of this, the early kings, and other governments since then, granted citizens the right to sue the king in some circumstances and under certain rules. If the citizen's circumstances were appropriate and all the conditions were met, it was said that he had "standing" to sue the government. The legal phrase "standing to sue" is still used in reference to suing the government and since suing to abate a public nuisance is in a sense trying to place oneself above or in place of the government, it's also used in such cases, even when the government is not actually the defendant.

The question of who has standing to sue polluters, or to sue to force the government to act against them, is currently one of the most rapidly changing elements of the law. From a purely practical standpoint, we can think of the question of standing in the context of a continuous line representing potential plaintiffs' differing amounts of interest or degree of involvement in a particular act of pollution. At one end of the scale, the pollution directly and noticeably affects a person's bodily health or property rights; this is the private nuisance situation, and anyone who can prove such injury has essentially unquestioned standing to sue.

The question currently involved in the active evolution of the law is just how far toward the other end, the point of no involvement at all, we go to draw the line; that is, how minimal an interest in the polluting act can a person have and still be allowed to bring suit? Viewed in these terms, it seems reasonable to try to improve one's chances of having standing by trying to think of various ways to increase the plaintiff's personal interest in the outcome, and this is often done by increasing the number and variety of plaintiffs in the suit. Also, of course, it helps if the plaintiffs have a certain amount of political clout. Thus, we find suits brought by groups of people put together to include some near neighbors of the polluter, some members of the general public, and some civic figures if possible. This helps "the court," i.e., the judge, see that it is a serious, nonfrivolous suit which should not be lightly dismissed on a technicality, although many such suits are in fact dismissed, usually for lack of standing.

Groups and Class-Action Suits

The tactic of increasing the number of plaintiffs has some severe logistical difficulties; the practical problems of getting even a dozen people together make suits brought by thousands generally impossible. The only serious possibilities for a very large number of citizens to sue as a group are to sue through an organization or to try to establish a class-action suit, a suit on behalf of an entire class of persons, all "similarly situated," without specifically naming everyone, getting all their signatures, etc. The first of these, suits by organizations, has been tried fairly often, mostly by such groups as the Sierra Club, the Environmental Defense Fund, or the Natural Resources Defense Council, often in conjunction with individual plaintiffs. The ploy has often been fairly successful in a number of ways; certainly, having an established organization as a plaintiff solves some of the problems of recruiting legal talent, marshalling resources and technical witnesses, and so on. Legally, however, even large organizations are treated in much the same way that an individual is, though they are less likely to be casually dismissed by the court.

To get the most benefit from sheer numbers, the class-action suit seems ideal, although only in recent years has it become relatively widespread. Generally, the plaintiff must first convince the court that there does exist a reasonable class of persons who are all harmed in a similar way, that they are too numerous to be individually listed, and that the plaintiff is a reasonable representative of all the others. *If* all this is granted by the court, the plaintiff then has legal standing to sue on behalf of the entire class and, because of the size of the class, a powerful suit. The problem is that to date, the courts have been most conservative in permitting classes to be formed for environmental suits. The class of all commercial shell-fisheries in a particular estuary, represented by their trade association, might be permitted to sue the source of pollution that ruined the shellfish grounds, but the formation of a class of all SO_2-breathers in New York City, represented by a group of individuals, probably wouldn't be permitted to file suit.

The Evolving Law—Handles and Principles

Much of the previous discussion about the various types of suits and all the "ifs" and "maybes" involved may well seem confusing, and one might be tempted to ask: Doesn't the law know what it wants to say? Isn't the law the same regardless of who is suing? The answer in this case is no; questions about citizen lawsuits are questions of common law, and there is no clear definition of what the common law is on environmental suits. Whereas many areas of the common law are so rigid and well known as to be musty, the area of environmental law is definitely not. The courts are getting questions they haven't heard before, questions for which they have few precedents, or at least few that can be obviously lifted from their origin and be made applicable to the environmental question at hand. Thus, this part of the common law is evolving rapidly. The various courts, finding no clear solutions in the law, try to find a legal justification for the solution that they see as the fair thing to do in any given case, and every such case thus becomes a possible precedent for the next one.

Some of you may find your belief in our judicial system somewhat shaken by these statements about the law changing and courts trying to find justification for what they want to do anyway. This should not be too disturbing, however; it is precisely by this means that our legal system has proved flexible enough to continue to work over many centuries.

David Sive of New York, one of the emerging group of environmental lawyers, has described environmental law as presently being somewhere between the point where it draws all its legal doctrines from already established fields of law and the point where it becomes established in its own right, as a separate body of law, with its own doctrines and theory. The first point was when an environmental nuisance, e.g., dirty, black smoke, was legally no different from other nuisances, e.g., the traffic jam that occurred when the smoke stopped and all the workers went home; the second point has not yet been reached.

The goal toward which the legal system is presently evolving will probably need to be some legal mechanism which openly guarantees citizens the right to protect and improve their environment through legal action. This is in distinction to the results in most of the recent successful suits, which have succeeded not because the court legally recognized the citizens' right to a clean environment, but because there was some other, more conventional handle by which the case could be decided, and this is often a minor technicality. For example, the filling in of part of the Hudson River for a highway was prevented, not because it was a crass destruction of the river, but because the court was persuaded that the highway constituted a dike on the river, which, under an obscure old law, required Congressional approval, whereas a highway didn't. Similarly, construction of the trans-Alaska oil pipeline was at least delayed because the Interior Department (presumably accidentally) granted a right-of-way slightly wider than was permitted by an obscure regulation. Such decisions, though the results may be good, do strain the rationality of the legal system.

A direct improvement has since become available in the National Environmental Policy Act (P.L. 91–190, signed January 1, 1970), which stated that it is national policy to conserve the environment and established the Council on Environmental Quality. More to our point here, this law requires a study of the possible environmental impacts, and a public statement about them, whenever a federal agency takes any major action. Since the federal government not only conducts its own activities, but also regulates many, many other things, these *environmental impact statements* are now legally required in a great many situations in which various actions may cause pollution. In each case, the adequacy of the environmental considerations that went into the statement then becomes a legal handle by which to challenge actions detrimental to the environment. Specific to air pollution, for example, would be the environmental impact of a new power plant licensed by the Federal Power Commission (though there are also statutory ways of controlling such a source). Still, the impact statements required under the NEPA are just a handle, or procedural device, that can be used if the situation fits; they aren't a clear-cut fundamental legal principle that can be universally applied.

However, serious attempts have been made to establish just such clear-cut principles. One such effort is based on the contention that citizens have an inalienable right to a clean environment and that this right is protected by the Constitution, just as are other basic human rights; even though it is not specifically mentioned there, it could be considered to be included under the Ninth Amendment, which states: "The enumeration in the Constitution of certain rights shall not be construed to deny or disparage others retained by the people." This contention has been asserted in several cases, but so far no court has ruled on it specifically, the cases having been decided on other issues. Actually, it is fairly unlikely that the courts will positively affirm such a far-reaching principle in the foreseeable future, although a constitutional right to privacy, protected by the Ninth Amendment, was recognized in a 1965 Supreme Court decision in a birth control case.

According to another view, the courts and legislatures should establish the legal principal that the public's right to public property be enforceable at law in much the same way that private property rights presently are.

This idea, propounded principally by Professor Joseph L. Sax of the University of Michigan Law School, has its basis in legal theory in the doctrine of public trust. This concept, rooted in Roman law, concerns the government's stewardship of the citizens' rights to such common public property as the air, navigable rivers and lakes, the seashore, and so on. The doctrine has become part of American common law, but is used only rarely—when a government has abridged public rights to a public property in order to benefit private interests, e.g., the sale of public parklands to private developers. The doctrine very clearly recognizes, however, that the public—as individuals—has rights to the common public property, and there seems no legal reason why these rights should not be just as defendable in court as private rights are.

In the long run, of course, it will probably make little difference with what legal theory citizens' rights to protect their environment is developed, so long as it is developed. In the meantime, however, individual citizens and groups are still encountering the public-nuisance provisions of the common law that deny them the right to sue. In taking their resulting frustration before the state legislative bodies, a number of groups have urged a very simple solution, namely, modifying the common law by statute to specifically permit this type of citizen-initiated suit. The first success toward this end was achieved in July 1970 in the Michigan legislature. The Anderson-Rockwell Environmental Protection Act specifically provides that:

> The attorney general, any political subdivision of the state, any instrumentality or agency of the state or of a political subdivision thereof, any person, partnership, corporation, association, organization or other legal entity may maintain an action ... against the state, any political subdivision thereof, any person, partnership, corporation, association, organization or other legal entity for the protection of the air, water, and other natural resources and the public trust therein from pollution, impairment, or destruction.*

The year 1970 also saw partial success in Congress. In December 1970, amendments to the federal air pollution law included a section granting citizens standing in federal courts to sue the federal Environmental Protection Agency (EPA), or anyone in violation of federally backed pollution control plans. The standing has been slightly weakened, however, because the law requires anyone planning a suit to give 60 days prior notice to the defendant. In effect, this gives the potential defendant, especially the EPA, 60 days to "shape up" and avoid an embarrassing lawsuit, although if the threat of a suit does bring the desired action, the purpose of the law is at

---

* Section 2(1), Public Act No. 127 of 1970, State of Michigan, 75th Legislative, Regular Session of 1970.

least partly served. This provision has been used several times to compel the EPA to take a very strict, hard-line view of their powers under the act. Since 1970, citizen-suit legislation has been enacted in Florida, Illinois, Massachusetts, Minnesota, and North Carolina, and a bill patterned after the Michigan bill has been introduced in Congress by Senators Hart and McGovern and Representative Udall, so that acceptance of that idea appears to be spreading.

The legal principles we've discussed here are, of course, applicable to the entire gamut of environmental problems, and this unity is certainly as it should be. Most of these ideas, however, have been applied less in air pollution situations than in others. Thus, although the legal basis for air pollution control seems firm, it remains to be seen just how successful suits based on these laws and principles will be in solving the overall problem of air pollution.

EXERCISES

Review Questions

1. What is "the common law"?
2. Under what category of common law is a pollution damage suit most often brought?
3. In the 1930 case involving the steel mill's galvanizing plant, what was the biggest factor in the plaintiff's success, the factor indicated as being frequently decisive?
4. Why is the private nuisance suit not relevant to modern urban pollution problems?
5. Distinguish between public and private nuisance actions. Who may bring suit in each case?
6. When were the first air pollution laws adopted in this country? What sorts of laws were they? On what legal principle were they based?
7. What other legal principle has been commonly used more recently as a basis for air pollution control laws? What legal limitations are there on such laws?
8. Of what use is the broad statement of public policy that often appears at the beginning of a pollution control law?
9. For what reasons were pollution control boards initially established? Why do some people now advocate their elimination?
10. How does dissatisfaction with government pollution control efforts fit into the development of environmental law?
11. What does "standing to sue" mean? What devices might you try to increase your standing to sue a polluter in your city?
12. Distinguish between the two legal arguments mentioned as attempts to establish citizens' rights to sue to protect their environment.
13. What are the provisions of the Anderson-Rockwell Environment Protection Act? What is its special historic significance?

Thought Questions

14. Under the older perspective of *private* nuisance suits, would you think suits against small or large industrial polluters would be more successful? Would it be different for injunctions and monetary damages?
15. Select the parts from the case about the galvanizing plant that you might use to support each of the two sides in a similar, subsequent case.
16. Consider the question of "standing" along a spectrum of the plaintiff's degree of involvement. Why is it assumed that a line should be drawn somewhere, that is, why shouldn't we let anyone sue, regardless of his stake in the outcome? Do you agree with this?
17. Can you think of areas of law, other than environmental, that have evolved rapidly in recent years?

Discussion Questions

18. To what extent is it good (or bad) that the judicial system bends with public opinion? Does this make the courts and judges just "a bunch of politicians"? How rapidly should courts bend? Should all courts bend the same?
19. Prepare a legal brief (one to two pages of tight reasoning) arguing that a private nuisance suit should succeed in gaining damages for your client and an injunction forcing a small, nearby factory to stop emitting black smoke. Or, prepare an opposing brief. The factory is prosperous, but the neighborhood is run down. The equipment to control the smoke is expensive (such equipment is *always* expensive). The plaintiff lives several blocks from the factory and feels that the factory is the biggest reason for the neighborhood deterioration.
20. To what extent do you feel that citizen suits are better (or worse) than government programs for ultimately reducing overall community pollution? What are the advantages and disadvantages of each? Is there a type of government program or type of government that could eliminate the need for citizens to sue on their own?

FURTHER READING

The works by Landau and Rheingold [11] and Reitze [130] contain many such specific case citations, in the form of legal texts. For a good narrative discussion of the entire legal area, see *Defending the Environment* [17] by Professor Sax, or his shorter article [217], which includes the history of the Michigan law. More recently, Carter has followed the history of the environmental-law movement in [184] and [185]. In addition to Sax's book, Ridgeway [15] and especially Esposito [8] should contribute to an opinion on whether the government agencies are doing their job. The suggestion about the statement of legislative purpose affecting the constitutionality of the law was made by Lawrence W. Pollack, in a useful chapter of [142] on the history of and constitutional limits on state and local air pollution laws; it is also a good source for the older, more traditional case citations.

For the reader interested in somewhat more technical discussions than the above, there are a number of articles in the various law reviews, legal journals published by the law schools. In [218], Sax gives a thorough treatment of the public trust concept; [191] provides a good discussion of the role injunctions may play in air pollution control. David Sive's description of the law's evolution comes from [223], which is worth reading for other reasons also. A number of law review articles discuss the state or local law where the author or law school is located. The law review journals are almost surely available in the nearest law school library, if not elsewhere; the *Michigan Law Review* includes in each issue a bibliography of articles in other law journals.

Some more current, less fundamental discussions of legal questions appear in nonlegal journals. Experience with the National Environmental Policy Act is discussed in several articles ([189], [194–195]) and more thoroughly in the 1971 CEQ Report [101]. An article by Stunkel [229] explores environmental law in Japan, while [188] discusses citizen-suit legislation in the United States.

11
GOVERNMENTAL AIR POLLUTION CONTROL PROGRAMS

EPA-Documerica, Gene Daniels

This is the first of two chapters about governmental programs to control air pollution. In this chapter we'll discuss the various agencies, their programs, and how they function at the federal, state, and local levels. In Chapter 12 we'll consider the nature of the pollution-reduction processes these agencies are conducting. As we mentioned in Chapter 10, many people feel that governmental programs have not worked well in the past, and in fact there is some basis for such a feeling. However, since the 1960s at least, there has also been a renewed effort to make such programs effective and thus to reduce our overall pollution problem in the most efficient way.

INTRODUCTION

Historically, the first governmental air pollution programs in this country were developed to enforce the early smoke-control laws in the major cities. By 1912, 23 of the 28 American cities with population over 200,000 had such laws, passed by city councils under their state-delegated authority to protect the public health and welfare. Typically, these smoke-control laws specified the type of fuel-burning equipment that was to be used, how such equipment should be operated, and sometimes specified the type of fuel that could be burned. Ultimately, many of these laws stipulated that emitting smoke darker than a particular level of the Ringelmann scale constituted a punishable offense. The laws were enforced by smoke inspectors, who patrolled the city, looking for smokestack emissions in violation of the law and by permit systems for installing and operating the equipment, as well as by inspection systems to ensure the use of acceptable equipment and firing procedures. By the late 1940s, these programs had been reasonably effective in eliminating or preventing serious smoke problems.

In 1947 California passed the first state law specifically directed at air pollution control. Developed out of the postwar concern about photochemical smog pollution in the Los Angeles Basin, this law provided specific enabling authority for countywide air pollution control districts. The Los Angeles County Air Pollution Control District was immediately formed under this law, with a mandate somewhat broader than that of the smoke-control departments in the eastern cities. More important, however, the California law set a precedent for state-level legislation and began a trend toward concern with pollutants other than smoke. In the following years, other states adopted specific air pollution control legislation, and by the end of the 1950s there were active and growing efforts in many areas.

As part of this trend, the federal government came under increasing pressure to play a role and, in particular, to put its financial resources and political weight behind the new state pollution control agencies in their struggle to expand the public concern beyond the old smoke problems. The ultimate result was the establishment, in 1955, of a federal air pollution program, devoted primarily to conducting research and providing technical assistance to the states. Since then, the federal role has expanded considerably; today, local, state, and federal agencies are all involved in a vigorous, if not always completely coordinated, national program of pollution control. Before discussing the federal program in more detail, however, we'll look more closely at the operational activities of a pollution control agency.

AIR POLLUTION CONTROL FUNCTIONS

If we were to visit a major air pollution control agency, we would see a variety of functions being carried on. A fairly large number of people would be involved in measuring ambient pollution levels, operating and maintaining samplers and instruments, and operating a chemical laboratory. Another sizable group would be processing records and forms submitted by the operators of major pollution sources, and some inspectors would be in the field, checking the operations of these sources. One person would be taking telephoned complaints from citizens, and other people would be investigating these complaints. There would probably be a group of legal experts preparing documents for court cases and almost surely a public information staff for assisting reporters and others making inquiries; this staff group might also be preparing slide shows, posters, and other educational materials.

An organizational chart of the agency would probably indicate such other functions as a chief (or director), perhaps a group doing "program planning and evaluation," a special assistant to the director for legislative matters, and (likely off to the upper corner) an Air Pollution Control Commission or Advisory Council. Figure 11–1 shows an organization chart for a hypothetical control agency.

Permits, Inspections, and Variances

The oldest function of pollution control agencies, at least of local agencies, has often been the most visible and has involved a large group of employees—the operation of a permit-and-variance system, with associated inspections of pollution sources. Typically, pollution control laws require that the operator of a potential pollution source have both an operating permit and a construction permit to modify the source or build a new one. Such a system is enforced by having engineers review construction plans to determine whether a new source will meet the laws and regulations; only after these plans have been approved can an operating permit be awarded. In addition, inspectors periodically visit existing sources to verify their continued compliance and to renew their operating permits.

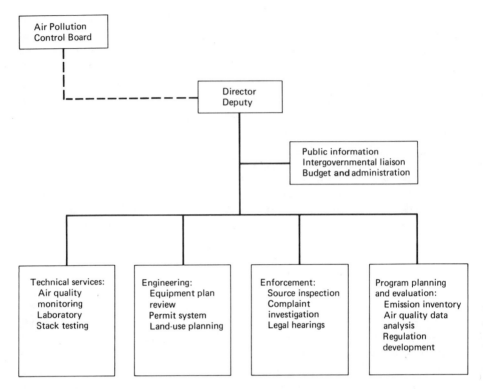

Fig. 11–1. Organization of a typical air pollution control agency.

In the early days, these permit systems were used as a means of enforcing smoke-control regulations; operators of fuel-burning equipment were required to have a permit from the control agency in order to operate their equipment, and the permit could be denied if the combustion equipment didn't meet the city's regulations. On the other hand, the operator could try to convince the agency or an appeals board that there was good reason for noncompliance, and such appeals were usually made on the basis of an undue hardship facing the operator. If the appeals board agreed, it awarded the operator a special dispensation, known as a "variance," a legal exception to the enforcement of the regulations.

The provision for issuing variances was made to give the laws a certain degree of flexibility in order to avoid genuine hardship, or at least that was usually the stated reason. Such a system, however, is just begging to be abused, and such was frequently the case, at least in the past. In some cities, enforcement officials issued warnings about violations, perhaps even hauled the polluter into court, forced him to file a petition for a variance, and then routinely granted the variance, leaving the agency with a new file folder and the citizens with the same pollution as before. In other cities and states, agencies routinely denied variances, only to have them granted on appeal to the air pollution control board's political appointees. Similar abuses no doubt continue today, but they're clearly declining, largely as a result of increased public awareness of the problem. When a variance must be renewed every year, with a full-dress public hearing every time, the polluter quickly finds it too embarrassing to continue the practice.

Regulatory Standards

Behind the permit-and-variance system are the laws or regulations with which the sources must comply. Originally, the requirements were usually spelled out in the smoke-control ordinance, but more recently most agencies have been delegated the authority to promulgate detailed regulations implementing a more general purpose expressed in the law. These regulations are promulgated according to a standard procedure, which often involves public hearings and usually requires the concurrence of the air pollution control board or commission, if there is such a body. The adopted regulations carry the full force of the enabling legislation and are the agencies' principal tool for effecting reductions in pollutant emissions. Some of the regulations are primarily administrative, specifying the requirements for permit applications, for instance, but the heart of the control program is in those regulations that specify the standards against which the sources' performance is to be compared.

There are two types of standards commonly specified: equipment standards, which have been used for many years and are thus relatively common, and emission standards, which are somewhat newer. An *emission standard* is a regulation specifying the maximum amount of pollutant permitted in the effluent from any source—so many pounds of particulate per million BTU heat input, so many grams of CO per mile, and so on. *Equipment standards*, on the other hand, specify the type of equipment that must be used. For example, a regulation might stipulate that apartment houses use only heating furnaces with mechanical stokers rather than hand-fired types, or that all power plants be equipped with electrostatic precipitators of at least 98% efficiency. Sometimes, equipment standards are expressed more vaguely, requiring the use of the "maximum feasible technology" to keep emissions to the lowest level "economically feasible," and then leaving the control agency to determine on a case-by-case basis whether a source is in fact employing maximum feasible control.

No matter how the standards are expressed, they are, of course, only legal instruments unless there is an enforcement effort which, operationally, is the function actually being carried out by the agency employees in operating the permit system and in conducting the source inspections. As we noted, the issuance of variances is becoming less and less common or routine; the recent trend has clearly been for potential polluters to comply with the regulations, albeit perhaps grudgingly. In a very real sense, this quasi-voluntary compliance is crucial to the success of the control effort. An air pollution inspector can fairly easily verify compliance with equipment standards by simply inspecting the boiler, furnace, or whatever; verifying compliance with emission standards, however, is much more difficult and often requires extensive stack sampling. As increasingly stringent reductions are required, the improvement that can be gained from changes in equipment is lessened, and add-on control devices become necessary. Thus, emission standards are becoming increasingly common, making it necessary for the control agencies to have stack-testing teams to verify compliance. In Los Angeles County (always a special case), the county Air Pollution Control District even has patrol cars, just as the police have, that are used to spot smoke violations from vehicles and that can provide rapid response to citizen complaints. Nonetheless, since it is impossible to inspect every source every week, some degree of cooperation by the pollutant sources is essential.

Emissions Inventories

A useful by-product of a permit system is that it facilitates another agency function—compiling and maintaining an inventory of the pollutant emissions in the area over which the agency has responsibility. A relatively new function within the last ten years, the practice of maintaining a running compilation of sources and their emissions is now followed by all the state agencies and most of the major local agencies. What would be desirable, aside from its cost, would be a complete list of all the pollutant sources and their location, together with the amount of each source's emissions, how the level of emissions has varied over time, and some provision for keeping up with any changes in these factors. In practice, the cost of such a program would be prohibitive; therefore, detailed emissions inventories are usually kept only for the medium and larger sources, typically those that are required to have permits. Emissions information about the multitude of small sources is kept only as aggregate estimates, usually for certain geographic areas, e.g., census tracts.

The inventory of large sources usually includes information about the nature of the source, details on the type of equipment used, the quantity and quality of fuel used, stack heights, emission controls (if any), and so on. Stack-sampling data on emission quantities would surely be included if available; however, since these data are seldom available, it has become routine procedure to estimate the emissions on the basis of an "emission factor" and more readily available information, e.g., data on fuel use or, in the case of manufacturing processes, data on the amount of raw material input or finished product output. The emission factor is the approximate proportionality constant between the emissions and the other data, e.g., 10 pounds of particulate matter per 1000 gallons of oil burned, 96 grams of CO per mile driven, and so on. Emission factors are usually determined in a field-research study, based on stack-sampling results from a few specific sources and are then used more widely; thus, emission factors produce only approximate, but reasonably good, figures for total emissions. The emissions quantities tabulated in Chapters 3, 8, and 9 were all estimated in this way.

Using this kind of information to make estimates of emissions, an agency can maintain a reasonably current estimate of the total emissions of each pollutant, as well as the distribution of emissions by geographical area, type of source, and so on. Most agencies get this information when sources apply for their annual renewals of operating permits. If a permit system isn's used by the agency, information to update the emission inventory, perhaps annually, must be gained by questionnaire, telephone inquiry, etc., a much more difficult task.

Air Quality Monitoring

Another ongoing responsibility of a pollution control agency is to monitor the ambient concentration of the various pollutants—the ambient air quality. Almost any assessment of the harm caused by pollution requires knowing the actual pollutant levels, as does any judgment about whether or not things are satisfactory, or are getting better or worse, and a pollution control agency needs to make both types of judgments. Consequently, a new agency's first action is usually to establish an air quality monitoring program. In addition, of course, monitoring remains an important function of a well-established program; in fact, cynics are fond of implying that governmental agencies spend all their effort measuring pollution in order to avoid doing anything about it. Although this may have been true in the past, at present it is clearly necessary to know in some detail what the pollutant levels are so that a realistic control program can be maintained. Beyond this, the investment of manpower in analyzing the data, its variations, trends, and so on, can provide valuable knowledge about pollution sources that isn't available otherwise. (The discussion in Chapter 7 offers an expanded view of monitoring programs, and particularly about various aspects of data use.)

Meteorology and Dispersion Models

Another parameter over which an agency needs to maintain surveillance in its area of jurisdiction is the meteorology, which determines the relationship between the pollutant emissions and the ambient concentrations they produce. A few of the largest agencies have become involved in the routine measurement of meteorological parameters, but most just make use of the data gathered by the National Weather Service as part of the air transportation system. In either case, the need is to develop, for each urban area, a meteorological dispersion model. Such a model is a means of estimating, at least approximately, the ambient concentrations that will be produced, after meteorological dispersion and mixing, from the quantity of pollution emitted. This is done through the use of the meteorological dispersion formula (see Chapter 8), which lets us calculate the ambient concentration produced at a receptor point by a specific, single pollutant source. A meteorological dispersion model applies this formula to each major source in turn, using the estimates of each source's emissions from the emissions inventory and the appropriate meteorological data. The emissions from sources too small to consider individually, e.g., individual residences, are generally lumped together as "area sources," and their contribution to the pollutant level at any given point is calculated by using a slightly modified equation. The totals of the individual source contributions are then added to any background concentration in the air coming in from the adjoining geographical areas to give a total—a prediction or estimate of the pollutant concentration at that receptor point.

The results of this type of urban-area diffusion modeling are not very precise by some standards, since predicted and actual values often differ by a factor of two. Considering all the approximations and assumptions that are unavoidably involved in such calculations, however, this degree of error isn't considered discouraging. If the results are inaccurate, the model can be adjusted, or calibrated, based on data from the air quality monitoring sites in the area, and the adjusted model will then better predict air quality at other points. In addition, the most important use of dispersion models is in comparing different hypothetical situations, so that errors in the model *per se* will cancel out and hence are of less concern.

Emergency Episode Control

One of the newest operational activities of a control agency is the ongoing effort to forecast and prevent or control emergency episodes arising when extreme meteorological conditions magnify the harmful potential of everyday pollution. The purpose, of course, is to try to prevent the type of disastrous incident that occurred in such cities as London and Donora. In the long run, a general reduction of pollution levels should make such instances increasingly rare, but in the meantime, the potential for a severe episode remains.

The control system, usually called an emergency action plan, is a preplanned sequence of contingency actions "triggered" by either a forecast of adverse meteorological conditions or the deterioration of air quality below a specified point. The plan, as sketched schematically in Fig. 11–2,

The first level occurs when either the Weather Service or the air pollution agency makes a forecast of adverse meteorological conditions; the forecast-level actions are designed to alert the relevant authorities to the possibility of an upcoming emergency situation. Those contacted are usually the air pollution control agencies and health departments in the affected jurisdictions, the major pollution sources, the police and fire departments, and the news media. The second stage occurs when the pollutant concentrations reach the preset "first alert," generally a level at which the most susceptible individuals should begin to take precautions. The appropriate agency actions are: first, a request that the news media alert the public to take precautions; and second, the initiation of feasible control actions, which are usually directed at the most significant sources and/or those which require the least effort to control. For example, power plants might be directed to switch to less-polluting fuels, and restrictions might be placed on incineration and various other semivoluntary polluting activities. Note that if the air quality reached the alert level specified, this stage might be reached without having gone through a forecast stage. Such a situation might occur simply because meteorological forecasting is not at all perfect, especially on a small geographical scale, and in such cases the actions appropriate to both levels are taken simultaneously.

Typically, actions at the third and fourth stages of the emergency action plan are aimed at shutting down as much pollution-causing activity as possible. The third stage might comprise those actions that can be taken without harming persons or equipment, even though they entail accepting some economic hardship. The fourth stage, then, consists of yet more stringent measures, e.g., shutting down all commercial and light-industrial activity except for essential food service, drug stores, police protection, etc. Depending on their nature, most heavy industries are already under the maximum possible short-term control at the third stage, since such industries typically cannot shut down abruptly without causing massive permanent damage to their capital plant. As the demand for electric power decreases with the fourth-stage reduction in other activity, the pollution contributions of power plants will automatically go down.

It is obvious that complex advance planning is needed to control emergency episodes and that various types of information are needed to make such a plan workable. For example, one must have at least a rough idea of the effects of pollution in order to select the air quality levels that will trigger action at the various stages. In order to forecast high levels of ambient air quality, one must have some facility in predicting future air quality, based on knowledge of emissions and meteorological predictions. One must also have a thorough knowledge of at least the major pollutant sources and of what pollution-reducing actions are available to each source. Finally, and most important in the short-term situation, one must have the ability to communicate rapidly with the groups involved, and this necessarily entails well-planned advance arrangements for direct phone contact with major polluters, news media, and other governmental jurisdictions.

The decision-making requirements in such situations are also obvious and should be made in advance; the choice of pollutant levels and the selection of actions to be taken at the various stages constitute the bulk of the decision functions, although some room for on-the-spot modificatins may well exist. In order to be effective, the authority to initiate alerts must be delegated in advance to a relatively low level. The image of the air pollution control officer waiting to get a call through to the public health commissioner, who in turn must get the ear of the governor, is a ridiculous, though sometimes realistic, picture; it certainly reflects the highly political nature of initiating alert actions.

The implementation of pollution-reducing actions also needs to be preplanned so that the plan goes into effect automatically once the alert is under way. Equipment operators and executives at the pollutant sources need to take their respective actions, and air pollution personnel need to verify that these actions have been taken. The communication and enforcement functions are, of course, limited by the duration of the alert, but the selection of appropriate abatement measures by the air pollution agency and the sources' responsibility for carrying them out are not much different from the similar functions usually performed on an ongoing basis.

Newer Agency Activities

In the last few years, some agencies have begun new types of activities, many of them associated with the longer-term management of our urban areas. Zoning, land-use regulations, and similar techniques of city planning are a much more basic approach to the pollution problem than are, say, emission standards; in general, however, such plans can have little or no immediate effect on already developed urban areas. Nonetheless, sound environmental planning for the next 15 to 20 years or more will require much better land-use planning, which can be accomplished, for instance, by including air pollution considerations in zoning decisions. In Chapter 9 we mentioned some of the possibilities in the planning of transportation facilities; these efforts are just now being started, and as they progress, they will likely become more and more prominent parts of the control agency's overall activities.

FEDERAL AIR POLLUTION FUNCTIONS

The air pollution program of the federal government is unlike that of state or local agencies. Until recently, the federal program had no direct authority to control or abate pollution sources, and even today its authority is limited. However, because of the federal government's ability to command public attention and financial resources far beyond those of the richest state or city, the federal program has a dominant influence on the nation's air pollution control efforts. In this section, we'll consider the federal program's functional authorities and responsibilities as they currently exist. Then, we'll discuss the history of the federal program, primarily as a vehicle for explaining the overall national control effort.

As we've noted previously, the federal air pollution effort is conducted by the Environmental Protection Agency (EPA), an agency independent of all the cabinet-level departments of the executive branch. A new agency, EPA was established in December 1970 to pull together the various federal environmental programs; previously, the Department of Health, Education, and Welfare was responsible for air pollution control programs. Since 1955, when federal air pollution programs were initiated, the title of the responsible agency has changed several times. We'll use the acronym EPA throughout, but older materials refer to APCO (Air Pollution Control Office) and NAPCA (National Air Pollution Control Administration), the two previous designations.

Since there is no common-law police power at the federal level, the existence of a program in the executive branch depends on laws passed by Congress; for this reason, we frequently speak of the congressional "authority" to do thus-and-so. In theory, the only limit on such authority is the Constitution, but in fact the limits imposed by practical politics are far more constraining. The law defining the federal program is the Clean Air Act, codified in Title 42 of the United States Code, beginning on p. 1857. The law includes the original Clean Air Act of 1963 and a number of amendments, most important of which were adopted in 1967 and 1970. The Act has three Titles which incorporate 52 Sections; these are summarized in Table 11–1. The "Findings and Purposes" are explicitly stated

TABLE 11–1
The Clean Air Act as amended December 31, 1970

Title I: Air Pollution Prevention and Control

Sec. 101. Findings and Purposes
Sec. 102. Cooperative Activities and Uniform Laws
Sec. 103. Research Investigations, Training, and other Activities
Sec. 104. Research Relating to Fuels and Vehicles
Sec. 105. Grants for Support of Air Pollution Planning and Control Programs
Sec. 106. Interstate Air Quality Agencies or Commissions
Sec. 107. Air Quality Control Regions
Sec. 108. Air Quality Criteria and Control Techniques
Sec. 109. National Ambient Air Quality Standards
Sec. 110. Implementation Plans
Sec. 111. Standards of Performance for New Stationary Sources
Sec. 112. National Emission Standards for Hazardous Air Pollutants
Sec. 113. Federal Enforcement

TABLE 11–1 (cont.)

Sec. 114. Inspections, Monitoring, and Entry
Sec. 115. Abatement by Means of Conference Procedure in Certain Cases
Sec. 116. Retention of State Authority
Sec. 117. President's Air Quality Advisory Board and Advisory Committees
Sec. 118. Cooperation by Federal Agencies to Control Air Pollution from Federal Facilities

Title II: Emission Standards for Moving Sources
Part A: Motor Vehicle Emission and Fuel Standards

Sec. 201. Short Title
Sec. 202. Establishment of Standards
Sec. 203. Prohibited Acts
Sec. 204. Injunction Proceedings
Sec. 205. Penalties
Sec. 206. Motor Vehicle and Motor Vehicle Engine Compliance Testing and Certification
Sec. 207. Compliance by Vehicles and Engines in Actual Use
Sec. 208. Records and Reports
Sec. 209. State Standards
Sec. 210. State Grants
Sec. 211. Regulation of Fuels
Sec. 212. Development of Low-Emission Vehicles
Sec. 213. Definitions for Part A

Part B: Aircraft Emission Standards

Sec. 231. Establishment of Standards
Sec. 232. Enforcement of Standards
Sec. 233. State Standards and Controls
Sec. 234. Definitions

Title III: General

Sec. 301. Administration
Sec. 302. Definitions
Sec. 303. Emergency Powers
Sec. 304. Citizen Suits
Sec. 305. Appearance
Sec. 306. Federal Procurement
Sec. 307. General Provision Relating to Administrative Proceedings and Judicial Review
Sec. 308. Mandatory Licensing
Sec. 309. Policy Review
Sec. 310. Other Authority not Affected
Sec. 311. Records and Audit
Sec. 312. Comprehensive Economic Cost Studies
Sec. 313. Additional Reports to Congress
Sec. 314. Labor Standards
Sec. 315. Separability
Sec. 316. Appropriations
Sec. 317. Short Title

in Section 1; briefly, Congress found that an air pollution problem did exist, that primary responsibility for solving it lay at the state and local governmental levels, but that "Federal financial assistance and leadership was necessary." This is in fact a fair statement of what the law tries to do.

The major elements of the federal program are a research, training, and technical-assistance program, the financial support of nonfederal programs, several mechanisms for controlling pollution in concert with the states, and the federal effort for controlling mobile-source pollution and regulating vehicular fuels.

Research, Training, and Technical Assistance

The research and training functions of the federal program have been conducted since the first 1955 law and still constitute a large portion of the agency's actual operating budget. The major research efforts are in the areas of pollutant effects and techniques for pollution control, although the program also includes projects in numerous other subject areas. The research program is conducted in a variety of ways; the most visible part is carried on by EPA employees in EPA laboratories and is hence known as "in-house," or intramural, research. In-house research has the advantage of being under close control and hence relevant to EPA policies and objectives. The primary disadvantage is the government's difficulty in recruiting and maintaining an adequate staff within legislative employment ceilings.

EPA also supports a sizable program of extramural research projects, which are conceived and conducted by outside researchers, primarily in the universities, and are funded as research grants. These research projects need not be closely related to specific governmental needs at any given time and are generally under less control by EPA. Research projects funded in this way are of considerable value in increasing the number of people and facilities involved in air pollution research, a major gain that perhaps even exceeds the value of the knowledge gained.

When caught between the limitations of in-house staff and the lack of direct control over grants, EPA can turn to a research contract with some organization to perform specified research work. Numerous profit and nonprofit firms do such contract research, often on a competitive basis, and often trade associations contract to do research work in their specific fields.

The manpower training and technical assistance functions have been part of the federal program from the beginning and have been an important stimulus to the development of the air pollution control effort in the United States, though that role has been decreasing as the competency of the nonfederal agencies increases. Presently, EPA supports the development of trained air pollution manpower in three ways. The Air Pollution Training Institute conducts excellent one- and two-week courses in various aspects of air pollution control, open to anyone employed or interested in the field. Less directly, EPA also supports air pollution training in university graduate schools, through both training grants to the universities for the development and maintenance of the programs and a limited number of fellowships for individual students.

The technical assistance function was very prominent in the late 1950s and early 1960s, when nonfederal agencies needed help much more than they do presently. Much of the early knowledge of community pollution problems came from cooperative studies conducted by federal air pollution staff and local agency personnel. More recently, EPA has conducted a program of demonstration grants, through which studies of a miscellaneous nature can be funded by, or conducted cooperatively between, EPA and other groups, usually nonfederal air pollution agencies or industrial firms. Imaginative use of such grants can be a valuable financial adjunct to the control agency that is willing to try new approaches.

Another important aspect of the technical assistance function is the federal air quality monitoring system, the source for most of the ambient air pollution concentration data in Chapter 3. Known as the National Air Surveillance Networks (NASN), this effort is a cooperative venture between the federal program and various state, local, and other federal agencies. The NASN operates 250–300 hi-vol samplers each year, a smaller number of bubbler gas samplers, and a few stations with continuous instruments for the major gaseous pollutants. The federal program provides sampling equipment and supplies, as well as laboratory and data-processing services; the cooperating agency in each locale provides a sampling site and, most crucially, the manpower to operate the system. In the 1950s the NASN represented essentially all the ambient air quality monitoring that existed in the country; today, hundreds of control agencies actively conduct pollution monitoring programs. The primary continuing value of the NASN lies in the uniformity of sampling method and quality control across the country and in the fact that it is the only source of historical data on air quality before the mid-1960s.

Operating Budget Support

Direct financial support of nonfederal air pollution control agencies accounts for the largest portion of the federal air pollution budget. This authority to grant funds to state, regional, and local control agencies was a new, major feature of the 1963 Clean Air Act and was intended to stimulate the development of new control programs and to encourage the evolution of the smoke-control efforts in large cities into broader, more comprehensive programs. EPA is authorized to grant up to two-thirds of the cost of developing new, or improving existing, programs and up to half the ongoing cost of maintaining them. These limits mean that in effect, the funds are granted to the agencies to match funds provided by the state or local governments, supplementing rather than totally supplanting local money.

This method of supplying federal financial aid has become a standard way of life during the last few decades; a nonfederal agency is greatly strengthened in its competition for a portion of the state or local budget if it can increase its appropriation significantly by attracting federal matching funds. Thus, the matching-grant mechanism is a way in which Congress can influence the priorities with which local tax monies are spent. The "revenue-sharing" efforts of recent years are attempts to partially modify this system by giving out at least some money that needn't be expended for specified purposes.

There is also one other way in which the control agency grant program affects nonfederal agencies. The power to draw up specifications for the type of pollution control eligible for support is one of the ways the EPA technical staff can influence the general direction and emphasis of the entire national effort; sometimes, this influence becomes fairly detailed in specific situations.

Federal-State Pollution Abatement

Pollution abatement is probably the most significant aspect of the current federal program. One element of this responsibility, the "Air Quality Criteria Documents," was discussed briefly in Chapter 4. Section 108 of the Clean Air Act directs the EPA Administrator to issue "air quality criteria" for major pollutants that "accurately reflect the latest scientific knowledge useful in indicating the kind and extent of all identifiable effects on public health or welfare which may be expected from the presence of such pollutant in the ambient air, in varying quantities." In addition, the administrator is required to publish information on the availability and cost of technology to control the sources of the pollutant, i.e., the "Control Technology Documents," referred to in Chapter 8. This authority and responsibility, an extension of the research function, requires that the EPA assemble and publish information about each pollutant so that judgments on the desirable level of air quality and the methodology for obtaining that level can be made

Actually, the publication of the criteria and control-technology documents has become part of one of the law's two approaches to cooperative federal-state abatement of pollution sources. The more important of the two approaches, the *air quality standards approach*, requires that EPA divide the country into "Air Quality Control Regions" (AQCRs), issue the criteria and control-technology documents, and establish minimum ambient air quality standards for the nation. It is then the responsibility of each state government to design specific legal-engineering plans for the implementation of these standards (or more stringent state standards) in each of the air quality control regions in its territory. The Clean Air Act makes certain requirements of these *implementation plans*, but leaves to the states most of the substantive choices (and hard decisions) about methods and priorities. Each implementation plan must be approved by the EPA; if a state refuses or fails to produce and enforce an acceptable plan, the EPA Administrator is required to do so. This part of the law has had a confused history, which we'll return to shortly, and has been operative in its present form only since December 1970; thus, although we say that it's the most important abatement approach, no really meaningful evaluation has yet been possible.

The second federal-state abatement method, aimed directly at interstate pollution problems, consists of a series of procedures for conferences, abatement hearings, and court action and is therefore called the conference-hearing approach. Under this procedure, federal abatement enforcement begins with a conference between federal representatives and state and local air pollution control agencies. If the problem cannot be resolved by this means, it may be brought into federal court. This approach, however, is cumbersome except in certain situations and has been used only a few times; since the enactment of the air quality standards approach, it is at best a minor weapon in the EPA's arsenal.

Motor Vehicle Emissions Regulation

In contrast to the two federal-state cooperative abatement approaches just discussed, the federal government has taken for itself sole authority to regulate emissions from motor vehicles. EPA is authorized to promulgate emission standards specifying the maximum pollutant concentrations from new motor vehicles; it is a federal crime to sell or distribute an automobile or engine which fails to meet the standards. The law specifically preempts any state from regulating motor vehicle emissions; California, the only exception, was ahead of the federal government in this area, as in others. The federal motor vehicle control program was discussed in some detail in Chapter 9.

Miscellaneous Provisions

The Clean Air Act also provides for several other federal abatement functions which, since their overall impact is somewhat less, have been labeled, perhaps unfairly, "miscellaneous." EPA has authority to establish emission standards for pollutants on the hazardous list (mentioned in Chapters 3 and 4). Currently, these "hazardous" pollutants are asbestos, beryllium, and mercury. EPA can also set "standards of performance" for *new* sources in those industrial categories that contribute "significantly" to air pollution, and for this purpose EPA has set emission limits for a number of different types of major sources. Note that this authority doesn't affect presently existing sources, which are regulated according to state implementation plans.

Since chemical additives to fuels can be a prominent factor in the pollution emitted from the fuel-burning equipment, EPA maintains a register of fuel additives and can, if necessary, control or prohibit their use. The primary example at the present is, of course, the lead in gasoline, which not only is a pollutant in its own right, but is also capable of damaging the catalytic mufflers that may be used as emission-control devices. The law specifically permits prohibition of an additive if it interferes with emission-control devices.

As a further contribution to promoting the availability of nonpolluting vehicles by 1975, Congress (and many others as well) has considered it desirable to pursue the engineering development of alternative low-emission vehicles, rather than rely solely on the success of the major auto manufacturers in meeting emission standards. Accordingly, the law stipulates that the federal government help support such research and development efforts not only by providing research grants, etc., but also by offering premium prices for low-pollution vehicles when buying cars for government motor pools.

Ephemeral Functions

Because of the pyramidal nature of our federal system, the federal government performs many functions that are not expressly stated in any law, merely because it is the group with the widest base. Thus, EPA supports the air pollution community in its various endeavors, not only by means of the research and training grants previously described, but also by such contributions as funding a literature-abstracting function and providing leadership toward standardization of analytical chemical methods and data-handling procedures. The federal agency has a major influence on both the technical and policy decisions of state and local programs. EPA's scheme as air quality standards and implementation plans gives it a major role in much of what is done; the states can implement their own plans for pollution control but only if they do so as quickly enough and as stringently as required by federal policy. But beyond this direct control, the federal government has a subtle but strong effect, through the media and public opinion, on the public policy which guides pollution control throughout the country. The tone, the degree of urgency, and the general thrust of the entire national effort are at least loosely governed by federal decisions.

A still more ephemeral influence, one that is often overlooked, is the very definition of things, technical things, such as the list of "major pollutants" we've used throughout our discussions. The inclusion of a pollutant on this list, and indeed the definition of what chemicals comprise what pollutant, depends on the way in which the federal criteria documents and standards are written. For example, a federal decision to include particulate sulfates in the sulfur oxide air quality standard would have changed the thrust of most control programs. The evolution of the hi-vol sampler into the definitive instrument for particulates and the question of using mass units for gases are further examples of the subtle power of certain types of federal decisions.

A SYSTEMATIC NATIONAL PROGRAM

A simple listing of the functions of the various agencies, such as our discussion so far, doesn't give much indication of any coherent, overall program to control air pollution, either nationally or on a local basis. It is, in fact, difficult to discern the difference between a well-organized, coherent program, dedicated to clear-cut objectives, and a mere collection of pollution-control functions assembled in a haphazard way.

On a local level, a good program is usually carried out by a single administrative agency, but this merely promotes efficiency, and is not strictly necessary; indeed, a good program may be carried out by several separate agencies, if they coordinate smoothly. Nor does the existence of a single agency ensure a coherent program as we speak of it here; a government agency can, and in the past most did, consist merely of groups of people performing air pollution control functions without any overall program. Since it is impossible to have a single agency on a national level, we have instead a loose federal-state partnership, involving a great variety of agencies with roughly corresponding goals and interlocking procedures. This is not to imply that the present national effort is completely "well-organized, coherent, and dedicated to clear-cut objectives," but rather that the national effort is much more nearly so than is apparent from the previous discussion, and much more so than it was only a few years ago.

In this section, we will first indicate how the various functions described previously fit into a coherent, overall program. We will then trace the development of the present national control effort, largely by considering the history of the federal program.

Agency Activities in the Abstract

In order to see how the functions fit together to make a program and in order to provide a certain degree of structure, we'll categorize the various agency activities as knowledge functions, decision functions, and implementation functions. This, of course, suggests a pattern—know the situation, make a decision, and then implement that decision. Various time scales can be superimposed on this pattern; a program's personnel should be able to know, decide, and implement a plan with respect to a problem of immediate concern, e.g., an emergency episode, and also to those involving long-term planning.

Knowledge functions are related to the gathering of information, both background and current, in order to have on hand all the knowledge possible pertaining to a particular decision. We need to know the sources, location, nature, and amount of pollution, the effects produced by the air quality, and meteorological information related to these other factors. Thus, emission inventory functions and the air quality and meteorological monitoring all fit in this category, as does research on the several effects of the various pollutants.

The second group of functions, decision functions, are essentially simpler, though crucial to the overall success or failure of the program. It is at this stage that someone assesses the available knowledge and decides whether pollution levels are too high; if in fact the ambient pollution levels are too high, someone must decide to require the reduction of pollution emissions or, more precisely, to select from among the numerous alternative ways of requiring various reductions from various sources. The third group, implementation functions, are simply those activities conducted to reduce the pollutant emissions after the decisions have been made. These activities include regulatory standards, permit systems, and the various legal and persuasive means used to encourage compliance.

On a short-term time scale, such as during an emergency episode, the three types of functions are quite obvious—short-term air quality and meteorological surveillance and the clear-cut abatement actions to be taken promptly. Even the decision functions are usually preplanned and highly visible, if not quite completely automatic.

On a long-term time scale, the knowledge and implementation functions are similar to those taken in the short run, but they're more a matter of research and do not involve short-term predictions. The major difference in the two time scales is in the decision functions. Mechanisms to make the necessary long-term decisions just did not exist until the late 1960s. Before then, various air pollution control agencies, primarily city agencies, had much the same knowledge and nearly all the same implementation tools that they have now. However, they rarely required any major pollution reduction. One of the benefits of taking an abstract view of the relationships among the various types of pollution control functions has been the realization that in the long-run time scale, the only thing missing has just been the will, the decision, to do something. The provision of a mechanism for making these decisions, however, has not been a simple task, for it has involved not only the existing city agencies, but also the state and federal governments and society as a whole, and the task has not yet been completed.

The Early History

Continuing to consider these three types of functions in the abstract, let's return to the early history of air pollution control programs in urban areas. The programs began when the obvious, widespread knowledge about smoke in the air finally produced a decision in the city council to pass a smoke-control law. The council then typically established a local smoke-control group to perform the implementation functions of inspecting fuel-burning equipment, using a Ringelmann chart to monitor for potential violations, or carrying out other activities stipulated by the law. The significant point was that the ongoing administrative entity—the Bureau of Smoke Control or whatever it might have been called—was vested only with implementation functions; this pattern was typical of all the early smoke-control programs, as well as of the clean-ups in several cities in the 1940s.

When California confronted its pollution problem in the late 1940s, the traditional approach failed to meet the need, and the resultant research and monitoring efforts were activities that come under the heading of "knowledge functions." As other states and urban areas followed suit, we came into the 1960s with growing agencies in many areas. However, all too often these agencies had power to monitor and gather data and to carry on the institutionalized functions of watching over the smoke polluters, but they lacked any effective power to actually decide to do anything. Typically, the decision-making power was still vested in a pollution control board, as described in Chapter 10, and the abuse of permit-and-variance systems was still rampant.

In the 15 years since 1960, however, a major change has taken place; in the abstract, this change amounts, simply, to a national decision to go ahead and *do it*, to build into the system a decision function between our knowledge of the problem and our ability to control it. This type of national decision typically occurs slowly, over a period of years, with false starts and minor mistakes, and air pollution control was no exception. Also typically, this decision was first crystallized at the federal level; to trace the evolution of our present national control effort is to run through the history of the federal program. Such a tour is valuable not only because of the political and social insights it brings, but also because it should help us keep our time perspective when evaluating the effectiveness of the present effort. The current popularity of environmental issues makes it easy to forget that just a few years ago, the national pollution control effort didn't have the nice organization and relatively potent laws that exist today.

The Federal Program

The 1948 smog episode that killed and sickened so many people in Donora is usually cited as the impetus that drove the federal government into the air pollution control field. After a great deal of urging in the public press and invitation by various groups, the Public Health Service (PHS) made a medical study in Donora, from which ultimately developed a PHS group interested in air pollution problems. Long before this time, however, the Bureau of Mines in the Commerce Department had been conducting engineering work on air pollution from coal and oil combustion, which in the early years was all there was to air pollution. But as the concept of air pollution broadened from just smoke pollution, and especially as its effects on health became cause for concern, the PHS group in the Department of Health, Education, and Welfare (HEW) became more prominent, and in 1955 the first federal air pollution law put the program in HEW.

The preceding sentences may evoke an image of two groups of scientists feuding over who should assume the responsibility for this new problem, and this description—unfortunately or maybe not so unfortunately—is accurate. The Bureau of Mines still does work in the field, and the two groups still periodically accuse each other of not cooperating, and so on. There is a valuable insight here—the federal agencies are not all-wise fountains of perfection, though they try to appear so; rather, they are composed of individuals whose professions and careers are important to them and who can generate rivalry, distrust, frustration, and even hate, no less than anyone else.

The 1955 federal air pollution law (P.L. 84–159) was entitled "An Act to Provide Research and Technical Assistance Relating to Air Pollution Control." Under this law, several authorities relating to air pollution control were given to the secretary of HEW, to be carried out by the Surgeon General of the PHS. The law provided authority to perform research and to provide technical assistance to state and local air pollution agencies and health departments. The law specifically stated that it was the policy of Congress "to preserve and protect the primary responsibilities and rights of the state and local governments in controlling air pollution." Accordingly, the law emphasized support of nonfederal programs and joint operations with the states, rather than the development of federal projects; quite reasonably, these functions were ultimately assigned to the Bureau of State Services within the PHS.

The primary thrust of the 1955 law, including its statement of policy, remained unchanged for eight years. Some minor laws, however, were passed in these years. P.L. 86–365 of 1959 extended the authority for an additional four years and added a section expressing the intent of Congress that other federal agencies cooperate with HEW and the state and local control agencies. The following year, P.L. 86–493, the Schenck Act, directed the Surgeon General to make a major study of the health effects of pollution from motor vehicles and to report back to Congress in two years. Late that same year, in September 1960, the first formal organizational structure for the air pollution activity was created within the Bureau of State Services by rearranging the groups of people working on air pollution into the Division of Air Pollution. In 1962 P.L. 87–761 extended the same authority for an additional two years; in addition, having in the meantime received the Schenck Act report of serious national health implications from automobile pollution, P.L. 87–761 instructed the Surgeon General to study ways and means of controlling pollution from motor vehicles.

Throughout this entire eight-year period, the most significant fact about the federal air pollution program was that it existed within the Public Health Service. The PHS is a bit of a bureaucratic misfit; its history outdates HEW by a century, it is run by a quasi-military Commissioned Officers Corps rather than by ordinary civil servants, and at that time it was a political power in its own right. The PHS is a medical group; its best-known unit is probably the National Institutes of Health, in Bethesda, Maryland, one of the biggest and most successful research organizations in the country. The PHS got involved with water pollution in the early 1900s, when drinking-water treatment, especially chlorination, was instrumental in eliminating typhoid, cholera, and similar epidemic diseases. Thus, it was natural enough for the PHS to become involved in the waste-treatment aspects of water pollution and then in air pollution. However, the Bureau of State Services was used to functioning more or less as a "big brother" to the state health departments, helping them in such matters as public vaccination programs, etc. Therefore, it was also natural for the PHS to try to attack air and water pollution by cooperating with the state health departments, and that's the way the early law was written. However, political forces in the states cared more about pollution than about vaccination programs, and accordingly the states often resisted pollution control in a way they had never resisted the more medically oriented PHS program. For its part, the natural predilection of the PHS was to be as cooperative as possible and not battle with their traditional colleagues at the state level.

As a result, the late 1950s and early 1960s were a time of increasing dissatisfaction with the PHS, mostly on matters pertaining to water pollution, and a number of attempts were made to reorganize the pollution functions out of the PHS. However, since the PHS also had powerful friends in Congress, a bureaucratic and legislative struggle ensued, continuing off and on for a number of years; it was finally resolved in 1968, with the ratification of an HEW reorganization that cleared out most of the excess hierarchy and left the PHS firmly within the control of HEW.

Through this same period, there was a parallel struggle between those who urged, "leave it to the states" and those who warned, "if the feds don't force them, the states will never do anything." From 1955 onward, the majority sentiment in Congress gradually shifted from the former to the latter viewpoint. By 1963, this majority was strong enough to pass a new basic law with some "teeth" in it, at least according to the 1963 perspective of what constituted teeth. Although the most important factor in this shift in policy was the change in congressional attitude, other factors also played a role. In 1960 John Kennedy was elected to succeed Dwight Eisenhower, who had opposed any federal effort to control pollution. In 1963 Senator Kerr of Oklahoma, a close friend of the oil industry, died, and a spokesman for the environmentalists, Senator Muskie of Maine, succeeded to his subcommittee chairmanship.

Money and Abatement Authority

Now, a major change in federal responsibility occurred. After two years of limbo in the House of Representatives, the Clean Air Act (P.L. 88–206) was passed in December of 1963. The act authorized federal abatement action in interstate situations by means of the conference-hearing procedure, as well as the granting of funds to nonfederal control agencies to support their activities. The act also provided authority for the publication of air quality "criteria," informational documents about the effects of pollutants, established a technical committee to deal with pollution from motor vehicles and make reports to Congress on the subject, and authorized the establishment of a permit system to regulate pollution sources operated by other federal agencies at their various facilities. The bill authorized appropriations for grants of $5 million in the current fiscal year (which was half gone when the law was passed) and for the next three years authorized annual expenditures of $25, $30, and $35 million, a most significant increase from the $5 million per year authorization of the previous several years. For the staff of the federal agency, it was indeed a heady atmosphere.

The operating grants certainly accomplished their goal of stimulating new, more comprehensive control programs. Of the 100 grants made in the first full year of the program, nearly half went to 10 state and 35 local programs that had not previously existed. Since then, every state and most large cities have either begun a program or upgraded the one they had.

The abatement authority contained in the 1963 Clean Air Act was not as simple, nor in the long run as effective, as the grants program. The conference-hearing approach was directed almost exclusively at interstate pollution situations and tried to use federal power primarily to compel the states to act. To initiate the procedure, the EPA administrator (originally the secretary of HEW) may call a conference to consider pollution, either at the request of the state governor or, in some cases, on his own initiative. Having called such an *abatement conference*, EPA publishes its assessment of the situation and then participates in the conference itself, along with representatives of the state and local agencies. After the conference members have discussed the existence of a pollution problem and the adequacy of efforts to abate it, the EPA administrator summarizes the results of the conference and may, if he believes it appropriate, make recommendations for abatement action. If the recommended abatement actions are not taken within six months, he may call a public hearing before a hearing board composed of representatives of the states involved and the federal government. If the hearing board also finds that pollution is in fact occurring and that adequate abatement efforts are not being carried out, it can make appropriate recommendations back to the EPA administrator, who then forwards them to all concerned parties. If after another six months, no appropriate abatement action has yet been taken, EPA may ask the Justice Department to file suit to compel abatement action. The law provides that the court shall receive in evidence the reports and recommendations of the hearing board and "giving due consideration . . . to the physical and economic feasibility of securing abatement of any pollution proved, shall have jurisdiction to enter such judgment and orders enforcing such judgment, as the public interest and the equities of the case require."

This approach is obviously cumbersome; although the 1963 act gave the authority to the HEW secretary rather than to the PHS Surgeon General, these ponderous procedures are a good example of the hesitancy of the PHS hierarchy. The procedure was very similar to the one which had previously been used for water pollution. The wording of the law obviously permits tough federal enforcement, at least in interstate situations; the similar water pollution law, however, had been used by the PHS for years with an unwritten rule that no conference proceedings ever reached the court house.

The air pollution law did a little better, a reflection of the changing attitudes and gradual erosion of PHS power. In the fall of 1965, nearly two years after the bill's passage, the first federal abatement action was taken under this provision. This action, which concerned odors from a chicken-rendering plant in Bishop, Maryland, was initiated at the request of the state of Delaware. The situation was pursued through all the appropriate steps, but the odor problem could not be solved, and the Department of Justice brought suit against the Bishop Processing Company, which lost the case. When the Supreme Court declined to hear an appeal, the company signed a consent decree, agreeing to shut down the plant if odors were again detected in Delaware. In March 1969 the District Court was asked to invoke the decree and order the closing of the plant, but it held that the evidence of the occurrence of odors in Delaware was inadequate; more evidence was needed. Ultimately, the Court did issue the injunction, and the rendering plant was closed in June 1970, four and a half years after the initial conference. At last report, the plant was operating again, supposedly with some less offensive methods.

Other abatement conferences have been held in the Washington, D.C., area, the New York–northern New Jersey metropolitan area, and in several smaller urban areas, but no major cases have ever gone to court. The record of this federal program is obviously not striking, and there are various reasons for this: the conference-hearing procedure is awkward, and only a few of the federal air pollution officials have had the necessary will to make the law work. In large areas, such as New York City, where the federal abatement people made their best try, the problem is just too big for such a cumbersome mechanism; federal pressure can move reluctant agencies, but it can't work quick miracles.

But even in the smaller areas, bureaucratic confusion among federal agencies and the recalcitrance of some of the state agencies have made the mechanism far from effective. After the 1967 amendments, when the use of air quality standards approach became predominant, the conferences that had been held were all considered to now be "recessed" rather than concluded. In 1970, when the law was again in the process of being amended, the conference-hearing procedure was almost eliminated, but was ultimately retained for use before the new procedures became effective. The present law still permits the calling of a conference for pollutants that haven't yet been covered by air quality criteria or for the small cases still pending. There is no doubt, however, that the air quality standards approach is presently the EPA's primary abatement tool.

Criteria, Standards, and Implementation Plans

The development of the air quality standards approach also has an interesting history that sheds some light on the political process by which such decisions are made. The idea that the federal government should compile some "criteria of air quality" had been mentioned in connection with the 1963 law and had been under discussion for some time at various technical meetings and similar forums; most striking was the 1966 National Conference on Air Pollution Control, at which state and local control officials and groups of citizens repeatedly requested, even demanded, that the federal government hurry up and publish such criteria. This open demonstration of support at a federally sponsored meeting was no doubt only partly spontaneous, but the existence of a consensus was evident, aside from the obvious fact that the industry lobbies weren't joining in.

In part, the consensus indicated a recognition that summarizing the vast literature on pollutant effects was a massive undertaking, well beyond the reach of most state and local control agencies. More important, however, there was also an obvious desire that the hot-potato issue of "Just how clean do we want the air to be?" be tossed into the hands of the federal government. It was presumed that the federal agency would prescribe as criteria some specific pollutant levels or concentrations; this was in fact the current interpretation of the word "criteria" in the water pollution program. Having a federally established criterion would, of course, be much easier and politically effective than the state and local control agencies' having to prepare and defend their own choice of some specific pollution level. In addition, the concept had the positive value of making the numbers uniform throughout the country and acknowledging the political realism of placing the responsibility at that level of government least subject to influence by industrial lobbying groups. The result of this climate of opinion was that in early 1967, the National Center for Air Pollution Control published a criteria document for sulfur oxides pollution. The publication met with much criticism, in part because it lacked information about control techniques and in part for legitimate disagreement over its content, but mostly because the overall import of the document, and its specific recommendation, was that only a very low level of sulfur oxides (an annual mean of 0.015 ppm) could be labeled "acceptable."

The interests that would have been the most hurt by such stringent control hadn't really believed that the criteria document would be issued and were therefore caught relatively unaware. However, a massive lobbying campaign by the electric power, coal, and oil lobbies, and their patron federal agencies, had an effect; later that year, the new 1967 act, which spelled out the criteria-air quality standards approach, specifically required that the criteria document be recalled, reevaluated after appropriate consultation with industry, and reissued in the form prescribed by the new law.

This was done, and the revised SO_x criteria, a similar document for particulate pollution, and control technology documents for both, were all issued in February 1969. In 1970 documents were issued for CO, hydrocarbons, and photochemical oxidants; in 1971, documents for NO_x. Significantly, however, none of the criteria documents issued (or reissued) since the 1967 law has interpreted the word "criteria" as meaning a specific number or standard; rather, the word has been interpreted to mean merely a description of pollutant levels at which effects occur. At the time, this seemed to be a victory for the industry lobbies, but subsequently it has proved to be less important than it seemed then.

Beyond the criteria and control techniques documents, the main elements of the new control scheme are federally defined air quality control regions and state-prepared implementation plans. EPA was to designate Air Quality Control Regions (AQCRs) in the major urban areas, according to specifications in the law, such that each core city and its suburbs would be included in one region, regardless of state boundaries. This regional approach was an outgrowth of the obvious failure of states in interstate urban areas to cooperate, even given sizeable financial incentives for doing so, and the general desire of the cities that they do so. In the early drafts of the bill, the regions so designated were to have a control program run by a regional pollution control board, on which the federal government would have a seat, though not total power. At the last moment, the Justice Department concluded that this plan amounted to a clearly unconstitutional federal-city alliance against the states; a hurried redraft retained the AQCRs as a part of the standard-setting procedure, but left the implementation to the states.

According to this scheme, after an AQCR had been designated and criteria issued, the states included in that air quality control region were to hold public hearings, adopt ambient air quality standards for their portion of the region, and submit their standards to HEW for approval. After HEW approval of the standards, the states were to submit implementation plans for achieving the standards.

The requirement of public hearings was, as it turned out, the most effectual part of this system. Since the criteria were not absolutely definitive, the lobbies presumed that they could persuade most states to adopt fairly lenient standards. However, largely because of good public-information work by the federal program, citizen groups had been organized in many of the urban areas, and those groups testified strongly at the hearings in favor of stringent air quality standards, urging significant factors of safety beyond the lowest levels specified in the criteria. This citizen testimony would have given HEW a basis for disapproving overly lenient standards, but more importantly, the hearings brought the state air pollution control boards into the spotlight of public scrutiny, for the first time in most cases. The result was that in almost all cases, the standards adopted by the states for SO_2 and particulates were reasonably low; in those states where pollution control boards did try to put through higher standards, the governor retreated before public opinion, with the result that generally good standards were adopted throughout the country.

Administratively, however, the scheme was working poorly. The federal program was very slow to designate regions, mostly because they tried to do a polished job of it, with nice published documents, but with too little staff. The criteria documents for pollutants other than the first two were delayed, and the standards-reviewing process was confused and slow, largely because of divided responsibility and understaffing. But the most telling criticism came from those state air pollution officials who were recognized as not being footdraggers. These men complained that the regions they'd set up in their states were adequate, that it was inefficient to have one set of procedures in the big cities and another elsewhere, and that they spent half their working hours in hearings and consultations with federal people or redoing things.

Thus, once broad public support for stringent air quality standards had been demonstrated and all the state governments had been awakened to take some action by going through the process at least once, the 1970 amendments modified the system so that there was only one set of national air quality standards and so that all of a state's area would be included in one air quality control region, enabling the agencies to handle all parts of the state in the same manner. This system is, of course, the one currently under way, with the longer-term results yet to come.

In December 1970, when the new law was passed, the reorganization forming EPA also took effect. A major rearrangement of the various agencies in the executive branch, the reorganization brought almost all the groups with environmental functions together into one independent agency. In the long run, the improved coordination of divergent programs should be very helpful. In terms of the air pollution program, the reorganization resulted in a final parting with the HEW/PHS bureaucracy and a much more direct line to Congress, the presidency, and public visibility.

The new EPA administrator had little time to organize things before the deadlines stipulated in the 1970 Clean Air Act began to impel action. In April 1971 the administrator promulgated the National Ambient Air Quality Standards, both primary standards related to health protection and secondary standards related to other pollution effects. The states had nine months, until January 1972, to prepare implementation plans for meeting at least the primary standards by 1975. The plans submitted were partially approved, amended, revised, etc., through 1972, and many enforcement efforts began, especially those aimed at SO_x and particulates.

As we noted in Chapter 9, the primary control strategy for automobile-related pollutants was the reduction in new-car emission levels as required by the federal regulatory program. In some large urban areas, where pollution levels were especially high, the states were required to adopt additional control measures directed at privately owned cars. These measures gained somewhat more publicity than did the controls directed at industry, and the summer of 1973 saw rather intensive public debates about gasoline rationing, catalytic mufflers, and plans to increase mass transit usage, as the EPA and the big cities tried to meet the CO and oxidants standards by 1975 (1977, with two-year extensions). Then the energy crisis of 1973–1974 again called into question some of the SO_2 and particulate controls applied to power plants and other energy-conversion installations.

Most of these questions and issues are still unresolved, and the "history" of government control programs has clearly dissolved into "current events." In fact, most of the ultimate results of the actions taken in response to the 1967 and 1970 amendments are not yet in. Society made a decision, and the effects are just now beginning to be felt; depending on the results, the law will be extended or possibly modified.

SUMMARY

In the last few years, many critics have condemned the overall national effort, and the federal leadership in particular, as being timid, ineffective, slow, and unresponsive. If we view the national air pollution program broadly, within the framework of our federal system of government, and if we accept the fact of the existence of strong industrial lobbies and their tangible influence on both federal and state governments, we find a scenario that contains a good bit of progress, though not necessarily enough. Historically, the police power to protect public welfare is a function of the states, not the federal government. Pollution control is one of a series of social problems that have been gradually taken over by the federal government, not because that's the best way, but because the states have failed, primarily for political and economic power reasons, to use their authority to meet their responsibilities. Only California can honestly claim to have attacked the air pollution problem earlier or better than did the federal government, though other states now have strong programs also.

The federal program has always operated by trying to help, assist, cajole, and "bribe" the states into exercising their power, and the history of federal legislation traces the escalating coercion applied to them. In the early years, technical assistance was thrust upon the states, whether or not they had requested it. When most states still had made no effort after eight years, the federal government tried to pave the way. The conference-hearing approach tried to get the states to work together, but failed. The 1967 act offered 100% funding if the states in an interstate area would simply organize a joint group to do no more than recommend regional standards, but there were no takers. Viewed in this light, the results of the air quality standards approach look a little better—there are now functioning, if not yet necessarily successful programs, in every state, large city, and many smaller cities. Lobbyists and politicians no longer can sabotage pollution control efforts with impunity, though they are by no means yet powerless. This is not necessarily to the credit of the federal program; there are many reasons for these changes, one of the major ones being the obvious increase in public awareness of, and interest in, environmental issues.

EXERCISES

Review Questions

1. How does a permit system operate? What function(s) does it perform?
2. What is a variance?
3. What is a regulatory standard? What are the different types?
4. What is an emission inventory? How does an agency typically compile one?
5. What is an emission factor? Where do they come from?
6. What is meteorological dispersion modeling? Why would a pollution control agency do it?
7. What is an emergency action plan? What types of actions might it include?
8. On what legal authority is the federal air pollution control program based? What limits are there on that authority?
9. What federal agency presently administers the air pollution program? How long has it done so? Where was the program previously?

10. List at least three major elements of the federal air pollution program.
11. With what three mechanisms is federal air pollution research conducted?
12. Identify the two major approaches to federal-state pollution abatement.
13. Explain briefly the various steps of the more important of the two approaches identified in question 12.
14. What entity operates the actual control program in an Air Quality Control Region?
15. In what two situations or cases does the federal program have authority to set emissions standards?
16. What can the federal program do about chemical additives in gasoline?
17. How can the federal government assist in the development of low-pollution automobiles?
18. Distinguish among an air pollution control program, an air pollution control agency, and air pollution control functions.
19. Into what three categories have we grouped air pollution control functions?
20. How did HEW get involved in air pollution?
21. When did Congress pass the first federal law regarding air pollution? Briefly, what were its provisions?
22. What was the role of the Public Health Service in air pollution history?
23. What was the role of the Bishop Processing Company in air pollution history?
24. What were the circumstances surrounding the fact that the criteria document for sulfur oxides was published twice?
25. Why were the public hearings on air quality standards particularly important?

Thought Questions

26. If you were a local pollution control official and you had developed your own emission factor for a certain type of source, what factors would influence your choice between using it and using the quasi-official one published by the federal program?
27. Would you expect accurate diffusion modeling of CO concentrations to be more or less difficult than modeling SO_2 levels?
28. Why is most air pollution research conducted by the federal program rather than by local control agencies?
29. The 1963 law permitted relatively effective use of federal power only in interstate situations, that is, when pollution from one state affected people in another. For a very good reason, this was not viewed as a major limitation. (*Hint*: In early America, urban commerce was heavily dependent on water transportation.)
30. Which of the political parties most often controls big-city governments? State governments? Congress? The presidency? How might this influence the relations among the various levels of government with respect to air pollution?
31. Why do you think it is so much easier for the federal government to raise large amounts of tax money than for the states to do so?

32. Consider the differences in the fate of the air pollution emissions and the water pollutants produced in your residence. Can you draw a logical connection between this difference and the fact that water pollution grants are typically much larger than those for air pollution? There is also a logical connection with the fact that the congressional clamor for action is louder in the case of water pollution.

Discussion Questions

33. To what extent do you feel that the federal government should either conduct or fund research into the effects and control of industrial pollutant emissions? Is the distinction between conducting the research and merely funding it important?
34. Emission standards are typically stated in terms of so much emission per unit of input to, or output from, the process. Alternatively, they could be expressed as so much per stack or per factory; or, if it was desirable to distinguish among plants of different sizes, they could be so much per unit of design capacity or maximum production capacity. Discuss these three approaches. Under what circumstances do they differ? Do you agree with the typical choice?
35. Discuss the question of how much the federal government should restrict the use of federal funds granted to state or local governmental authorities. Should the money be granted for any use, as the recipient sees fit? Should it be rigidly restricted? How might the answer differ for, say, welfare, urban renewal, or pollution control funds?
36. As a citizen, do you consider the present federal law an appropriate balance of state and federal power? What if you were an official of your state? Of your city? If you were a federal official, do you think you would be satisfied?

Problems

37. Consider pollution sources that are uniformly distributed over an area, e.g., residential housing, or distributed along a line, e.g., highway, rather than being concentrated at a single point; make mathematical modifications to the point-source diffusion equation to facilitate projections of air quality levels resulting from such area or line sources.

Project Suggestions

38. The thicket of lobbying, pro and con, surrounding all the federal laws is much greater than can be even hinted at here. Congressional records, committee hearings, and other books provide much of the information that could be used for a more detailed political science study of one of them. Also, as the political climate changes and time passes, the possibility of getting honest statements from the principals involved increases.

FURTHER READING

There is not much literature on the overall aspects of control programs, other than that on specific functions. J. J. Schueneman's Chapter 52 in Vol. III of Stern [162] is one good source. Emissions-inventorying procedures are heavily dependent on the federal compilation of emission factors in Publication AP-42 [79]. Meteorological modeling has produced a variety of literature, but no good summary work. Turner's *Workbook* [77] permits one to make hand calculations for a single source.

The federal laws are well worth reading; although it's difficult to integrate them into a picture of the federal program, it's very interesting to get a sense of the legislative process. These laws are cited [166] by P.L. number, and the latest revised version is contained in [167]. These references are generally available in law school or very large libraries; reprints of single laws are often available through congressmen, from EPA, or from the Superintendent of Documents of the Government Printing Office. State and local laws and regulations are usually available from the pollution control agencies.

Comprehensive histories of the federal program are less common than one might expect; the book by Davies [5] is certainly the best and is also noteworthy for its frank recognition of the politics involved. Ridgeway's book [15] has a good discussion of early PHS water pollution politics. The Esposito book [8] provides a major critique of the air pollution program, citing specific instances of both history and politics. The proceedings of the Second and Third National Conferences on Air Pollution [118] and [119], provide summaries of technical knowledge and professional opinion just prior to the 1963 and 1967 laws, respectively. An article from *Environmental Science & Technology* [177] summarizes some of the criticism leveled at the Clean Air Act later, in the process of debating the 1970 amendments, and an article by Stern [227] collects criticisms as of 1973.

Summaries of the functions of the federal program are quite plentiful, although all but the most recent are outdated. News articles in technical journals or scientific magazines are the best way to keep an up-to-date overview of current activities, proposed new legislation, and so on.

12

CONTROL STRATEGY: ECONOMICS AND PUBLIC POLICY

INTRODUCTION

In the latter part of Chapter 11, we considered the history of governmental air pollution programs, particularly the evolution of the present national control effort. Following as it did from the discussion of the control agency functions, that narrative logically adopted the viewpoint of the control agencies and emphasized their responsibilities. There are two other relatively distinct viewpoints that need to be considered, and both are involved, though in different ways, in the decisions that go into a detailed pollution control program. One viewpoint is the social science perspective, whereby events are viewed as the development of a public policy through collective, public decision-making. The other viewpoint focuses on the technical decisions involved in carrying out the details of that policy.

In considering the social aspects of public policy, we'll to some extent be reviewing the ground we covered earlier, and this will bring us up to the late 1960s, when the present public policy was defined. From then on, the decisions grow more and more detailed, ultimately coming down to the development of detailed plans for the control of individual pollution sources. These detailed decisions, typically made by an agency's technical staff, have come to be known as a control strategy, since they are essentially tactical decisions on what sources to control, how much, and when.

This chapter is subtitled "Economics and Public Policy" to emphasize the fact that choosing a control strategy is not by any means an esoteric function of the pollution control professionals; rather, it is a matter of evolving public policy, in which nearly every segment of society is involved in one way or another. In addition, this phase is the point in the pollution control process where economics plays its principal role. Economic considerations enter into the determination of control strategy in two very distinct ways. First, if the decisions are to be quantitatively rational, e.g., produced by a cost-benefit analysis, they must be made so at this point. More significantly, but less obviously, economics comes to play in this public decision-making process through the way in which decision-makers accept inputs from various segments of society. There can be little question but that the weight given to one's opinions is correlated with one's amount of economic power, although this is less true today than in former years.

We have emphasized that the determination of policy with respect to pollution control should be viewed as a process of collective, public decision-making, although the fact that it is so is perhaps not obvious. Although it is true that the laws seem to be written by legislatures and the detailed regulations by civil servants, it's also true that these groups pay attention to the opinions of other groups—the legislators because they have to be re-elected, and the bureaucrats because they need to keep their programs in favor with the legislators. The "other groups" to which attention is paid include the special-interest groups, or lobbies, the environmentalists as well as the polluters; however, the "general public" is always included among these "other groups" also, and it always comes near the head of the list, *if* the general public cares about the issue. Thus, the public debate always includes serious efforts to influence public opinion, as well as the efforts to privately persuade influential legislators or other officials. Those lobbying for more stringent limitations on pollutant emissions have always tried to convince the public that their health is in danger and that the control of pollution will bring more benefit than harm. In times past, those who opposed stringent pollution control did so only to the limits of their behind-the-scenes power, being unwilling to publicly appear too blatant in disregard of public health; more recently, they have emphasized to the public the economic cost of pollution control, hoping to convince some portion of the general public that the cost will be too high. The current climate is one of waiting; some initial decisions have been made, and are being carried out, and the crucial question is whether public opinion will support the results or demand a change.

Underlying all our consideration of questions that need to be answered and choices that need to be made in developing a control strategy, there is one fundamental necessity in our approach to air pollution control—the fact that air pollution must be prevented at the source rather than being removed from the air after it has once been emitted. Despite humorous references to the effect of greatly increased hi-volume air sampling, the intrinsic nature of the atmosphere is such that we can't seriously consider cleaning the air once it has been polluted; there is no way to collect the air and run it through a treatment plant. Note that this is unlike the situation with water pollution; waste water can be collected and cleaned at a central treatment plant, and this is commonly done, as is the cleaning of water in a water treatment plant prior to distribution for use. Thus, one of the major choices is removed from our discretion, and we are left only with questions about whether, how much, how, and by whom emissions should be prevented, or controlled, at the source.

HOW MUCH CONTROL DO WE NEED?

The first question that requires society's answer is: "Are we polluting too much?" or, as some might prefer: "How much pollution can we stand?" However the question is phrased, it first arises when some people come to believe, and then begin to vocally assert, that we are in fact polluting too much and that we should do something about it.

The answer has tended to come in two parts, distinguished largely by the nature of the arguments offered in opposition. To the first, relatively simple question of whether we need any control of pollution at all, opponents of pollution control tend to argue that the proponents are crackpots, health nuts, physical fitness fanatics, and so on. This argument was made in a long, drawn-out fashion, largely as described in Chapter 1, and reached full strength just as World War II broke out. In the postwar years, the question increasingly has become the more sophisticated: "O.K., so we need some control of pollution, but precisely how much do we need?" At this point the debate turns seriously scientific. The opponents of pollution control argue that the proponents are emotional and have little knowledge of the true problem and that what we really need is more information, more research. We need to know exactly how much pollution we can tolerate; we need to have "scientifically rigorous criteria" by which to judge the cleanliness of our air. Since the 1950s, the national debate has taken this line, and the provisions of the federal law reflect, of course, the desire to at least appear to try to be totally rational and scientific.

When the question of how much pollution we want to tolerate is phrased in precise, scientific terminology, it suggests the need for a careful, economic cost-benefit analysis, a careful weighing of the economic value of society's losses against the cost of controlling the pollution. There are various ways of stating such an issue, one of which is explained in Fig. 12–1. Without necessarily opposing the idea of the careful, quantitative decision-

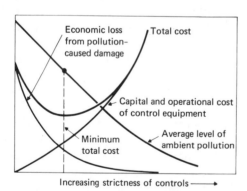

Fig. 12–1. Schematic relationship between economic costs and benefits. Note that as more stringent controls are applied, the economic costs of pollution damage decrease, but the cost of controlling the pollution increases. The U-shaped curve is the sum of the two, or the total cost to society. Because one cost curve rises as the other falls, their sum has a minimum, as indicated. Presumably, this would be the degree of stringency to strive for. (S. J. Williamson, *Fundamentals of Air Pollution*, Reading, Mass.: Addison-Wesley, 1973, p. 347.)

making represented by cost-benefit analysis, however, most workers in environmental fields generally dismiss this notion as impractical. The data needed to make such an analysis even approximately accurate is generally lacking, except in special, narrow situations. Not only is it impossible to put a dollar value on some aspects of human health, but the estimates of the other variables are also pretty crude.

Given the impracticality of letting the economists' algebra determine how much we want to reduce pollution, the debate then turns to whether we want to spend our money on determining the data necessary for such a detailed analysis or whether, at the other extreme, we should just use our common sense to make some estimates and get on with the business of reducing the pollution. The result of this type of public discussion, so far, has been the system of criteria, standards and implementation plans defined in the federal law, and it is in the federal law that any change will need to be expressed.

Our decision-making process actually consists of three distinct concepts: air quality goals, criteria, and standards. Each of these components merits a brief discussion as a concept, particularly because their definitions are often vague or vary with the user. By air quality goals, we mean an expression of society's choices about what it wants; conceivably, these choices could be expressed quantitatively, but usually, these are only vague declarations. However, they tend to be much more rigid than one might expect, because they are expressed through public opinion, which is often fairly difficult to change. At present, it is clear that our society has accepted the goal of having air sufficiently clean so that it has no effects on human health. Other goals, such as might relate to economic and aesthetic values, are less generally accepted. This is not to say that society's goals might not change; in fact, many people feel that when the economic cost of installing pollution control equipment is fully felt, especially when some marginal plants close and people lose jobs, human health may seem a good bit less sacred. If this does in fact happen, it will be reflected in public opinion, and one can expect the government to be quite sensitive to it.

The phrase "air quality criteria," as used in the air pollution field at the present, differs significantly from the common, everyday concept of criterion; rather than being specific rules for deciding whether the air is good or bad, clean or dirty, air quality criteria are simply the collected data on pollutant effects that are mandated by the Clean Air Act. Whatever the Act intended thom to be, in practice these criteria are not as scientifically rigorous as some might like them to be; rather, they have a very definite sociopolitical component, as we recall from the history of the first SO_2 criteria document.

Note that the word "criterion," in its everyday usage, embodies both scientific fact and society's wishes. A criterion which defines whether or not the air is clean incorporates not only the facts about how bad the effects might be, but also society's identification of a certain level of pollution and its effects as being "clean" or "acceptable." In this sense, the common concept of criteria is what we call "air quality standards," the specific ambient pollutant levels defined as the point at which the quality of air becomes "unacceptable." Such values are determined by a sociopolitical process based on both society's choice of goals, e.g., the protection of health, and the scientific facts relating amounts of pollution to specific effects. The concept allows room for variation in air quality standards, since different states might choose different goals, or perhaps might prefer a different margin of safety.

We need to distinguish carefully between the air quality standards just mentioned and the emission or equipment standards described as implementation tools in Chapter 11. An air quality standard specifies the presently acceptable level of pollutant concentration in the air, i.e., quantitatively, so many ppm for a certain period of time. Since all sources contribute pollution to the same overall concentration, this standard, as such, cannot be met or violated by any specific source. The concept of air quality standards makes sense with respect to society's goals, criteria, and the decision-making process, but it does not make sense with respect to the enforceable implementation of specific controls by specific sources. For this reason, some people feel that the word "standard" is not appropriate and prefer to call the quantitative "target concentration" a goal to be met by enforcing standards. Nonetheless, the federal law refers to "air quality standard," so "air quality standard" it is.

There is a gap between the two concepts, however; although an air quality standard tells us how large a reduction in pollution we need, it doesn't give us any help in deciding how to obtain that reduction. What we need, therefore, is some way of relating the air quality standards to specific emission standards. As we've seen, the task of making the choices about what reduction is to be required from various sources falls to the state or local control agencies, since they're the ones who must ultimately write the emission standards.

WHICH SOURCES? THE IMPLEMENTATION PLAN

The next question, that of deciding which sources should reduce their emissions by how much, is the most difficult part of the whole process, since it's a lot of work, it's not clear what basis one should be using to make the decisions, and the freedom of choice is often limited by powers beyond the local agency's control. From a national viewpoint, the most immediate need for reduction is in the urban areas, where the problem is greatest. There the pollution levels must be reduced, often significantly, in order to attain the level of air quality specified by the standards. In relatively undeveloped areas, in contrast, it is only necessary to maintain a level of air quality that already meets the standards. Since regulations such as emissions standards must by law apply equally to all similar parties, both air quality standards and emission standards are needed. From a national viewpoint, the question is one of achieving equity between urban and nonurban Air Quality Control Regions.

In a relatively nonurban AQCR, containing only isolated pollution sources, e.g., a solitary ore smelter or power plant, emission standards are the only way to keep the overall emissions of society's activities down as much as is feasible; such standards can be determined so as to require a reasonable control effort on the part of the source, without requiring massive expenditures to achieve really clean effluents. On the other hand, that same emission standard in an urban AQCR would likely be woefully inadequate. Therefore, it may be necessary to have much more stringent emission controls so that the overall pollution concentration produced by all the sources does not exceed the desired air quality standard. This situation thus leads us to a system based on both air quality standards and emission standards, arranged in such a way as to permit emission standards of varying stringency in various AQCRs or other geographical areas, so long as the result is consistent with the air quality standard.

Although our examples have been stationary sources, the point also applies to pollutants from motor vehicles. The Clean Air Act requires that emissions from each automobile be limited to a specific degree by the manufacturer; this may or may not be enough reduction to ensure that the ambient standards for the vehicular pollutants are met, depending on the number of vehicles and the extent of their usage in the area in question. If the air quality standards cannot be met in a given Air Quality Control Region because the people in that area drive more than people do in other areas, it's appropriate that they reduce their emissions by other means applicable only in that region, so that people elsewhere don't bear extra costs for which they get no benefits.

As a side effect, the use of air quality standards may to some extent lead to the dispersal of stationary pollution sources from urban areas out into presently less developed areas. Originally, EPA did not assume that this was bad, but the courts have since interpreted the Clean Air Act as requiring that there be no significant degrading of the air. What this may mean depends, of course, on how "significant" is ultimately interpreted by EPA and the various states.

Presently, the Clean Air Act requires the states to design and enforce a plan of source reductions in order to implement the air quality standards. Nonetheless, there are some national aspects to the overall decision in that the answer to the question "Which sources?" may involve emissions control strategies that have national repercussions or that are influenced by the repercussions of other areas of national policy. In other words, it is apparent whatever choices are made, they will need to be coordinated on a national basis.

The principal example of this need for a nationally coordinated effort is the currently critical question of the fuels to be used for generating electric power and the attendant questions concerning a national energy policy. Since the SO_2 emissions of major fuel-burning sources are a function of the sulfur content of the fuel burned, the adoption of restrictions on the sulfur content is both effective and popular. Frequently, for example, the most efficient way for a large power plant to meet tight emission standards has been to change from coal to low-sulfur oil as a fuel. Yet, as we saw in Chapter 8, the supply of low-sulfur fuels is limited, particularly with recent concern about importing oil. In the interest of economic and energy efficiency, various decisions about the required use of particular fuels need to be reconciled at the national level. However, when the Federal Power Commission and the Federal Energy Administration exert this authority over the fuels used by steam electric-power plants, state and local air pollution control agencies sometimes find themselves in the position of negotiating with a federal agency to allocate adequate clean fuel to serve their urban area in order to maintain their control strategy. Another side of the same question relates to the use of nuclear power plants; these are regulated by the federal government. Although nuclear power plants may seem to be a solution to an area's air pollution problem, they often present a serious water pollution problem and, some people feel, radiation problems as well; thus, they are often opposed by environmental groups.

In both of these cases, a possible means of reducing the emissions from electric-power generation is taken out of the hands of the state or local pollution control agency and becomes part of the policies of federal regulatory agencies whose primary concern is not the protection of the environment. There are many other factors of federal policy that impinge upon the flexibility with which fuel users can adjust their pollutant emissions—policy on coal mine safety regulations, research on fuels, the oil and gas depletion allowance allowed against corporate tax liabilities—and all of these factors influence the economics of the fuel-supply situation in which the sources must operate, which in turn affect their ability to cooperate with agencies in developing and implementing a planned schedule of pollution controls. These factors and others, especially concerns about the simple availability of adequate energy supplies, have necessitated some sort of overall national energy policy. This need, however, has only recently made itself felt in Congress, with the establishment of the Federal Energy Administration and the development of energy policy as a political issue.

Beyond these rather broad questions of national policy, there remains the question of which sources should reduce their emissions in order to meet the standards; most urban areas need to reduce at least SO_2 and particulates by 30% to 50%. The Clean Air Act requires simply that the states submit an implementation plan for each Air Quality Control Region, indicating the reductions that are planned for the various sources and demonstrating that this will in fact (or at least in a diffusion model) reduce the ambient air quality to the level of the national ambient air quality standards. Precisely how the choices are made is left to the states, which in turn need to cooperate with, if not completely rely on, the local agencies in the major urban areas.

In abstract terms, the problem seems relatively simple; given known emission quantities and source locations, on what basis do we allocate permissible emissions among these sources, or how do we decide which sources must reduce their emissions more and which less? The simplest, and intuitively the most equitable, way to decide has come to be known as the "roll-back" method, whereby all sources are required to reduce, or roll back, their emissions by the same percentage, as determined by using the formula:

$$\frac{\text{Percent}}{\text{reduction}} = \frac{\left(\begin{array}{c}\text{existing}\\\text{level}\end{array}\right) - \left(\begin{array}{c}\text{air quality}\\\text{standard}\end{array}\right)}{\left(\begin{array}{c}\text{existing}\\\text{level}\end{array}\right) - \left(\begin{array}{c}\text{background}\\\text{level}\end{array}\right)} \times 100$$

This formula simply gives algebraic expression to the very logical assumption that if every source reduces its emission by a certain percent, then the average pollutant concentration will be similarly reduced by that percent, with the appropriate adjustment for background concentration. This formulation presumes that the background level (from outside the AQCR) will be the same when the standard is achieved as it is now. If there are other major urban areas nearby, different background levels should be subtracted from the two figures in the numerator.

There are problems with the roll-back method, primarily because it is too simplistic. First, it is impossible to get all sources to reduce their emissions by the same percentage; some simply are physically unable to do so, and for others the cost would be prohibitive. The simplest example is the fuel used for residential space heating. In many areas residences are heated almost exclusively by natural-gas furnaces; the amount of pollution from such furnaces is very small, and there is no reasonable way that it can be further reduced, other than by replacing the gas furnace with electric heating units. This latter, of course, simply moves the pollution from the residential neighborhood to the location of the power plant, and unless the power plant also burns gas, the overall level of pollution will increase. Although this latter shift might be sensible in some cases, it too conflicts with the idea of having all sources reduce their emissions by the same percentage.

In an attempt to get around these problems, judgmental choices are made that one type of source be required to control more stringently than another type, and these choices are made in such a way that the total emissions, or at least the total of the emissions inventory, are reduced by the desired percentage. This method solves the problem of the low feasibility of reducing pollution from the very small source and seems quite logical. However, when this is done, it is no longer necessarily true that the percentage emission reduction will be followed by a similar reduction in the ambient pollution levels. For example, this problem is particularly extreme when the desired percentage reduction in total emissions is obtained largely by planning reductions of the largest sources. This approach is quite appealing to an agency, because it is a great deal easier to negotiate and then later enforce reductions by a few large sources that have technical staffs than it is to deal with a much larger number of smaller, unknowledgeable sources. The difficulty arises principally because the largest sources tend to have the highest stacks, and since their larger emissions are therefore dispersed over a wider area, they frequently contribute much less than their proportionate share to the ambient air quality levels in the local area. In such a situation, one could reduce total emissions by, say 40% by requiring controls on two power plants and one major factory and nonetheless obtain a reduction of only 10% to 20%, or even no measurable reduction, in the air quality at sampling sites for several miles around.

In order to avoid this problem, many experts feel that the effect of emission reductions on air quality should be calculated not on a simple percent basis, but according to an urban-area meteorological diffusion model (described in Chapter 11). Such a model can take into account the differences in stack heights and the exact geographical locations of sources and can thereby eliminate the problem just discussed. However, such diffusion models are complicated and expensive, are less than precise, and thus are sometimes not readily accepted by wary pollution control officials. The federal government has pressed the states to make use of diffusion modeling in preparing their implementation plans and in fact has developed and provided computerized models for use by the states.

One of the positive aspects of diffusion models for the planning of control strategy is that an operating diffusion model provides the necessary flexibility to do a great many additional things. One can, for instance, simply plug into the model a large variety of possible strategies for reducing emissions—different combinations of emission standards for various types of sources, hypothetical situations with certain sources removed, and so on—and then choose the combination that appears, on the basis of the model's calculations, to produce the pollutant concentrations closest to the standard to be met. One can go further, if there are estimates of the cost of implementing the various pieces of control strategy, and simply program the computer to calculate the cost of the various strategies, as well as the reduced pollution concentrations. This, of course, enables the agency to choose the strategy that is able to meet the standard at the lowest cost.

Given these possibilities, it's not difficult to see why computer modeling appears quite attractive to a large number of people. On the other hand, there are problems, largely those of introducing the use of computers to people unfamiliar with them, along with questions of cost, etc. It is generally agreed that at the present, at least the cost-estimating aspects falter because of the poor cost data available; the scheme of selecting the best from among a large number of possible control strategies also frequently fails, apparently because of the difficulty of devising a wide variety of control strategies, though this latter is probably more attributable to lack of imagination than to any genuine difficulty. Overall, however, it is clear that computer models, if they can be developed for the topography of a given urban area, are at least a definite plus in evaluating the opposing control strategies and often are, indeed, a necessity.

HOW FAST SHOULD WE DO IT?

Once we decide who must reduce their emissions and by how much, the next question that arises is how soon the reductions should be required. Typically, air quality standards specify a time by which they are to be attained. The desire to have the standards met as soon as possible must be balanced against the time required to conduct the necessary engineering studies and to design and build the pollution control devices. Thus, emission regulations usually provide for periods of six months to two or three years before compliance is required. Those in opposition to this view offer the logical argument that there is no reason why a pollution source should wait to begin planning its pollution control activities until it is compelled to do so by law or regulation. Nonetheless, regulations with immediate compliance deadlines are rare, and the writers of standards typically recognize this and require the standard to be met at a later date. The National Primary Air Quality Standards are to be met within three years from the time the implementation plan is approved, which for most urban AQCRs falls during the period 1975–1977.

There are two situations, however, that call into question the requirement to implement control measures within a year or two. Sometimes, a company may find the expense of meeting the emission standards prohibitive. Actually, the view prevalent among pollution sources is that *all* controls are too expensive; but here, we have in mind the possible situation in which the order of magnitude of control costs for a year or two is roughly comparable to the total capital worth of the company which has been accumulated over many years. Such situations will likely occur only when an entire industry has for many years assumed little responsibility for investment in any kind of process control, so that now they are forced to catch up quickly; although the amount of sympathy that is due such firms is a matter of one's own philosophy, as a matter of practical necessity it appears that the speed of implementation will in fact have to be a function of the financial capabilities of the industry, regardless of how the standards are phrased.

The second problem with respect to the timing of emission controls arises when the requisite technology to achieve the necessary emission standards does not yet exist; then, the economic need is not simply to buy equipment, but to buy knowledge, i.e., conduct research, which can't necessarily be speeded up by even massive influxes of money. In this case, the control agency has two options. One is to require the immediate installation of the best equipment presently available and so, in effect, to settle for less than the originally desired reduction from that particular type of source. This philosophy is known as requiring "maximum feasible control," and it does have connotations of stringency to those firms that formerly were under no restrictions whatsoever. On the other hand, "maximum feasible control" means accepting the status quo, and to some extent the federal government has been maneuvered into sponsoring research on pollution control technology in order to provide industry with the answer to its problem.

The alternative to this, and what your author feels is the generally more desirable course, is to "force the technology," that is, to set emission standards for some years ahead, thus giving tangible goals for research in control technology. This is the approach adopted for national automobile emission standards, as we saw in Chapter 9. This approach doesn't completely eliminate the questions of who pays for the research, who conducts the research, and what happens if the research program fails, but it does apply pressure to the industry to do some research on its own. Indeed, industry generally conducts extensive research on its own initiative only when forced to do so.

All told, there are probably no clear, overall principles of developing a control strategy that will apply uniformly in the various urban areas. The agencies involved in each area must work out the best compromise possible, given imperfect emissions knowledge, imperfect knowledge of the effects of one's proposals, nearly nonexistent information on the economic cost of the measures being required, and must try to devise an implemen-

tation plan that is at least a good approximation of the ideal of an equitable distribution of the necessary burdens.

During 1971 and early 1972, the states devised such a plan for particulates and sulfur dioxides; in mid-1972, EPA approved most parts of
most of the plans. Since then, the states have undertaken to modify the
rejected portions of the plans and have begun to implement the approved
portions. Few people believe that the eventual results will be precisely
those forecast by the various implementation plans, though everyone
clearly expects the results to be in the right direction. It is presumed that
the measured results from the air quality monitoring stations will need
to be carefully watched and that the plans will have to be modified if
they don't seem to be working. Since 1974 EPA has also required the
states to begin modifying their implementation plans to provide for the
long-term maintenance of the air quality standards after they have been
initially attained and to regulate the potential future development in areas
that are presently very clean, so that they do not just automatically become polluted up to the level of the secondary air quality standards.

WHO PAYS FOR THE CONTROL, AND HOW?

The question of deciding who should pay the costs of reducing emissions
is closely related to the problem of deciding how much control is needed.
Those who argue against stringent controls generally do so because they
expect to have to pay; many of those who advocate reducing emissions
greatly do so with the belief that they won't have to pay, or at least not
directly. Taken literally, there's no question who pays—the corporations
or individuals who operate the sources pay, because they have to write
the purchase orders or sign the contracts with the firms that build and
sell the pollution control equipment. The real question is whether the
sources absorb the cost through lower profits or whether they pass it on,
either to their customers in the form of higher prices or to the general
public through a tax break, an indirect subsidy that reduces their tax
liability. Just as it is the source that pays immediately, however, it is
also equally correct to say that the general public pays, in one way or
another, in the long run.

The general public, however, is not a single coherent whole, but rather
a collection of overlapping groups, each with its own interests. A group
of "taxpayers" may be composed of the same people who are customers
for a widespread product or service, e.g., automobiles or electricity; however, General Motors' stockholders and an ore smelter's customers are very
special groups indeed, and their interest in these matters is obviously different from that of the general public. To date, the struggle among special-
interest and the "general public" groups has produced a mixed, and most

likely still evolving, decision. Generally, the economic forces of the market place are permitted to work, free from government intervention. Thus, each source can make its own choice whether to reduce profits or charge higher prices; the only constraints are those of competition. In actual practice the vast majority of pollution control costs are passed on to the customers, since the overall level of profits for a business as a whole is typically not high enough to easily absorb the cost of air pollution control. EPA's 1971 Economic Report to Congress [108] estimated that of the 14 industrial categories tabulated in Table 8–6, five could be expected to absorb a portion of pollution control costs, and one (petroleum) would save enough through reclaimed materials to offset the control costs entirely.

In small part, the costs of pollution control are also borne by the tax-payers, through special tax privileges mostly at the state and local level, granted to industry. These tax breaks usually consist of exemptions from real estate taxes or the state sales tax. Typically, if the state pollution control authority certifies that a construction program is for pollution control, the amount by which the construction improves the property is not added to the assessed value of the property, and the sales tax is not levied on the relevant purchases.

The second part of the question "Who pays for the control, and how?" refers to how the industry pays, not to how the customer pays; the customer pays the same way he always has for the product or service, only more. The question of how the industry pays was raised briefly in Chapter 11, when we mentioned applying economic pressures, such as effluent charges, as an alternative to setting emission regulations. We'll now pursue this question in a bit more detail.

In considering the economics of a business operation, economists list and try to measure accurately the various inputs—raw materials, labor, etc.—and the outputs—such as the manufactured goods—and try to quantify the relationships among these factors. Some factors, however, which the economists call "free goods," never enter the calculations, because they're free. Air, for example, and the oxygen it contains are a vital input to many processes, especially combustion, but it has always been considered a free good. In fact, however, the use of the air does result in some economic costs, as the quality of the air is degraded. However, these costs are paid not by the user who dirties the air, but by the next user. Such an economic effect is called an "external diseconomy," a diseconomy because it works against the goal of increasing the economic value of things, but "external" because the cost accrues to those who did not cause it. If the economic effect were an internal cost, on the other hand, the polluter would make serious efforts to reduce it in order to maximize overall economic gain. Thus, it seems logical that the law try to "internalize" these costs so that the economic pressures would encourage the source to reduce pollution, and the various proposals for fines, effluent fees, and so on, are meant to do just that.

HOW DO WE ORGANIZE TO DO IT?

The question of how society organizes itself to accomplish a task has many facets and occurs in various depths. With respect to air pollution control, the broadest organizational decisions involve the difference between achieving pollution control through the courts, largely via citizen-initiated lawsuits and control by governmental programs, largely by regulation and quasi-coerced "voluntary" cooperation, with the use of government-initiated court action only as a last resort. Society has pretty much decided this question, clearly if not explicitly, in favor of carefully maintaining both avenues toward solution, each to apply where it works best. The present federal-state program of criteria, standards, and implementation plans clearly has the potential for making much more progress in a fairly short time than could be achieved in our overcrowded courts. On the other hand, it's equally clear that the courts and a corps of environmental attorneys will be needed to press the attack against other minor or esoteric pollutants, to provide a means for relief in individual special situations, and, most particularly, to make sure that the gov ment program is in fact carried out.

Two rather distinct organizational decisions must be made about structure of governmental programs—the division of responsibility among federal, state, and local governments, and the organizational structure of the agencies charged with the task of each level of government. Here, questions about the most effective use of power to curb pollution and the most effective administrative arrangement are mixed with questions pertaining to personal publicity for office holders, interagency rivalries (both substantive and trivial), and sometimes even the power to offer special favors to industrial contributors. This comment, however, is not meant as a condemnation of the participating agencies or individuals; except for dishonesty or blatant corruption, all these factors are an essential part of the give-and-take flexibility that makes democracy work. Although it may seem wasteful and unseemly for office-holders to fight over the credit for each minor advance against pollution, this competition (given a free and alert press) acts to ensure that the steps are in fact advances. Furthermore, it does seem clear that there is far less dishonesty and corruption in pollution control agencies than in many other areas of government activity; pollution control, as a relatively new major activity, generally attracts a younger, more technical, and often more committed staff and elicits a high degree of public interest, which in turn makes it more difficult for the worst abuses to occur.

The question of federal as opposed to state and local programs has been an ongoing policy question for two decades or more, but the Air Quality Act of 1967 seems to have decided the issue in favor of federal-state cooperation. The 1970 amendments simply ironed out some administrative details about the division of responsibility between the federal government and the states. Although it seems largely imposed by federal law, this division of responsibility is also dictated by practical organizational necessity; Congress actually had much less choice than it might at first seem. Given the complexity of reducing air pollution on a national basis, the federal government could not possibly effect a striking reduction in emissions without participation by the states. For example, the effectiveness of emission-control regulations depends largely on willing compliance; it is just not possible to forcibly compel compliance from more than a small portion of those affected. As it is, the state and local control programs have a difficult time dealing with firms that have chosen noncooperation. If the federal program were to attempt to do the entire job, the requisite bureaucracy would almost certainly lead to insensitivity, at best, to local variations and to chaos or paralysis at worst. Legal questions would arise from the extension of federal power via the Constitution's interstate commerce clause into tiny, intrastate, noncommercial sources, e.g., schools or individual residences; in addition, centralization would likely work to minimize the effect of public opinion and to maximize the chance that industrial lobbies could sabotage control efforts by influencing Congress to gut the budget.

On the other hand, there is equally clear evidence that the state and local governments cannot do the job alone, or at least that they in fact didn't do the job in the past. One of the principal reasons for this poor record is simply that the major national corporations are much bigger and more powerful than almost any local governmental unit and, in fact, most states. In the early 1960s, when public opinion led to more stringent pollution control requirements in some states, other states were more than willing to try to lure industries by promising lax pollution control, tax advantages, etc. Since shifts in the economy are closely linked to jobs for the voters, it was clear that unless all states attempted an approximately equal control effort, no state would be able to conduct a truly effective program.

Out of these two conflicting situations has come the series of federal laws, in which Congress has become increasingly specific that the states shall in fact conduct pollution control programs sufficient to at least protect the health of their own citizens; basically, the laws provide that if a state does so, it will be supported by federal power, but if it doesn't the federal government will do it for them. These escalating congressional decisions, most clear in the 1967 law, represent a national recognition that the long-range decision to actually control the pollution had not really been made. Although stringent pollution control was being advocated by a growing number of citizen activists and was being pursued by a few state governments, only California's program had much success. In most states and municipalities, pollution control agencies were merely performing the same, routine functions they had always performed, with no overall plan or purpose and leaving it to others to provide any stimulus for change. In those instances when change did invade the control agency, it was effectively squelched when the air pollution control boards vetoed any control actions that were attempted. The effect of the evolving federal policy has been to shift authority from the municipalities, to the states, with the flat proviso that the federal government is watching to see that the states really assume their responsibility.

Once the division of responsibility among various levels of government has been decided, the only organizational questions remaining are which agency should run the program at each level and how that agency should organize itself internally. On the federal level, the selection of an agency to conduct air pollution control activities—the PHS and the Bureau of Mines, the reorganization of the PHS within the HEW, and the formation of EPA—has been inseparable from the question: "What sort of federal program shall we have?" The most recent answer to this question has given us, of course, an integrated agency in which air pollution is included along with most of the other federal environmental programs. This decision has set the pattern for state programs as well; this reflects similar policy decisions in response to public opinion, as well as the fact that state programs have become so interrelated with the federal programs that parallel agency structure has become a communications necessity. Thus, more and more state programs are emerging from Public Health or Public Works Departments and are being placed in broader, integrated environmental agencies.

When we reach the level of organizational structure within an agency, we finally reach a level at which organizational decisions become almost separate from any effective policy decisions. Almost. There is still some distinction between organization within an agency and the ties it has with other agencies at the same level, especially at the federal and state levels. Within the local agency, little affects the organization except human convenience, which typically results in the pattern of relationships as shown in the organization chart depicted in Fig. 11–1. Similarly, within the federal or a large state agency, the agency head has a great deal of leeway to organize the agency's operations into groups and chains of authority so as to maximize the agency's effectiveness. The principal limits on the agency head's freedom to organize and reorganize are the practical matters of distributing the abilities and career interests of his principal staff and increasing efficiency while decreasing the confusion that may accompany organizational changes. Confusion is most likely to occur when the reorganization involves merging different substantive agencies, e.g., those dealing with air and water pollution. In such a case, it often becomes appropriate to divide and reassemble even the lowest-level working groups, which in itself causes a good bit of confusion and difficulty. The EPA has been experiencing these reorganizational problems ever since its formation.

For our purposes here, however, it is more important to consider the problems an agency may face because of limitations imposed by its relationships with other agencies or by policies that involve providing support services. Typically, both federal and state laws set up either support agencies or general policies regarding personnel and civil service systems, purchasing, bookkeeping, etc., that dictate how an agency must perform these functions. This type of limitation on the agency's freedom is meant to, and generally does, work in the interest of efficiency and overall equity, but there are situations when they can be used to assert quiet, undue influence, and there have been cases when they have worked violent havoc on the common-sense operation of the program.

The best example of the problem of outside influence is the federal practice of centralizing the daily practice of courtroom law within the Department of Justice. When any federal agency has need to go to court, e.g., the suit against Bishop Processing under the Clean Air Act, the agency uses the Justice Department's lawyers in the various district attorney offices around the country. This introduces an additional liaison effort, but this is generally a small price to pay to save the cost and trouble of requiring every agency to maintain its own set of attorneys. However, if the President or factions in Congress wish to minimize the effectiveness of some federal program without taking public responsibility for doing so, this arrangement provides an ideal way of doing it. The President or his immediate staff can effectively cripple a federal program, e.g., civil rights or a specific antitrust case, by simply passing down the word to the Justice Department to go slow in enforcement, and they can do so with relative immunity from public backlash. Even if the facts are made public by, say, the indignant resignation of a prominent official, the confusion of the two-agency liaison arrangement makes it difficult for the public to grasp the facts and assign the blame. A more serious, though less undercover and dramatic, threat to an enforcement program is the control exerted by Congress over the staff and budget of the Justice Department. By seriously restricting the staff available for enforcement tasks, the Appropriations and Judiciary committees of Congress can emasculate a program, and do so with no embarrassing policy memos or midnight meetings, and the agency operating the program and the congressional committees that oversee it are nearly helpless to stop it. In the case of EPA's air pollution program, this highly likely possibility was foreseen by the drafters of the 1970 amendments to the Clean Air Act, which includes a very brief provision that the EPA administrator can hire his own lawyers if the Justice Department is unable to provide sufficient staff. On such little things are effective government programs often built.

The second example, a case of bureaucratic interference with the operation of a control program, comes from the state level, where abuses seem to be more common, no doubt because of the low level of public interest and visibility that most state governments generate. In one of the largest states, the state air pollution control agency was in the process of purchasing a number of automatic instruments in order to expand its monitoring network and wanted to purchase Brand X so as to match the instruments already in use in the agency's network. The state purchasing agent's office, however, insisted on purchasing Brand Y instruments because they were cheaper, even though they were not comparable in methodology and performance to the agency's other instruments. The state agency appealed to the federal staff for help (federal grant money was paying for the instruments), and the federal agency tactfully tried to explain why a network had to consist of uniform instrumentation so that the data would be comparable, etc. They all lost, however, to the power of the purchasing agent, who saved several hundred dollars; the network is now part Brand X and part Brand Y, to the consternation of the people working with the data. Although it is perhaps conceivable that the purchasing agent took a bribe, it is far more likely that he was merely exercising the power given him to keep costs down, and the fault lies less with him than with a bureaucratic organization that fails to distinguish between scientific instruments and paper clips.

EXERCISES

Review Questions

1. Why do we assert that the determination of pollution-control policy is a matter of collective, public decision-making?
2. Since World War II, along what lines has the debate run over how stringent our control policy should be?
3. Why do most environmentalists feel that economic cost-benefit analysis is not appropriate at the present?
4. Distinguish carefully among air quality goals, criteria, and standards. What is our current air quality goal?
5. Distinguish between air quality standards and emission standards.
6. Describe the rationale of the "roll-back" method of determining necessary pollutant reductions. What is wrong with this method?
7. What is wrong with simply eliminating the emissions from the major sources?

8. What is urban-area diffusion modeling? Why do we use it?
9. Explain how emission and air quality standards complement each other in rural and urban areas.
10. List several policy areas of federal activity that affect the fuels and energy market.
11. What is the usual time lag between the promulgation of a new emission regulation and the compliance deadline?
12. In what two different ways can the cost of industrial pollution control reach the typical consumer-taxpayer?
13. What is an external diseconomy?
14. Why did Congress have little choice but to adopt the cooperative state-federal-approach that presently exists?

Thought Questions

15. What benefits does a business or factory get by being in an urban area that might compensate for more stringent air pollution controls there?
16. What, if anything, prevents the states from ignoring the Clean Air Act, thus forcing the federal government to undertake the entire process and, presumably fail?
17. If you oppose a particular program, it is often easier to hurt it by restricting funds at the federal level than at the state level. Explain why.

Discussion Questions

18. To what extent do you feel that air quality standards should be based on "scientifically rigorous criteria"?
19. If an individual is accused of a criminal act, the law is rather clear that the criminality of his act must depend on the act, not on the identity of the person. Consider the parallel between this idea and the concept of different standards in urban and rural areas, both of which seem to be fair and equitable. Do you feel that there is an inconsistency? Why or why not?
20. If you were the President, with a functioning majority in Congress, what kind of national energy policy would you propose?
21. The idea behind not including pollution-control equipment and construction in a plant's tax base is, of course, that such additions to the physical plant bring in no additional profit and hence are different from other things the industry might build. If the basis for taxing the industry's real estate were its profitability rather than its construction costs, this distinction would disappear. What other ramifications might such a policy have? Would you like to see it adopted?

Problem

22. Since achieving the objectives of a control program presumably take a few years, it might be appropriate to take the general growth in emissions into account when figuring the desired emission reduction. Modify the formula on p. 331 to do this.

13

EPILOGUE: WHY?

At the end of Chapter 4, which dealt with the effects on air pollution on human health, we mentioned that most people's first reaction to the topic of air pollution is to ask: "Is it really as bad as they say?" When this question is answered affirmatively, their next thoughts are frequently along the line of: "Why now? How did it get so bad all of the sudden? Who let it happen?" In this chapter, we will try to contribute toward the answers to those and similar questions, questions that prove more fundamental than they would at first appear.

This chapter is unusual in that it touches briefly on a number of topics about the nature of our society and ourselves; these subjects aren't usually included in a discussion of air pollution, but are nonetheless important, even crucial, to a real solution of the air pollution problem. In fact, the close fundamental relationship between environmental issues and the nature of our society is one of the reasons why environmental issues have attracted so much general public attention and why there is as much room for the philosopher as for the engineer. If it seems that we're getting too far from the classical topics of pollution material, it is only necessary to recall Commoner's first law of ecology: "Everything is connected to everything else"; so it often is with viable thoughts, as well as with living organisms.

This chapter is also unusual in other ways. By the very nature of the material, it is necessarily somewhat less structured and organized than that in the other chapters. In addition, many of the thoughts on the following pages are offered without supporting evidence; this is because they are not facts, but ideas. The evidence on which these ideas are based is daily all around us, the reader no less than the writer, and each person must interpret this evidence personally. On topics of government, history, and especially psychology, most people become convinced of the validity of an idea not by the arguments of others, but by their own experiences and beliefs. Thus, our function here is merely to point out various thoughts for your consideration and personal evaluation.

Let us begin by exploring the nature of our country—not the United States of the civics books, but the United States as people actually perceive it. If we were to take a sidewalk poll and ask what kind of country are we, we would likely get such responses as "big," "democratic," "free," "rich," "fascist," etc. Trying to categorize these adjectives, we find that they fit into three distinct groups: (1) concern about the degree of personal freedom that we have; (2) the form of economic organization in this country; and (3) our wealth. The ideas of personal freedom, contained in such adjectives as "free," "democratic," "totalitarian," and "dictatorship," are not clearly separate from terms that describe economic structure, e.g., "capitalist" and "free-enterprise," although there is some distinction. There is little question about how most Americans feel on each of these questions; most people consider the United States to be a free, democratic country, as opposed to a totalitarian country, a dictatorship.

The principal ramification of this fact for air pollution control is the manner in which public decisions are made. We have emphasized throughout the book the strong impact that public opinion can have if in fact the public cares about an issue. In a very real sense, this is at the heart of what most people mean by "democracy," a system in which everyone is free to agitate and proselytize for his views or for those decisions that he feels will benefit him and equally free to ignore public issues that he does not care about. Those who feel that we are not a democratic country frequently offer as evidence the strong influence that major corporations and other powerful economic interests can have on the governmental process, and there is little doubt that the history of air pollution control is replete with examples of such situations. Those who would rebut this viewpoint point out that this type of influence occurs only when no major segment of the public cares and that, in fact, it is probably good that the government listens to the specialists when the public does not care. There are, of course, valid arguments that this is an idealistic view, that in fact the average citizen is not listened to and that this inability to be heard permits incredible abuse by the government and by special interests. Although this is quite likely true to some extent, it is also true that there are few other countries whose governmental systems work even approximately as well as ours does.

In the category of adjectives about economic organization, it is a bit more difficult to precisely establish the position of the United States. The simplistic spectrum often offered has at one end laissez-faire capitalism, whereby everything is left to the individual enterprise, from the corner grocery to the largest corporation, and at the other end the totally planned economy, whereby all decisions about the production, consumption, and allocation of goods are made by central policy-makers and implemented through an elaborate system of economic planning. In actuality, the United States is not at the extreme free-enterprise end of the spectrum; indeed, it is fairly easy to demonstrate that the option of being free to either get rich or fail is available only for the smallest economic entities in the system. Under our system, the largest economic enterprises, the major corporations, have pretty much lost the "freedom to fail," as has been amply demonstrated in the cases of Lockheed Aircraft and the Penn Central Railroad. This distinction between free enterprise for the small business and subsidized protection for the major corporation is a basic argument of those who believe that economic interests run the country. On the other hand, one can offer the comment that since these major corporations have become such a large part of our life, society as a whole cannot permit them to collapse, for then, it is argued, it will be the workers, the stores

that are supported by the workers' wages, and in this sense society in
general, that will be hurt, rather than "the wealthy capitalists who have
been making grandiose profits." This interdependence aspect of free enterprise relates to the complexity of our society, a topic to which we'll return shortly.

The one single decision that can be considered to be at the heart of
our belief in the free-enterprise system is the assumption that people and
institutions will work best if they personally profit from their efforts. The
opposite view, which seems to be taken by advocates of centrally planned
economies, is that people can and will work effectively, even though their
personal profit may be slight, as long as they are adequately motivated by
belief in some longer-term goal.

The third category of terms applied to the United States deals with
our relative affluence. The United States is described as "big," "wealthy,"
"rich," etc., and no one would question this. The relative affluence we enjoy
is commonly attributed to our free-enterprise system; the man on the street,
in response to any criticism of our way of government or economic organization, will almost assuredly answer, "Yes, but look at the standard of
living it has brought us." This standard of living is a major aspect of our
pollution problem; there is little question but that much of our problem
stems from our prodigious consumption of energy and resources to create
that way of life. Of particular concern is not just our present consumption,
but the prospect of continuously increasing growth in this consumption;
the "growth" of our economy is often portrayed as a major villain.

The cause of this tremendous growth in consumption and pollution
is the source of some controversy within the environmental movement.
Some people say that the principal problem in this nation, and certainly
in the world at large, is overpopulation; as a species, *homo sapiens* has
succeeded too well, has grown too great in numbers, and is about to be
submerged in his own effluents. Other people, however, argue that it is
not population that causes our problem, but inappropriate technology
causing too much pollution per person; we have failed to live in harmony
with our environment, we have invented synthetic materials that the environment cannot handle, we have disrupted balances, negligently spread
our wastes around, and in general done what we have done badly. (Although I want to encourage you to consider seriously both of these viewpoints, I can't resist commenting that this argument seems a great deal
like arguing whether it's the length or the width of a rectangle that makes
its area large.)

Suppose, now, that we were to ask in our hypothetical sidewalk poll,
not what kind of country, but what kind of society, we have. Many people,
probably, would be unable to give any real answer. The word "free" fits
with society, and many people might say "free society," whereas many

others might offer "permissive society." From those who have considered "society" in a deeper sense, we might get several answers that are relevant to our pollution situation. We are a competitive society by and large, which, of course, is consonant with centuries of emphasis on free enterprise. By way of refining what we mean by this, we note first that many people feel that the competitive nature of man is an instinctive heritage from the days of hunting for food in competition with other men and other species. On the other hand, some people feel that the Chinese culture is distinguished by having become, presumably over several centuries, a society characterized by emphasis on mutual dependence and cooperation rather than by competition. I have found this topic a relevant question for introspective moments. Do you see yourself as an individual confronted with a largely human environment, or do you see yourself as one of a group of humans, interacting with other, nonhuman, elements of the natural environment? The difference is relevant to one's view on environmental protection in general.

Another major effect of competitiveness on the environment is its effect on our standard of living. The need to succeed, to achieve, is one of the driving forces behind our economic growth.

Also accurate as a description of our society is that it is complicated, interrelated, and highly specialized; we noted earlier, for example, that the economic health of corporations is so crucial to our lives that we can't let them fail. We have, in effect, divided the work to be done into very small pieces; perhaps not all as small as an individual bolt on an automotive assembly line, but sufficiently small that we have not doctors, but surgeons, cardiologists, anesthetists, etc., not inventors, but interdisciplinary teams. There is a high degree of specialization in almost any field, because as our society gets more and more complicated, specialization becomes increasingly necessary; no one is able to maintain sufficient information to precisely perform any broad spectrum of functions in our society. Thus, the argument goes, we must expect to depend on more and more people to perform various tasks for us, and we must expect to find our own role in life becoming increasingly narrow and specialized. The groups of people who have chosen to live communally or who have adopted some other form of withdrawal are in part reacting against this viewpoint.

The automobile provides several interesting examples of how complexity affects the way we do things. Our efforts to reduce carbon monoxide and hydrocarbons, for example, produce more NO_x, and vice versa. In order to obtain smoother performance, we add lead to gasoline, which leaves deposits in the engine; to remove the lead deposits, we add halogens, and to mitigate the halogens' adverse effects, we add still other additives. In each case, additional complexity is favored over making a wholesale, fresh start. Each such decision is made for reasons that are very compelling in the context of that one decision; why risk a major change when just this one more effort will do it?

The opponents of complexity, however, argue that the process has to stop somewhere. They offer the analogy that in building a house of cards or a pile of blocks, it is very easy, even trivial, to successfully place one card upon another, one block upon another. Yet it is essentially impossible to build a pile of blocks, say, eight feet high. The conflict between these two statements arises because as the pile grows higher or the house of cards more intricate, the precision and delicacy with which each new increment must be added increases, ultimately, to the point at which we are no longer able to be so precise and delicate. Opponents of technological solutions to the problems caused by technology are in effect arguing that the complexity of our system is already such that most additional changes bring more complex ramifications and new problems than they do solutions to previous problems.

Another adjective often applied to our society is "idealistic." Although at first thought it may seem ridiculous to speak of idealism, given the widespread alienation and disaffection that has been evidenced in the last few years, it isn't really; the disaffection with the country, which many people feel to be relatively temporary, is in large measure produced because we establish idealistic goals and then do not in fact live up to them. Our educational system, for example, teaches a highly idealistic view of our democracy and freedom, the free-enterprise system, and so on, a view which has probably never been accurate. Thus, each generation must discover anew the inaccuracies of what they have been taught and must make their own adjustments to this fact.

With the advent of television, the current generation has been able to discover the inaccuracies of an idealistic view of America before they have begun to participate in a permanent way, rather than after they have spent much of their life in acccommodating to the social system and coming to feel a part of it. It is the people with this view, no matter their age, that have provided the moving force behind the "environmental movement" of recent years. They have been sufficiently uninvolved in the social structure as to have some capacity for criticism, to give voice to some of their idealism. The future course of environmental decisions will depend in large part on whether and how much that idealism is either smothered or maintained.

BIBLIOGRAPHY

GENERAL

1. Louis J. Battan, *The Unclean Sky*, Garden City, N.Y.: Doubleday, 1966. A readable account by a meteorologist of some of the technical aspects of air pollution meteorology.

2. Virginia Brodine, *Air Pollution*, New York: Harcourt Brace Jovanovich, 1973. This highly readable book by one of the editors of *Environment* magazine discusses the atmospheric system, its pollution by man, the health effects of pollution, and closes with an excellent section on the philosophical bases for pollution control and the social obstacles.

3. Rachel Carson, *Silent Spring*, Boston: Houghton Mifflin, 1962. The classic discussion of pesticides and wildlife that began the early awakenings of the current environmental movement.

4. Barry Commoner, *The Closing Circle*, New York: Knopf, 1971. A thought-provoking discussion by one of the more prominent scientists in the environmental movement; a biologist, Commoner considers environmental problems in the context of ecology and argues that the nature of our technology, rather than population growth or simple affluence, is the ultimate villain.

5. J. Clarence Davies, III, *The Politics of Pollution*, New York: Pegasus, 1970. An excellent discussion of the activities of Congress, the executive agencies, public interest groups, etc., by a political scientist with first-hand experience in the federal government.

6. Garrett DeBell, ed., *The Environmental Handbook*, New York: Ballantine/ Friends of the Earth, 1970. A collection of papers published as source material for Earth Day; includes many useful contributions and thoroughly portrays the activist tone of the times.

7. Paul R. Ehrlich, *The Population Bomb*, New York: Sierra Club/Ballantine, 1968. The classic, and frightening, treatise on the consequences of population growth.

8. John C. Esposito, *Vanishing Air*, New York: Grossman, 1970. The report of Ralph Nader's Study Group on Air Pollution; a definitive and generally valid indictment of the national air pollution control effort, somewhat dated now, but excellent for historical perspective.

9. R. Buckminster Fuller, Eric A. Walker, and James R. Killian, Jr., *Approaching the Benign Environment*, London: Collier-Macmillan, 1970. One

349

of the very few discussions of environmental problems that is optimistic about the future.

10. Huey D. Johnson, ed., *No Deposit—No Return,* Reading, Mass.: Addison-Wesley, 1970. Collection of contributions to a 1969 UNESCO conference; includes most of the best-known authors and a wide sampling of opinions and topics.

11. Norman J. Landau and Paul D. Rheingold, *The Environmental Law Handbook,* New York: Ballantine/Friends of the Earth, 1971. A relatively activist text on how to protect the environment through the courts; includes discussion of the various legal approaches, theories, and techniques in clear, layman language.

12. National Tuberculosis and Respirable Disease Association, *Breathing—What You Need to Know,* New York: NTRDA, 1968. Describes lung function and physiology, breathing control mechanisms, and respiratory hazards.

13. ———, *Introduction to Respiratory Diseases,* New York: NTRDA, 1969. Describes respiratory diseases and treatment in layman's language.

14. Sheldon Novick and Dorothy Cottrell, eds., *Our World In Peril—An Environment Review,* Greenwich, Conn.: Fawcett, 1971. A collection of reprints from *Environment* magazine on a wide range of topics, including asbestos, health effects, automobile pollution, and alternative vehicles.

15. James Ridgeway, *The Politics of Ecology,* New York: E. P. Dutton, 1970. An exposé by a radical journalist, directed primarily at water pollution, but with a major section on fuels monopolies and exploitation.

16. Breton Roueché, *Eleven Blue Men,* Boston: Little, Brown, 1953. A series of instances of medical detective work, including a chapter on the Donora smog episode.

17. Joseph L. Sax, *Defending the Environment,* New York: Knopf, 1971. A well-done, readable treatise on the failure of existing legal and regulatory mechanisms to deal effectively with environmental problems; recommends citizen suits as an effective alternative.

18. Richard Scorer, *Air Pollution,* Oxford: Pergamon Press, 1968. A narrative emphasizing the meteorological aspects, thoroughly illustrated with photographs.

19. Jerome Spar, *Earth, Sea, and Air—A Survey of the Geophysical Sciences,* 2d ed., Reading, Mass.: Addison-Wesley, 1965. An elementary, highly readable discussion of basic geology, oceanography, and meteorology.

20. George R. Stewart, *Not So Rich As You Think,* Boston: Houghton Mifflin, 1967; New York: New American Library (paper), 1970. A general discussion of environmental problems, including the concept that mankind has been intrinsically sloppy, through evolutionary time, since the days of the apes.

21. Subcommittee on Environmental Improvement, Committee on Chemistry and Public Affairs, *Cleaning Our Environment: The Chemical Basis for Action,* Washington D.C.: American Chemical Society, 1969.

22. William Wise, *Killer Smog,* New York: Audubon/Ballantine, 1968. A fictionalized account of the 1952 London smog episode.

GOVERNMENT PUBLICATIONS

Reports and documents published by the government are made available by the GPO Superintendent of Documents (using AP, APTD, EPA numbers or title) and/or by the National Technical Information Service (using the PB numbers), the latter in microfiche if desired.

Publications from EPA and predecessors

Air Quality Criteria for:

23. *Particulate Matter,* Jan. 1969, AP–49, FS 2.93/3:49, PB 190–251.

24. *Sulfur Oxides,* April 1970, AP–50, FS 2.93/3:50, PB 190–252.

25. *Carbon Monoxide,* March 1970, AP–62, HE 20.1309:62, PB 190–261.

26. *Photochemical Oxidants,* March 1970, AP–63, HE 20.1309:63, PB 190–262.

27. *Hydrocarbons,* March 1970, AP–64, HE 20.1309:64, PB 190–489.

28. *Nitrogen Oxides,* Jan. 1971, AP–84, EP 4.9:84, PB 197–333.

Control Techniques for:

29. *Particulate Air Pollutants,* Jan. 1969, AP–51, FS 2.93/3:51, PB 190–253.

30. *Sulfur Oxide Air Pollutants,* Jan. 1969, AP–52, FS 2.93/3:52, PB 190–254.

31. *Carbon Monoxide Emissions from Stationary Sources,* March 1970, AP–65, HE 20.1309:65, PB 190–263.

32. *Carbon Monoxide, Nitrogen Oxides and Hydrocarbon Emissions from Mobile Sources,* March 1970, AP–66, HE 20.1309:66, PB 190–264.

33. *Nitrogen Oxides Emissions from Stationary Sources,* March 1970, AP–67, HE 20.1309:67, PB 190–265.

34. *Hydrocarbons and Organic Solvent Emissions from Stationary Sources,* March 1970, AP–68, HE 20.1309:68, PB 190–266.

Preliminary Air Pollution Survey of:

35.	Aeroallergens	APTD-23	PB 188–076
36.	Aldehydes	APTD-24	PB 188–081
37.	Ammonia	APTD-25	PB 188–082
38.	Arsenic and Its Compounds	APTD-26	PB 188–071
39.	Asbestos	APTD-27	PB 188–080
40.	Barium and Its Compounds	APTD-28	PB 188–083
41.	Beryllium and Its Compounds	APTD-29	PB 188–078
42.	Biological Aerosols	APTD-30	PB 188–084

43. Boron and Its Compounds	APTD-31	PB 188–085
44. Cadmium and Its Compounds	APTD-32	PB 188–086
45. Chlorine Gas	APTD-33	PB 188–087
46. Chromium and Its Compounds	APTD-34	PB 188–075
47. Ethylene	APTD-35	PB 188–069
48. Hydrochloric Acid	APTD-36	PB 188–067
49. Hydrogen Sulfide	APTD-37	PB 188–068
50. Iron and Its Compounds	APTD-38	PB 188–088
51. Manganese and Its Compounds	APTD-39	PB 188–079
52. Mercury and Its Compounds	APTD-40	PB 188–074
53. Nickel and Its Compounds	APTD-41	PB 188–070
54. Odorous Compounds	APTD-42	PB 188–089
55. Organic Carcinogens	APTD-43	PB 188–090
56. Pesticides	APTD-44	PB 188–091
57. Phosphorus and Its Compounds	APTD-45	PB 188–073
58. Radioactive Substances	APTD-46	PB 188–092
59. Selenium and Its Compounds	APTD-47	PB 188–077
60. Vanadium and Its Compounds	APTD-48	PB 188–093
61. Zinc and Its Compounds	APTD-49	PB 188–072

Air Quality Data Reports

62. *Continuous Air Monitoring Program in Cincinnati, Ohio, 1962–1963,* Jan. 1965, AP–21, FS 2.300:AP–21, PB 168–863.

63. *Continuous Air Monitoring Program in Washington, D.C., 1962–1963,* Sept. 1966, AP–23, FS 2.300:AP–23, PB 173–987.

64. *Continuous Air Monitoring Program in Philadelphia, 1962–1965,* August 1969, APTD–69–14, PB 194–863.

65. *Air Quality Data for 1967 from the National Air Surveillance Network and Contributing State and Local Networks, Revised,* August 1971, APTD–0741, PB 203–546.

66. *Air Quality Data for 1968 from the National Air Surveillance Network and Contributing State and Local Networks,* August 1972, APTD–0978, PB 213–830.

67. *Air Quality Data for Suspended Particulates, 1969, 1970, and 1971, from the National Air Surveillance Networks and Contributing State and Local Networks,* Nov. 1972, APTD–1353.

68. *Air Quality Data for Sulfur Dioxide, 1969, 1970, and 1971, from the National Air Surveillance Networks and Contributing State and Local Networks,* Nov. 1972, APTD–1354, PB 214–167.

69. *Air Quality Data for Organics, 1969 and 1970, from the National Air Sur-veillance Networks and Contributing State and Local Networks,* June 1973, APTD–1465, PB 224–822/AS.

70. *Air Quality Data for Non-Metallic Inorganic Ions, 1969 and 1970, from the National Air Surveillance Networks and Contributing State and Local Networks,* June 1973, APTD–1466, PB 223–630/AS.

71. *Air Quality Data for Metals, 1968 and 1969, from the National Air Sur-veillance Networks and Contributing State and Local Networks,* June 1973, APTD–1467, PB 244–823/AS.

72. *The National Air Monitoring Program: Air Quality and Emission Trends— Annual Report,* August 1973; *Volume I,* EPA–450/1–73–001A; *Volume II,* EPA–450/1–73–001B.

73. *Monitoring and Air Quality Trends Report, 1972,* Dec. 1973, EPA–450/ 1–73–004.

74. *Monitoring and Air Quality Trends Report, 1973,* Oct. 1974, EPA–450/ 1–74–007.

Miscellaneous Technical Reports

75. D. A. Lynn, B. J. Steigerwald, and J. H. Ludwig, *The November–Decem-ber 1962 Air Pollution Episode in the Eastern United States,* Sept. 1964, AP–7, FS 2.300:AP–07, PB 168–878.

76. T. B. McMullen and R. Smith, *The Trend of Suspended Particulates in Urban Air 1957–1964,* Sept. 1965, AP–19, FS 2.300:AP–19, PB 170–475.

77. D. B. Turner, *Workbook of Atmospheric Dispersion Estimates,* 1970, AP– 26, EP 4.9:26, PB 191–482.

78. *Air Pollution Engineering Manual,* 2d ed., May 1973, AP–40, EP 4.9:40/2, PB 225–130/OAS.

79. *Compilation of Air Pollution Emission Factors,* 2d ed., April 1973, AP–42, EP 4.9:42/2; *Supplement No. 1,* July 1973, EP 4.9:4/2/Supp; *Supplement No. 2,* September 1973, EP 4.9:42/2/Supp.

80. J. G. Fensterstock and R. K. Fankhauser, *Thanksgiving 1966 Air Pollution Episode in the Eastern United States,* July 1968, AP–45, FS 2.93/3:45; PB 190–248.

81. J. T. Peterson, *The Climate of Cities,* Oct. 1969, AP-59, HE 20.1309:59, PB 190–260.

82. I. J. Hindawi, *Air Pollution Injury to Vegetation,* 1970, AP–71, HE 20.1309:71, PB 193–480.

83. *Guide for Air Pollution Episode Avoidance,* June 1971, AP–76, EP 4.9:76, PB 201–456.

84. L. B. Barrett and T. E. Waddell, *Cost of Air Pollution Damage: A Status Report,* Feb. 1973, AP–85, EP 4.9:85, PB 222–040.

85. R. E. Engel, *et al., Environmental Lead and Public Health,* March 1971, AP–90, EP 4.9:90, PB 199–058.

86. G. Holzworth, *Mixing Heights, Wind Speeds, and Potential for Urban Air Pollution in the Contiguous United States,* Jan. 1972, AP–101, EP 4.9:101, PB 207–103.

87. *Federal Air Quality Control Regions,* Jan. 1972, AP–102, EP 4.9:102.

88. T. R. Lewis, *et al., Toxicology of Atmospheric Sulfur Dioxide Decay Products,* July 1972, AP–111, EP 4.9:111, PB 212–744.

89. *SAROAD Parameter Coding Manual,* July 1971, APTD–0633, PB 207–348.

90. *SAROAD Users' Manual,* July 1971, APTD–0663, PB 201–408.

91. *SAROAD Station Coding Manual,* Feb. 1972, APTD–0907, PB 211–747.

92. J. H. Cavender, D. S. Kircher, and A. J. Hoffman, *Nationwide Air Pollutant Emission Trends 1940–1970,* Jan. 1973, AP–115, PB 222–739.

93. *Background Information: Proposed National Emission Standards for Hazardous Air Pollutants: Asbestos, Beryllium, and Mercury,* Dec. 1971, APTD–0753, PB 204–876.

94. *Guide for Compiling a Comprehensive Emission Inventory,* June 1972, APTD–1135, PB 212–231.

95. *Projected Utilization of Stack Gas Cleaning Systems by Steam-Electric Plants (SOCTAP Report),* April 1973, APTD–1569, PB 221–356.

96. *A Survey of Air and Population Lead Levels in Selected American Communities,* Dec. 1972, R1–73–005, PB 222–459.

97. R. Spirtas and H. J. Levin, *Characteristics of Particulate Patterns 1957–1966,* March 1970, AP–61, HE 20.1309:61, PB 192–223.

98. *Proposed Implementation Plan for the Control of Particulates and Sulfur Oxides for the State of Ohio Portion of the Metropolitan Cincinnati Interstate AQCR,* Sept. 1970, APTD–0598, PB 195–758.

99. *Health Consequences of Sulfur Oxides: A Report from CHESS, 1970–1971,* May 1974, EPA–650/1–74–004.

Publications of the Council on Environmental Quality

100. *Environmental Quality–1970: The First Annual Report of the Council on Environmental Quality,* August 1970, GPO S/N 4111–0001. This first report discusses the nature of environmental problems, the federal organization, and the environmental philosophy.

101. *Environmental Quality–1971: The Second Annual Report of the CEQ,* August 1971, GPO S/N 4111–0005. Includes sections on the year's developments in environmental activities, the economic cost of pollution controls, and legal aspects.

102. *Environmental Quality–1972: The Third Annual Report of the CEQ,* August 1972, GPO S/N 4111–0011. Includes discussion of environmental indices and forecasting, the year's developments, economic impact (industry by industry), and useful appendixes, including the National Environmental Policy Act and other laws and executive orders.

103. *Environmental Quality–1973: The Fourth Annual Report of the CEQ,* Sept. 1973, GPO S/N 4111–00020. Includes case studies, review of federal programs, sections on economics, land-use regulation, and environmental trends.

104. *Environmental Quality–1974: The Fifth Annual Report of the CEQ,* Dec. 1974, GPO S/N 4000–00327. Highlights land use, the energy crisis, and a five-year review of the National Environmental Policy Act, as well as a survey of the year's events.

Congressional Documents

105. *Some Environmental Implications of National Fuels Policies, Report by Staff of Senate Committee on Public Works,* Committee Print, Dec. 1970. Outlines the policy issues and includes useful statistics on fuels and fuel uses, with emphasis on sulfur oxides emissions.

106. *The Economy, Energy, and the Environment, A Background Study for the Joint Economic Committee,* Legislative Reference Service, Library of Congress, Committee Print, September 1970. An excellent resource on fuels, the economics of energy, and the environmental impact of fuel production and use, especially by the electric power industry.

The Cost of Clean Air, Annual Economic Reports of the EPA Administrator to the Congress:

107. *Second Annual Report* (of Secretary of HEW), March 1970, Senate Document 91–65.

108. *Third Annual Report,* March 1971, Senate Document 92–6.

109. *Fourth Annual Report,* March 1972, Senate Document 92–67.

110. *Fifth Annual Report,* October 1973, Senate Document 93–40.

111. *Sixth Annual Report,* Sept. 1974, Senate Document 93–122.

112. *Alternative to the Gasoline-Powered Internal Combustion Engine,* Hearing before the Panel on Environmental Science and Technology of the Senate Committee on Public Works, March 14, 1972, Serial No. 92–H23. Includes technical testimony from alternative-engine proponents.

113. *Development of Systems to Attain Established Motor Vehicle and Engine Emission Standards,* Report of the Administrator of the EPA to Congress in Compliance with Public Law 90–148, Senate Document No. 92–39, September 1971. This report includes a history of motor vehicle regulation and standards, discussion of emission test cycles and emission control technology, and a summary of federal programs, including research on alternative power systems.

Air Quality and Automobile Emission Control, A Report by the Coordinating Committee on Air Quality Studies of the National Academy of Sciences and National Academy of Engineering for the Senate Committee on Public Works, Committee Print, Serial No. 93–24, USGPO, 1974:

114. Volume 1: *Summary Report.*

115. Volume 2: *Health Effects of Air Pollutants.*

116. Volume 3: *The Relationship of Emissions to Ambient Air Quality.*

117. Volume 4: *The Costs and Benefits of Automobile Emission Control.*

Miscellaneous federal documents

118. *National Conference on Air Pollution Proceedings,* Public Health Service Publication No. 1022, 1963.

119. *Proceedings: The Third National Conference on Air Pollution,* Public Health Service Publication No. 1649, 1967.

120. *Symposium: Air Over Cities,* U.S. Public Health Service, R. A. Taft Sanitary Engineering Center, Technical Report A62–5, 1962. An early summarization of the impact of urbanization on the air.

121. *Federal Register.* Published daily by the Office of the Federal Register, National Archives and Records Service, General Services Administration, as a vehicle for the formal publication of official government rules and regulations; reference to Volume 99, page 9999, is customarily made in the form 99FR9999.

122. *Code of Federal Regulations,* Washington, D.C.: U.S. Government Printing Office. Codifies regulations published in the Federal Register; EPA regulations are in Title 40.

123. *Cumulative Regulatory Effects on the Cost of Automotive Transportation (RECAT), Final Report of the ad hoc Committee,* Office of Science and Technology, Feb. 1972. Includes a number of specific contributions debating the stringency of vehicle regulations; also similar material on auto safety standards.

124. *Minerals Yearbook 1972,* Vol. 1: *Metals, Minerals, and Fuels,* Bureau of Mines, Department of the Interior, 1974. A valuable reference on properties, production, etc., for various fuels and minerals.

TEXTBOOKS

125. John A. Day and Gilbert L. Sternes, *Climate and Weather,* Reading, Mass.: Addison-Wesley, 1970. A readable meteorology text for nonscience majors; emphasizes clouds, precipitation, and forecasting rather than atmospheric mechanics and physics.

126. Frank P. Grad, *Environmental Law: Sources and Problems,* New York: Bender, 1971. Designed as a law-school text; considers both legislative and regulatory matters concerning air and water pollution and other environmental topics, and background material, primarily by quoting legal decisions, laws and regulations, and other public documents.

127. Howard E. Hesketh, *Understanding and Controlling Air Pollution,* Ann Arbor, Mich.: Ann Arbor Science Publishers, 1972. Broad coverage at a relatively detailed technical level.

128. Albert Miller and Jack C. Thompson, *Elements of Meteorology,* Columbus, Ohio: Chas. E. Merrill, 1970. A well-written text emphasizing the mechanics of forces and energy rather than precipitation.

129. Frederick Mosteller and Robert E. K. Rourke, *Sturdy Statistics–Nonparametrics and Order Statistics,* Reading, Mass.: Addison-Wesley, 1973. Considers statistical tools that help provide stable judgments in the face of extreme errors, departures from assumptions, and similar situations; very readable, at a very accessible mathematical level.

130. Arnold W. Reitze, Jr., *Environmental Law,* 2d ed., Vol. 1, Washington, D.C.: North American International, 1972. Covers legal aspects of environmental policy, solid waste, air and water pollution; a general text, it includes more narrative discussion and less case law than a typical law text.

131. Arthur C. Stern, Henry C. Wohlers, Richard W. Boubel, and William P. Lowry, *Fundamentals of Air Pollution,* New York: Academic Press, 1973. A comprehensive but concise technical text with a traditional engineering viewpoint.

132. Samuel J. Williamson, *Fundamentals of Air Pollution,* Reading, Mass.: Addison-Wesley, 1973. A broad text by a physicist, emphasizing the physical science fundamentals of air pollution; especially good on atmospheric physics and meteorology, and aerosol (particle) physics.

ANTHOLOGIES AND MONOGRAPHS

133. Robert U. Ayres and Richard P. McKenna, *Alternatives to the Internal Combustion Engine: Impacts on Environmental Quality,* Baltimore: Resources for the Future/Johns Hopkins University Press, 1972. A technical but readable survey of the engineering and scientific aspects of the internal combustion and various alternative engines.

134. Paul W. Barkley and David W. Seckler, *Economic Growth and Environmental Decay,* New York: Harcourt Brace Jovanovich, 1972. A readable treatise addressing the issue of whether continued economic growth and environmental quality are compatible.

135. Robert Dorfman and Nancy S. Dorfman, eds., *Economics of the Environment,* New York: Norton, 1972. A collection of selected readings, including many well-known authors. Sections on overview, formal analysis, policy issues, causes, and measuring costs and benefits, along with a bibliography and an excellent introduction by the editors.

136. Paul B. Downing, ed., *Air Pollution and the Social Sciences,* New York: Praeger, 1971. Consideration of the role various social sciences can play in various aspects of air pollution; overviews and literature assessments in fields of psychology, political science, economics, and law.

137. Matthew Edel, *Economics and the Environment,* Englewood Cliffs, N.J.: Prentice-Hall, 1973. Considers the economic methods of approaching environmental problems and expresses concern that such problems cannot be solved within our present economic institutions.

138. *Energy and Power; A Scientific American Book,* San Francisco: Freeman, 1972. A reprint of the September 1971 issue of *Scientific American;* articles on various aspects of energy, including the abstract flow of energy through the biosphere and human society.

139. *Federal Reporter,* New York: West. Periodic volumes containing selected cases from federal courts, compiled as a standard legal reference.

140. John C. Fisher, *Energy Crises in Perspective,* New York: Wiley, 1974. Useful and readable background material on fuels and energy questions, especially with respect to electric power generation.

141. A. Myrick Freeman, III, Robert H. Haveman, and Allan V. Kneese, *The Economics of Environmental Policy,* New York: Wiley, 1973. A thorough discussion of environmental problems viewed as economic policy issues; the "market system" of economic theory and why it has failed to correct environmental problems; revisions and new approaches to internalize environmental costs.

142. Clark D. Havighurst, ed., *Air Pollution Control,* Dobbs Ferry, N.Y.: Oceana, 1969; originally published as the Spring 1968 issue of *Law and Contemporary Problems,* Duke University School of Law. An early compendium of articles on all aspects of air pollution, with emphasis on legal and administrative problems.

143. Allen L. Hammond, William D. Metz, and Thomas H. Maugh, III, *Energy and the Future,* AAAS, Washington, 1973. A well-written book by three of the editorial staff of *Science* magazine; excellent survey of energy from fossil fuels, nuclear, and other alternative sources of energy transmission, storage, and conservation.

144. *Inadvertent Climate Modification,* Report of the Study of Man's Impact on Climate, Cambridge, Mass.: M.I.T. University Press, 1971. A major review study, considering geological-scale climatic history, climatic theory and modeling, and man's potential impact, all in as much quantitative detail as possible with present knowledge.

145. Henry D. Jacoby and John D. Steinbrunner, *Clearing the Air: Federal Policy on Automotive Emissions Control,* Cambridge, Mass.: Ballinger, 1973. Analyses of the public policy and decision-making issues involved in the federal legislation of new-car emission standards.

146. Allan V. Kneese and Blair T. Bower, eds., *Environmental Quality Analysis,* Baltimore: Johns Hopkins University Press, 1972. Based on a 1970 conference conducted by Resources for the Future, Inc.; the papers are collected into groups on environment and economic growth, developing plans for environmental management, and designing political and legal institutions. The general level of the work is somewhat abstract and theoretical, though most is accessible and useful.

147. Herbert F. Lund, ed., *Industrial Pollution Control Handbook,* New York: McGraw-Hill, 1971. Chapters on various industries' pollution problems and control approaches; more emphasis on water than air pollution.

148. Gleb Mamantov and W. D. Shults, eds., *Determination of Air Quality,* New York: Plenum, 1972. The proceedings of an April 1971 American Chemical Society Symposium, this volume contains chapters on monitoring, network design, the CHESS program, and a weighting system for

combining pollutant levels into a single index, as well as a number of more technical discussions on specific monitoring and instrumentation topics.

149. *Man's Impact on the Global Environment*, Report of the Study of Critical Environmental Problems, Cambridge, Mass.: M.I.T. University Press, 1970. A major assessment study aimed at identifying critical global problems; considers global climatic and ecological effects of man's activities, global monitoring, and specific human activities.

150. B. M. McCormac, ed., *Introduction to the Scientific Study of Atmospheric Pollution*, Dortrecht, Holland: D. Reidel, 1971. A slightly technical book, with chapters on the pollutants, meteorology (good), health effects, vegetation effects, and air quality surveillance.

151. Dinella Meadows, *et al.*, *The Limits to Growth*, New York: Potomac Assoc./Universe Books, 1972. The well-publicized "Club of Rome" computer-model study conducted at M.I.T.; projections of population, resource use, pollution, etc., led to conclusions of impending catastrophe and to intense debate and rebuttal.

152. Kenneth Noll and Joseph Duncan, eds., *Industrial Air Pollution Control*, Ann Arbor, Mich.: Ann Arbor Science Publishers, 1973. Good discussions of pollution control practices and problems in the electric power, metallurgical, materials handling, chemical, and wood products industries.

James N. Pitts, Jr., and Robert L. Metcalf, eds., *Advances In Environmental Science and Technology*, New York: Wiley. A series of volumes with contributions on current technical issues:

153. Volume 1, 1969: Federal pollution control policy, several photochemistry topics, aeroallergens, and catalytic control of vehicular pollutants.

154. Volume 2, 1971: Air pollution health effects, mercury pollution, motor vehicle emissions, and measurement methods.

155. *Proceedings of the IBM Scientific Computing Symposium on Water and Air Resource Management*, Form No. 320–1953, IBM Data Processing Division, White Plains, New York, 1968. A collection of 20-odd papers on automatic telemetering of data, computerized storage and retrieval systems, and data analysis. More are water- than air-oriented, and some are dated, but many are useful.

156. S. I. Rasool, ed., *Chemistry of the Lower Atmosphere*, New York: Plenum, 1973. Several pertinent, though rather technical, contributions on photochemistry and other atmospheric chemistry topics.

157. Ronald G. Ridker, *Economic Costs of Air Pollution*, New York: Praeger, 1967. One of the better early treatments of air pollution as an economic topic.

158. Sam H. Schurr, ed., *Energy, Economic Growth, and the Environment*, Baltimore: Resources for the Future/Johns Hopkins University Press, 1972. Excellent papers by prominent authors on economic growth and its impact on the environment, environmental-energy production interactions,

and related policy issues. Also includes an extensive appendix of energy production and consumption statistics.

159. Ernest S. Starkman, ed., *Combustion-Generated Air Pollution*, New York: Plenum, 1971. Varied papers, mostly on pollution from motor vehicle fuel combustion; two sections on the fundamental thermodynamics of combustion.

Arthur C. Stern, ed., *Air Pollution*, New York: Academic Press, 1968. The most comprehensive technical reference in the field:

160. Volume I: *Air Pollution and Its Effects*

161. Volume II: *Analysis, Monitoring, and Surveying*

162. Volume III: *Sources of Air Pollution and Their Control*

Werner Strauss, ed., *Air Pollution Control*, New York: Wiley:

163. *Part I*, 1971. Atmospheric dispersion, the control of NO_2, SO_2 and particulate emissions, and internal combustion engines.

164. *Part II*, 1972. Air pollution legislation and literature, radioactive emissions from reactors, and a good chapter by Robinson and Robbins on the global emissions and fate of gaseous pollutants.

165. Shigeto Tsuru, ed., *Proceedings of the International Symposium on Environmental Disruption*, March 1970, International Social Science Council, 1970. A general collection of contributions on various topics; includes a discussion of Pittsburgh's 1950s clean-up campaign and a good discussion of air pollution law by Prof. J. L. Sax.

166. *United States Laws*, Washington, D.C.: U. S. Government Printing Office. Periodic compilation of public laws as passed in each congressional session.

167. *United States Code*, New York: West. Periodic compilation of United States laws as most recently amended or modified; compiled as a standard legal reference.

168. Albert E. Utton and Daniel H. Henning, *Environmental Policy: Concepts and International Implications*, New York: Praeger, 1973. Originally published in the July 1971 and April 1972 issues of *Natural Resources Journal*, University of New Mexico School of Law. A good collection of papers on the national and international political science aspects of environmental protection.

Mosby, 1973. A relatively nontechnical discussion of pollutants and health
169. George L. Waldbott, *Health Effects of Environmental Pollutants,* St. Louis: effects, well illustrated with scanning electron micrographs.

JOURNALS

170. *Archives of Environmental Health*, American Medical Association, 535 North Dearborn Street, Chicago, Illinois 60610. An official AMA publication, the *Archives* frequently contains articles on air pollution health effects.

171. *Atmospheric Environment,* Pergamon Press, Headington Hill Hall, Oxford OX3 OBW, England. A somewhat technical journal; the best source for studies of atmospheric physics, etc., but includes scientific air pollution work.

172. *Environment,* Scientists' Institute for Public Information, 438 N. Skinker Blvd., St. Louis, Missouri 63130. Published by a public-interest scientific group; has a strong antipollution, environmentalist viewpoint on topics of air and water pollution, resource conservation, and nuclear hazards.

173. *Environmental Science & Technology,* American Chemical Society, 1155 16th Street N.W., Washington, D.C. 20036. Both general-interest articles and technical papers; best source for analytical methodology papers and good for timely awareness of current events.

174. *Journal of the Air Pollution Control Association,* Air Pollution Control Association, 4400 Fifth Avenue, Pittsburgh, Pa. 15213. APCA is the primary technical organization devoted to air pollution, and its *Journal* is the best source for specific material on air pollution engineering and control.

175. *Science,* American Association for the Advancement of Science, 1515 Massachusetts Ave. N.W., Washington, D.C. 20005. The principal general science journal in the United States, *Science* occasionally contains both general and fairly technical articles on air pollution, but is more valuable for its in-depth coverage of the public policy aspects of major environmental decisions and the progress of important bills in Congress.

176. *Science News,* Science Service, Inc., 1719 N Street N.W., Washington, D.C. 20036. A weekly current-awareness magazine, *Science News* provides broad up-to-date coverage of current events in the environmental fields as well as other scientific areas.

ARTICLES

177. "Air Pollution Control Hits Red Tape," *ES&T* 4 (Oct. 1970):802–804.

178. Lydon R. Babcock, "A Combined Pollution Index for Measurement of Total Air Pollution," *JAPCA* 20 (Oct. 1970):653–659.

179. R. J. Bazell, "Lead Poisoning: Zoo Animals May Be the First Victims," *Science* 173 (9 July 1971):129–131.

180. "Beryllium—Hazardous Air Pollutant," *ES&T* 5 (July 1971):584–585.

181. Henry C. Bramer, "Pollution Control in the Steel Industry," *ES&T* 5 (Oct. 1971):1004–1008.

182. Irwin M. Brodo, "Lichen Growth and Cities: A Study on Long Island, New York," *Bryologist* 69 (1966):427–449. One of a number of studies using lichens as indicators or monitors of the extent of pollution beyond cities.

183. J. R. Brough and W. A. Carter, "Air Pollution Control of an Electric Furnace Steelmaking Shop," *JAPCA* 22 (March 1972):167–171.

184. Luther J. Carter, "Environmental Law (I): Maturing Field for Lawyers and Scientists," *Science* 179 (23 March 1973):1205–1209.

185. ———, "Environmental Law (II): A Strategic Weapon Against Degradation?" *Science* 179 (30 March 1973) :1310, 1350.

186. S. A. Changnon, "The LaPorte Weather Anomaly—Fact or Fiction?" *Bulletin American Meteorological Society* 49 (1968) :4.

187. ———, "Recent Studies of Urban Effects on Precipitation in the United States," *Bulletin American Meteorological Society* 50 (June 1969) :411–421.

188. "Citizens Gain Ground in Right to Sue," *ES&T* 5 (July 1971) :586–587.

189. "Courts Say NEPA Is a Law for All People," *ES&T* 6 (March 1972:209–211.

190. Janice Crossland, "Cars, Fuel, and Pollution," *Environment* 16, 2 (March 1974) :15, 27. Discusses alternative engines in the light of both pollution problems and the energy crisis; chastizes the auto industry for failing to pursue such alternatives.

191. "Equity and the Eco System: Can Injunctions Clear the Air?" *Michigan Law Review* 68 (1970) :1254–1293.

192. (William Forester), "States Doubt Clean Air Achievement," *ES&T* 8, 6 (June 1974) :498–505. State-by-state survey of likelihood of meeting National Ambient Air Quality Standards by 1975 or 1977 deadlines.

193. (Lena C. Gibney), "Catalytic Converters: An Answer from Technology," *ES&T* 8, 9 (Sept. 1974) :793–799. Summarizes the control approaches adopted by manufacturers for 1975 vehicles, discussing in particular catalytic converters, the most common choice.

194. Robert Gillette, "National Environmental Policy Act: Signs of Backlash are Evident," *Science* 176 (7 April 1972) :30–33.

195. ———, "National Environmental Policy Act: How Well Is It Working?" *Science* 176 (14 April 1972) :146–150.

196. Richard H. Gilluly, "A Home on a Range for a Vast Industry," *Science News* 101 (4 March 1972) :156–158.

197. Steven K. Hall, "Lead Pollution and Poisoning," *ES&T* 6 (Jan. 1972) :31–35.

198. Edward B. Hanf, "A Guide to Scrubber Selection," *ES&T* 4 (February 1970) :110–116.

199. Earl T. Hayes, "Paying for New Car Emission Controls," *ES&T* 8, 9 (Sept. 1974) :807–809. Summarizes the arguments against the federal new-car emission standards in terms of cost and reduced fuel economy.

200. Joel L. Horowitz, "Transportation Controls Are Really Needed in the Air Cleanup Fight," *ES&T* 8, 9 (Sept. 1974) :800–805. Summarizes types of transportation control measures available and which are being applied in each of various urban areas requiring a transportation control plan.

201. Frank Kreith, "Lack of Impact," *Environment* 15 (Jan./Feb. 1973) :26–33.

202. Emanuel Landau, Raymond Smith, and David A. Lynn, "Carbon Monoxide and Lead—An Environmental Appraisal," *Journal APCA* 19(Sept. 1969): 684–689.

203. Lester Lave and Eugene Seskin, "Air Pollution and Human Health," *Science* 169(1970):723–732.

204. J. Lear, "The Home-Brewed Thunderstorms of LaPorte, Indiana," *Saturday Review,* 6 April 1968, pp. 53–55.

205. Gene E. Likens and F. Herbert Bormann, "Acid Rain: A Serious Regional Environmental Problem," *Science* 184(14 June 1974):1176–1179. A technical article on acid rain in the New York–New England area.

206. Gene E. Likens, F. Herbert Bormann, and Noye M. Johnson, "Acid Rain," *Environment* 14, 2(March 1972):33–40. A nontechnical article on acid rain both in the United States and in northern Europe.

207. T. H. Maugh, "Air Pollution Instrumentation: A Trend Toward Physical Methods," *Science* 177(25 August 1972):685–687.

208. "Mercury in the Air," *Environment* 13, 4(March 1971):24, 33.

209. "Metals Focus Shifts to Cadmium," *ES&T* 5(Sept. 1971):754–755.

210. I. Michelson and B. Tourin, *(U.S.) Public Health Report* 81, 6(1966): 505.

211. Gerald J. Nehls and Gerald G. Akland, "Procedures for Handling Aerometric Data," *JAPCA* 23(March 1973):180–184.

212. G. J. Nehls, D. H. Fair, and J. Clements, "National Air Data Bank Open for Business," *ES&T* 4(Nov. 1970):902–905.

213. S. Oden, "Nederbordens forsurning-ett generellt hot mot ekosytemem," in Mysterud, ed., *Forurensning og biologisk miljovern,* Oslo: Universitetsforlaget, 1971.

214. Sabert Oglesby, Jr., "Electrostatic Precipitators Tackle Air Pollutants," *ES&T* 5(Sept. 1971):766–770.

215. James H. Onnen, "Wet Scrubbers Tackle Pollution," *ES&T* 6(Nov. 1972):994–998.

216. D. Rush, J. C. Russell, and R. E. Iverson, "Air Pollution Abatement on Primary Aluminum Potlines: Effectiveness and Cost," *JAPCA* 23(Feb. 1973):98–104.

217. Joseph L. Sax, "Environment in the Courtroom," *Saturday Review* (3 Oct. 1970):55–57.

218. ———, "The Public Trust Doctrine in Natural Resources Law: Effective Judicial Intervention," *Michigan Law Review* 68(Jan. 1970):473–566.

219. Henry A. Schroeder, "A Sensible Look at Air Pollution by Metals," *Arch. Env. Health* 21(Dec. 1970):798–806.

220. ———, "Metals in the Air," *Environment* 13, 8(Oct. 1971):18, 32. A less technical version of [219].

221. I. J. Selikoff, "Asbestos," *Environment* 11, 2 (March 1969). Also reprinted in [14].

222. Carl M. Shy and John F. Finklea, "Air Pollution Affects Community Health," *ES&T* 7, 3 (March 1973) : 204–208.

223. David Sive, "Securing, Examining, and Cross-Examining Expert Witnesses in Environmental Cases," *Michigan Law Review* 68 (1970) : 1175. Also reprinted in [11] without legal footnotes.

224. A. V. Slack, "Removing SO_2 from Stack Gases," *ES&T* 7 (Feb. 1973) : 110–119.

225. R. Spirtas and H. J. Levin, "Patterns and Trends in Levels of Suspended Particulate Matter," *JAPCA* 21 (June 1971) : 329–333.

226. Arthur M. Squires, "Clean Power From Coal," *Science* 169 (28 August 1970) : 821–828.

227. A. C. Stern, "Strengthening the Clean Air Act," *JAPCA* 23, 12 (Dec. 1973) : 1019–1022. Considers the problems arising since 1970 and recommends corrective amendments.

228. Richard D. Stewart, *et al.*, "Carboxyhemoglobin Levels in American Blood Donors," *JAMA* 229, 9 (26 August 1974) : 1187–1195.

229. Kenneth R. Stunkel, "New Hope In Japan," *Environment* 16, 8 (Oct. 1974) : 18–20. Describes how recent pollution negligence cases in Japan have shifted the burden of proof onto the pollution source rather than the victim.

GLOSSARY

Adiabatic lapse rate   A particular value of lapse rate corresponding to the rate at which a rising parcel of air would change temperature if it did not exchange any heat with the surrounding air.

Absorbed   Taken up, assimilated, into the interior of a material, as opposed to being adsorbed onto the surface of the material.

Adsorbed   Taken up onto the surface of a material, as opposed to being absorbed into the interior.

Anticyclone   A weather system circulating clockwise (in the Northern Hemisphere) about a high-pressure center; generally fair-weather systems, but can stagnate over an area to cause elevated pollutant levels.

Atom   The smallest fragment of matter that maintains the identity of one of the chemical elements, e.g., a single atom of sulfur.

Baghouse   A fabric filter installation, a particulate control device that filters the stack gas through fabric bags.

Biosphere   The aggregate of the various portions of the earth that sustain on-going life and intertwined ecological systems.

Btu   British thermal unit, a unit of energy equivalent to 252 calories, 0.293 watt-hours, or 1054.8 joules.

Carcinogen   A substance capable of causing cancer formation.

Chemiluminescence   A measurement principle based on the emission of minute amounts of light during certain chemical reactions.

Cellulose   A complex carbohydrate substance, the main constituent of all plant tissues and fibers.

Climatology   The study of climate, or meteorology, over a very long time scale.

Combustion   Burning; the chemical reaction of a substance with oxygen, usually from air.

Concentration   The amount of one substance contained in a unit volume of another substance, e.g., the mass or volume of a pollutant in a unit volume of air.

Cosmic rays   Radiation of various types that originates beyond the atmosphere.

Cupola   A cylindrical type of melting furnace used for melting scrap metal.

Cyclone   A weather system circulating counterclockwise (in the Northern Hemisphere) about a low-pressure center; in the extreme, cyclone or tornado in the lay sense.

Density   Mass per unit volume of a substance, e.g., grams per cubic centimeter.

Deuterium   An isotope of hydrogen having a neutron in the nucleus in addition to the normal single proton.

Distillate fuel oil   The portion of crude oil distilled away after the lighter portions used in gasoline; distillate oil, used as a fuel by small fuel-burning installations, is cleaner and more expensive than residual fuel oil.

Diurnal   Pertaining to the 24-hour cycle of day and night.

Dust devil   A small, transient whirlwind that can pick up and carry along leaves and similar debris.

Elastomer   An elastic organic material, either a natural rubber or a synthetic compound.

Emission standard   A standard set for a pollution source that places a specific limit on the quantity of emissions permitted.

Episode   A short-term occurrence of severe air pollution caused by stagnation or other adverse meteorological conditions.

Equipment standards   A standard set for a pollution source that requires the use of a certain type of equipment.

Fossil fuels   Fuels, such as coal, oil, and natural gas, that were formed from the fossilized remains of prehistoric organisms.

Free radical   An atom or molecule that has an unpaired electron that actively seeks to react with another electron.

Heat island   An area of elevated temperatures associated with an urban area, caused by increased absorption and retention of solar energy by the physical environment of the city.

Hygroscopic   Having the property of attracting moisture from the atmosphere.

Inversion   A condition of the vertical temperature profile wherein temperature increases, rather than decreases, with height.

Ion   An atom or molecule that has either gained one or more extra electrons (negatively charged ion) or lost electrons (positive ion).

Isotope   One of two or more types of atoms of the same element that have the same number of protons in the nucleus, but different numbers of neutrons.

Lachrymator   A substance capable of causing the eyes to tear, water, or become irritated.

Lapse rate   The rate at which the temperature of the air changes (usually decreases) with height.

Lichen   Simple plants consisting of a fungus and an algae living in close association; form a blue or gray green crusty growth on rocks and trees.

Lignin   A complex noncarbohydrate constituent of woody plant tissue that binds together and supports the cellulose fibers.

London smog   The type of air pollution generally found in London and other large coal-burning industrial cities, consisting primarily of particulate matter and sulfur oxides.

Los Angeles smog   *See* Photochemical smog.

Microgram   A unit of mass equivalent to one millionth of a gram, or about one thirty-millionth of an ounce.

Micron   A unit of length, equivalent to one millionth of a meter.

Mixing depth   The depth of the lowest layer of the atmosphere, through which pollutants are mixed and diluted.

Molecule   The smallest fragment of a chemical compound that maintains the identity of the compound, e.g., a single molecule of sulfur dioxide, a compound of one sulfur and two oxygen atoms.

Nanogram   A unit of mass equivalent to 10^{-9} grams, or one thousandth of a microgram.

Necrotic collapse   The death and subsequent physical collapse of a cell.

Oxidation   A type of chemical reaction typified by combustion, wherein oxygen atoms are combined with another element.

Ppm   Parts per million, a ratio measure of volume concentration, i.e., the number of parts of pollutant in a million parts of air.

Photochemical   Pertaining to chemical reactions that utilize light to provide the needed energy.

Photochemical smog   The type of air pollution typically found in Los Angeles, characterized by an oxidizing atmosphere with high ambient levels of oxidants.

Photosynthesis   The biochemical process by which green plants form organic material using energy from the sun.

Plasmolysis   Shrinking of cells due to loss of water through the cell walls.

Pollutant rose   A graphical presentation in which the concentrations of a pollutant associated with winds from various compass points are represented by bars of different lengths extending in the various directions.

Pressure   The force applied per unit area of surface, e.g., pounds per square inch.

Primary pollutant   A pollutant emitted into the air directly from a source.

Proteinuria   The abnormal excretion of protein in the urine.

Pyrites   Metallic sulfide compounds, often the source of the sulfur in coals.

Radiant energy   Energy transmitted by electromagnetic radiation, e.g., light, heat, radio waves.

Radiational cooling   The cooling of the earth's surface on clear nights as radiant energy from the earth is lost into space in the absence of cloud cover.

Residual fuel oil   That heavy, thick portion of crude oil that is left after lighter, more desirable portions are distilled away; used as a fuel by large installations with relatively sophisticated burners.

Retrofit   Used to describe a pollution control device retroactively fitted into an existing automobile, combustion operation, or other source; retrofitted control devices are more costly than similar controls on new sources.

Scrubber   A particulate control device that operates by mixing or spraying water through the stack gas to collect the particles.

Secondary pollutants   A pollutant formed in the air from other substances, as opposed to being emitted directly from sources.

Sinks   In a context of global dispersion, those locations or substances (e.g., oceans or plant matter) that can accept and absorb large amounts of a substance without significantly reducing their ability to absorb more (as a kitchen sink accepts water to be drained away).

Smelter   A processing plant where a metal such as zinc or lead is purified from its ore by heating and roasting the ore.

Smog   Originally, a contraction of smoke and fog, the major components of London's pollution problem.

Stagnation   Meteorological situation occurring when a large air mass slows its forward movement and remains stagnant over an area, permitting pollutants to accumulate to abnormal levels.

Stoichiometric point   The point in the balance between amounts of different chemicals in a reaction where the quantities are precisely those needed to react, without any amount of any reactant left over.

Synergism   Phenomenon wherein two pollutants acting simultaneously have an effect greater than the sum of their separate effects.

Tetraethyl lead   An organic lead compound used as an antiknock additive in gasoline.

Thermal convection   Motion in an air mass caused by differential heating, with warm air rising in one location, to be replaced by cooler air descending at another location.

Thermal pollution   The discharge of waste heat to a body of water beyond the water's capacity to absorb it without a serious temperature rise.

Threshold level   A level of pollutant concentration below which no effect occurs.

Ultraviolet light   Electromagnetic radiation with energy and wavelength just beyond the violet end of the range of visible light.

Wind roses   A graphical presentation in which the frequency of wind from various compass points is represented by bars of different lengths extending in the various directions.

INDEX

(Italic numerals indicate pages on which tables or figures appear.)

Abatement authority, 312–314
Absenteeism, studies of, 84, 98
Absorption method of separating gases, 159, 205–206, 220
Acidity of precipitation, 134–*135*
"An Act to Provide Research and Technical Assistance Relating to Air Pollution Control" (1955), 310
Acute effects of exposure, 83
Adiabatic lapse rate, *30*–32
Adsorption method for separating gases, 159–160, 205
Aerodynamic equivalent diameter, 43
Afterburner, 225, 233, 248
Agencies, pollution control (*See also* Governmental control programs)
  activities of, 307–308
  authority and responsibility of, 277–278
  organization, typical, *292*
  state and local, functions of, 291–299
  strategy, 324–341
Air (*See also* Atmosphere)
  composition of dry, *3*
  uses of, 2
Air flow rate, 153
Air-fuel ratio, in internal combustion engine, 239, 248–250, 253
  pollutant emissions related to, *249*
Air intake modifications, 255, 257
"Air movers," 153
Air Pollution Control Office (APCO)
  (*See* Environmental Protection Agency)
Air Pollution Division of State Services Bureau, 311
Air pollution problem, 2–14
  definition of, 9–10
  effects of, 12–13
  history of, 3–9
  major pollutants, 10–12
  scope of topic, 14
  sources of pollutants, 13–14
Air Pollution Training Institute, 302
Air Quality Act (1967), 338
Air Quality Control Regions (AQCRs), 304, 315–316, 329, 331, 333
Air quality criteria, 314–317, 327–328
  documents, 304, 312, 315
Air quality goals, 327
Air quality standards, 327–329 (*See also* Standards)
Air quality standards approach, 304–305, 314–318
Aircraft, 242, 244
Airways resistance, 95–97
Alaska, 223, 283
Alerts, emergency, 296–299
Algae, 131
Aluminum, 71n
  primary industries, 231
  smelters, 136
Aluminum oxides, 73, 231
Alveoli, 87–88, 90–91, 93, 100, 114–115
  pulmonary capillaries intertwining with, *101*

Ambient air quality, 153, 258–259, 295

Ammonia, 89

Ammonium, 71, 221

Analysis, of data, 189–194
  of gases, 160–163
  of particulate pollution, 157–159

Andersen impactor, *158*

Anderson-Rockwell Environmental Protection Act, 284

Anemia, 108

Animals, experimentational studies on, 85, 95, 105, 114
  pollution affecting, 71, 136–138, 147

Antagonism of particles and gases, 96

Anthracite coal, 208–210, *209, 212,* 218

Anticyclone, 27–34

Antiknock additives, 71, 241, 253–254, 306, 347

Appalachia, 47, 210

Appropriations Committee, congressional, 340

"Area sources," 296

Arsenic, 113–114

Arsenic compounds (As), 136–137

Arsenic poisoning, 136–137

Arsenic trioxide, 113

Asbestos, health effects of, 95, 110–111
  as pollutant, 71–73, 305

"Asbestos bodies," 110

Asbestosis, 95, 110, 111

Ash content of a fuel, 209

Asphalt batching, 230

Aswan High Dam, 223

Athletic performance, reduction in, 105–106

Atlantic high, 24, 26, 35

Atmosphere, air pollution climatology, 36
  composition of dry, *3*
  functions of, 18
  global temperature imbalances, *20*
  motion, 21–28
    scales of, *23*–28
  physical nature of, 18–*19*
  radiation and heat balance, 19–21
  vertical structure of, *19*
  vertical temperature inversions, 29–35

Atomic age, 5

Atomic Energy Commission, 223

Atomic fission, 223

Atomic power, 222–223

Automatic data processing systems, 180

Automatic sampler-analyzers, 154–155, 160, 162–163, 165–173, *166,* 178–179, 181, *191*

Automobiles (*See also* Mobile sources of air pollution)
  alternative power plants, 256–258
  alternatives to conventional internal combustion engine, 254–258
  controlling conventional internal combustion engine emissions, 246–254
  emission quantities, 243–245
  performance and emissions related to air-fuel ratio, *249*
  as pollution source, 7, 11, 52–53, 62, 239–241

Back-scatter effect, 133

"Bag sampling," 160, 163

Baghouse, 202–*203,* 205, 230

Basic oxygen process of refining iron, 229

Bauxite, 231

Beehive ovens, 229

Belgium, episode in, 4, 50, 98, 136

Benzene, 104

Benzene-soluble organic matter, 72

Benzo-a-pyrene, concentrations, *73*
  health effects of, 112
  molecular structure, *72*
  volatility of fuel and, 210

Bermuda high, 24, 26–27

Berylliosis, 111

Beryllium, health effects of, 95, 111
  as pollutant, 71, 305

Bessemer converter, 229

Beta absorption method, 172

Bethesda, Maryland, 311

Biochemical respiration, 139

Biosphere (*See also* Ecological effects of air pollution)
atmospheric function and, 18
carbon dioxide role in, 131
defined, 13

Bishop, Maryland, 313

Bishop Processing Company, 313

Bituminous coal, 208–210, *209*, *212*, 221

Blast furnace, 229

Blowby emissions, 240, 247, 256

"Body burdens" of a pollutant, 82, 109

Boston, 260

Bottled gas, 254

Brain, pollution affecting, 100–102, 108

Breeder reactors, 222–223

Bromine, 71*n*

Bronchi, 87, 96, 115

Bronchial carcinoma, 93–*94*

Bronchioles, 87, 90

Bronchitis, chronic, 91–93, 98
mild, 113

Bubbler, 160–161, 163, 220, 303

Bureau of Mines, 310, 339

Buses, 242, 260

By-product coke ovens, 229

Cadmium, health effects of, 95, 114
as heavy metal, 134
as pollutant, 71

Cadmium oxide, 114

Calcium, 73, 221

California, climate and wind pattern, 25
controlling pollution, 8, 246, 250–251, 275, 290, 305, 309, 318, 339
geothermal steam plant in, 224

California Agriculture Department, 147

California Institute of Technology, 6

California Motor Vehicle Pollution Control Board, 246–247

Calories, defined, 20*n*

Canada, 214

Cancer, 93–*94*, 98, 112–114, *113* (*See also* Carcinogens)

Car pooling, 8

Carbon, 214–215

Carbon dioxide (CO_2), atmospheric function and, 18
ecological effects of, 131–134
from fossil fuels, 10
interfering, 170
sources, 131, 215

Carbon monoxide (CO), controlling emissions of, *248*–255, 257, 317
criteria document, 315
diurnal variations in levels of, *54*
emissions of, annual, *53*
emissions from motor vehicles, trend in, *252*
health effects of, 11, 13, 83, 100–103, 116
as major pollutant, 11
measuring, 163, 165, 169–170
from mobile sources, 13, 238, 240–243
properties and prevalence of, 52–55
sources and sinks, 130–131
from stationary sources, *198*, 205, *208*, 213, 215–216, 222, *225*, 229, 232–233

Carboxyhemoglobin (COHb), 100–103
level related to test results, *103*

Carburetor, 239–240, 251, 253

Carcinogens, 72, 95, 111–114

"Carrier" gas, 171

Cars (*See* Automobiles)

Cascade impactor, 157–*158*

Catalytic converter, 253–255

Catalytic cracking, 232

Causes of pollution (*See also* pollutants by name)
fuel combustion, 207–224
industrial processes, 227–233
mobile sources, 238–*245*
solid-waste disposal, 224–227

Cellulose, 232

Cement industry, 230

Cerium, 71*n*

Cesium, 71n
Changnon, Stanley A., Jr., 128
Charcoal, activated, 159, 205, 251
Chattanooga, 104
Chemiluminescence, 58, 169
CHESS (Community Health and Environment Surveillance System), 86
Chicago, 4, 27, 260, 273
Chlorine, 71n
Chlorine gas, 269
Chlorophyll, 139
Chlorosis, 139–140
Choking mechanism, 89
Chromatography, 171
Chronic bronchitis, 91–93
Chronic effects of exposure, 83, 85
Chrysotile, 73
Cilia, 90, 96–97
Cincinnati, 186, 191, 194, 273
Circulations, global air, 24
    horizontal motions of air and, 21–28
    planetary, 24–26
Citizen-suit legislation, 284–285
Citizen suits, 279–285
Class-action suits, 281–282
"Classic episode," (See also Episodes)
    defined, 4
    meteorological conditions associated with, 28, 32
Clean Air Act, England's, 8
Clean Air Act, United States, 11, 148, 227, 253, 299–307, 300–301, 312, 327, 329, 331, 341
Clerical data-processing operations, 181–182
Cleveland, 260
Climate, air pollution and, 36
    defined, 36
    wind patterns and, 25
Climatology, air pollution, 36
Clinical studies, 84
Clinton, Massachusetts, 267
Cloudiness, 133
Coal, composition and characteristics, 209
    deposits in United States, 211

equipment for burning, 143, 214–217
    as pollution source, 3, 13, 47, 51, 112–114, 208–212
    reserves, distribution of, by sulfur content, 212
    smoke-control problem, 5
Coal cleaning, 230
Coal furnace, hand-fired, 214–215, 217
Coal gasification processes, 222
Coal lobby, 315
Coal mine safety regulations, 330
Coding data, 182–183
Coefficient of haze (COH), 172
Coke, 212, 218, 228–229, 233
Colds, common, 91, 98
Colorado, 214
Colorimetry and colorimetric method, 161–163, 167
Combustion method of gaseous pollutant removal, 205
Combustion techniques, alternative, 222 (See also Fuel combustion)
Commerce Department, United States, 310
Common law, changing, 279, 282–285
    defined, 266
    police power of state and, 274
    traditional, remedies for air pollution, 266–272
Competitiveness of society, 347
Complexity of pollution problem, 347–348
Compliance, 333, 338
Compression ratios, 253
Concentrations of pollution, atmospheric movement and, 23, 29
    of benzo-a-pyrene, 73
    of carbon monoxide, diurnal variations in, 54
    of dustfall, 46
    of oxidants, 65, 68
    of particulate pollution, 48
    stagnation increasing, 68
    standards, 328
    of sulfur dioxide and particulates, 51–52
Condensation nuclei, 128

Conductometric method for sulfur dioxide, 162, 168
Conference-hearing approach, 305, 312–314, 318
Congress, 148, 247, 251–254, 283–284, 300, 306, 310–312, 330, 338, 340
Constitution, United States, 274, 277, 283, 300, 338
Construction permit, 291
Contamination, differentiated from pollution, 10
Continuous instruments, 165, 180
Control of air pollution (*See also* Governmental control programs)
  basic approaches to, 198–206
  citizen suits, 279–285
  exhaust emissions, *248*–251
  governmental programs, 272–279, 290–318
  legal basis for, 266–285
  from mobile sources, 246–254
  particulate, from fuel combustion, 217–218
  particulate, from solid-waste incineration, 225–227
  strategy, 324–341
  sulfur dioxide, from fuel combustion, 219–221
Control strategy, 324–341
  degree of control, 325–328
  financing, 335–337
  organizing, 337–341
  sources to be controlled, 328–333
  timing of, 333–335
Control technology documents, 304, 315
Cooking, 207
Copper, corrosion of, 145
  as heavy metal, 134
  smelting, 231
Corona discharge, 204–205
Corrosion caused by pollution, 144–145
Cosmic rays, upper atmosphere and, 18
Cost-benefit analysis, 324, *326* (*See also* Economic effects of air pollution)

"Cost of clean air," 142–143, 148
"Cost of dirty air," 142–143, 147
Costs, economic (*See* Economic effects of air pollution)
Cough, chronic, 92
  mechanism, 90
Council on Environmental Quality, 283
Country grain elevators, 230
Crankcase, 239–240, 246–247
Criteria of air quality, 304, 312, 314–317, 327–328
Crude oil, 212–214
Cryolite, 231
Cupola and cupola emissions, 233
Cyclone, 27
Cyclone particle separator, 201–205, *202*, 228
Cylinder, design changes in, 255

Damage(s), economic caused by air pollution, 142–*148*
  legal proof of, 267
  monetary, awarded to plaintiff, 272
Data analysis, 189–194
Data processing, 179–189
Day, Mr. Justice, 273
DDT, 129
DeBlois v. *Bowers,* 267–271
Decision functions of agency, 308–309, 324–341
Delaware, 313
Depletion allowances, oil and gas, 330
Dermatitis, 113–114
Desulfurization processes, for flue gas, 220
  for fuel, 221–222
Deterioration of substances, caused by pollution, 144–147
Detroit Municipal Smoke Abatement Ordinance, 275
Deuterium isotope of hydrogen, 223
Dichlorosulfitromercurate, 161
Diesel, engine, 241–242, 244, 246
  railway locomotives, 143
Diffusion equation, meteorological, *200*
Dispersion, formula, *200*, 296

global, 129–131
models, 295–296, 332
tall stack, 199–201
Dispersive spectroscopic technique,
    169
Distillate fuel oil, 213
Diurnal variation patterns, *54, 66–67,*
    190, 193
Donora (Pennsylvania) episode, 6,
    50, 98, 309
Dosage of pollutant, defined, 83
Dose-response curve, 82–83
Driving patterns, *243–244*
"Due process of law," 274, 277
Dust devils, 23, 28
Dustfall, ecological effects of, 127
    economic effects of, 143
    levels, downward trend in, *44*
    measurement, 152, 154
    as particulate pollution, 11,
        44–45
Dustfall jar, 44, 154–155
Duststorms, 10
Dynamometer, 244

Ecological effects of air pollution, 13,
    124–142
    acidity of precipitation, 134–*135*
    on animals, 136–138
    global balance, sources and sinks,
        129–131
    heavy metals, 134–136
    on micro-organisms, 141–142
    radiation balance, carbon dioxide,
        particulates and, 131–134
    urban atmosphere, 124–128, *127*
    on vegetation, 138–141
    weather, regional, 128–129
Economic effects of air pollution, 13,
    45, 71, 142–148
    corrosion and materials damage,
        144–146
    costs, totalling, 147–*148*
    smoke, soot, and soiling, 143–144
Economic effects of pollution control,
    costs and benefits relationship,
        326

financing control, 335–337
of smoke-control laws, 5
Economic Report to Congress, EPA's
    (1971), 336
Economics, control strategy and,
    324–341
Economy of United States, form of,
    344–345
Edema, pulmonary, 93, 95, 104
Effluent charges, 336–337
Effluent cleaning, 198, 201–205
Effluent dispersal, 198–201
Eisenhower, Dwight D., 312
Elastomers, air pollution affecting, 146
Electric arc furnace, 229
Electric power lobby, 315
Electric power plants, in emergency
    action, 298
    during energy crisis, 8, 317
    fuel combustion, 199, *207–208,* 221,
        330–331
    as pollution source, 46, 62, 201
    uranium-processing industry and, 5
Electromagnetic spectrum, *132*
Electrostatic precipitators, 202, 204–
    205, 217, 230, 293
Elevation, mountain-valley wind and,
    28
Emergency action plan, 296–299, *297*
Emission factor, defined, 295
Emission standards, 293–294, 328–329
Emissions, of carbon monoxide, *53*
    control (*See* Control of air pollu-
        tion)
    exhaust standards, federal, *248*
    of hydrocarbons, *64*
    inventories, 294–296
    from mobile sources, *198,* 238–261,
        243–244
    of nitrogen oxides, *63*
    of particulate matter, *47*
    from stationary fuel combustion
        sources, *207*
    from stationary sources, *198*–233
    of sulfur oxides, *51*
Emphysema, pulmonary, 91–93, 104,
    114

Energy, consumption, 346
crisis, environmental decisions and, 8, 220–221, 261, 317
national policy on, 330
sources, 208, 222–224
Energy content of a fuel, 209
England (*See* United Kingdom)
English Factory Act, 269
Environment, physical, effects of air pollution on, 124–142
Environmental Defense Fund, 281
Environmental law, 279–285, 337
Environmental Protection Agency (EPA), control strategy, 329, 335
on economic aspects of pollution, 148, 336
on emissions from mobile sources, 253–254
establishing standards for major pollutants, 11, 56, 117–*118*, 258–259
functions, 299–307, 312–313
on industrial emissions, 227–*228*
minor pollutants emphasized by, 71
organization of, 6, 8, 300, 317, 339–341
reference methods, 155, 157, 161, 168–170, 172
SAROAD codes, 183
suits against, 284–285
Enzyme-interference mechanism, 108
Epidemiological studies, 84
Epidermal cells of plants, 138
Episodes, air pollution, defining, 7
in Donora, Pennsylvania, 6, 50, 98, 309
emergency control plan, 296–299
health effects of, 97–98
ingredients in, 11, 42, 50
in London, 7, 50, 98, 136
meteorological conditions associated with, 28, 32, 35
in Meuse River valley, 4, 50, 98, 136
in Poza Rica, Mexico, 115
worldwide (1962), 8
Epithelium, 88, 93

"Equal protection under the law," 274
Equator, heat energy from, 20–21, 24, 26
Equipment standards, 293, 328
Ethylene, 141, 169
Europe, acidity of precipitation, *135*
air pollution episode in, 8
Europium, 71*n*
Evaporative emission from fuel system, 240, 251
Evelyn, John, 3, 218
Exhaust emissions, 7, 109, 246 (*See also* Mobile sources of air pollution)
air-fuel ratio related to, *249*
controlling, *248*–251
standards, federal, *248*
Exhaust system, 239–240
Experimental studies, 85
External diseconomy, 336
Extreme values, 185, 187–189, *188*
Eye irritation, 59, 61–62, 104–106, 116
oxident levels and, *107*

Fay v. *Whitman*, 270
Federal Energy Administration, 330
Federal government air pollution functions, 299–307
cooperating with state, 304–305
motor vehicle emissions regulation, 305
operating budget support, 303–304
research, training, and technical assistance, 302–303
Federal government air pollution program (*See* Governmental control programs)
Federal Power Commission, 283, 330
Felt processing, 112*n*
Fibrosis, pulmonary, 95, 104, 114
Filter, fabric, 202–*203*, 205
Filtration, 155, 201–202
Financial support of control agencies, 303–304, 312, 335–337
Finite-difference formulae, 193
First-generation exhaust standard, 250

Fixed carbon, 209

Flagged values, verification of, 185, 187–189, *188*

Flame ionization detection (FID), 170–172

Florida, 285

Flue-fed incinerator, *225–226*

Fluorides (F), 71, 73–74, 136–137, 141, 231

Fluorosis, 136

Fly ash, 42, 44, 217–218

Fog, 125

Food chain or cycle, *137*–139

Ford Motor Company, 256

Forecast-level actions, 298

Forest fires, 10

Formaldehyde, 161

Fossil fuels, 133, 208–214
  alternatives to, 222–224

Foundries, 52

Four-stroke Otto cycle, 238–*239, 255*

Fourteenth Amendment to United States Constitution, 274

Free enterprise, 345–347

"Free goods," 336

Free radical reactions, 59*n*, 104

Freon, 257

Frequency distribution, 190, *192*–193

Friction, atmospheric motion and, 27–28

Frontal inversions, *34*

Fuel-burning devices, 143, 214–*217*, *215*

Fuel combustion, economic cost of, 143–144
  emissions from stationary sources, 207–224
  as pollution source, 13, 42, 44, 46, 50, 62, *198*

Fuel desulfurization, 221–222

Fuel economy, 143

Fuel injection systems, 255

Fuel oil, 6, 8, 13, 51, 208, 212–213

Fuels, rocket, 111

Fumigation, 33

Fusion reactors, 223

Gas chromatographic techniques, 159, 163, 171–172

Gas turbine engine, 241–243, *242,* 256–257

Gaseous hydrocarbon fuel, 254–255

Gaseous pollutants, concentration increase during stagnation, *68*
  major (*See pollutants by name*)
  measuring, 159–165
  minor, 73–74
  removal of, from effluent stack stream, 205–206

Gasoline, as pollution source, 13, 71, 114 (*See also* Mobile sources of air pollution)

Gastro-intestinal effects of pollution, 112, 114

General Motors, 256, 258

General Services Administration, 219

Geothermal energy, 223–224

Geysers, 224

Glaciers, 133–134

Global balance, sources and sinks, 129–131

Governmental control programs, 272–279, 290–318
  agency authority and responsibility, 277–278
  agency organization, typical, *292*
  criteria, standards, and implementation plans, 314–317
  evaluation of, 317–318
  federal, history of, 309–312
  federal functions, 291, 299–307
  history of, 290–291
  money and abatement authority, 312–314
  police power of the state, 273–275
  regulatory boards and commissions, 278–279, 291, 293, 309, 339
  smoke ordinances, 4, 45–46, 273, 290, 293, 309
  state and local agency functions, 291–299
  state and local, history of, 309
  state laws, modern, 275–278

strategy, 324–341
Grain handling industry, 230
Gravimetric technique, 161
Gravity, vertical temperature inversions and, 29
Great Britain (*See* United Kingdom)
Great Depression, pollution during, 4–5
Great Plains, 27, 212
Greenhouse effect, 131
Greenland glacier, 133–134
Grey iron foundries, 232–233
Griess-Saltzman method, 162, 167

Haagen-Smit, A. J., 6, 59
Hadley, George, 24
Hadley cells, 24
Halogens, 347
Hand-fired coal furnace, 214–*215*, 217
Hart, Senator, 285
Harvard School of Public Health, 152
Hazardous air pollutants, 111, 305
Haze, 56, 125, 127
Haze, coefficient of (COH), 172
Health, Education, and Welfare Department (HEW), 250, 252–253, 300, 310–311, 313, 316, 339
Health (human), carbon monoxide affecting, 100–103
  effects of pollution on, 82–83
    economic cost of, 147
    severity of, 115–118
  hydrocarbon affecting, 104
  minor pollutants affecting, 107–115
  nitrogen oxides affecting, 104
  particulate matter affecting, 95–99
  photochemical oxidants affecting, 104–107
  physiological effects mechanisms, 83–84
  pollution affecting, 12–13, 44–45, 50, 71
  respiratory diseases, 91–95
  respiratory system, 86–91
  studying pollution's effects on, 84–86
  sulfur dioxide affecting, 96–99

Heart, carbon monoxide affecting, 100–101, 103
  disease, 114
  failure, 93
Heat balance, in atmosphere, 19–*22*
Heat energy, atmospheric function and, 18
  nocturnal radiation inversions and, 33
"Heat island," 125
Heating boilers, as pollution source, 46, 48
Heavy metals, 134–136
Helium atom, 223
Heme, 108, 110
Hemoglobin, 100, 108
High pressure systems, global, 24–*26*
  moving, 26–27, 34–35
High-volume air sampler (hi-vol), 45, 152, *156*–157, 159, 172, 179, 303
"Hi-vol" (*See* High-volume air sampler)
Honda Motor Company, 255
"Hot soak period," 240
Hot water heating, 207
Houston, 279
Humidity, 126, 128, 133
Huron Portland Cement Company v. *City of Detroit,* 275
Hurricane, 27
Hydrocarbons, controlling emissions of, *248*–257
  criteria document, 315
  ecological effects of, 139, 141
  emissions of, annual, *64*
  health effects of, 104, 116
  as major pollutant, 12
  measuring, 159, 163, 165, 170–172
  from mobile sources, 238, 240–243, 247
  in photochemical smog, 7, 12
  prevalence of, 62–63
  properties of, 56–57
  sources of, 13
  from stationary sources, *198*, 205, *208*, 213–214, 225, 232

Hydroelectric power sources, 223
Hydrofluoric acid, in classic episode, 4
Hydrogen, 214, 223
Hydrogen fluoride, 73
Hydrogen sulfide (H_2S), ecological effects of, 134
 economic effects of, 145
 health effects of, 115
 as minor pollutant, 74
Hygroscopic substances, 158
Hypertension, 114

Idealism in United States society, 348
Ignition systems, 251, 253
Illinois, 210, 285
Impact statements, environmental, 283
Implementation functions of agency, 308–309
Implementation plans, 305, 314–317, 328–333
Incinerators, 225–227
Industrial fuel use, 207
Industrial hygiene, 9
Industrial process loss emissions, 228
Industrial processes, 13–14, 45–46, 50, 52, 198, 227–233, 228
Industrial Revolution, 3, 145
Industrial studies, 84
Inertial separation, 155, 157, 201–202, 205
Influenza, 91, 98
Infrared absorption method, 163
Infrared energy, 131, 133
Infrared spectroscopy, 169–170
Injunctions, 272, 313
Input data forms and formats, 181
Inspection-maintenance programs, 259
Inspections, 290–292
Insulation and energy waste, 224
Interferences, 162–163, 168, 170
Interior Department, United States, 214, 221, 283
Internal combustion engine (ICE), controlling, 246–254
 conventional, 238
  alternatives to, 254–258
 producing carbon monoxide, 11

Inversion, 29–35
 condition in Los Angeles Basin, 32
 defined, 31
 frontal, 34
 nocturnal radiation, formation and breakup of, 33
 subsidence, 34
Iodine, 163
Iron, 71, 73, 145, 222, 228–229
Iron oxides, 229
Iron and steel industry, 212, 228–229

Jacobs-Hochheiser method, 162
Japan, air pollution episode in, 8
 cutting off rubber supplies, 5
 mercury poisoning in, 112
 modifying engine, 255–256
Jet engine, 242
Judiciary Committee, congressional, 340
Justice Department, United States, 313, 315, 340–341

Kennedy, John F., 312
Kentucky, 210
Kerosene, 257
Kerr, Senator, 312
Kidney, damage to, 114, 280
 malfunction, 108
Killer smog (See Episodes, air pollution)
Knowledge functions of agency, 307–309
Kraft-pulping industry, 232

Lachrymator, 105 (See also Eye irritation)
Land-sea breeze, 27–28
Land use, changing patterns of, 261
 regulations, 299
Lanthanum, 71n
La Porte anomaly, 128–129
Lapse rate, adiabatic, 30–31
 defined, 29
 superadiabatic, 31
Laws on air pollution (See also Clean Air Act, United States; Legal

basis for air pollution control)
on auto emissions, 8
England's Clean Air Act, 8
federal, 310–311
on fuel quality, 5
on petroleum refineries and back-yard burning, 7
on smoke and sulfur dioxide emissions, 6
Lead, in air and blood, *109*
antiknock additives, 241, 253–254, 306, 347
ecological effects of, 134, 136, 142
health effects of, 83, 95, 108–110, 279–280
as pollutant, 71
reclaiming, 232
Lead candles, 164–165
Lead peroxide, 164
Lead plate, *164*
Lead sulfate, 164
Leather, air pollution affecting, 145
Legal basis for air pollution control, citizen suits, 279–285
governmental control programs, 272–279
traditional common-law remedies, 266–272
Legal definition of air pollution, 276
Legal standing, 280–281, 284
Lichens, 142
Light energy, in formation of photochemical smog, 59
Lignin, 232
Lignite, 208–210, *209, 212*
Lime, 206, 221, 231
Lime industry, 231
Limestone, 206, 221–222, 229–231
Liquefaction of coal, 222
Liquefied petroleum gas (LPG), 254
Liquid impinger system, 160
Living standard, 346–347
Lobbying groups, 315–318, 324–325
Lockheed Aircraft, 345
London, coal problem in, 3, 218
episode in, 7, 50, 98, 136
London smog, defined, 7

economic effects of, 144–146
pollutants in, 11, 42–51
Los Angeles (city, county, and Basin), ecological effects of pollution in, 139–140
economic effects of pollution in, 146–147
measurement of pollution in, 152, 170
meteorology and, 26–27, 32
pollution control, 6, 246, 290
prevalence of photochemical pollutants, 63, 65
studies on carbon monoxide effects, 103
studies on photochemical smog effects, 105–106
Los Angeles County Air Pollution Control District, 6, 170, 246, 290, 294
Los Angeles smog, differentiated from London smog, 6–7 (*See also* Photochemical smog)
Louisville, Kentucky, 5
Low pressure systems, 26–27
Low-sulfur fuels, 212–213, 218–221, 330
Low-volatile coal, 218
Lung cancer, 93, 98, 110
in bronchial lining, *94*
urban-rural difference in deaths from, *113*
Lung function, 95, 105, 115
Lungs, 87
inside surface of passages, *89*
pollutants' effects on, 96, 104

McGovern, Senator, 285
Macrophages, 90–91
Magnesium, 221
Magnesium oxide, 73
Maine, 223
Manual data-processing systems, 180–181
Mass, of atmosphere, 18
Mass transit, 8, 65, 260, 317

Mass units, 49, 55

Massachusetts, 285

Matching-grant mechanism, 303–304

"Maximum feasible control," 334

Mazda cars, 256

Measurement of air pollution, 152–174
  (*See also* Monitoring programs)
  automatic sampler-analyzers, 165–173, *166*
  gases in ambient air, 159–165
  particulate pollution in ambient air, 155–159
  process of, steps in, 153–154
  sensor types, 154–155
  at source, 173–174

Measurement units, 48–50, 55

Mechanical stokers, 216–*217*, 293

Mechanized samplers, 154–157, 160, 179, 181

Mellon Institute, 152

Membrane filter samplers, 157

Mercury, ecological effects of, 134, 142
  health effects of, 111–112
  as pollutant, 71, 129, 305

Mesoscale motions, 27–28

Metals, corrosion of, 144–145 (*See also metals by name*)
  heavy, 134

Metastasis, 93

Meteorology, air pollution and, 18–36
  diffusion equation, *200*, 296
  models, 295–296, 332

Methane, 56, 63
  measuring, 170–172
  in natural gas, 213

Methyl mercury, 111

Meuse River valley episode, 4, 50, 98, 136

Michigan, 284–285
  University of, Law School, 284

Micrograms of particulate matter per cubic meter of air ($\mu g/m^3$), 45, 48–50

Micro-organisms, pollution affecting, 141–142

Microscale motions, 28

Microwave spectroscopy, 169

Minnesota, 210, 285

Mixing depth, 29

Mobile sources of air pollution, 238–261
  alternatives to conventional internal combustion engine, 254–258
  alternatives to engine changes, 258–261
  controlling conventional internal combustion engines, 246–254
  pollutants from, *245*
  regulating emissions from, 305, 334
  vehicular emissions, 238–*245*

Moisture content of a fuel, 209

Molecular motions, 28

Molten iron, 222

Monitoring programs, 178–194, 295, 335
  data analysis, 189–194
  data processing, 179–189
  networks, 178–179

Monongehela River, 6

Morbidity, 98

Mortality, 98
  lung cancer, *113*
  particulate matter and sulfur oxide related to, *99*

Mosses, 142

Motor vehicles (*See also* Automobiles; Mobile sources of air pollution)
  cost of pollution, 147
  emission control devices, 205
  emissions regulation, 305, 310–311
  as pollution source, 70

Mountain-valley wind, *27–28*

Mucous membranes, 88, 111

Mucus, 88–92, 96–97

Mufflers, catalytic, 248, 253–255, 306, 317

Multiple-chamber incinerators, 225

Muskie, Senator, 312

Myocardial infarctions, 103

Nasal cavity, 87–88, 90

Nasal irritation, 113
Nasser, Lake, 223
National Academy of Science, 147
National Air Pollution Control Administration (NAPCO) (*See* Environmental Protection Agency)
National Air Surveillance Network (NASN), 156–157, 187, 303
National Ambient Air Quality Standards, 11, 56, 117–*118*, 317, 333
National Center for Air Pollution Control, 315
National Conference on Air Pollution (1962), 8
National Conference on Air Pollution Control (1966), 314
National Environmental Policy Act (NEPA) (1970), 283
National Institutes of Health, 311
National Weather Service, 126, 296, 298
Natural air pollution, 10
Natural gas, 208
  controlling pollution from, 221
  furnaces, 143, 331
  as gaseous hydrocarbon fuel, 254–255
  pollution and, 13, 62, 213
Natural Resources Defense Council, 281
Negligence, 266
Nervous system, effects of pollution on, 112, 115–116
New York City, ecological effects of air pollution in, 136, 142
  meteorology and topography affecting pollution, 36
  pollution in, 314
  rapid transit, 260
New York State, 247
News media, 298–299, 306
Nickel, health effects of, 114
  as heavy metal, 134
Nickel carbonyl [$Ni(CO)_4$], 114
Ninth Amendment to United States Constitution, 283

Nitrate, 71
Nitric acid plant, as pollution source, 232
Nitric oxide (NO), conversion into nitrogen dioxide in presence of reactive hydrocarbon molecules, *61*
  in formation of photochemical smog, 58–*61*
  interfering, 168
  measuring, 163, 167, 169
  as pollutant, 12
  properties of, 55
Nitrogen dioxide (NO_2), chemical reaction cycle initiated by, *60*
  in formation of photochemical smog, 58–*60*
  health effects of, 96, 104
  interfering, 162
  as major pollutant, 12
  measuring, 162–163, 167
  prevalence of, 62
  properties of, 55–56
Nitrogen oxides (NO_x), controlling emissions of, *248*, 250–251, 253–255, 257
  criteria document, 315
  diurnal variation patterns of, *66–67*
  ecological effects of, 139–140
  emissions of, annual, *63*
  in formation of photochemical smog, 7, 58–62
  health effects of, 104, 116
  as major pollutant, 12
  measuring, 162–163, 165, 167–168
  from mobile sources, 238, 240–242
  prevalence of, 62–64
  properties of, 55–56
  sources of, 13
  from stationary sources, *198*, 206, 232
Nitrogen-fixing bacteria, 142
Nocturnal radiation inversions, *33*
Noise pollution, 8, 10
Nondispersive infrared (NDIR) spectroscopic technique, 170

Nondispersive spectroscopic technique, 169–170

Nonferrous metals industries, 231–232

Nonmethane hydrocarbons (*See also* Hydrocarbons)
measurement of, 56–57, 170–172
in photochemical smog, 58–59, 61–62

Nonspecific irritants, 83

North Africa, climate and wind pattern, 25

North Carolina, 285

North Dakota, 187–*188*

North Pacific high, 24–25, 35

Northwestern Laundry v. *City of Des Moines,* 273

Nuclear power plants, 330

Nuisance suits, 266, 279–280
private, 267–272, 279
public, 272–273

Observational studies, 85

Occupational hazards, 109–110, 112

Occupational health, 9

Ocean-ice balance, 133–134

Odorous compounds, 74

Ohio, 210

Ohio Valley, 47

Oil, fuel, 6, 8, 13, 51, 208, 212–213

Oil lobby, 315

Oil shale, 213–214

Open-hearth process, 229

Operating permit, 291–292

Ore sintering, 228

Organic carcinogens, 112–113

Organizations, suits by, 281

Overpopulation, 346

Oxidant, defined, 12 (*See also* Photochemical oxidants)

Oxidation, 57n, 163, 167–168

Oxygen, atmospheric function and, 18
in photochemical smog formation, 59, 61

Oxygen–carbon dioxide distribution cycle, atmospheric function and, 18

Ozone (O_3), ecological effects of, 139–141
economic effects of, 146
health effects of, 105
interfering, 162
as major pollutant, 12
measuring, 168–169
in photochemical smog formation, 59–62
properties and prevalence of, 58
radiation absorption by, 29

"Packed column," 171

Palisade cells of plant, 138, 140

Paper, air pollution affecting, 145–146

Paper mills, 52

Pararosaniline dye, 161

Pararosaniline methylsulfonic acid, 161

Parenchyma cells of plant, 138–140

Particle size, spectrum of, *43*

Particulate matter, concentration, typical, 49–50
controlling emissions of, 217–218, 227–228, 230, 317, 331, 335
criteria document, 315
distribution of levels of, by city size, *48*
ecological effects of, 125–126, 131–134
economic effects of, 143–144
emissions of, annual, *47*
frequency distribution of, *192*
health effects of, 83, 95–99, 115
levels in selected cities, *52*
levels in urban and nonurban areas, long-term trend in, *129*
as major pollutant, 11
measuring, 155–159, 172
as minor pollutant, *70*–73
from mobile sources, 241
mortality and, equations relating, *99*
properties and prevalence, 42–50
separation methods for effluent cleaning, 201–205
sources of, 13

from stationary sources, *198, 207–* 209, 225–233

substances in, *70*

trends at nonurban site, *188*

Particulate sulfates (SO_4), as pollutant, 11, 70, 126

Parts per million (ppm), 49

Peat, 208–210, *209*

Penn Central Railroad, 345

Pennsylvania, 210

Permit-and-variance system, 290–293, 309

Permits, 290–293, 312

Peroxyacetyl nitrate (PAN), ecological effects of, 139–140

measuring, 168

in photochemical smog, 62

as pollutant, 12

Personal freedom, degree of, 344–345

Pesticides, 113, 129

Petroleum and petroleum products, 212–213, 238

Petroleum refineries, pollution control, 336

as pollution source, 6–7, 50–52, 232

refinery process, 212–213

Phagocyte, 91

Pharynx, 87

Philadelphia, 260

Phosphate fertilizer plants, 71, 136, 231

Phosphate industry, 231

Phosphorus, 231

Photochemical oxidants, concentration variations from amount of sunlight, *68*

control program, 317

criteria document, 315

ecological effects of, 139–140

in formation of photochemical smog, *58–59,* 62

health effects of, *104–107,* 116

as major pollutant, 12

measuring, 163, 165, 168

prevalence of, 64–65

properties of, 57–58

Photochemical smog, control of, 290

defined, 7

ecological effects of, 126

economic effects of, 144–146

formation, chronology of, *58*

health effects of, 104–107

pollutants in, 11–12, 55–58, 171

prevalence of, 62–65

reactions involved in, *58–62, 60, 61,* 171

as secondary pollutant, 9, 55

Photosynthesis, 139

Pig iron, 233

Pipeline, trans-Alaska, 283

Pittsburgh, 5, 44, 143, 244, 273

Planetary circulations, 24–26

Plankton, 131

Plants, pollution damage to, 138–141, 147, 231

Plasmolysis, 139

Pleural mesothelioma, 93, 110

Plumbism, 108, 110

Plutonium, 223

Pneumoconiosis, 95

Pneumonia, 91

Poles, heat energy to, 20, 24

Police power of the state, 273–275

Policy statement, 276

Pollen, 72*n*

"Pollutant rose" analysis, 193–*194*

Pollutants (*See also* Concentrations of pollution; Emissions; *pollutants by name*)

air, air quality standards for, 117–*118*

major, 10–12, 42–67

minor, 70–74

properties and prevalence of, 42–76

relative significance of, 74–76, *75*

sources of, 13–14

Polycyclic aromatic hydrocarbons, 72

Polynuclear aromatic hydrocarbons, 56*n*

Portland cement, 230

Positive crankcase ventilation (PCV), 247

Potassium iodide (KI), 163, 168
Poza Rica (Mexico) episode, 115
Precipitation, 36, 128, 134–*135*
Preventive legal action, 274, 276
Preventive techniques for reducing emissions, 198–199, 250
Primary burner, 226
Primary pollutants, 9
Private nuisance, 267, 279–280
Producer gas, 213
Propane, 254
Proteinuria, 114
Public health laws, 275
Public Health Service (PHS), United States, 6, 143, 310–311, 313, 339
Public hearings, 316
Public nuisance suits, 272–273
Public policy, control strategy and, 324–341
Public property, public's right to, 283
Public trust, doctrine of, 284
Pulmonary capillaries, alveoli intertwining with, *101*
Pulmonary function, 95
Pulverized-coal units, 216–217

Quality of life, 8
Quantitative dosage concept, 83
Quantities of emissions, from vehicles, *243*–245, *244* (*See also* Emissions)

Radiant energy, 131
Radiation, balance, atmospheric, 19–20
    carbon dioxide, particulates and, 131–134
  hazards, 8, 330
  upper atmosphere and, 18
Radiation inversion, 34–35
Radiation wavelength, 131–*132*
Radioactivity dispersal, 200
Railroads, 143, 244
Rain, 34, 36, 134–*135*
Rankine-cycle engine, 256–258
Rapid transit systems, 260
Rationing gasoline, 260, 317
Reactive hydrocarbons, 56 (*See also*

Hydrocarbons; Nonmethane hydrocarbons)
Reagents, 160–163, 166–167, 169, 220
Recycling and reuse, 206
Reference methods, EPA, 155
    for carbon monoxide, 170
    for hydrocarbons, 170
    for oxidants, 169
    for ozone, 168
    for sulfur dioxide, 161, 168
    for suspended particulate matter, 157, 172
Regulatory boards and commissions, 278–279, 291, 293, 309, 339
Regulatory standards, 293–294
Research, intramural and extramural, 302, 310 (*See also* Health, human)
Residual fuel oil, controlling pollution from, 221
  as pollution source, 50, 213
"Resistant" measures, 189
Respiratory diseases, 91–95, 104–105
    death rate trends in United States, *92*
Respiratory irritation, 115
Respiratory system, breathing, mechanics of, *87*
  diseases of, 91–95
  human, 86–91, *88*
Retrofit devices, 259
Revenue sharing, 304
Ringelmann chart, 45–*46*, 152, 290, 309
"Roll-back" formula, 331
Roman law, 284
Rubber, air pollution affecting, 146
"Rubbertown," 5
Rusting, 145

St. Louis, 4–6, 44, 143, 273
Sampling devices, for gases, 160
  for particulate pollution, 155–157
Sampling methods and equipment, 152–174
San Francisco, 260
Sanitary landfills, 199, 224–225
SAROAD codes, 183

Sax, Joseph L., 284
Scandium, 71n
Schenck Act, 246–247, 310–311
Sea breeze, 27–28
Second-generation exhaust standards, 250–251
Secondary nonferrous industries, 232
Secondary pollutants, 9, 57, 62
Selenium, 71n
Semiautomatic data-processing systems, 180–181
Sensors, basic types of, 152, 154–155
Separation techniques, 154
  for gases, 159–160
  for particulate pollution, 155, 201–205
Sequential impactor, 157–158
Sequential sampler, 160, 178
Settleable dust (dustfall), 11, 44–45, 127, 143, 152, 154
Sierra Club, 281
Silica, 73
Silica gel, 159
Silicosis, 95
Silver, 71n, 145
Silver sulfide, 145
Silverman, Leslie, 152, 156
Sinks, environmental, 130–131, 133, 142
Sintering plant, 228–229
Sinuses, 88, 114
Sive, David, 282
Slag, 229
Slurry, 206, 220
Smelters, pollution control in, 221
  as pollution source, 50–51, 113, 136–138, 231
Smog, coinage of word, 4 (See also London smog; Photochemical smog)
Smoke, black, 45–46, 72, 95, 125, 143–144, 152, 210, 218, 241, 273 (See also Particulate matter)
Smoke control laws, 4, 45–46, 273, 290, 293, 309
Smoking, 86
Sneezing mechanism, 90

Sniffing mechanism, 89
Societal factors in problem of pollution and its control, 344–348
Sodium, 71n, 221
Sodium tetrachloromercurate, 161
Soiling, caused by air pollution, 143–144
Solar energy radiation, 19–21, 64, 131, 223
Solid waste, combustion, 52, 114, 224–225
  disposal, 8, 198–199, 224–227, 226
  emission factors for incineration of, 226
Solvent-refining processes, 222
Soot, 42, 44–45, 98, 143–144
Sources of air pollution (See also sources and pollutants by name)
  chosen for emission reduction, 328–333
  mobile, 238–261, 329
  stationary, 198–233, 329
Southeast Asia, climate and wind pattern, 25
Space heating, 51, 97, 143, 207, 213–214, 218, 331
Spain, climate and wind pattern, 25
Specialization, 347
Specificity, 162, 168–169
Spectroscopy, 169–170
Spores, 72n
Spot-tape sampler, 172
Spray tower, 203–204
Sputum production, 98
Stack sampling, 153, 173–174, 294
Stack-gas cleaning processes, 220–221
Stagnation, atmospheric, 27, 35–36
  increasing gaseous pollutant concentration, 68
  in killer smog episodes, 97
"Standard test cycle," 243–244, 247
Standards, air quality, 11, 56, 117–118, 304, 314–317, 328–329, 331
  emission, 293–294, 328–329
  equipment, 293, 328
  performance, 305–306

"Standing to sue," 280–281, 284
State, federal government cooperating
        with, 304–305, 312
    laws of, modern, 275–278
State Services Bureau of Public
        Health Service, 310–311
Static sensors (or monitors), 154–155,
        164–165, 179, 181
Stationary sources of air pollution,
        198–233
    control of emissions, basic ap-
        proaches to, 198–206
    fuel combustion, 198, 207–224
    industrial processes, 227–233, 228
    solid-waste disposal, 224–227, 226
Steam electric-power plants, 224, 330
Steam engine, 256–258
Steel mills, 6, 228–229
Steubenville, Ohio, 47, 143
Stoichiometric point, 248–249
Stone, carbonate, 145
Storage and Retrieval of Aerometric
        Data (SAROAD) codes, 183
Storage and retrieval of data, 182–183
Strachan v. Beacon Oil Company, 269–
        270
Stratified-charge engine, 255
Subbituminous coal, 208–210, 209, 212,
        221
Subsidence inversion, 34–35
Subsidies for major companies, 345
Sulfates, properties and prevalence of,
        50–51, 70
Sulfation index, 164
Sulfhydryl (−SH) groups, 108
Sulfur content, of coal, 210
        distribution of reserves by, 212
    controlling, 219–220, 330
    of fuel oil, 213
    of natural gas, 213
Sulfur dioxide (SO_2), in classic epi-
        sode, 4
    concentration, typical, 49–50
    controlling, 6, 205–206, 219–221,
        317, 330–331, 335
    ecological effects of, 134, 138, 140
    economic effects of, 144, 146

health effects of, 83, 89, 96–99
    interfering, 163, 168
    levels at Cincinnati CAMP station,
        186
    levels in selected cities, 52
    levels in Washington, D.C., decrease
        in, 219
    as major pollutant, 11
    measurement of, 161–162, 165, 168
    pollutant rose, 194
    properties and prevalence of, 50–51
    seasonal variations in concentra-
        tions, 51, 53
    from stationary sources, 205–208,
        207, 210, 231–232
Sulfur oxides (SO_x), controlling, 317
    criteria document, 315
    economic effects of, 143–146
    emissions of, annual, 51
    health effects of, 115–116
    measuring, 164–165
    mortality and, equations relating, 99
    as pollutant, 11, 71
    properties and prevalence of, 50–51
    sources of, 13–14
    from stationary sources, 198, 227
Sulfur trioxide (SO_3), as pollutant, 11
    properties and prevalence of, 50–51
Sulfuric acid mist, ecological effects of,
        134
    economic effects of, 144–146
    health effects of, 96
    properties and prevalence of, 50–51
Sulfuric acid plants, in Donora, Penn-
        sylvania, 6
    pollution control in, 221
    as pollution source, 232
    recovery, 231–232
Summarization of data, 189–193, 191,
        192
Superadiabatic lapse rate, 31
Supreme Court, United States, 273–
        275, 313
Surgeon General, 310–311, 313
Suspended particulates, 11, 45, 47
        (See also Particulate matter)
Sweden, forest damage in, 201

Synergism, of particles and gases, 96
  of particulate matter and sulfur
      oxides, 42
  of sulfur dioxide and nitrogen diox-
      ide, 140
  of sulfur dioxide and ozone, 140–*141*
Synoptic motions, 26–27
Synthetic fibers, air pollution affecting,
      146
Systemic poisons, 83, 108, 111

"T, T, T, and O" conditions, 215, 225
Tall-stack dispersion, 199–201, 272
Tar sands, 213–214
Target concentration, 328
Tax privileges, 330, 335–336
Technical assistance, 302–303, 310
Technology, inappropriate, 346
Telemetering, 180
Temperature, affecting pollution, 36
  global imbalances caused by uneven
      distribution of incoming solar
      radiation, *21*
  imbalances and air motion, 23–24,
      27–29
  La Porte anomaly and, 128
  radiation and heat balance in at-
      mosphere, 19–*22*
  radiation balance and, 131–134
  vertical inversions, 29–35
  vertical variation in atmosphere, *19–*
      20
Temperature gradient, 29–32
  atmospheric mixing and pollutant
      dispersal, relationship of, *31*
Terminal grain elevators, 230
Tetraethyl lead, 71
Textiles, air pollution affecting, 146
Thermal convection cells, 24
Thermal pollution, 125
Thermal precipitation, 205
Thermal reactor, 255
Thermodynamic processes of internal
      combustion engine, 238–239
Thermonuclear fusion reactions,
      223
"Third pollution," 224

Third-generation exhaust standards,
      253
Threshold, level of exposure, 82–83,
      117
  taste and odor for sulfur dioxide, 97
Thunderstorms, 27
Tidal power sources, 223
Tolerance levels, 117
Topography, atmospheric motion and,
      27, 32
"Toxic," usage of word, 84
Trachea, 87–88
Traffic, 58, 63, 65, 114, 260
Training manpower, 302–303
Transportation (*See also* Mobile
      sources of air pollution)
  control plans, 259–261
  sources of emissions, *198*
Traveling grate spreader-stoker, 216–
      217
Trees, 142, 201
Trespass, 266
Tropopause, 29
Troposphere, 19
Trucks, 242, 244
Tuberculosis, 91
Tuttle v. *Church,* 270
Two-stroke gasoline engine, 241

Udall, Representative, 285
Ultraviolet light, 6–7
Ultraviolet spectroscopy, 169
Uniontown, Pennsylvania, 143
United Kingdom, cancer in, 113
  chronic bronchitis in, 92–93
  climate and pollution, 125
  common law, 266, 271
  pollution from, 201
  smog problem, 4, 218
United States, air pollution control
      strategy, 324–341
  air pollution episode in, 8
  air pollution functions, 299–307
  air pollution problem in twentieth
      century, 4–9
  air pollution program, 307–318
  climate and wind patterns, 25

coal deposits in, *211*
fuel-combustion emissions, regional, 50–51
particulate levels, variation in, 48
societal factors in problem of pollution and its control, 344–348
Uranium-fuel fission plants, 222–223
Uranium-processing industry, 5
Urban atmosphere, 124–128, *127*
"Urban effect" in cancer incidence rates, 112–*113*
Urban effluents, precipitation effect of, 128
Utah, 214

Validation of data, 183–189, *186*
Variances, 291–294
Vegetation, leaf cross-section, *138*
pollution affecting, 138–141
Vehicle-use restraints, 260
Vehicular emissions, 238–245 (*See also* Automobiles; Mobile sources of air pollution)
from light-duty motor vehicles, *244*
rates for various engine-operating modes, *243*
Venezuela, 221
Ventilatory function, 104
Venturi scrubber, *204*
Vertical temperature inversions, 29–35
Viral infections, 91
Visibility, low, frequency of, 1930s to 1950s, *127*
reduction of, 125–*127*
sulfur oxides reducing, 50
Visible radiation, 131, 133
Volatile carbonaceous matter, 209–210

Wade v. *Miller*, 270
Wankel engine, 255–*256*

Ward County, North Dakota, *188*
Washington, D.C., 260
sulfur dioxide levels in, *219*
"Washout," 36
Water pollution, 8, 112, 204, 232, 311, 325, 330
Water vapor, atmospheric function and, 18
interfering, 170
Wealth of United States, 344, 346
Weather effects, regional, of pollution, 128–129
Weather systems, 26–27
West-Gaeke method, 161–162, 168
West Virginia, 210
Wet chemical analysis, 160–163
Wet chemical instruments, 166–168, *167*
Wet scrubbers, 202–204, 220, 232–233
"Whiskey brown haze," 56
White smoke plume, 50
Wickwire Spencer Company, 267
Wind, 21, 27–28
data and pollutant rose analysis, 193
patterns, 25
Wind rose, 193
Windpipe, 87–88
Wood, as fuel, 3, 208
World War II, affecting air pollution, 5
Wyoming, 214

Yellowstone National Park, 224

Zero-effects exposure, 82
Zinc, corrosion of, 145
as heavy metal, 134
Zinc smelter, 6
Zoning, 299
Zoo animals, lead poisoning of, 136